PENGUIN

CW00539625

GEORGE HERBERT:
THE COMPLETE POETRY

GEORGE HERBERT was born in Montgomery in 1593, the seventh of ten children in an aristocratic family. Initially he showed worldly ambition and seemed sure of high public office and a career at court, becoming Orator of the University of Cambridge in 1620. However, four years later he was ordained a deacon in the Church of England and for a time he 'lost himself in a humble way', devoting himself to the restoration of the church at Leighton Bromswold in Huntingdonshire. Later he settled in the parish of Bemerton, near Salisbury. Herbert published some Latin poetry in his lifetime, but his English verse remained unknown until his death, at the age of thirty-nine, in 1633. In that year his friend Nicholas Ferrar, leader of the quasi-monastic community at Little Gidding, had Herbert's English poems published under the title *The Temple*, and his fame as one of the great English poets was soon established.

JOHN DRURY is Chaplain and Fellow of All Souls College, Oxford. He began as a biblical scholar and, while Dean of King's College, Cambridge, worked with Frank Kermode on the Gospels for *The Literary Guide to the Bible* (1987), which sharpened his sense of the role of imagination in the formation of the Gospel stories. He took this interest further, and into the realm of Christian paintings and their meaning, in *Painting the Word* (1999), written while he was Dean of Christ Church, Oxford. His biography of Herbert, *Music at Midnight*, which was published to great acclaim in 2013, is the culmination of a lifetime's interest in the poet.

VICTORIA MOUL is Lecturer in Latin Literature and Language at King's College London. She works mainly on classical poetry and its reception, and has published widely on the translation and imitation of Virgil, Horace and Pindar in the sixteenth and seventeenth centuries, as well as on neo-Latin poetry of the period. She is the author of *Jonson, Horace and the Classical Tradition* (2010) and the editor of *Neo-Latin Literature* (2015).

GEORGE HERBERT

The Complete Poetry

Edited by
JOHN DRURY *and* VICTORIA MOUL

with translations from the Latin by
VICTORIA MOUL

PENGUIN BOOKS

PENGUIN CLASSICS

UK | USA | Canada | Ireland | Australia
India | New Zealand | South Africa

Penguin Books is part of the Penguin Random House group of companies
whose addresses can be found at global.penguinrandomhouse.com.

First published in Great Britain by Penguin Classics 2015

009

Set in 10.25/12.25 pt PostScript Adobe Sabon
Typeset by Jouve (UK), Milton Keynes
Printed in Great Britain by Clays Ltd, Elcograf S.p.A.

ISBN: 978-0-141-39204-2

www.greenpenguin.co.uk

MIX
Paper from
responsible sources
FSC™ C018179

Penguin Books is committed to a sustainable
future for our business, our readers and our planet.
This book is made from Forest Stewardship
Council™ certified paper.

Contents

Chronology

1613 Herbert graduates as Bachelor of Arts.
Campion, *Two Books of Airs*.

1614 Herbert elected minor fellow of Trinity College.

1616 Herbert elected major fellow of Trinity College as Master of Arts.

1617 Herbert Sublector Quartae Classis (Junior Lecturer of the fourth-year class).

1618 Herbert elected praelector in rhetoric in the University.
Writes letter of congratulation to Earl of Buckingham on being made marquess.

1619 Herbert delivers Latin oration *vice* Sir Francis Nethersole, Orator.
Edward Herbert Ambassador in Paris. Manuscript of his work of philosophy *De Veritate*.
Lancelot Andrewes becomes Bishop of Winchester. Herbert visits him there later.

1620 Herbert elected Orator of the University.
John Williams becomes Dean of Westminster.

1621 Donne becomes Dean of St Paul's.
Burton, *The Anatomy of Melancholy*.
John Williams becomes Bishop of Lincoln, also succeeds Bacon (dismissed from office) as Lord Keeper of the Great Seal.

1623 Herbert's orations for Honorary Degrees conferred on the Spanish ambassadors, for the king's departure after a visit, and for the return of Prince Charles and Buckingham from Spain.
Shakespeare's First Folio dedicated to the Herbert (Earls of Montgomery and Pembroke) brothers, distant senior relatives of George Herbert.

1624 Herbert becomes Member of Parliament for Montgomery, sits on committee to consider petitions against schoolmasters and heads of colleges.
Granted six months leave from his duties as Orator.
Ordained deacon in the Church of England.
Comportioner ('sharer') of the revenues of the Rectory of Llandinam.

Edward Herbert, *De Veritate* published in Paris. He is recalled to London.

Donne, *Devotions*.

1625 Herbert and Donne at Chelsea.

Bacon dedicates his *Translation of Certain Psalms* to Herbert.

James I dies.

John Williams excluded from Charles I's coronation.

1626 Herbert made canon of Lincoln Cathedral and prebendary (entitled to the income) of Leighton Bromswold.

Latin memorial poem on Sir Francis Bacon.

Death of Lancelot Andrewes.

1627 Herbert's mother, Magdalen, Lady Danvers, dies. Donne preaches her memorial sermon, published together with Herbert's Latin poems in her memory, *Memoriae Matris Sacrum*.

1628 Herbert's stepfather Sir John Danvers remarries. His brother, Sir Henry Danvers, Earl of Danby, accommodates Herbert in an apartment in his house at Dauntsey, Wiltshire.

1629 Herbert marries Jane Danvers of Baynton in Edington Church, Wiltshire.

1630 Herbert made rector of Fugglestone with Bemerton between Wilton and Salisbury.

1631 Donne dies.

1633 Herbert dies at Bemerton having sent his English poems to Nicholas Ferrar at Little Gidding.

The Temple published in Cambridge. Six editions up to 1641.

Donne, *Poems* published.

1634 *A Treatise of Temperance and Sobriety: Written by Lud. Cornarus, Translated into English by Mr George Herbert* published at Cambridge.

1640 *Outlandish Proverbs, Selected by Mr G. H.* published in London.

Christopher Harvey, *The Synagogue or, The Shadow of The Temple*.

1646 Crashaw, *Steps to the Temple*.

General Introduction

Izaak Walton published his *Life of Mr George Herbert* in 1670: thirty-seven years after Herbert's death and ten years after the end of the Commonwealth and the restoration of the monarchy. Walton himself had never met Herbert and set him up as a model for the restored Church of England, with a hagiographical enthusiasm which makes him suspect. But he did consult eyewitnesses, among them a Hertfordshire clergyman called Edmund Duncon, who had had a crucial role in the transmission of Herbert's poetry. Walton narrates that on his deathbed Herbert, 'with a thoughtful and contented look', gave Duncon this instruction:

> Sir, I pray you deliver this little book to my dear brother Ferrar, and tell him he shall find in it a picture of the many spiritual conflicts that have passed betwixt God and my soul, before I could subject mine to the will of Jesus my Master; in whose service I have now found perfect freedom; desire him to read it; and then, if he can think it may turn to the advantage of any dejected poor soul, let it be made public; if not, let him burn it; for I and it are less than the least of God's mercies.

Nicholas Ferrar had known of Herbert from their student days at Cambridge. He had withdrawn from London with his family to live a quasi-monastic life at Little Gidding in Huntingdonshire, and had helped Herbert with the restoration (which can still be seen and admired) of the church at nearby Leighton Bromswold, from which Herbert derived an income. Ferrar was moved to tears by the contents of the little book delivered to him by Duncon and set the women in his Writing Room to work on a fair copy, now in the Bodleian Library at Oxford. He presented this to the authorities of the University of Cambridge, who in turn licensed it to be printed – all within the year – under the title of *The Temple*. It went through six editions between 1633 and 1641.

The dying Herbert's charge to Duncon points up several things which need to be understood for a full appreciation of his poetry: the nature of his 'spiritual conflicts' within an otherwise quiet and orderly life; just what God and 'Jesus my Master' meant to him; whether poetry should be kept private in manuscript or made public in print; Herbert's personal character as shown and passed over in this anecdote; the uses of poetry.

What, first, were the 'many spiritual conflicts' pictured in the book? The major crises in Herbert's life were protracted and profound, lasting from 1619 to 1630, between the ages of twenty-six and thirty-seven. They need to be set in the context of his whole life.

Herbert was born in 1593, the seventh child of Richard and Magdalen Herbert, in Montgomery, where the ancestral Herbert Castle had its back to the Welsh mountains and looked east over a gentler English landscape. His father's death when he was only three had two determinative effects. It focused George's affection on his beautiful, clever and commanding mother, Magdalen. And it released him and his family from the remote and wild border of Wales, where his Herbert forebears had kept order with more than necessary violence, a good table and no great aspirations towards culture. Magdalen and her brood then moved east: first to the stately home of her mother, Lady Newport, at Eyton-upon-Severn, south-east of Shrewsbury, where the exemplary poet of the previous age, Philip Sidney, had lodged when at Shrewsbury School; from there to Oxford, where she could keep an eye on her eldest son Edward, the future diplomat, poet, philosopher and boastful autobiographer – and where her friendship with John Donne began; and from Oxford to settle at last in London at Charing Cross. This was an excellent address, a green riverside interval between the great houses of the political/ecclesiastical establishment along the Strand, with the commercial City of London beyond, and Westminster with the royal palace of Whitehall, the Abbey and the royal foundation of Westminster School. The last of these gave the young Herbert a superb education in the classical languages and literature, fostered by the great linguist and preacher Lancelot Andrewes as dean and alleviated by an afternoon a week of instruction in music. His mother was a cultivated hostess of note. Music and cards were played. The composers John Bull and William Byrd were frequent guests. There was dancing and the poor were fed. Her son Edward accused her of keeping 'a greater family than became either my mother's widowed estate or such young beginners as we were'.

From Westminster Herbert went to Trinity College, Cambridge, as a scholar in 1609. He was to spend the next fourteen years of his life there: too fastidious in dress and distant in manner to be popular with his peers, but so outstandingly able intellectually as to rise steadily through the ranks of college and university life. In his first year his mother married again: to a handsome, rich and agreeable young man called Sir John Danvers. In the same year Herbert sent her two sonnets (see p. 197–8) announcing his intention to have nothing to do with secular love poetry but to write for God. Eight years later he was a major fellow of his college, writing to Danvers to tell him that he was 'setting foot into Divinity' and asking for money to buy books. Fellows of Trinity were expected to be ordained into the ministry of the Church. Theological study was a responsible preparation for it. But Herbert's religious intentions were mixed with secular ambition in another direction. He longed to be the University Orator. In a lobbying letter he explained to his stepfather with only a slight touch of irony:

> The Orator's place (that you may understand what it is) is the finest place in the University . . . the Orator writes all the University Letters, makes all the Orations, be it to King, Prince or whatever comes to the University; to requite these pains, he takes place next the Doctors, in all their Assemblies and Meetings, and sits above the Proctors . . . and such like Gaynesses, which will please a young man well.

More than that, an Orator could expect to be preferred to high office at court, such as Secretary of State. Herbert had already deputized for the retiring Orator, Sir Francis Nethersole, whom the king was sending on an urgent diplomatic mission to Prague. He had written Latin letters and speeches for Nethersole and was his inevitable successor. But he was panicked by a letter in which Nethersole put his finger on the problem with his predicted career path. Herbert wrote to Danvers again:

> I understand by Sir Francis Nethersole's letter, that he fears I have not fully resolved the matter, since this place [of Orator] being civil may divert me too much from Divinity, at which, not without cause, he thinks I aim; but I have wrote him back, that this dignity hath no such earthiness in it, but it may very well be joined with Heaven.

That was an opportunistic version of the purer thought in his poem 'The Elixir':

> All may of thee partake:
> Nothing can be so mean,
> Which with his tincture (for thy sake)
> Will not grow bright and clean.

Anyhow, in 1620 (he consulted Lancelot Andrewes about his dilemma) Herbert got the job. Three years on he may well have regretted that he had not taken more care over what he wished for. The climax of his Oratorship was a Latin speech on the return in 1623 of Prince Charles and the Duke of Buckingham from Spain, where they had failed farcically to get the hand of the Spanish Infanta in marriage to the English prince. The Protestant public was delighted and celebrated with bonfires. Buckingham was furious and wanted to go to war. James I did not, and was simply relieved to have his two 'dear boys' back. All this had to be navigated by the Orator with erudition, wit and flattery. Only in an urgent plea for peace did Herbert speak from the heart – and that would have excluded him from the favour of the distributor of favours, Buckingham. The oration was admired, but can only have grated on the conscience of the poet, who valued above all transparent simplicity and sincerity. However well thought of in Cambridge, it would not have done him much good at court. His feelings are described in his auto-biographical poem 'Affliction (1)' – he wrote five with that title.

'Affliction (1)' is set in Cambridge and is precisely a poem of 'the spiritual conflicts that have passed betwixt God and my soul'. He complained that God (the director of human lives) had seduced him into his service with prospects of a good life, only to mistreat him with 'consuming agues' and the deaths of friends and family. As a result he felt useless: 'a blunted knife'. His life had turned sour, entangling him in 'the world of strife' and palliating his rage with 'academic praise'. And all the time he was aware that 'my birth and spirit rather took/The way that takes the town . . .' He felt stuck, prevented from settling for his lot by recurrent illness. Surrounded by books which failed to tell him 'what thou wilt do with me', he envied the usefulness of trees. He first considered sticking it out, then quitting to serve 'some other master' than this hostile deity. The last two lines of the poem are an extraordinary reference to St Paul at Romans 12:9: 'let love be without dissimulation':

> Ah my dear God! though I am clean forgot,
> Let me not love thee, if I love thee not.

Herbert and his God have pitted themselves against each other with mounting savagery up to this point, and we might now expect some resolution or capitulation. Instead we get a vehe-ment prayer or vow that the poet's love for his adversary should be erased rather than tainted by fawning insincerity. It is an heroic assertion: both of the poet's individual identity and of the crucial primacy, for both parties, of loving in truth. As an introduction to both Herbert's life and his poetic achievement it serves to contradict the conventional image of him as sweet and tame.

Not to believe in God would, in Herbert's time and place, have been extraordinary: something like not believing in trees. The natural world could only be understood as God's work – as the first pages of the Bible, now widely available in English, testified. Herbert's poem 'Providence' shares with the biblical Psalms, such as Psalm 104, an admiring delight in the Creator's handiwork. There was no problem of belief in creation for people then, with their bibles in a stable, pre-Darwinian world. But the problems of history proliferated and tormented: both on the micro-level of individual life lamented in Herbert's 'Affliction (1)' and on the macro-level of international events. The Psalms are full of such agonies: the sufferings of the just and the triumphs of the wicked, the absence of the God who had promised to be present, the everlasting 'why?' of the afflicted. Christianity had loosened the tyrannical grip of monotheism by its heartfelt belief in Jesus Christ as God yet man. He was the incarnation of the supremacy of love: the divine Son of the old Father, and he had surrendered himself to extreme, sacrificial affliction for love of the human race. This at least broke the isolation which is the psychological sting of suffering and acknowledged love as supreme over God and man.

Herbert's ardent devotion to Jesus's sacrifice is evident at the outset of his arrangement of his poems in *The Temple*, which are organized into headed sections. After the prolonged secular wisdom of *The Church-Porch* (seventy-seven stanzas), *The Church* is entered via 'The Altar' of sacrifice. There follow the sixty-three stanzas of Christ's monologue in 'The Sacrifice'. Neither of these long poems makes easy reading. *The Church-Porch* is prosy, though spiced with wit and acute observation. 'The Sacrifice' is relentless though majestic in its tragic irony. But they are the twin pillars and poles of all Herbert's thinking: the one common-sensical, empirical, relaxed and quotidian; the other mysterious, tense, relentlessly double-edged and transcendent. He is a realist and a mystic. 'The Sacrifice' is followed by the nine poems devoted to Christ's redeeming death and resurrection. Herbert's personal devotion to Christ is, typically, as everyday as it is intense. In his preface 'The Printers to the Reader' Ferrar related of his friend the poet that

> he used in his ordinary speech, when he made mention of the blessed
> name of our Lord and Saviour Jesus Christ, to add, *My Master*.

Ships, colleges, hospitals, trades and the great host of servants –
they all had masters. They were part of the fabric of a society of
hierarchical belonging, and nothing mattered more to Herbert
than the mutual belonging of himself and his saviour-master. 'A
true Hymn' testifies to it.

> My joy, my life, my crown!
> My heart was meaning all the day,
> Somewhat it fain would say:
> And still it runneth mutt'ring up and down
> With only this, *My joy, my life, my crown.*

Preoccupation with that spiritual relationship carried Herbert
through the seven years of rootlessness and perplexity which
followed the high point of his oration on the return of Prince
Charles. The bitterness of these years is evident in the two
'Employment' poems – in fact about unemployment – written
early on in this period, along with 'Affliction (1)'. 'The Answer'
testifies to the disappointment of his acquaintances:

> Who think me eager, hot, and undertaking,
> But in my prosecutions slack and small.

He got leave from Cambridge in 1624 and served briefly as MP
for Montgomery: a family duty. He spent time with his mother
and stepfather at Chelsea, John Donne being a fellow-guest, in
1625. In 1626 his patron John Williams, Bishop of Lincoln, made
him a canon of Lincoln with the prebend (salary without duties)
of the church at Leighton Bromswold in Huntingdonshire. The
Ferrar family lived nearby in their quasi-monastic family
community at Little Gidding and took on most of the actual
work entailed in Herbert's project of restoring the dilapi-
dated church. The result, completed shortly after Herbert's
death, is an interior eloquent of the Ferrars' and Herbert's
churchmanship: pulpit and prayer desk on either side of the
aisle balanced in equal height, pews all on a level, and abun-
dant light.

    When his mother died in 1627 Herbert put his heartbreak

into the Latin poems *Memoriae Matris Sacrum*, whose title means 'A Sacred Gift in Memory of My Mother'. In the same year he finally resigned the Oratorship that he had once so avidly desired and then neglected (no oration from him on the death of James I in 1625). John Danvers soon remarried but, solicitous for his stepson, he got his elder brother Henry, Earl of Danby, to put Herbert up in an apartment at his house at Dauntsey in Wiltshire. It stood cheek by jowl with the parish church, which Danby was restoring and adorning with a new tower: a project of interest to Herbert as the restorer of Leighton Bromswold. Having been made a deacon in 1624, with no concomitant duties, Herbert started worrying about being a priest, as recorded in his inconclusive poem 'The Priesthood'. Then happiness supervened. On 5 March 1629 Herbert married Jane Danvers, favourite daughter of Charles Danvers's large family living at Baynton, a few miles from stepfather Sir John Danvers's house and garden at West Lavington and twenty from Dauntsey. Like so many of the Wiltshire gentry, she was related to the biographer John Aubrey, who noted that 'my kinswoman was a handsome *bona roba* [literally "good stuff"] and ingenious [clever].' A few months later the head of the vastly ramifying Herbert family, William Earl of Pembroke, solved Herbert's employment problem by getting the king to appoint him rector of Fugglestone with Bemerton. These parishes lay between the great Pembroke house, Wilton, where Sir Philip Sidney had stayed with his sister the Countess Mary while writing *Arcadia*, and Salisbury with its cathedral music. It was an ideal placement. Herbert took his duties seriously, writing *The Country Parson* to describe them to himself as 'a mark to aim at'. Useful at last, married, living in an ample rectory with three orphaned nieces from Wales, writing and making music, the last four years of Herbert's previously anxious life were fulfilled. At the very last he handed to Edmund Duncon the 'little book' of his poems, which was to be published within the year.

   Its quality and variety – in both forms and contents – put it immediately and for ever among the masterpieces of English verse. Herbert, the contemporary of Shakespeare and friend of

Donne, drew on a century of achievement when he opened
'The Son' with ingenuous patriotic chutzpah:

> Let foreign nations of their language boast,
> What fine variety each tongue affords:
> I like our language, as our men and coast:
> Who cannot dress it well, want wit, not words.

Wyatt and Surrey had experimented with forms. They had
been included in Richard Tottel's popular *Miscellany* (1557),
which went through nine subsequent editions in the century. In
his preface Tottel, having noticed the achievements of Latin
and Italian poetry, 'yea, and in small parcels', asserted:

> That our tongue is able in that kind to do as praiseworthily as
> the rest, the honourable style of the noble Earl of Surrey, and
> the weightiness of the deep-witted Sir Thomas Wyatt the elder's
> verse, with several graces in sundry good English, do show
> abundantly.

In 1589 George Puttenham, a lawyer, provided a kind of en-
cyclopaedia of poetic forms in English:

> our language being no less copious, pithy and significative than
> [Greek or Latin], our conceits [ideas] the same, and our wits no
> less apt to devise and imitate than theirs were.

In 1595 Sir Philip Sidney's *Apology for Poetry* was published,
again insisting that 'our tongue is most fit to honour Poesy, and
to be honoured by Poesy'. Poetry could be used 'with the fruit
of comfort by some, when, in sorrowful pangs of their death-
bringing sins, they find the consolation of the never-leaving
goodness' of God, who, since the Psalms of biblical antiquity,
could be praised in 'that lyrical kind of songs and sonnets'
which abounded in England. It was a scrupulous craft, weigh-
ing 'each syllable of each word by just proportion' to make 'a
speaking picture', true to the soul's passions. Poetry in English
was abundantly resourceful, popular and self-confident.

Herbert's poetry was, as he said to Duncon, 'a picture' or series of pictures of what 'passed betwixt God and my soul': a sort of private record or journal. Much of his Latin poetry was published, but he kept his English poems private and in manuscript. He was certainly not alone in choosing to keep his poetry private: his friend Donne's *Songs and Sonnets* and *Divine Poems* were published posthumously in 1633, while *La Corona*, dedicated to Magdalen Herbert, remained in manuscript in her cabinet until then. Nevertheless, Herbert's thought that the records of his own inner life-experiences might be helpful to other people did not occur to him all of a sudden on his deathbed. '*The Dedication*' is there on the first page of the Williams Manuscript written some seven or eight years before his death (see A Note on the Texts at p. xlviii) and its final couplet expects readers other than himself to:

> *Turn their eyes hither, who shall make a gain:*
> *Theirs, who shall hurt themselves or me, refrain.*

The last stanza of 'Obedience' shows that he hoped for them and their sympathy.

> How happy were my part,
> If some kind man would thrust his heart
> Into these lines . . .

A certain modesty, even a withdrawn aristocratic vanity, such as Walton records of him as an undergraduate ('at too great a distance with all his inferiors'), may have kept Herbert from exposing his inmost soul to the world at large. But it is difficult to believe that when he had written masterpieces such as 'Redemption', 'Virtue', 'The Collar' or 'Love (3)' his just sense of achievement did not impel him to show them to someone, not least the mother who taught him how to write ('*literae hoc debent tibi / Queîs me educasti*' ['this my letters owe to you / The letters you taught me'], *Memoriae Matris Sacrum* 2) or his elder brother and fellow-poet Edward. He certainly exchanged

Latin and English verses with their mutual friend John Donne. Sir Francis Bacon dedicated his translation of the Psalms to Herbert as the best judge of 'divinity and poesy met'. An intimate and controlled readership of friends and family looks most likely for Herbert's English poetry in his lifetime.

We may assume that the fundamental reason that impelled Herbert to write his poems and revise them over and over again is the value he put on his own experience. He had read books of 'divinity' (theology) and found them tedious ('ling'ring' in 'Affliction (1)'). An exception was St Augustine, the theologian of love whose works, particularly his deeply experiential *Autobiography*, Herbert owned at his death and bequeathed to his curate. In his poem 'Divinity' he derided speculative theology as of no more use in living a life than astronomy. Experience was the thing, as Montaigne had insisted in his essay 'Of Experience': 'I study myself more than any other subject. It is my supernatural metaphysic, it is my natural philosophy.' And like Montaigne he found that to study the self was to study a being in constant flux: the subject of 'The Flower' (a favourite of Coleridge's) with its *cri de coeur* 'O that I once past changing were' denied by experience – and the denial accepted. The Psalms in his Bible agreed on all this with St Augustine and Sir Francis Bacon, whom Herbert praised in the Latin poem as the *pontifex* (high priest) of truth and Lord of induction: induction in which thinking starts with the observation of the specific and actual, in which experience and experiment are in command.

Herbert encouraged Ferrar to publish his poetry 'if he can think it may turn to the advantage of any dejected poor soul'. One can think of various ways in which this might come about. Poetry can be a reminder of happier times past or a hope of happier times to come. Herbert has both in 'The Glance', recalling the 'sug'red strange delight' when God first turned his 'sweet and gracious eye' upon him in his youthful past. Now, in his adult present it is a memory which can control 'surging griefs'. For the future it is a prospect and promise, captivatingly put in lines reminiscent of childhood hurts and their maternal comforting:

> What wonders shall we feel, when we shall see
> Thy full-ey'd love!
> When thou shalt look us out of pain . . .

The reciprocity, the loving exchange in those lines, sustains the best echo-poem ever written (they were a fashionable form in his time), Herbert's 'Heaven'. It is about the promise of future happiness in terms of perfectly reciprocal speech – not mere repetition but a taking up, adjusting and turning around. Its last lines are:

> Then tell me, what is that supreme delight?
>   *Echo.*   *Light.*
> Light to the mind: what shall the will enjoy?
>   *Echo.*   *Joy.*
> But are there cares and business with the pleasure?
>   *Echo.*   *Leisure.*
> Light, joy and leisure: but shall they persever?
>   *Echo.*   *Ever.*

Helen Vendler comments with Herbertian spirit that

> when we find words of the right sort to ask about the divine –
> words like 'delight,' 'enjoy,' 'pleasure' and 'persever' – God can
> do nothing better than answer us in our own vocabulary.
>   (*The Poetry of George Herbert* (Cambridge, MA.:
>   Harvard University Press, 1975, p. 227).

Herbert's heart's desire – the answering word, the answering look – is achieved in 'The Glance' and 'Heaven' with a precision of form and diction which looks ultimate until one reads the poem which follows 'Heaven' and closes the collection, 'Love (3)'. After it Herbert wrote 'Finis'. Vendler closes her book with it too:

> Sublime as 'Heaven' is, with its ethereal evocation of 'light, joy,
> and leisure', we conclude by preferring to it, as Herbert himself
> did, the heaven in which a welcome, a smile, a colloquy, a taking
> by the hand, and a seat at the table stand for all the heart can wish.
>   (p. 276)

In both 'Heaven' and 'Love (3)' complexity of form and feeling
is conveyed with the utmost, direct simplicity – the thing desired
and proposed in his two 'Jordan' poems.

Herbert is as great a poet of pain and grief as of happiness,
and here, too, reciprocity is the key. The sting of affliction in
the poems of that name is isolation:

> Thus thin and lean without a fence or friend,
> I was blown through with ev'ry storm and wind.

Sometimes Herbert is able to overcome it by recalling the suf-
ferings of Jesus, his Master.

> Thy life on earth was grief, and thou art still
> Constant unto it, making it to be
> A point of honour, now to grieve in me,
>   And in thy members suffer ill.
>   They who lament one cross,
> Thou dying daily, praise thee to thy loss.

Thus 'Affliction (3)'. The same thought resolves 'The Cross' –
more dramatically for following upon longer agonies at the
hands of the Father God, who makes 'my hopes my torture'.
But sometimes there is no consolation, no alleviation:

> Verses, ye are too fine a thing, too wise
>   For my rough sorrows . . .

And the poem ('Grief') ends with an unrhymed, out-of-metre
line, 'Alas, my God!' In 'Denial' each of the six verses ends with
such a line, except for the last, aspiring rather than actual:

> That so thy favours granting my request,
>   They and my mind may chime,
>   And mend my rhyme.

Deliberate distortions of this sort so dominate 'The Collar' as to
make it a sort of anti-poem. A poem usually engages its readers

by holding something lightly but firmly, simultaneously letting it be itself and keeping it under control. 'The Collar' is a tour de force, outbursts of rage being themselves so outrageously as to push control to breaking point – until the very end. This extraordinary threat to poetry's hold on its material, this triumph of descriptive form when form is disintegrating, contradicts the false image of Herbert as the tamer counterpart to his ferocious friend John Donne, a misapprehension for which William Dyce's sentimental picture in London's Guildhall, *George Herbert at Bemerton*, must bear some responsibility.

The therapeutic 'advantage' to the 'dejected reader' of Herbert's descriptions of physical and psychological pain is complex: the company of the poet as a fellow-sufferer, the poet's own comfort by his divine fellow-sufferer, the force and accuracy of the description or diagnosis of pain, the aptness of the form in metre and rhyme to the matter – even the possibility that the reader can forget his pain for a while in admiration of the poet's art. In 'Confession' his chosen metaphors of the carpenter's bradawl and burrowing moles induce a sympathetic wince:

> No screw, no piercer can
> Into a piece of timber work and wind,
> As God's affliction into man
> When he a torture hath designed.
> They are too subtle for the subtlest hearts;
> And fall, like rheums, upon the tend'rest parts.
>
> We are the earth; and they,
> Like moles within us, heave, and cast about:
> And till they foot and clutch their prey,
> They never cool, much less give out.

The isolation and the lack of reciprocity, most urgently desired, hurts in such lines as this verse of 'Denial':

> O that thou shouldst give dust a tongue
> To cry to thee,

> And then not hear it crying! all day long
> My heart was in my knee,
> But no hearing.

Once again, the last line fails to rhyme. Enjambement (the urgent voice and sense ignoring line endings) gives unbroken thrust, only for it to be brought up short in the third line and again in the fifth. Over against the divine torturer and frustrater is the divine sufferer, Christ, for whom Herbert invents a particularly palpable description of pain in 'The Agony':

> Sin is that press and vice, which forceth pain
> To hunt his cruel food through ev'ry vein.

So why should poems about psychological and physical pain 'turn to the advantage' of a poet's fellow-sufferers? When a baffling and mysterious illness is at last named, however drastic the diagnosis, it is some sort of comfort to the patient that what had weighed so inexplicably within, what had been dumbly confined to the personal, is known and named in the world outside. The poetry of affliction, especially when it touches the depths and heights of tragedy, can claim a similar therapeutic value, enhanced by the quality of art which takes care to make precision and beauty out of the destructive ugliness.

That is something, but not an answer to the sufferer's question of 'why?' and 'why to me?' Belief in a single omnipotent and benevolent God as the whole world's creator and director, enforced in the Christian Bible, gave those questions a destination but by no means a solution. If anything it made them more painful by suggesting that one's troubles were personally meant – perhaps as some sort of punishment – as well as personally felt. There was no way out of this for Herbert and his contemporaries, no alternative explanation of the world to challenge theism's explanatory power, no grounds or footings from which to do it. Atheists were rebels who opposed God morally rather than intellectually. Herbert, the unwavering believer, showed himself capable of such opposition in his poem 'Discipline':

> Throw away thy rod,
> Throw away thy wrath:
>   O my God,
> Take the gentle path.

Love is the lesson God needs to learn, or rather remember:

> Who can scape his bow?
> That which wrought on thee,
>   Brought thee low,
> Needs must work on me.

There is an adroitly witty syncretization here. Cupid, the classical archer god of love, hits the Christian God and – the reference is to the descent of his Son as God made man – brings him down to earth like a shot bird. The image is daring enough, and pleasing to readers as learned in classical paganism as in their own religion and ready to treat both with the freedom of familiarity. The implication is bolder still: there is a divine power over and above the great creator and director of the world, evident in the self-sacrifice of his 'son' Jesus Christ, Herbert's 'my Master'. It is love. And it is time that the Almighty recognized it. In effect, the whole of Herbert's deepest religious conviction is held in the buoyant imagery and light-footed metre of this miraculous poem.

T. S. Eliot was well aware of Herbert's Little Gidding connections when he wrote in his poem of that name that:

> Love is the unfamiliar Name
> Behind the hands that wove
> The intolerable shirt of flame
> Which human power cannot remove.

Stern but positive comfort: and like Herbert, Eliot was weaving together classical myth, the fiery shirt of Nessus that killed Heracles in Greek legend, with Christian conviction. William Cowper, an exceptional admirer of Herbert in the eighteenth century, found that his depression 'never seemed so much alleviated as while I was reading him', and Coleridge got 'substantial comfort' against his 'tendency to self-contempt'. Elizabeth Bishop, writing to thank Joseph Summers for sending her his *George Herbert: His Religion and Art* at a time when her lover was in hospital with a self-inflicted overdose, congratulated him on 'a beautiful job' which had sent her back to the poems: 'some even help a bit, I think'. Herbert is the idealized possibility haunting the imagination of Ford Madox Ford's long-suffering lover Christopher Tietjens in the latter pages of *Parade's End.*

'The only end of writing is to enable the readers better to enjoy life, or better to endure it,' declared Samuel Johnson, reviewing *A Free Enquiry into the Nature and Origin of Evil* by Soame Jenyns (1757). If Herbert had much to endure psychologically and physically in an apparently easy and comfortable life, he also had plenty to enjoy. He loved music. Aubrey was told by someone who knew Herbert at Dauntsey that 'he had a very good hand on the lute, and that he set his own lyrics or sacred poems'. Herbert described its mysteriously delightful effect in 'Church-music'.

> Now I in you without a body move,
> > Rising and falling with your wings:
> We both together sweetly live and love . . .

Language was another intense pleasure, with its 'sweet phrases, lovely metaphors':

> Lovely enchanting language, sugar-cane,
> Honey of roses . . .
> > ('The Forerunners')

Nature could delight him on a fine morning with the lifting vowels of the first line of 'Virtue' and its marriage of earth with sky:

> Sweet day, so cool, so calm, so bright,
> The bridal of the earth and sky . . .

And the sensual enjoyment of nature unites with the joy of writing in the famous lines about convalescence from 'The Flower':

> I once more smell the dew and rain,
> And relish versing . . .

Herbert's sensuality is at its height in 'The Odour' when he relishes the sheer sound of his favourite appellation for Christ, 'my Master':

> How sweetly doth *My Master* sound! *My Master!*
> As ambergris leaves a rich scent
> Unto the taster:
> So do these words a sweet content,
> An oriental fragrancy, *My Master*.

Ambergris is, according to *The Oxford English Dictionary*, 'a wax-like substance of ashy colour, found floating in tropical seas, and as a morbid secretion in the intestines of the sperm-whale. Used in perfumery, and formerly in cookery.' It has, in any case, a luscious sonority. Herbert was keen on smell, although, or perhaps because, it ranked lowest in the current hierarchy of faculties.

Between enjoying life and enduring it, with a touch of each in its essence, is the sense of its permanent ambivalence and muta-bility. It haunts three of the four stanzas of 'Virtue', which begin in rapturous sensuousness by addressing the 'sweet day', 'sweet rose' and 'sweet spring' and end with the reiterated 'must die'. 'There is but joy and grief' ('Affliction (5)') and Herbert blends them in 'Joseph's coat', a title derived from the 'coat of many colours' which Jacob, a metaphor for God in the poem, made for his darling son Joseph in Genesis 37. It starts with:

> Wounded I sing, tormented I indite,
> Thrown down I fall into a bed, and rest:
> Sorrow hath changed its note: such is his will,
> Who changeth all things, as him pleaseth best.

It ends with the conviction that God has:

> giv'n to anguish
> One of Joy's coats, 'ticing it with relief
> To linger in me, and together languish.
> I live to show his power, who once did bring
> My *joys* to *weep*, and now my *griefs* to *sing*.

That last word, along with 'note' in the previous extract, hints that music is making itself felt here with its ability to make sadness into pleasure. Both songs (Schubert's come to mind) and poems share the description of 'lyric'. When they are treading this borderline between grief and joy they are most effective when they are short. They walk a tightrope requiring an exquisite balance. Herbert's eight-line 'Bitter-sweet', each line being of a mere three feet, keeps that balance perfectly.

Such miniatures are one of Herbert's specialities. 'Iesu' tells of heartbreak and healing in ten lines. It depends on that old spelling in which the letter 'I' is interchangeable with 'J', because 'Iesu' broken into bits sounds the same as 'I ease you', reassembling the letters scattered by the breakage: 'a great affliction' finding its apt metaphor in a domestic accident, and a grief crafted into a delightful toy made of words and their letters. Other miniatures include the nine-line 'Trinity Sunday', its three three-line stanzas covering past, present and future, the last verse made up of three bodily nouns, three abstract nouns and three verbs. It could hardly be neater, but for all that it is a heartfelt prayer. 'Hope' is as neat and even shorter. Its sprightly allegory is unravelled in the notes included in this book. The title is deliberately misleading (Herbert likes to tease his readers in this way: see 'Discipline' and 'Employment (1)' and '(2)'). The poem is about hope's repeated disappointments.

Allegory consists of metaphors extended into series or sets. With Spenser's *Faerie Queene* of 1596 it was very extended indeed. This long poem was, as its poet himself said in 'A Letter of the Authors', 'cloudily enwrapped in allegorical devices'. Bunyan's allegorical *Pilgrim's Progress*, of 1678 and 1684 (Part 2), was to be somewhat less extended and highly popular.

Between the two, Herbert's allegorical poems show brevity to be the soul of wit. In 'The Pilgrimage', as with Bunyan later, inner biography becomes a journey through the English landscape, its meadows, woods, heaths, hills and ponds all marking episodes of the soul's progress with a homely realism surpassing Bunyan's and unusual in allegory. Its conclusion is bitter. Two of Herbert's allegorical poems are conversational: the poet unburdening himself to a friend who answers him in 'Love unknown' and the 'good old man' in 'Peace' telling his agricultural allegory of Christian history. Christian writers, not least those of the New Testament, were accustomed to treat the Old Testament scriptures allegorically. Herbert continues that tradition in 'The Bunch of Grapes' after a comically domestic start. 'The Family' is an entirely domestic allegory of the disorderly heart and its peacemakers.

Among Herbert's most enjoyable qualities is his wit, particularly when it is deployed on his religion – so much part and parcel of his inner and outer worlds that on occasion he can treat it lightly. 'Discipline' (see above) shows him using it against God, no less, 'Giddiness' and 'Vanity (1)' against human perversities and failings, and 'Divinity' against theological speculation. His clever devising of forms to picture their content, as in 'The Altar' and 'Easter-wings', was derided by Hobbes and Dryden, but when these poems are read aloud it is clear that there is nothing forced about them – rather that their shapes assist both sense and feeling. Herbert's creative intelligence, his wit at his most inventive and original, enabled him to make, in short compass, convincing stories of creation and redemption to put beside their orthodox and biblical counterparts. Of 'Redemption' Louis MacNeice wrote in *Varieties of Parable* (Cambridge: Cambridge University Press, 1965, p. 50) that Herbert was 'able quite naturally to express his feelings about Redemption in an out-and-out allegorical sonnet in everyday diction and with images drawn from something so prosaic as real estate'. For Seamus Heaney in his investigation of the relation of poetry to life in *The Redress of Poetry* (London: Faber and Faber, 1995, p. 10), 'Herbert's work ... is an example of that fully realized poetry I have attempted to define,

a poetry where the coordinates of the imagined thing corres-
pond to and allow us to contemplate the complex burden of
our own experience.' 'Fully realized poetry' – that is what the
reader will find here in abundance.

It was Coleridge's view that to appreciate Herbert's poetry
the reader must be not only 'a devotional Christian' but also
'an affectionate and dutiful child of the Church'. T. S. Eliot was
just such a reader. But in his British Council pamphlet *George
Herbert* (1962) Eliot dismissed that line of thinking as 'a gross
error'. Herbert was for everybody: not just because of his
'exquisite craftsmanship' but for 'the *content* of the poems
which make up *The Temple*'. Eliot was speaking from his own
experience when he wrote in the same essay that

> The great danger, for the poet who would write religious verse,
> is that of setting down what he would like to feel rather than
> be faithful to the expression of what he really feels. Of such
> pious insincerity Herbert is never guilty . . . What we can confi-
> dently believe is that every poem in the book is true to the poet's
> experience.

With Herbert, craftsmanship and content are always inte-
grated, as the notes in this edition try to show. The fourth
stanza of 'Denial' is a case – one among so many – in point. It
is addressed to his inattentive, even deaf, God. To quote it
again:

> O that thou shouldst give dust a tongue
>   To cry to thee,
> And then not hear it crying! all day long
>   My heart was in my knee,
>   But no hearing.

From the religious point of view, that is not remote from the
passionate bleakness of Samuel Beckett. In Herbert our dust is
given a tongue of exceptional eloquence. You have only to look
at this stanza to notice the aptness of its form to its content: the
lines all broken by inequality but impelled by enjambement,

and the last line showing by its stark non-rhyming the lack of that reciprocity, that echo, which was Herbert's (and is everybody's) heart's desire. *The Temple* is full of lyrics which are true to life, recording common mental processes with honest precision. They bring 'a constant wit' to bear on occasions of anger, shame, desperation, sorrow, submission, protest, wonder, praise, gratitude, nostalgia, contentment – the list could go on, but in any case must end, as *The Temple* itself does, with love.

John Drury, 2015

Introduction to the Latin Poems

Many readers may be unaware that Herbert wrote almost as much Latin poetry as he did English; that only the Latin verse was published in his lifetime; and that his brother Edward, a poet himself, considered the Latin poetry his best work. But in his commitment to Latin poetry Herbert was in fact typical of his day: a few major English poets of the late sixteenth and seventeenth centuries, including Shakespeare and Jonson, appear to have written little or no Latin verse, but they are the exception. By contrast, Campion, Donne, Herbert, Crashaw, Marvell, Milton and Cowley all wrote important poems in Latin as well as English, poems which both they and their contemporaries took as a serious element of their literary career. Modern surveys of seventeenth-century literature tend to obscure this fact, but anyone who begins to look at the manuscript notebooks and miscellanies in which so much of the poetry of this period was circulated and recorded quickly realizes that Latin poetry of all kinds – classical excerpts and translations of classical excerpts, as well as contemporary Latin verse – was an essential part of literary culture.

There are several reasons for this aspect of Renaissance English literature, which now seems so alien. Education, at both school and university, was strongly classical, focused intensely on the translation, memorization and production of Latin and Greek poetry and prose: all poets of this period had experience at school of writing verse in Latin, and often also in Greek, and many of them continued to turn to Latin verse throughout their adult lives. The study of 'literature' at school and university meant, almost exclusively, the study of the literature of Greece and Rome – and, in poetry, Homer, Virgil, Horace and Ovid above all.

Writing in Latin was also a route to professionalization of a kind: English in the early seventeenth century was still a relatively minor European language, and just as writers and thinkers in many countries today who wish to secure a worldwide audience are likely to write in English, or arrange for the translation of their work into English, so ambitious men across early modern Europe wrote in Latin to ensure that their work could be read as widely as possible. The Latin poems of the Welsh poet John Owen (*c.*1564–*c.*1622) and of the Polish poet Casimir Sarbiewski (1595–1640), for instance, were read, translated and imitated right across Europe; it is hard to think of a Polish author today with a similar international profile.

These are both practical factors, but there were literary reasons, too, for turning to Latin. The tradition of neo-Latin poetry – that is, Renaissance Latin poetry written in the classical style – offered a rich range of forms and genres which were in many cases quite different, both in their literary and cultural associations and in their technical challenges, from vernacular forms. To honour a friend, patron or monarch with a long Horatian ode, for instance, was not only an effective display of technical linguistic skill (as the metres of these poems are challengingly rigid), but also allowed the poet to bring into play the long history of that genre: rooted in Horace, and his expressions of love and respect for a host of famous Romans, including Virgil, their patron Maecenas and Augustus himself; but also participating in a tradition to which revered Christian writers from Prudentius to Sarbiewski had contributed.

So much for why poets of this period, Herbert among them, wrote in Latin. Why, then, should a modern reader be interested in this work, even if they have no Latin themselves, and little or no knowledge of the classical literature by which it is so strongly informed?

One answer to this question is the 'completist' one: if you love and admire Herbert's English poetry, there is both interest and satisfaction in gaining some knowledge of this 'hidden' half of his poetic identity, and there are plenty of connections

between the English and Latin poetry to satisfy you – I have
pointed out such connections wherever possible. A second
answer to that question is a biographical or psychological one:
if you find Herbert's life, Herbert the man, compelling, the
Latin verse includes several glimpses of his domestic life – such
as his cottage and garden in the seventh poem of *Memoriae
Matris Sacrum* (A Sacred Gift in Memory of My Mother) –
which are unlike anything in the English verse. That sequence,
a series of poems written in the immediate aftermath of his
mother's death, applies to a human subject the intensity of
emotion that we associate in the English Herbert only with the
divine. Other pieces – such as the enigmatic love lyric *Aethio-
pissa ambit Cestum Diuersi Coloris Virum* (included in 'Other
Latin Poems') or the brutal invective of *Memoriae Matris Sacrum*
(*MMS*) 12, display a side of Herbert that is barely represented
in the English writing.

But the best reason of all – the most important and enduring
one – is that Herbert is an excellent Latin poet. Many of these
poems are beautiful in Latin, and moving even in translation in
their blend of lived emotion and resonant allusion. Technically
they are of a very high quality: the early collection *Musae
Responsoriae* (*MR*) showcases Herbert's mastery of ten different
Latin metres. Some of what is beautiful about these poems will
always be lost in translation. But not all of it. Herbert's Latin
poetry offers the reader both what he or she already loves most
about his English poetry – a dazzling series of images, for
instance, or a nuanced expression of religious feeling – and also
new aspects to him: invective, eroticism, grief for his mother and
the clear-voiced confidence of a young man's literary ambition.

KEY FEATURES OF HERBERT'S
LATIN POETRY

I offer below a very brief guide to four aspects of Herbert's
Latin poetry that readers new to this material may find particu-
larly helpful to bear in mind.

1. Relationship to Scripture

As we might expect from such a famously religious poet, Herbert's Latin poetry has a close relationship to scripture, both the Old and New Testaments. This is most obvious in the collection of epigrams *Passio Discerpta* (*PD*, The Passion in Pieces), which follows the events of the crucifixion in the order in which they appear in the Gospel accounts. Many of the poems can be understood as meditations upon particular verses: poems 7 ('On the Reed, the Thorns, the Bowing Down and the Scarlet') and 8 ('On the Slaps') allude to particular verses from Matthew 27 and Mark 14 and 15. But the importance of scripture is evident throughout Herbert's Latin verse – his poem in honour of Francis Bacon ('In Honour of the Illustrious Lord Verulam') ends by comparing Bacon's project to the mustard seed (line 26), an allusion to the parable of the mustard seed found in three of the four Gospels (Matthew 13, Mark 4, Luke 13). The comparison suggests that Bacon's work is the scientific equivalent of the Kingdom of God.

2. Epigrams

The majority of Herbert's Latin poems are best described as epigrams: that is, short poems, usually in elegiac couplets, iambic trimeter or hendecasyllables (all metres used for short poems by the classical Latin poets; see also p. 349), on a very wide range of topics, but characterized by their concision and 'point' – their focus, often sharpened by wordplay, upon a single quality, person or idea. Typical subjects include abstract qualities or stock characters ('Avarice', *Lucus* 7; 'Love', *Lucus* 16; 'On the Worldly and the Unworldly', *MR* 27), historical, mythological or contemporary personages ('Doubting Thomas', *Lucus* 30; 'To the King. The Reason for Writing Epigrams', *MR* 1) or important concepts, moments or actions ('Man, a Statue', *Lucus* 1; 'Homeland', *Lucus* 2; 'On the Pierced Side', *PD* 4, 'On His Birthday and Good Friday Falling on the Same Day', 'Other Poems' 2; 'To Scotland. An Exhortation to Peace', *MR* 35).

Epigrams are a classical genre – the Latin form is indebted in particular to Catullus and Martial – but they are a much more significant element of early modern Latin literature than they are of the classical canon. Collections of epigrams – often combined with some longer forms, such as elegies or odes – were enormously popular in Herbert's time, in both English and Latin. The short Latin epigrams of the Welsh poet John Owen (c.1564–1622), for instance, were translated into English, French, German and Spanish. In English, Ben Jonson's *Epigrams* were published in 1616. Particularly popular epigrams often circulated individually – contemporary notebooks and manuscript miscellanies are full of them, with the most amusing or provocative examples found in dozens of surviving collections, often accompanied by a personal translation (for instance, of a fashionable Latin epigram into English rhyming couplets). The short form and rhetorical focus made them easy to memorize and well suited to witty quotation, whether in written correspondence or in conversation.

3. The Poetry Book

It is important to appreciate that epigram *collections* were designed to be read and appreciated as a whole. Poems which seem slight, unrewarding or even inappropriately flippant on their own may gather a different sort of resonance when read as one element, perhaps a single contributing image or motif, to the larger pattern of an entire book. Individual epigrams on 'stock characters' such as 'the good man' or 'the greedy man', for instance, may, read cumulatively over the course of an entire epigram collection, suggest the variety of characters and attributes to be found in society as a whole. Other collections suggest the various aspects of a fulfilling life, both public – epigrams to a patron, on political events and on the poet's own ambitions – and more private poems to friends, or on the loss of loved ones.

All four of Herbert's collections of Latin verse (like *The Temple*) show evidence of careful construction and organization. The most obvious example of this is *Passio Discerpta*, a series of devotional epigrams which follows the sequence of the

Gospel accounts of the crucifixion. *Memoriae Matris Sacrum* is unified by its theme – Herbert's attempts to come to terms with the loss of his mother – but it is also linked to his other work by its imagery: the first poem of the collection associates tears, ink and sin in a similar combination of images to the opening poem of *Passio Discerpta*. Similarly, the prefatory poem to James I in *Musae Responsoriae* uses an image of the Nile, and Herbert returns to the Nile in the final prayer, addressed this time to God himself (*MR* 40).

4. Characteristic Imagery

The image of the Nile in *Musae Responsoriae* is a structural device – it both opens and closes the collection, and in so doing associates the address to James I with God himself. But it is also an example of Herbert's marked interest in liquid imagery. Rivers, streams, seas, tears – and even blood, sweat, milk and saliva – flow throughout his Latin verse. *Passio Discerpta* 1–5 link Herbert's tears (at the thought of the crucifixion) with the ink (of his verse on the subject), the blood, sweat and water that flows from Christ on the cross, and finally even the saliva of the men who spit at Jesus as he is crucified. In the second half of *PD* 5 ('On the Spitting and the Mockery') this dense series of liquid motifs returns, as it were, to its wellspring: the 'Waters of life' from which all Christians drink – that is, Christ himself. In a remarkable epigram (*Lucus* 34) Herbert imagines himself suckling at Christ's wounded side, like a baby at the breast – an image that connects this powerful devotional poem with an equally powerful piece (*MMS* 7) in which an image of Herbert's dead mother taunts him with her empty breasts. This sequence of images draws part of its power from the traditional classical association between poetic inspiration and the motif of drinking water from the well or spring of the Muses.

This is just one of several such productive clusters of imagery; others include medical language and imagery – as in *Passio Discerpta* 8, where Christ is compared to a healing balm; *Lucus* 9, on the apostle Luke, who was a doctor; and *Memoriae Matris Sacrum* 6, which describes Herbert's intense grief as a physical illness cured only by the writing of poetry – and a persistent association between female fertility and the writing of poetry itself. *Memoriae Matris Sacrum* twice imagines Herbert himself transformed into a labouring mother, his offspring the poems of the collection (*MMS* 1 and 6). Poetic inspiration is also linked with fertility in the first poem of *Musae Responsoriae* (to James I).

The present book is the first edition of Herbert's poetry, aimed at the general reader, to print all the Latin poetry as well as the English, with a complete translation and some notes for guidance. The Latin is printed alongside the English, and the notes at the back of the volume refer to the English text, but with references to the Latin where relevant. The notes assume no prior knowledge of Latin or of classical literature. The translations are intended to be clear but not simplifying: Herbert's Latin is quite often very compressed, and his Latin poetry is operating within an allusive framework – a set of assumed shared reference-points, including classical myth and literature – often quite different from the English verse. The translations aim to give a sense of that poetic texture, using the notes where necessary to explicate names and allusions. Cross-references in the notes to both the English and the Latin poetry encourage readers to move between these two bodies of work which have so often been kept rigidly and artificially distinct.

Readers new to Herbert's Latin, but who are familiar with the English work, may wish to begin by following up cross-references in the notes to the English poetry, 'following their noses' from the poems they already know to Latin pieces that are new to them. The dazzling series of epithets applied to Francis Bacon in Herbert's poem 'In Honour of the Illustrious Baron Verulam', for instance, employs a stylistic motif familiar from several well-known English poems (such as 'Prayer (1)'). Otherwise, readers interested particularly in Herbert as a devotional poet might wish to start with the epigram collection *Passio Discerpta*, a meditation on the crucifixion; those with a historical interest in the culture and politics of the period could begin with *Musae Responsoriae* and the political epigrams in *Lucus* (6, 15–18); those interested in particular in Herbert's own life and experiences could try *Memoriae Matris Sacrum*, the moving collection written in memory of his mother in the weeks immediately after her death. From a literary perspective, the combination of emotional honesty and lyric form in *Memoriae Matris Sacrum* makes it the most appealing Latin collection for the majority of modern readers, while *Lucus* ('A Sacred Grove') is the most interestingly representative of the typical range and variety of seventeenth-century verse collections. But there are fine poems in each of Herbert's books of Latin verse, and they deserve a great deal more attention than they have so far received. I hope that this edition will allow more readers who have come to know and love the English Herbert to appreciate something of the mastery of his Latin poetry as well.

Victoria Moul, 2015

A Note on the Texts

THE ENGLISH TEXTS

The best edition of all Herbert's writings in verse and prose, English, Latin and Greek, remains *The Works of George Herbert*, edited with a commentary by F. E. Hutchinson (Oxford: Oxford University Press, 1941 and subsequently reprinted, but now out of print). Hutchinson's textual notes are full and immaculate, but his commentary can be disappointing. The remedy for this, though it copes only with Herbert's English poetry, is Helen Wilcox's *The English Poems of George Herbert* (Cambridge: Cambridge University Press, 2007), with its notes on the sources of every poem and on modern criticism of it, along with detailed commentary. Izaak Walton's *The Life of Mr George Herbert* (1670) and Herbert's own *A Priest to the Temple or, the Country Parson, his Character and Rule of Holy Life* are best consulted in *George Herbert: The Complete English Works*, edited and introduced by Ann Pasternak Slater (London: Everyman's Library, 1995).

Herbert's English poetry was first published in the year of his death, 1633, in Cambridge by Thomas Buck and Roger Daniel with the title *The Temple. Sacred Poems and Private Ejaculations*: a small duodecimo book, elegant and accurate. Appropriately to the intimacy of its contents, it could be slipped into a pocket. Italics were added to help the reader. It is the foundation of all subsequent editions, of which no fewer than six appeared in the next seven years, thirteen by 1709. After a long hiatus editions started to appear again in 1799 – some popular, some visually ornate, some increasingly scholarly and elaborate (notable if eccentric was G. H. Palmer's 1905 attempt to rearrange the poems in a biographical order, suggested by their origins in the circumstances of Herbert's life) up to and including the achievements of Hutchinson and Wilcox.

Now we need to go backwards to a point earlier in 1633. In the Bodleian Library at Oxford is a folio in which all the poems printed by Buck and Daniel are inscribed in the unmistakable, florid calligraphy of the Writing Room at Little Gidding, the Christian family community in Huntingdonshire. It was presided over by Herbert's friend Nicholas Ferrar and was only six miles from Leighton Bromswold Church, of which Herbert was prebendary: the recipient of its revenues but not its vicar. The title page of this fine manuscript is interesting. Herbert's introductory poem 'The Dedication' is written in the same fluent, curvaceous and sloping style as in the rest of the book. Above it, in a different hand recognizable as Ferrar's own trying to harmonize with the work of his scribes, is written 'The Temple: Psal: 29:8. In his Temple doth every man speake of his honour.' So the title seems to be Ferrar's, derived from the Psalm and the architectural references (The Church-Porch and so on) of the first poems. Below the dedication are the various signatures of five men: the Vice-Chancellor of the University of Cambridge, three heads of colleges and a secretary. These are explained by a subsequent owner of the book, William Sancroft, a collector eventually to become Archbishop of Canterbury, in an inscription above Ferrar's: 'The Original of Mr George Herbert's Temple as it was at first Licenced for the presse.' The signatories were granting that licence, at the disposal of the University. Buck and Daniel took advantage of it. But is it 'The Original'?

Edmund Duncon took the 'little book' which Herbert had entrusted to him, as related in the General Introduction of this book, to Little Gidding. John Ferrar, in his life of his brother Nicholas, confirms that he got it and 'which when N. F. had many & many a time read over, & embraced, & kissed again & again, he said, he could not sufficiently admire it, as a rich Jewel & most worthy to be in the hands & hearts of all true Christians'.

However, the Little Gidding manuscript in the Bodleian Library is by no stretch of the imagination a 'little book'. The likelihood is that it is a copy from it, in grandiose style to impress the Cambridge authorities, by the scribes in Ferrar's Writing Room. This little book itself has disappeared.

But another has survived. It contains, mostly in a different order, 69 of the 164 poems in the Bodleian manuscript and Buck and Daniel's 1633 printing, written by a scribe and corrected by Herbert himself. These are followed by two collections of Herbert's Latin poems, *Passio Discerpta* and *Lucus*, written in his own hand. It measures somewhat less than 6 by 4 inches, is bound in leather and is the sort of workaday notebook available from stationers' shops. It is now in Dr Williams's Library in London, having got there via two eighteenth-century collectors, the first of whom, John Jones, wrote on the fly-leaf that he got it from the library of Hugh Mapletoft of Huntingdon. Mapletoft was the grandson of Susanna Ferrar, sister of Nicholas Ferrar and a member of the family and community at Little Gidding. Internal evidence dates it around 1623 or soon after. There are three poems addressed to the poet-pope Urban VIII, who became pope in 1623; the unresolved disillusionment with academic life of 'Affliction (1)', included in this little book, confirms that it should be dated at the end of Herbert's Cambridge years and is not the other little book which Herbert entrusted to Duncon.

It was published in facsimile, introduced by Amy Charles, by Scholars' Facsimiles and Reprints of Delmar, New York in 1977. Herbert's own corrections are of obvious fascination for seeing him at work, in addition to which the poems in this little manuscript can be compared to Herbert's final versions as they appeared in their first printed edition, under the title of *The Temple*, in 1633. So major readings from the Williams manuscript which are absent from the Bodleian's Little Gidding manuscript are included in the notes of this book. Hutchinson can be consulted for minor ones.

The spelling here is modernized, with one exception which is important for pronunciation and reading. When Herbert finished a word, such as a past participle, with *ed*, he expected it to be pronounced as a syllable and not elided. Thus 'I looked on thy furniture so fine' in 'Affliction (1)' is a five-beat pentameter in which the *ed* is indispensable to the metre and rhythm – so it is marked with a grave accent in the text. When Herbert wants the *e* to be silent he indicates it with an apostrophe, as with 'quick-ey'd love' in 'Love (3)'. The original spelling can always be found in Hutchinson. The punctuation here is not modernized. I have retained the occasional italics, which seem to have been introduced by the Cambridge printers of 1633 to help the reader: they are not in the Williams or the Bodleian manuscripts. They indicate quotation or emphasis.

THE LATIN TEXTS
AND TRANSLATIONS

The text for this edition has been taken from Hutchinson's expertly edited text.

None of Herbert's English poetry was printed in his lifetime, but several of the Latin pieces gathered here in *Alia Poemata Latina* (Other Latin Poems) were, as was his book of Latin poems on the death of his mother, *Memoriae Matris Sacrum* (1627), the only complete collection of Herbert's poetry, English or Latin, to be published while he was alive. Autograph copies of *Passio Discerpta* and *Lucus* survive in the Williams MS.

Existing commentary on Herbert's Latin verse is in short supply. Hutchinson offers brief notes, especially to points of historical background or biblical allusion, but they are extremely concise and include no guide to, for instance, Herbert's accomplished and varied use of Latin lyric metres.

Memoriae Matris Sacrum, in many respects the most impressive of Herbert's Latin verse collections, now has a strong edition with parallel translation, literal gloss and extensive commentary, edited by Catherine Freis, Richard Freis and Greg Miller (Fairfield, Conn.: George Herbert Journal, Special Studies and Monographs, 2012). The reader interested in this fine collection in particular should certainly consult the more extensive interpretative essays, and meticulous guide to grammar, syntax and metre, offered by this edition.

For the rest of Herbert's Latin poetry, we have only the brief notes in Hutchinson, the even briefer comments to be found at the back of M. McCloskey and P. Murphy, *The Latin Poems of George Herbert: A Bilingual Edition* (Athens, OH: Ohio University Press, 1965; now long out of print, though still available on the second-hand market), plus scattered remarks in various works of secondary literature. The single most useful of these is the essay on Herbert's Latin poetry by W. Hilton Kelliher included in J. W. Binns's fine 1974 collection *The Latin Poetry of English Poets*, which has happily just been reissued by Routledge.

Further Reading

EDITIONS

George Herbert, The Temple: A Diplomatic Edition of the Bodleian Manuscript (Tanner 307) with Introduction and Notes by Mario A. di Cesare, Medieval and Renaissance Texts and Studies, Volume 54 (Binghampton, NY, 1995).

The Williams Manuscript of George Herbert's Poems: A Facsimile Reproduction with an Introduction by Amy M. Charles, Scholars' Facsimiles and Reprints (Delmar, NY, 1977).

The Works of George Herbert, ed. with a Commentary by F. E. Hutchinson (Oxford: Oxford University Press, 1945).

The English Poems of George Herbert, ed. Helen Wilcox (Cambridge: Cambridge University Press, 2007).

George Herbert: The Complete English Works, ed. and introduced by Ann Pasternak Slater (London: Everyman's Library, 1995).

George Herbert: Verse and Prose, ed. and selected by Wendy Cope (London: Society for Promoting Christian Knowledge, 2003).

A Choice of George Herbert's Verse, ed. with an introduction by R. S. Thomas (London: Faber and Faber, 1967).

George Herbert, selected and introduced by W. H. Auden (Harmondsworth: Penguin, 1973).

George Herbert: Memoriae Matris Sacrum . . . A Critical Text, Translation, and Commentary, ed. Catherine Freis, Richard Freis and Greg Miller (Fairfield, CT: George Herbert Journal, Special Studies and Monographs, 2012).

Selected Poems of George Herbert with a Few Representative Poems by his Contemporaries, ed. Douglas Brown (London: Hutchinson, 1960).

McCloskey, M. and Murphy, P., *The Latin Poetry of George Herbert: A Bilingual Edition* (Athens, OH: Ohio University Press, 1965).

LIFE

Aubrey, J., *Brief Lives*, ed. Oliver Lawson Dick (London: Secker & Warburg, 1949).

Charles, A., *A Life of George Herbert* (Ithaca, NY: Cornell University Press, 1977).

Drury, J., *Music at Midnight: The Life and Poetry of George Herbert* (London: Allen Lane, 2013).

Walton, I., *The Life of Mr George Herbert* (London, 1670), reprinted in *George Herbert: The Complete English Works*, ed. and introduced by Ann Pasternak Slater (London: Everyman's Library, 1995).

CONCORDANCE

A Concordance to the Complete Writings of George Herbert, ed. Mario di Cesare and Rigo Mignani (Ithaca, NY: Cornell University Press, 1977).

CRITICAL AND CONTEXTUAL

Augustine, *Confessions*, trans. Henry Chadwick (Oxford: Oxford University Press, 1992).

Bloch, C., *Spelling the Word: George Herbert and the Bible* (Berkeley: University of California Press, 1985).

Bottrall, M., *George Herbert* (London: John Murray, 1954).

Carey, J., *John Donne: Life, Mind and Art* (London: Faber and Faber, 1990).

Clarke, E., *Theory and Theology in George Herbert's Poetry* (Oxford: Oxford University Press, 1997).

Collinson, P., *The Religion of Protestants: The Church in English Society 1559–1625* (Oxford: Oxford University Press, 1982).

Crashaw, R., *The Verse in English of Richard Crashaw* (New York and London: Grove Press, 1949).

Doeksen, D. W., *Conforming to the Word: Herbert, Donne and the English Church before Laud* (Lewisburg, PA: Bucknell University Press, 1997).

Donne, J., *The Major Works*, ed. John Carey (Oxford: Oxford University Press, 1990).

——, *A Sermon of Commemoration of the Lady Danvers* (Ann Arbor, MI: Scholars' Facsimiles and Reprints, 2006).

Eliot, T. S., *George Herbert* (London: Longmans Green, 1962).

Empson, W., *Seven Types of Ambiguity* (London: Chatto & Windus, 1930).

Fenton, J., *An Introduction to English Poetry* (London: Viking, 2002).

Fincham, K., *The Early Stuart Church: 1603–1642* (London: Routledge, 1993).

Fish, S., *Self-Consuming Artefacts: The Experience of Seventeenth-Century Literature* (Berkeley: University of California Press, 1972).

——, *The Living Temple: George Herbert and Catechizing* (Berkeley: University of California Press, 1978).

Free, C., *Music for a King: George Herbert's Style and the Metrical Psalms* (Baltimore: Johns Hopkins University Press, 1972).

Green, I., *Print and Protestantism in Early Modern England* (Oxford: Oxford University Press, 2000).

Heaney, S., *The Redress of Poetry* (London: Faber and Faber, 1995).

Herbert, E., *De Veritate*, trans. and ed. Meyrick Carre (Bristol: J. W. Arrowsmith, 1937).

——, *The Poems of Lord Herbert of Cherbury*, ed. G. Moore Smith (Oxford: Oxford University Press, 1923).

——, *Autobiography* (London: Walter Scott, 1888).

Hooker, R., *Works*, ed. John Keble (Oxford: Oxford University Press, 1836).

Hyde, A. G., *George Herbert and his Times* (London: Methuen, 1906).

King, Bishop H., *The Poems*, ed. John Sparrow (London: Nonesuch Press, 1925).

Knights, L. C., *Explorations: Essays in Criticism Mainly on the Literature of the Seventeenth Century* (London: Chatto & Windus, 1946).

Lull, J., *The Poem in Time: Reading George Herbert's Revisions of 'The Church'* (Newark, DE: University of Delaware Press, 1990).

McCullough, P., ed., *Lancelot Andrewes: Selected Sermons and Lectures* (Oxford: Oxford University Press, 2005).

Mack, P., *Elizabethan Rhetoric: Theory and Practice* (Cambridge: Cambridge University Press, 2002).

MacNeice, L., *Varieties of Parable* (Cambridge: Cambridge University Press, 1965).

Martin, J., *Walton's Lives: Conformist Commemorations and the Rise of Biography* (Oxford: Oxford University Press, 2001).

Martz, L., *The Poetry of Meditation* (New Haven, CT: Yale University Press, 1962).

Maycock, A., *Nicholas Ferrar* (London: Society for Promoting Christian Knowledge, 1938).

Nicolson, A., *Power and Glory: Jacobean England and the Making of the King James Bible* (London: HarperCollins, 2003).

Novarr, D., *The Making of Walton's Lives* (Ithaca, NY: Cornell University Press, 1958).

O'Day, R., *Education and Society 1500–1800: The Social Foundations of Education in Early Modern Britain* (London: Longman, 1982).

Patrides, C. A., *George Herbert: The Critical Heritage* (London: Routledge, 1983).

Powers-Beck, J., *Writing the Flesh: The Herbert Family Dialogue* (Pittsburgh, PA: Duquesne University Press, 1998).

Puttenham, G., *The Art of English Poesy*, ed. Frank Wigham and Wayne A. Rebhorn (Ithaca, NY: Cornell University Press, 2007).

Schonfeldt, M., *Prayer and Power: George Herbert and Renaissance Courtship* (Chicago: University of Chicago Press, 1991).

Sidney, Sir P., *An Apology for Poetry*, ed. Geoffrey Shepherd (London: Thomas Nelson and Sons, 1965).

——, *The Old Arcadia*, ed. Katherine Duncan-Jones (Oxford: Oxford University Press, 1999.

Singleton, M. W., *God's Courtier: Configuring a Different Grace in George Herbert's 'Temple'* (Cambridge: Cambridge University Press, 1987).

Stubbs, J., *Donne: The Reformed Soul* (London: Viking, 2006).

Summers, J., *George Herbert: His Religion and Art* (London: Chatto & Windus, 1954).

Tottel, R., *Miscellany: Songs and Sonnets of Henry Howard, Earl of Surrey, Sir Thomas Wyatt and Others*, ed. Amanda Holton and Tom Macfaul (London: Penguin, 2011).

Tuve, R., *A Reading of George Herbert* (London: Faber and Faber, 1952).

Vaughan, H., *The Complete Poems*, ed. Alan Rudrum (London: Penguin, 1995).

Vendler, H., *The Poetry of George Herbert* (Cambridge, MA: Harvard University Press, 2005).

——, *Invisible Listeners: Lyric Intimacy in Herbert, Whitman and Ashbery* (Princeton, NJ: Princeton University Press, 2005).

White, J. B., *'This Book of Starres': Learning to Read George Herbert* (Ann Arbor: University of Michigan Press, 1994).

Woudhuysen, H. R., *Sir Philip Sidney and the Circulation of Manuscripts 1558–1640* (Oxford: Oxford University Press, 1996).

THE ENGLISH VERSE

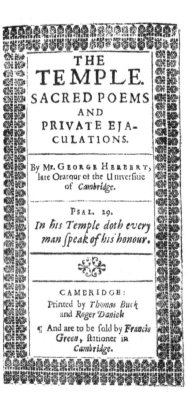

THE
TEMPLE.
SACRED POEMS
AND
PRIVATE EJA-
CULATIONS.

By Mr. GEORGE HERBERT,
late Oratour of the Universitie
of *Cambridge.*

PSAL. 29.
In his Temple doth every
man speak of his honour.

CAMBRIDGE:
Printed by *Thomas Buck*
and *Roger Daniel.*
¶ And are to be sold by *Francis*
Green, stationer in
Cambridge.

THE TEMPLE

SACRED POEMS
AND PRIVATE EJACULATIONS[1]

The Printers to the Reader.

The dedication of this work having been made by the author to the Divine Majesty only, how should we now presume to interest any mortal man in the patronage of it? Much less think we it meet to seek the recommendation of the Muses, for that which himself was confident to have been inspired by a diviner breath than flows from Helicon. The world therefore shall receive it in that naked simplicity with which he left it, without any addition either of support or ornament more than is included in itself. We leave it free and unforestalled to every man's judgement, and to the benefit that he shall find by perusal. Only for the clearing of some passages we have thought it not unfit to make the common Reader privy to some few particularities of condition and disposition of the Person.

Being nobly born, and as eminently endued with gifts of the mind, and having by industry and happy education perfected them to that great height of excellency, whereof his fellowship of Trinity College in Cambridge, and his Oratorship in the University, together with that knowledge which the King's Court had taken of him, could make relation far above ordinary. Quitting both his deserts and all the opportunities that he had for worldly preferment, he betook himself to the Sanctuary and Temple of God, choosing rather to serve at God's Altar, than to seek the honour of State employments. As for those inward enforcements to this course (for outward there was none) which many of these ensuing verses bear witness of, they detract not from the freedom but add to the honour of this resolution in him. As God had enabled him, so he accounted him meet not only to be called but to be compelled to this service: wherein his faithful discharge

was such as may make him justly a companion to the primitive
Saints, and a pattern or more for the age he lived in.

To testify his independency upon all others and to quicken
his diligence in this kind, he used in his ordinary speech, when
he made mention of the blessed name of our Lord and Saviour
Jesus Christ, to add, *My Master*.

Next God, he loved that which God himself has magnified
above all things, that is, his Word: so as he has been heard to
make solemn protestation, that he would not part with one leaf
thereof for the whole world, if it were offered him in exchange.

His obedience and conformity to the Church and the discip-
line thereof was singularly remarkable. Though he abounded in
private devotions, yet went he every morning and evening with
his family to the Church; and by his example, exhortations and
encouragements drew the greater part of his parishioners to
accompany him daily in the public celebration of Divine Service.

As for worldly matters, his love and esteem to them was so
little, as no man can more ambitiously seek than he did ear-
nestly endeavour the resignation of the Ecclesiastical dignity,
which he was possessor of. But God permitted not the accom-
plishment of this desire, having ordained him his instrument
for re-edifying of the Church belonging thereunto that had lain
ruinated almost twenty years. The reparation whereof, having
been uneffectually attempted by public collections, was in the
end by his own and some few others' private free-will offerings
successfully effected. With the remembrance whereof, as of an
especial good work, when a friend went about to comfort him
on his deathbed, he made answer, *It is a good work, if it be
sprinkled with the blood of Christ*: otherwise than in this
respect he could find nothing to glory or comfort himself with,
neither in this nor in any other thing.

And these are but a few of many that might be said, which
we have chosen to premise as a glance to some parts of the
ensuing book, and for an example to the Reader. We conclude
all with his own Motto, with which he used to conclude all
things that might seem to tend any way to his own honour:

Less than the least of God's mercies.

The Dedication.

Lord, my first fruits present themselves to thee;
Yet not mine neither: for from thee they came,
And must return. Accept of them and me,
And make us strive, who shall sing best thy name.
    Turn their eyes hither, who shall make a gain:
    Theirs, who shall hurt themselves or me, refrain.

The Church-porch.

PERIRRHANTERIUM

1

Thou, whose sweet youth and early hopes enhance
Thy rate and price, and mark thee for a treasure;
Harken unto a Verser, who may chance
Rhyme thee to good, and make a bait of pleasure.
   A verse may find him, who a sermon flies,   5
   And turn delight into a sacrifice.

2

Beware of lust: it doth pollute and foul
Whom God in Baptism washt with his own blood.
It blots thy lesson written in thy soul;
The holy lines cannot be understood.   10
   How dare those eyes upon a Bible look,
   Much less towards God, whose lust is all their book?

3

Abstain wholly, or wed. Thy bounteous Lord
Allows thee choice of paths: take no byways;
But gladly welcome what he doth afford;   15
Not grudging, that thy lust hath bounds and stays.
   Continence hath his joy: weigh both; and so
   If rottenness have more, let Heaven go.

4

If God had laid all common, certainly
20   Man would have been th' incloser: but since now
God hath impaled us, on the contrary
Man breaks the fence, and every ground will plough.
    O what were man, might he himself misplace!
    Sure to be cross he would shift feet and face.

5

25   Drink not the third glass, which thou canst not tame,
When once it is within thee; but before
Mayst rule it, as thou list; and pour the shame,
Which it would pour on thee, upon the floor.
    It is most just to throw that on the ground,
30   Which would throw me there, if I keep the round.

6

He that is drunken, may his mother kill
Big with his sister; he hath lost the reins,
Is outlaw'd by himself: all kind of ill
Did with his liquor slide into his veins.
35   The drunkard forfeits Man, and doth devest
    All worldly right, save what he hath by beast.

7

Shall I, to please another's wine-sprung mind,
Lose all mine own? God hath giv'n me a measure
Short of his can, and body; must I find
40   A pain in that, wherein he finds a pleasure?
    Stay at the third glass: if thou lose thy hold,
    Then thou art modest, and the wine grows bold.

8

If reason move not gallants, quit the room,
(All in a shipwrack shift their several way)
45   Let not a common ruin thee entomb:
Be not a beast in courtesy; but stay,
    Stay at the third cup, or forgo the place.
    Wine above all things doth God's stamp deface.

9

Yet, if thou sin in wine or wantonness,
Boast not thereof; nor make thy shame thy glory.   50
Frailty gets pardon by submissiveness;
But he that boasts, shuts that out of his story.
  He makes flat war with God, and doth defy
  With his poor clod of earth the spacious sky.

10

Take not his name, who made thy mouth, in vain: 55
It gets thee nothing, and hath no excuse.
Lust and wine plead a pleasure, avarice gain:
But the cheap swearer through his open sluice
  Lets his soul run for nought, as little fearing.
  Were I an *Epicure*, I could bate swearing.   60

11

When thou dost tell another's jest, therein
Omit the oaths, which true wit cannot need:
Pick out of tales the mirth, but not the sin.
He pares his apple, that will cleanly feed.
  Play not away the virtue of that name,   65
  Which is thy best stake, when griefs make thee tame.

12

The cheapest sins most dearly punished are;
Because to shun them also is so cheap:
For we have wit to mark them, and to spare.
O crumble not away thy soul's fair heap.   70
  If thou wilt die, the gates of hell are broad:
  Pride and full sins have made the way a road.

13

Lie not; but let thy heart be true to God,
Thy mouth to it, thy actions to them both:
Cowards tell lies, and those that fear the rod;   75
The stormy working soul spits lies and froth.
  Dare to be true. Nothing can need a lie:
  A fault, which needs it most, grows two thereby.

14

Fly idleness, which yet thou canst not fly
80   By dressing, mistressing, and compliment.
If those take up thy day, the sun will cry
Against thee: for his light was only lent.
    God gave thy soul brave wings; put not those feathers
    Into a bed, to sleep out all ill weathers.

15

85   Art thou a magistrate? then be severe:
If studious; copy fair, what time hath blurr'd;
Redeem truth from his jaws: if soldier,
Chase brave employments with a naked sword
    Throughout the world. Fool not: for all may have,
90   If they dare try, a glorious life, or grave.

16

O England! full of sin, but most of sloth;
Spit out thy phlegm, and fill thy breast with glory:
Thy gentry bleats, as if thy native cloth
Transfused a sheepishness into thy story:
95   Not that they all are so; but that the most
    Are gone to grass, and in the pasture lost.

17

This loss springs chiefly from our education.
Some till their ground, but let weeds choke their son:
Some mark a partridge, never their child's fashion:
100   Some ship them over, and the thing is done.
    Study this art, make it thy great design;
    And if God's image move thee not, let thine.

18

Some great estates provide, but do not breed
A mast'ring mind; so both are lost thereby:
105   Or else they breed them tender, make them need
All that they leave: this is flat poverty.
    For he, that needs five thousand pound to live,
    Is full as poor as he, that needs but five.

19

The way to make thy son rich, is to fill
His mind with rest, before his trunk with riches: 110
For wealth without contentment, climbs a hill
   To feel those tempests, which fly over ditches.
      But if thy son can make ten pound his measure,
      Then all thou addest may be called his treasure.

20

When thou dost purpose ought (within thy power),   115
Be sure to do it, though it be but small:
Constancy knits the bones, and makes us stour,
When wanton pleasures beckon us to thrall.
   Who breaks his own bond, forfeiteth himself:
   What nature made a ship, he makes a shelf.   120

21

Do all things like a man, not sneakingly:
Think the king sees thee still; for his King does.
Simp'ring is but a lay-hypocrisy:
Give it a corner, and the clue undoes.
   Who fears to do ill, sets himself to task: 125
   Who fears to do well, sure should wear a mask.

22

Look to thy mouth; diseases enter there.
Thou hast two sconces, if thy stomach call;
Carve, or discourse; do not a famine fear.
Who carves, is kind to two; who talks, to all.   130
   Look on meat, think it dirt, then eat a bit;
   And say withal, Earth to earth I commit.

23

Slight those who say amidst their sickly healths,
Thou liv'st by rule. What doth not so, but man?
Houses are built by rule, and common-wealths.   135
Entice the trusty sun, if that you can,
   From his Ecliptic line: beckon the sky.
   Who lives by rule then, keeps good company.

24

Who keeps no guard upon himself, is slack,
140 And rots to nothing at the next great thaw.
Man is a shop of rules, a well truss'd pack,
Whose every parcel underwrites a law.
  Lose not thyself, nor give thy humours way:
  God gave them to thee under lock and key.

25

145 By all means use sometimes to be alone.
Salute thyself: see what thy soul doth wear.
Dare to look in thy chest; for 'tis thine own:
And tumble up and down what thou find'st there.
  Who cannot rest till he good fellows find,
150   He breaks up house, turns out of doors his mind.

26

Be thrifty, but not covetous: therefore give
Thy need, thine honour, and thy friend his due.
Never was scraper brave man. Get to live;
Then live, and use it: else, it is not true
155   That thou hast gotten. Surely use alone
  Makes money not a contemptible stone.

27

Never exceed thy income. Youth may make
Ev'n with the year: but age, if it will hit,
Shoots a bow short, and lessens still his stake,
160 As the day lessens, and his life with it.
  Thy children, kindred, friends upon thee call;
  Before thy journey fairly part with all.

28

Yet in thy thriving still misdoubt some evil;
Lest gaining gain on thee, and make thee dim
165 To all things else. Wealth is the conjurer's devil;
Whom when he thinks he hath, the devil hath him.
  Gold thou mayst safely touch; but if it stick
  Unto thy hands, it woundeth to the quick.

29

What skills it, if a bag of stones or gold
About thy neck do drown thee? raise thy head;   170
Take stars for money; stars not to be told
By any art, yet to be purchasèd.
   None is so wasteful as the scraping dame.
   She loseth three for one; her soul, rest, fame.

30

By no means run in debt: take thine own measure.   175
Who cannot live on twenty pound a year,
Cannot on forty: he's a man of pleasure,
A kind of thing that's for itself too dear.
   The curious unthrift makes his cloth too wide,
   And spares himself, but would his tailor chide.   180

31

Spend not on hopes. They that by pleading clothes
Do fortunes seek, when worth and service fail,
Would have their tale believèd for their oaths,
And are like empty vessels under sail.
   Old courtiers know this; therefore set out so,   185
   As all the day thou mayst hold out to go.

32

In clothes, cheap handsomeness doth bear the bell.
Wisdom's a trimmer thing, than shop e'er gave.
Say not then, This with that lace will do well;
But, This with my discretion will be brave.   190
   Much curiousness is a perpetual wooing
   Nothing with labour; folly long a-doing.

33

Play not for gain, but sport. Who plays for more,
Than he can lose with pleasure, stakes his heart;
Perhaps his wife's too, and whom she hath bore;   195
Servants and churches also play their part.
   Only a herald, who that way doth pass,
   Finds his crack'd name at length in the church glass.

34

If yet thou love game at so dear a rate,
Learn this, that hath old gamesters dearly cost:
Dost lose? rise up: dost win? rise in that state.
Who strive to sit out losing hands, are lost.
  Game is a civil gunpowder, in peace
  Blowing up houses with their whole increase.

35

In conversation boldness now bears sway.
But know, that nothing can so foolish be,
As empty boldness: therefore first assay
To stuff thy mind with solid bravery;
  Then march on gallant: get substantial worth.
  Boldness gilds finely, and will set it forth.

36

Be sweet to all. Is thy complexion sour?
Then keep such company; make them thy allay:
Get a sharp wife, a servant that will lour.
A stumbler stumbles least in rugged way.
  Command thyself in chief. He life's war knows,
  Whom all his passions follow, as he goes.

37

Catch not at quarrels. He that dares not speak
Plainly and home, is coward of the two.
Think not thy fame at ev'ry twitch will break:
By great deeds show, that thou canst little do;
  And do them not: that shall thy wisdom be;
  And change thy temperance into bravery.

38

If that thy fame with ev'ry toy be pos'd,
'Tis a thin web, which poisonous fancies make:
But the great soldier's honour was compos'd
Of thicker stuff, which would endure a shake.
  Wisdom picks friends; civility plays the rest.
  A toy shunn'd cleanly passeth with the best.

39

Laugh not too much: the witty man laughs least:
For wit is news only to ignorance.   230
Less at thine own things laugh; lest in the jest
Thy person share, and the conceit advance.
   Make not thy sport, abuses: for the fly
   That feeds on dung, is colourèd thereby.

40

Pick out of mirth, like stones out of thy ground,   235
Profaneness, filthiness, abusiveness.
These are the scum, with which coarse wits abound:
The fine may spare these well, yet not go less.
   All things are big with jest: nothing that's plain,
   But may be witty, if thou hast the vein.   240

41

Wit's an unruly engine, wildly striking
Sometimes a friend, sometimes the engineer.
Hast thou the knack? pamper it not with liking:
But, if thou want it, buy it not too dear.
   Many, affecting wit beyond their power,   245
   Have got to be a dear fool for an hour.

42

A sad wise valour is the brave complexion,
That leads the van, and swallows up the cities.
The giggler is a milk-maid, whom infection,
Or a fir'd beacon frighteth from his ditties.   250
   Then he's the sport: the mirth then in him rests,
   And the sad man is cock of all his jests.

43

Towards great persons use respective boldness:
That temper gives them theirs, and yet doth take
Nothing from thine: in service, care or coldness   255
Doth rateably thy fortunes mar or make.
   Feed no man in his sins: for adulation
   Doth make thee parcel-devil in damnation.

44

Envy not greatness: for thou mak'st thereby
Thyself the worse, and so the distance greater.
Be not thine own worm: yet such jealousy,
As hurts not others, but may make thee better,
    Is a good spur. Correct thy passions' spite;
    Then may the beasts draw thee to happy light.

45

When baseness is exalted, do not bate
The place its honour, for the person's sake.
The shrine is that which thou dost venerate;
And not the beast, that bears it on his back.
    I care not though the cloth of state should be
    Not of rich arras, but mean tapestry.

46

Thy friend put in thy bosom: wear his eyes
Still in thy heart, that he may see what's there.
If cause require, thou art his sacrifice;
Thy drops of blood must pay down all his fear:
    But love is lost; the way of friendship's gone,
    Though *David* had his *Jonathan*, *Christ* his *John*.

47

Yet be not surety, if thou be a father.
Love is a personal debt. I cannot give
My children's right, nor ought he take it: rather
Both friends should die, than hinder them to live.
    Fathers first enter bonds to nature's ends;
    And are her sureties, ere they are a friend's.

48

If thou be single, all thy goods and ground
Submit to love; but yet not more than all.
Give one estate, as one life. None is bound
To work for two, who brought himself to thrall.
    God made me one man; love makes me no more,
    Till labour come, and make my weakness score.

49

In thy discourse, if thou desire to please:
All such is courteous, useful, new, or witty.   290
Usefulness comes by labour, wit by ease;
Courtesy grows in court; news in the city.
  Get a good stock of these, then draw the card
  That suits him best, of whom thy speech is heard.

50

Entice all neatly to what they know best;   295
For so thou dost thyself and him a pleasure:
(But a proud ignorance will lose his rest,
Rather than show his cards.) Steal from his treasure
  What to ask further. Doubts well raised do lock
  The speaker to thee, and preserve thy stock.   300

51

If thou be Master-gunner, spend not all
That thou canst speak, at once; but husband it,
And give men turns of speech: do not forestall
By lavishness thine own, and others' wit,
  As if thou mad'st thy will. A civil guest   305
  Will no more talk all, than eat all the feast.

52

Be calm in arguing: for fierceness makes
Error a fault, and truth discourtesy.
Why should I feel another man's mistakes
More than his sicknesses or poverty?   310
  In love I should: but anger is not love,
  Nor wisdom neither: therefore gently move.

53

Calmness is great advantage: he that lets
Another chafe, may warm him at his fire:
Mark all his wand'rings, and enjoy his frets;   315
As cunning fencers suffer heat to tire.
  Truth dwells not in the clouds: the bow that's there,
  Doth often aim at, never hit the sphere.

54

Mark what another says: for many are
Full of themselves, and answer their own notion.
Take all into thee; then with equal care
   Balance each dram of reason, like a potion.
     If truth be with thy friend, be with them both:
     Share in the conquest, and confess a troth.

55

Be useful where thou livest, that they may
Both want, and wish thy pleasing presence still.
Kindness, good parts, great places are the way
   To compass this. Find out men's wants and will,
     And meet them there. All worldly joys go less
     To the one joy of doing kindnesses.

56

Pitch thy behaviour low, thy projects high;
So shalt thou humble and magnanimous be:
Sink not in spirit: who aimeth at the sky,
   Shoots higher much than he that means a tree.
     A grain of glory mixt with humbleness
     Cures both a fever and lethargicness.

57

Let thy mind still be bent, still plotting where,
And when, and how the business may be done.
Slackness breeds worms; but the sure traveller,
   Though he alight sometimes, still goeth on.
     Active and stirring spirits live alone.
     Write on the others, Here lies such a one.

58

Slight not the smallest loss, whether it be
In love or honour: take account of all;
Shine like the sun in every corner: see
   Whether thy stock of credit swell or fall.
     Who say, I care not, those I give for lost;
     And to instruct them, twill not quit the cost.

59

Scorn no man's love, though of a mean degree;
(Love is a present for a mighty king).   350
Much less make anyone thy enemy.
As guns destroy, so may a little sling.
　　The cunning workman never doth refuse
　　The meanest tool, that he may chance to use.

60

All foreign wisdom doth amount to this,   355
To take all that is given; whether wealth,
Or love, or language; nothing comes amiss:
A good digestion turneth all to health:
　　And then as far as fair behaviour may,
　　Strike off all scores; none are so clear as they.   360

61

Keep all thy native good, and naturalise
All foreign of that name; but scorn their ill:
Embrace their activeness, not vanities.
Who follows all things, forfeiteth his will.
　　If thou observest strangers in each fit,   365
　　In time they'll run thee out of all thy wit.

62

Affect in things about thee cleanliness,
That all may gladly board thee, as a flower.
Slovens take up their stock of noisomeness
Beforehand, and anticipate their last hour.   370
　　Let thy mind's sweetness have his operation
　　Upon thy body, clothes, and habitation.

63

In Alms regard thy means, and others' merit.
Think heav'n a better bargain, than to give
Only thy single market-money for it.   375
Join hands with God to make a man to live.
　　Give to all something; to a good poor man,
　　Till thou change names, and be where he began.

64

Man is God's image; but a poor man is
380   Christ's stamp to boot: both images regard.
God reckons for him, counts the favour his:
Write, So much giv'n to God; thou shalt be heard.
    Let thy alms go before, and keep heav'n's gate
    Open for thee; or both may come too late.

65

385   Restore to God his due in tithe and time:
A tithe purloin'd cankers the whole estate.
Sundays observe: think when the bells do chime,
'Tis angels' music; therefore come not late.
    God then deals blessings: If a king did so,
390   Who would not haste, nay give, to see the show?

66

Twice on the day his due is understood;
For all the week thy food so oft he gave thee.
Thy cheer is mended; bate not of the food,
Because 'tis better, and perhaps may save thee.
395   Thwart not th' Almighty God: O be not cross.
    Fast when thou wilt; but then 'tis gain, not loss.

67

Though private prayer be a brave design,
Yet public hath more promises, more love:
And love's a weight to hearts, to eyes a sign.
400   We all are but cold suitors; let us move
    Where it is warmest. Leave thy six and seven;
    Pray with the most: for where most pray, is heaven.

68

When once thy foot enters the church, be bare.
God is more there, than thou: for thou art there
405   Only by his permission. Then beware,
And make thyself all reverence and fear.
    Kneeling ne'er spoil'd silk stocking: quit thy state.
    All equal are within the church's gate.

69

Resort to sermons, but to prayers most:
Praying's the end of preaching. O be dresst;   410
Stay not for th' other pin: why thou hast lost
A joy for it worth worlds. Thus hell doth jest
   Away thy blessings, and extremely flout thee,
   Thy clothes being fast, but thy soul loose about thee.

70

In time of service seal up both thine eyes,   415
And send them to thine heart; that spying sin,
They may weep out the stains by them did rise:
Those doors being shut, all by the ear comes in.
   Who marks in church-time others' symmetry,
   Makes all their beauty his deformity.   420

71

Let vain or busy thoughts have there no part:
Bring not thy plough, thy plots, thy pleasures thither.
Christ purg'd his temple; so must thou thy heart.
All worldly thoughts are but thieves met together
   To cozen thee. Look to thy actions well: 425
   For churches are either our heav'n or hell.

72

Judge not the preacher; for he is thy Judge:
If thou mislike him, thou conceiv'st him not.
God calleth preaching folly. Do not grudge
To pick out treasures from an earthen pot.   430
   The worst speak something good: if all want sense,
   God takes a text, and preacheth patience.

73

He that gets patience, and the blessing which
Preachers conclude with, hath not lost his pains.
He that by being at church escapes the ditch,   435
Which he might fall in by companions, gains.
   He that loves God's abode, and to combine
   With saints on earth, shall one day with them shine.

74

Jest not at preacher's language, or expression:
How know'st thou, but thy sins made him miscarry?
Then turn thy faults and his into confession:
God sent him, whatso'er he be: O tarry,
    And love him for his Master: his condition,
    Though it be ill, makes him no ill Physician.

75

None shall in hell such bitter pangs endure,
As those, who mock at God's way of salvation.
Whom oil and balsams kill, what salve can cure?
They drink with greediness a full damnation.
    The Jews refusèd thunder; and we, folly.
    Though God do hedge us in, yet who is holy?

76

Sum up at night, what thou hast done by day;
And in the morning, what thou hast to do.
Dress and undress thy soul: mark the decay
And growth of it: if with thy watch, that too
    Be down, then wind up both; since we shall be
    Most surely judg'd, make thy accounts agree.

77

In brief, acquit thee bravely; play the man.
Look not on pleasures as they come, but go.
Defer not the least virtue: life's poor span
Make not an ell, by trifling in thy woe.
    If thou do ill; the joy fades, not the pains:
    If well; the pain doth fade, the joy remains.

SUPERLIMINARE

Thou, whom the former precepts have
Sprinkled and taught, how to behave
Thyself in church; approach, and taste
The church's mystical repast.

Avoid, Profaneness; come not here: 5
Nothing but holy, pure, and clear,
Or that which groaneth to be so,
May at his peril further go.

The Church

The Altar.

A broken ALTAR, Lord, thy servant rears,
Made of a heart, and cemented with tears:
   Whose parts are as thy hand did frame;
   No workman's tool hath touch'd the same.
          A HEART alone   5
          Is such a stone,
          As nothing but
          Thy pow'r doth cut.
          Wherefore each part
          Of my hard heart   10
          Meets in this frame,
          To praise thy name:
   That if I chance to hold my peace,
   These stones to praise thee may not cease.
O let thy blessed SACRIFICE be mine,   15
And sanctify this ALTAR to be thine.

The Sacrifice.

O, all ye, who pass by, whose eyes and mind
To worldly things are sharp, but to me blind;
To me, who took eyes that I might you find:
              Was ever grief like mine?

The Princes of my people make a head   5
Against their Maker: they do wish me dead,
Who cannot wish, except I give them bread:
              Was ever grief like mine?

Without me each one, who doth now me brave,
Had to this day been an Egyptian slave.   10
They use that power against me, which I gave:
                    Was ever grief, & c.

Mine own Apostle, who the bag did bear,
Though he had all I had, did not forbear
To sell me also, and to put me there: 15
                    Was ever grief, & c.

For thirty pence he did my death devise,
Who at three hundred did the ointment prize,
Not half so sweet as my sweet sacrifice:
                    Was ever grief, & c.   20

Therefore my soul melts, and my heart's dear treasure
Drops blood (the only beads) my words to measure:
O let this cup pass, if it be thy pleasure:
                    Was ever grief, & c.

These drops being tempered with a sinner's tears,   25
A Balsam are for both the Hemispheres:
Curing all wounds, but mine; all, but my fears:
                    Was ever grief, & c.

Yet my Disciples sleep: I cannot gain
One hour of watching; but their drowsy brain   30
Comforts not me, and doth my doctrine stain:
                    Was ever grief, & c.

Arise, arise, they come. Look how they run.
Alas! what haste they make to be undone!
How with their lanterns do they seek the sun!   35
                    Was ever grief, & c.

With clubs and staves they seek me, as a thief,
Who am the way of truth, the true relief;
Most true to those, who are my greatest grief:
                    Was ever grief, & c.   40

Judas, dost thou betray me with a kiss?
Canst thou find hell about my lips? and miss
Of life, just at the gates of life and bliss?
                          Was ever grief like mine?

45   See, they lay hold on me, not with the hands
Of faith, but fury: yet at their commands
I suffer binding, who have loos'd their bands:
                          Was ever grief, & c.

All my Disciples fly; fear puts a bar
50   Betwixt my friends and me. They leave the star,
That brought the wise men of the East from far.
                          Was ever grief, & c.

Then from one ruler to another bound
They lead me; urging, that it was not sound
55   What I taught: Comments would the text confound.
                          Was ever grief, & c.

The Priest and rulers all false witness seek
'Gainst him, who seeks not life, but is the meek
And ready Paschal Lamb of this great week:
60   Was ever grief, & c.

Then they accuse me of great blasphemy,
That I did thrust into the Deity,
Who never thought that any robbery:
                          Was ever grief, & c.

65   Some said, that I the Temple to the floor
In three days razed, and raisèd as before.
Why, he that built the world can do much more:
                          Was ever grief, & c.

Then they condemn me all with that same breath,
70   Which I do give them daily, unto death.
Thus *Adam* my first breathing rendereth:
                          Was ever grief, & c.

They bind, and lead me unto *Herod*: he
Sends me to *Pilate*. This makes them agree;

But yet their friendship is my enmity: 75
               Was ever grief, & c.

Herod and all his bands do set me light,
Who teach all hands to war, fingers to fight,
And only am the Lord of hosts and might:
               Was ever grief, & c.   80

Herod in judgement sits, while I do stand;
Examines me with a censorious hand:
I him obey, who all things else command:
               Was ever grief, & c.

The *Jews* accuse me with despitefulness;   85
And vying malice with my gentleness,
Pick quarrels with their only happiness:
               Was ever grief, & c.

I answer nothing, but with patience prove
If stony hearts will melt with gentle love.   90
But who does hawk at eagles with a dove?
               Was ever grief, & c.

My silence rather doth augment their cry;
My dove doth back into my bosom fly,
Because the raging waters still are high: 95
               Was ever grief, & c.

Hark how they cry aloud still, *Crucify*:
It is not fit he live a day, they cry,
Who cannot live less than eternally:
               Was ever grief, & c.   100

Pilate a stranger holdeth off; but they,
Mine own dear people, cry, *Away, away*,
With noises confusèd frighting the day:
               Was ever grief, & c.

Yet still they shout, and cry, and stop their ears,   105
Putting my life among their sins and fears,
And therefore wish *my blood on them and theirs*:
               Was ever grief, & c.

See how spite cankers things. These words aright
110   Usèd, and wishèd, are the whole world's light:
But honey is their gall, brightness their night:
                      Was ever grief, & c.

They choose a murderer, and all agree
In him to do themselves a courtesy:
115   For it was their own cause who killèd me:
                      Was ever grief, & c.

And a seditious murderer he was:
But I the Prince of peace; peace that doth pass
All understanding, more than heav'n doth glass:
120   Was ever grief, & c.

Why, Caesar is their only King, not I:
He clave the stony rock, when they were dry;
But surely not their hearts, as I well try:
                      Was ever grief, & c.

125   Ah! how they scourge me! yet my tenderness
Doubles each lash: and yet their bitterness
Winds up my grief to a mysteriousness:
                      Was ever grief, & c.

They buffet me, and box me as they list,
130   Who grasp the earth and heaven with my fist,
And never yet, whom I would punish, miss'd:
                      Was ever grief, & c.

Behold, they spit on me in scornful wise,
Who by my spittle gave the blind man eyes,
135   Leaving his blindness to mine enemies:
                      Was ever grief, & c.

My face they cover, though it be divine.
As *Moses'* face was veilèd, so is mine,
Lest on their double-dark souls either shine:
140   Was ever grief, & c.

Servants and abjects flout me; they are witty:
Now prophesy who strikes thee, is their ditty.
So they in me deny themselves all pity:
                    Was ever grief, & c.

And now I am deliver'd unto death,   145
Which each one calls for so with utmost breath,
That he before me well nigh suffereth:
                    Was ever grief, & c.

Weep not, dear friends, since I for both have wept
When all my tears were blood, the while you slept: 150
Your tears for your own fortunes should be kept:
                    Was ever grief, & c.

The soldiers lead me to the common hall;
There they deride me, they abuse me all:
Yet for twelve heav'nly legions I could call: 155
                    Was ever grief, & c.

Then with a scarlet robe they me array;
Which shows my blood to be the only way,
And cordial left to repair man's decay:
                    Was ever grief, & c.   160

Then on my head a crown of thorns I wear:
For these are all the grapes *Sion* doth bear,
Though I my vine planted and wat'red there:
                    Was ever grief, & c.

So sits the earth's great curse in *Adam's* fall   165
Upon my head: so I remove it all
From th' earth unto my brows, and bear the thrall;
                    Was ever grief, & c.

Then with the reed they gave to me before,
They strike my head, the rock from whence all store   170
Of heav'nly blessings issue evermore:
                    Was ever grief, & c.

They bow their knees to me, and cry, *Hail king*:
Whatever scoffs or scornfulness can bring,
175   I am the floor, the sink, where they it fling:
                    Was ever grief, & c.

Yet since man's sceptres are as frail as reeds,
And thorny all their crowns, bloody their weeds;
I, who am Truth, turn into truth their deeds:
180   Was ever grief, & c.

The soldiers also spit upon that face,
Which Angels did desire to have the grace
And Prophets once to see, but found no place:
                    Was ever grief, & c.

185   Thus trimmèd forth they bring me to the rout,
Who *Crucify him*, cry with one strong shout.
God holds his peace at man, and man cries out:
                    Was ever grief, & c.

They lead me in once more, and putting then
190   Mine own clothes on, they lead me out again.
Whom devils fly, thus is he toss'd of men:
                    Was ever grief, & c.

And now weary of sport, glad to engross
All spite in one, counting my life their loss,
195   They carry me to my most bitter cross:
                    Was ever grief, & c.

My cross I bear myself, until I faint:
Then Simon bears it for me by constraint,
The decreed burden of each mortal Saint:
200   Was ever grief, & c.

O all ye who pass by, behold and see;
Man stole the fruit, but I must climb the tree;
The tree of life to all, but only me:
                    Was ever grief, & c.

Lo, here I hang, charg'd with a world of sin,   205
The greater world o' th' two; for that came in
By words, but this by sorrow I must win:
       Was ever grief, & c.

Such sorrow, as if sinful man could feel,
Or feel his part, he would not cease to kneel   210
Till all were melted, though he were all steel:
       Was ever grief, & c.

But, *O my God, my God!* why leav'st thou me,
The son, in whom thou dost delight to be?
My God, my God –   215
        Never was grief like mine

Shame tears my soul, my body many a wound;
Sharp nails pierce this, but sharper that confound;
Reproaches, which are free, while I am bound.
       Was ever grief, & c.   220

Now heal thyself, Physician; now come down.
Alas! I did so, when I left my crown
And father's smile for you, to feel his frown:
       Was ever grief, & c.

In healing not myself, there doth consist   225
All that salvation, which ye now resist;
Your safety in my sickness doth subsist:
       Was ever grief, & c.

Betwixt two thieves I spend my utmost breath,
As he that for some robbery suffereth.   230
Alas! what have I stolen from you? death:
       Was ever grief, & c.

A king my title is, prefixed on high;
Yet by my subjects am condemned to die
A servile death in servile company: 235
       Was ever grief, & c.

They gave me vinegar minglèd with gall,
But more with malice: yet, when they did call,
With Manna, Angel's food, I fed them all:
240   Was ever grief, & c.

They part my garments, and by lot dispose
My coat, the type of love, which once cured those
Who sought for help, never malicious foes:
                          Was ever grief, & c.

245   Nay, after death their spite shall further go;
For they will pierce my side, I full well know;
That as sin came, so Sacraments might flow:
                          Was ever grief, & c.

But now I die; now all is finishèd.
250   My woe, man's weal: and now I bow my head.
Only let others say, when I am dead,
                          Never grief was like mine

The Thanksgiving.

O King of grief! (a title strange, yet true,
        To thee of all kings only due)
O King of wounds! how shall I grieve for thee,
        Who in all grief preventest me?
5   Shall I weep blood? why, thou hast wept such store
        That all thy body was one door.
Shall I be scourgèd, flouted, boxèd, sold?
        'Tis but to tell the tale is told.
My God, my God, why dost thou part from me?
10   Was such a grief as cannot be.
Shall I then sing, skipping, thy doleful story,
        And side with thy triumphant glory?
Shall thy strokes be my stroking? thorns, my flower?
        Thy rod, my posy? cross, my bower?
15   But how then shall I imitate thee, and
        Copy thy fair, though bloody hand?

Surely I will revenge me on thy love,
    And try who shall victorious prove.
If thou dost give me wealth, I will restore
    All back unto thee by the poor.   20
If thou dost give me honour, men shall see,
    The honour doth belong to thee.
I will not marry; or, if she be mine,
    She and her children shall be thine.
My bosom friend, if he blaspheme thy name,   25
    I will tear thence his love and fame.
One half of me being gone, the rest I give
    Unto some Chapel, die or live.
As for thy passion – But of that anon,
    When with the other I have done.   30
For thy predestination I'll contrive,
    That three years hence, if I survive,
I'll build a spittle, or mend common ways,
    But mend mine own without delays.
Then I will use the works of thy creation,   35
    As if I used them but for fashion.
The world and I will quarrel; and the year
    Shall not perceive, that I am here.
My music shall find thee, and ev'ry string
    Shall have his attribute to sing;   40
That all together may accord in thee,
    And prove one God, one harmony.
If thou shalt give me wit, it shall appear;
    If thou hast giv'n it me, 'tis here.
Nay, I will read thy book, and never move   45
    Till I have found therein thy love;
Thy art of love, which I'll turn back on thee,
    O my dear Saviour, Victory!
Then for thy passion – I will do for that –
    Alas, my God, I know not what.   50

The Reprisal.

I have consider'd it, and find
There is no dealing with thy mighty passion:
For though I die for thee, I am behind;
    My sins deserve the condemnation.

5   O make me innocent, that I
May give a disentanglèd state and free:
And yet thy wounds still my attempts defy,
    For by thy death I die for thee.

Ah! was it not enough that thou
10   By thy eternal glory didst outgo me?
Couldst thou not grief's sad conquests me allow,
    But in all vict'ries overthrow me?

Yet by confession will I come
Into the conquest. Though I can do nought
15   Against thee, in thee I will overcome
    The man, who once against thee fought.

The Agony.

Philosophers have measur'd mountains,
Fathom'd the depths of seas, of states, and kings,
Walk'd with a staff to heav'n, and tracèd fountains:
    But there are two vast, spacious things,
5   The which to measure it doth more behove:
Yet few there are that sound them; Sin and Love.

Who would know Sin, let him repair
Unto Mount Olivet; there shall he see
A man so wrung with pains, that all his hair,
10   His skin, his garments bloody be.
Sin is that press and vice, which forceth pain
To hunt his cruel food through ev'ry vein.

Who knows not Love, let him assay
    And taste that juice, which on the cross a pike
    Did set again abroach; then let him say   15
        If ever he did taste the like.
Love is that liquor sweet and most divine,
Which my God feels as blood; but I, as wine.

The Sinner.

Lord, how I am all ague, when I seek
    What I have treasur'd in my memory!
    Since, if my soul make even with the week,
Each seventh note by right is due to thee.
I find there quarries of pil'd vanities,   5
    But shreds of holiness, that dare not venture
    To show their face, since cross to thy decrees:
There the circumference earth is, heav'n the centre.
In so much dregs the quintessence is small:
    The spirit and good extract of my heart   10
    Comes to about the many hundredth part.
Yet Lord restore thine image, hear my call:
    And though my hard heart scarce to thee can groan,
    Remember that thou once didst write in stone.

Good Friday.

    O my chief good,
How shall I measure out thy blood?
How shall I count what thee befell,
    And each grief tell?

    Shall I thy woes   5
Number according to thy foes?
Or, since one star showed thy first breath,
    Shall all thy death?

Or shall each leaf,
Which falls in Autumn, score a grief?
Or cannot leaves, but fruit, be sign
            Of the true vine?

Then let each hour
Of my whole life one grief devour;
That thy distress through all may run,
            And be my sun.

Or rather let
My several sins their sorrows get;
That as each beast his cure doth know,
            Each sin may so.

Since blood is fittest, Lord, to write
Thy sorrows in, and bloody fight;
My heart hath store, write there, where in
One box doth lie both ink and sin:

That when sin spies so many foes,
Thy whips, thy nails, thy wounds, thy woes,
All come to lodge there, sin may say,
No room for me, and fly away.

Sin being gone, O fill the place,
And keep possession with thy grace;
Lest sin take courage and return,
And all the writings blot or burn.

Redemption.

Having been tenant long to a rich Lord,
            Not thriving, I resolved to be bold,
            And make a suit unto him, to afford
A new small-rented lease, and cancel th' old.
In heaven at his manor I him sought:
            They told me there, that he was lately gone
            About some land, which he had dearly bought

Long since on earth, to take possession.
I straight return'd, and knowing his great birth,
    Sought him accordingly in great resorts;   10
    In cities, theatres, gardens, parks, and courts:
At length I heard a raggèd noise and mirth
    Of thieves and murderers: there I him espied,
    Who straight, *Your suit is granted*, said, and died.

Sepulchre.

O Blessed body! Whither art thou thrown?
No lodging for thee, but a cold hard stone?
So many hearts on earth, and yet not one
               Receive thee?

Sure there is room within our hearts good store;   5
For they can lodge transgressions by the score:
Thousands of toys dwell there, yet out of door
               They leave thee.

But that which shows them large, shows them unfit.
Whatever sin did this pure rock commit,   10
Which holds thee now? Who hath indicted it
               Of murder?

Where our hard hearts have took up stones to brain thee,
And missing this, most falsely did arraign thee;
Only these stones in quiet entertain thee,   15
               And order.

And as of old, the law by heav'nly art
Was writ in stone; so thou, which also art
The letter of the word, find'st no fit heart
               To hold thee.   20

Yet do we still persist as we began,
And so should perish, but that nothing can,
Though it be cold, hard, foul, from loving man
               Withhold thee.

Easter.

Rise heart; thy Lord is risen. Sing his praise
                  Without delays,
Who takes thee by the hand, that thou likewise
                  With him mayst rise:
5   That, as his death calcinèd thee to dust,
His life may make thee gold, and much more, just.

Awake, my lute, and struggle for thy part
                  With all thy art.
The cross taught all wood to resound his name,
10   Who bore the same.
His stretchèd sinews taught all strings, what key
Is best to celebrate this most high day.

Consort both heart and lute, and twist a song
                  Pleasant and long:
15   Or since all music is but three parts vied
                  And multiplied,
O let thy blessed Spirit bear a part,
And make up our defects with his sweet art.

    I got me flowers to straw thy way;
20   I got me boughs off many a tree:
    But thou wast up by break of day,
    And brought'st thy sweets along with thee.

    The Sun arising in the East,
    Though he give light, and th' East perfume;
25   If they should offer to contest
    With thy arising, they presume.

    Can there be any day but this,
    Though many suns to shine endeavour?
    We count three hundred, but we miss:
30   There is but one, and that one ever.

Easter-wings.

Lord, who createdst man in wealth and store,
    Though foolishly he lost the same,
        Decaying more and more,
           Till he became
             Most poor: 5
             With thee
           O let me rise
        As larks, harmoniously,
    And sing this day thy victories:
Then shall the fall further the flight in me.   10

My   tender   age   in   sorrow   did   begin:
    And still with sicknesses and shame
        Thou didst so punish sin,
           That I became
             Most thin.   15
             With thee
           Let me combine,
    And feel this day thy victory:
For, if I imp my wing on thine,
Affliction shall advance the flight in me.   20

Holy Baptism (1).

As he that sees a dark and shady grove,
    Stays not, but looks beyond it on the sky;
    So when I view my sins, mine eyes remove
More backward still, and to that water fly,
Which is above the heav'ns, whose spring and rent   5
    Is in my dear Redeemer's piercèd side.
    O blessed streams! either ye do prevent
And stop our sins from growing thick and wide,
Or else give tears to drown them, as they grow.
    In you Redemption measures all my time,   10
    And spreads the plaster equal to the crime:

You taught the Book of Life my name, that so
  Whatever future sins should me miscall,
  Your first acquaintance might discredit all.

Holy Baptism (2).

                              Since, Lord, to thee
                    A narrow way and little gate
  Is all the passage, on my infancy
                    Thou didst lay hold, and antedate
5   My faith in me.

                              O let me still
                    Write thee great God, and me a child:
  Let me be soft and supple to thy will,
                    Small to myself, to others mild,
10   Behither ill.

                              Although by stealth
                    My flesh get on; yet let her sister
  My soul bid nothing, but preserve her wealth:
                    The growth of flesh is but a blister;
15   Childhood is health.

Nature.

          Full of rebellion, I would die,
          Or fight, or travel, or deny
        That thou hast ought to do with me.
                O tame my heart;
5   It is thy highest art
        To captivate strong holds to thee.

If thou shalt let this venom lurk,
And in suggestions fume and work,
My soul will turn to bubbles straight,
    And thence by kind   10
   Vanish into a wind,
Making thy workmanship deceit.

O smooth my rugged heart, and there
Engrave thy rev'rend law and fear;
Or make a new one, since the old   15
    Is sapless grown,
   And a much fitter stone
To hide my dust, than thee to hold.

Sin (1).

Lord, with what care hast thou begirt us round!
 Parents first season us: then schoolmasters
 Deliver us to laws; they send us bound
To rules of reason, holy messengers,
Pulpits and Sundays, sorrow dogging sin,   5
 Afflictions sorted, anguish of all sizes,
 Fine nets and stratagems to catch us in,
Bibles laid open, millions of surprises,
Blessings beforehand, ties of gratefulness,
 The sound of glory ringing in our ears: 10
 Without, our shame; within, our consciences;
Angels and grace, eternal hopes and fears.
 Yet all these fences and their whole array
 One cunning bosom-sin blows quite away.

Affliction (1).

When first thou didst entice to thee my heart,
        I thought the service brave:
So many joys I writ down for my part,
        Besides what I might have
5   Out of my stock of natural delights,
Augmented with thy gracious benefits.

I lookèd on thy furniture so fine,
        And made it fine to me:
Thy glorious household-stuff did me entwine,
10   And 'tice me unto thee.
Such stars I counted mine: both heav'n and earth
Paid me my wages in a world of mirth.

What pleasures could I want, whose King I served?
        Where joys my fellows were.
15   Thus argued into hopes, my thoughts reserv'd
        No place for grief or fear.
Therefore my sudden soul caught at the place,
And made her youth and fierceness seek thy face.

At first thou gav'st me milk and sweetnesses;
20   I had my wish and way:
My days were straw'd with flow'rs and happiness;
        There was no month but May.
But with my years sorrow did twist and grow,
And made a party unawares for woe.

25   My flesh began unto my soul in pain,
        Sicknesses cleave my bones;
Consuming agues dwell in ev'ry vein,
        And tune my breath to groans.
Sorrow was all my soul; I scarce believ'd,
30   Till grief did tell me roundly, that I liv'd.

When I got health, thou took'st away my life,
        And more; for my friends die:
My mirth and edge was lost; a blunted knife
        Was of more use than I.
Thus thin and lean without a fence or friend,   35
I was blown through with ev'ry storm and wind.

Whereas my birth and spirit rather took
        The way that takes the town;
Thou didst betray me to a ling'ring book,
        And wrap me in a gown.   40
I was entangled in the world of strife,
Before I had the power to change my life.

Yet, for I threat'ned oft the siege to raise,
        Not simp'ring all mine age,
Thou often didst with academic praise   45
        Melt and dissolve my rage.
I took thy sweet'ned pill, till I came where
I could not go away, nor persevere.

Yet lest perchance I should too happy be
        In my unhappiness,   50
Turning my purge to food, thou throwest me
        Into more sicknesses.
Thus doth thy power cross-bias me, not making
Thine own gift good, yet me from my ways taking.

Now I am here, what thou wilt do with me   55
        None of my books will show:
I read, and sigh, and wish I were a tree;
        For sure then I should grow
To fruit or shade: at least some bird would trust
Her household to me, and I should be just.   60

Yet, though thou troublest me, I must be meek;
        In weakness must be stout.
Well, I will change the service, and go seek
        Some other master out.

65   Ah my dear God! though I am clean forgot,
      Let me not love thee, if I love thee not.

Repentance.

      Lord, I confess my sin is great
        Great is my sin. O! gently treat
    With thy quick flow'r, thy momentary bloom;
                    Whose life still pressing
5   Is one undressing,
        A steady aiming at a tomb.

      Man's age is two hours' work, or three:
        Each day doth round about us see.
    Thus are we to delights: but we are all
10   To sorrows old,
                    If life be told
        From what life feeleth, Adam's fall.

      O let thy height of mercy then
        Compassionate short-breathed men.
15   Cut me not off for my most foul transgression:
                    I do confess
                    My foolishness;
        My God, accept of my confession.

      Sweeten at length this bitter bowl,
20   Which thou hast poured into my soul;
    Thy wormwood turn to health, winds to fair weather:
                    For if thou stay,
                    I and this day,
        As we did rise, we die together.

25   When thou for sin rebukest man,
        Forthwith he waxeth woe and wan:
    Bitterness fills our bowels; all our hearts
                    Pine, and decay,
                    And drop away,
30   And carry with them th' other parts.

But thou wilt sin and grief destroy;
That so the broken bones may joy,
And tune together in a well-set song,
      Full of his praises,
        Who dead men raises.   35
Fractures well cured make us more strong.

Faith.

Lord, how couldst thou so much appease
Thy wrath for sin as, when man's sight was dim,
And could see little, to regard his ease,
    And bring by Faith all things to him?

Hungry I was, and had no meat: 5
I did conceit a most delicious feast;
I had it straight, and did as truly eat,
    As ever did a welcome guest.

There is a rare outlandish root,
Which when I could not get, I thought it here: 10
That apprehension cured so well my foot,
    That I can walk to heav'n well near.

I owèd thousands and much more:
I did believe that I did nothing owe,
And liv'd accordingly; my creditor   15
    Believes so too, and lets me go.

Faith makes me anything, or all
That I believe is in the sacred story:
And where sin placeth me in Adam's fall,
    Faith sets me higher in his glory.   20

If I go lower in the book,
What can be lower than the common manger?
Faith puts me there with him, who sweetly took
    Our flesh and frailty, death and danger.

25 If bliss had lien in art or strength,
      None but the wise or strong had gain'd it:
      Where now by Faith all arms are of a length;
          One size doth all conditions fit.

      A peasant may believe as much
30 As a great clerk, and reach the highest stature.
      Thus dost thou make proud knowledge bend and crouch
          While grace fills up uneven nature.

      When creatures had no real light
      Inherent in them, thou didst make the sun,
35 Impute a lustre, and allow them bright;
          And in this show, what Christ hath done.

      That which before was dark'ned clean
      With bushy groves, pricking the looker's eye,
      Vanisht away, when Faith did change the scene:
40   And then appear'd a glorious sky.

      What though my body run to dust?
      Faith cleaves unto it, counting ev'ry grain
      With an exact and most particular trust,
          Reserving all for flesh again.

Prayer (1).

      Prayer the Church's banquet, Angels' age,
          God's breath in man returning to his birth,
          The soul in paraphrase, heart in pilgrimage,
      The Christian plummet sounding heav'n and earth;
5   Engine against th' Almighty, sinners' tower,
          Reversèd thunder, Christ-side-piercing spear,
          The six-days world-transposing in an hour,
      A kind of tune, which all things hear and fear;

Softness, and peace, and joy, and love, and bliss,
  Exalted Manna, gladness of the best,   10
  Heaven in ordinary, man well dresst,
The milky way, the bird of Paradise,
  Church-bells beyond the stars heard, the soul's blood,
  The land of spices; something understood.

The Holy Communion.

Not in rich furniture, or fine array,
    Nor in a wedge of gold,
    Thou, who for me wast sold,
  To me dost now thyself convey;
For so thou shouldst without me still have been,   5
    Leaving within me sin:

But by the way of nourishment and strength
    Thou creep'st into my breast;
    Making thy way my rest,
  And thy small quantities my length;   10
Which spread their forces into every part,
    Meeting sin's force and art.

Yet can these not get over to my soul,
    Leaping the wall that parts
    Our souls and fleshly hearts;   15
  But as th' outworks, they may control
My rebel-flesh, and carrying thy name,
    Affright both sin and shame.

Only thy grace, which with these elements comes,
    Knoweth the ready way,   20
    And hath the privy key,
  Op'ning the soul's most subtle rooms;
While those to spirits refin'd, at door attend
    Dispatches from their friend.

25   Give me my captive soul, or take
              My body also thither.
       Another lift like this will make
              Them both to be together.

       Before that sin turn'd flesh to stone,
30   And all our lump to leaven;
       A fervent sigh might well have blown
              Our innocent earth to heaven.

       For sure when Adam did not know
              To sin, or sin to smother;
35   He might to heav'n from Paradise go,
              As from one room t'another.

       Thou hast restored us to this ease
              By this thy heav'nly blood;
       Which I can go to, when I please,
40   And leave th' earth to their food.

Antiphon (1).

Cho.   Let all the world in ev'ry corner sing,
                         My God and King.

        Vers.   The heav'ns are not too high,
                  His praise may thither fly:
5   The earth is not too low,
                  His praises there may grow.

Cho.   Let all the world in ev'ry corner sing,
                         My God and King.

        Vers.   The church with psalms must shout,
10   No door can keep them out:
                  But above all, the heart
                  Must bear the longest part.

Cho.   Let all the world in ev'ry corner sing,
                         My God and King.

Love (1).

Immortal Love, author of this great frame,
    Sprung from that beauty which can never fade;
    How hath man parcell'd out thy glorious name,
And thrown it on that dust which thou hast made,
While mortal love doth all the title gain!   5
    Which siding with invention, they together
    Bear all the sway, possessing heart and brain
(Thy workmanship), and give thee share in neither.
Wit fancies beauty, beauty raiseth wit:
    The world is theirs; they two play out the game,   10
    Thou standing by: and though thy glorious name
Wrought our deliverance from th' infernal pit,
    Who sings thy praise? only a scarf or glove
    Doth warm our hands, and make them write of love.

Love (2).

Immortal Heat, O let thy greater flame
    Attract the lesser to it: let those fires,
    Which shall consume the world, first make it tame;
And kindle in our hearts such true desires,
As may consume our lusts, and make thee way.   5
    Then shall our hearts pant thee; then shall our brain
    All her invention on thine Altar lay,
And there in hymns send back thy fire again:
Our eyes shall see thee, which before saw dust;
    Dust blown by wit, till that they both were blind: 10
    Thou shalt recover all thy goods in kind,
Who wert disseisèd by usurping lust:
    All knees shall bow to thee; all wits shall rise,
    And praise him who did make and mend our eyes.

The Temper (1).

How should I praise thee, Lord! how should my rhymes
    Gladly engrave thy love in steel,
    If what my soul doth feel sometimes,
       My soul might ever feel!

5   Although there were some forty heav'ns, or more,
    Sometimes I peer above them all;
    Sometimes I hardly reach a score,
       Sometimes to hell I fall.

O rack me not to such a vast extent;
10   Those distances belong to thee:
    The world's too little for thy tent,
       A grave too big for me.

Wilt thou meet arms with man, that thou dost stretch
    A crumb of dust from heav'n to hell?
15   Will great God measure with a wretch?
       Shall he thy stature spell?

O let me, when thy roof my soul hath hid,
    O let me roost and nestle there:
    Then of a sinner thou art rid,
20   And I of hope and fear.

Yet take thy way; for sure thy way is best:
    Stretch or contract me, thy poor debtor:
    This is but tuning of my breast,
       To make the music better.

25   Whether I fly with angels, fall with dust,
    Thy hands made both, and I am there:
    Thy power and love, my love and trust
       Make one place ev'ry where.

The Temper (2).

It cannot be. Where is that mighty joy,
   Which just now took up all my heart?
   Lord, if thou must needs use thy dart,
Save that, and me; or sin for both destroy.

The grosser world stands to thy word and art;   5
   But thy diviner world of grace
   Thou suddenly dost raise and race,
And ev'ry day a new Creator art.

O fix thy chair of grace, that all my powers
   May also fix their reverence: 10
   For when thou dost depart from hence,
They grow unruly, and sit in thy bowers.

Scatter, or bind them all to bend to thee:
   Though elements change, and heaven move,
   Let not thy higher Court remove,   15
But keep a standing Majesty in me.

Jordan (1).

Who says that fictions only and false hair
Become a verse? Is there in truth no beauty?
Is all good structure in a winding stair?
May no lines pass, except they do their duty
   Not to a true, but painted chair?   5

Is it no verse, except enchanted groves
And sudden arbours shadow coarse-spun lines?
Must purling streams refresh a lover's loves?
Must all be veil'd, while he that reads, divines,
   Catching the sense at two removes?   10

Shepherds are honest people; let them sing:
Riddle who list, for me, and pull for Prime:
I envy no man's nightingale or spring;
Nor let them punish me with loss of rhyme,
15   Who plainly say, *My God, My King*.

Employment (1).

If as a flower doth spread and die,
    Thou wouldst extend me to some good,
Before I were by frost's extremity
            Nipt in the bud;

5   The sweetness and the praise were thine;
    But the extension and the room,
Which in thy garland I should fill, were mine
            At thy great doom.

For as thou dost impart thy grace,
10   The greater shall our glory be.
The measure of our joys is in this place,
            The stuff with thee.

Let me not languish then, and spend
    A life as barren to thy praise,
15 As is the dust, to which that life doth tend,
            But with delays.

All things are busy; only I
    Neither bring honey with the bees,
Nor flow'rs to make that, nor the husbandry
20   To water these.

I am no link of thy great chain,
    But all my company is a weed.
Lord place me in thy consort; give one strain
            To my poor reed.

The Holy Scriptures (1).

O Book! infinite sweetness! let my heart
    Suck ev'ry letter, and a honey gain,
    Precious for any grief in any part;
To clear the breast, to mollify all pain.
Thou art all health, health thriving till it make   5
    A full eternity: thou art a mass
    Of strange delights, where we may wish and take.
Ladies, look here; this is the thankful glass,
That mends the looker's eyes: this is the well
    That washes what it shows. Who can endear   10
    Thy praise too much? thou art heav'n's lidger here,
Working against the states of death and hell.
    Thou art joy's handsel: heav'n lies flat in thee,
    Subject to ev'ry mounter's bended knee.

The Holy Scriptures (2).

O that I knew how all thy lights combine,
    And the configurations of their glory!
    Seeing not only how each verse doth shine,
But all the constellations of the story.
This verse marks that, and both do make a motion   5
    Unto a third, that ten leaves off doth lie:
    Then as dispersèd herbs do watch a potion,
These three make up some Christian's destiny:
Such are thy secrets, which my life makes good,
    And comments on thee: for in ev'ry thing   10
    Thy words do find me out, and parallels bring,
And in another make me understood.
    Stars are poor books, and oftentimes do miss:
    This book of stars lights to eternal bliss.

Whitsunday.

Listen sweet Dove unto my song,
And spread thy golden wings in me;
Hatching my tender heart so long,
Till it get wing, and fly away with thee.

5   Where is that fire which once descended
On thy Apostles? thou didst then
Keep open house, richly attended,
Feasting all comers by twelve chosen men.

Such glorious gifts thou didst bestow,
10   That th' earth did like a heav'n appear:
The stars were coming down to know
If they might mend their wages, and serve here.

The sun, which once did shine alone,
Hung down his head, and wisht for night,
15   When he beheld twelve suns for one
Going about the world, and giving light.

But since those pipes of gold, which brought
That cordial water to our ground,
Were cut and martyr'd by the fault
20   Of those, who did themselves through their side wound,

Thou shut'st the door, and keep'st within;
Scarce a good joy creeps through the chink:
And if the braves of conqu'ring sin
Did not excite thee, we should wholly sink.

25   Lord, though we change, thou art the same;
The same sweet God of love and light:
Restore this day, for thy great name,
Unto his ancient and miraculous right.

Grace.

My stock lies dead, and no increase
Doth my dull husbandry improve:
O let thy graces without cease
                Drop from above!

If still the sun should hide his face,   5
Thy house would but a dungeon prove,
Thy works night's captives: O let grace
                Drop from above!

The dew doth ev'ry morning fall;
And shall the dew out-strip thy Dove?   10
The dew, for which grass cannot call,
                Drop from above.

Death is still working like a mole,
And digs my grave at each remove:
Let grace work too, and on my soul   15
                Drop from above.

Sin is still hammering my heart
Unto a hardness, void of love:
Let suppling grace, to cross his art,
                Drop from above.   20

O come! for thou dost know the way.
Or if to me thou wilt not move,
Remove me, where I need not say,
                Drop from above.

Praise (1).

To write a verse or two, is all the praise,
                That I can raise:
    Mend my estate in any ways,
                Thou shalt have more.

5   I go to Church; help me to wings, and I
                                Will thither fly;
                        Or, if I mount unto the sky,
                                I will do more.

       Man is all weakness; there is no such thing
10   As Prince or King:
                        His arm is short; yet with a sling
                                He may do more.

       An herb distill'd, and drunk, may dwell next door,
                                On the same floor,
15   To a brave soul: Exalt the poor,
                                They can do more.

       O raise me then! Poor bees, that work all day,
                                Sting my delay,
                        Who have a work, as well as they,
20   And much, much more.

Affliction (2).

                        Kill me not ev'ry day,
              Thou Lord of life; since thy one death for me
                  Is more than all my deaths can be,
                        Though I in broken pay
5   Die over each hour of Methusalem's stay.

                        If all men's tears were let
              Into one common sewer, sea, and brine;
                  What were they all, compared to thine?
                        Wherein if they were set,
10   They would discolour thy most bloody sweat.

Thou art my grief alone,
Thou Lord conceal it not: and as thou art
All my delight, so all my smart:
Thy cross took up in one,
By way of imprest, all my future moan.   15

Matins.

I cannot ope mine eyes,
But thou art ready there to catch
My morning-soul and sacrifice:
Then we must needs for that day make a match.

My God, what is a heart?   5
Silver, or gold, or precious stone,
Or star, or rainbow, or a part
Of all these things, or all of them in one?

My God, what is a heart,
That thou shouldst it so eye, and woo,   10
Pouring upon it all thy art,
As if that thou hadst nothing else to do?

Indeed man's whole estate
Amounts (and richly) to serve thee:
He did not heav'n and earth create,   15
Yet studies them, not him by whom they be.

Teach me thy love to know;
That this new light, which now I see,
May both the work and workman show:
Then by a sunbeam I will climb to thee.   20

Sin (2).

O that I could a sin once see!
We paint the devil foul, yet he
Hath some good in him, all agree.
Sin is flat opposite to th' Almighty, seeing
It wants the good of *virtue*, and of *being*.

But God more care of us hath had:
If apparitions make us sad,
By sight of sin we should grow mad.
Yet as in sleep we see foul death, and live:
So devils are our sins in perspective.

Evensong.

Blest be the God of love,
Who gave me eyes, and light, and power this day,
Both to be busy, and to play.
But much more blest be God above,
Who gave me sight alone,
Which to himself he did deny:
For when he sees my ways, I die:
But I have got his son, and he hath none.

What have I brought thee home
For this thy love? have I discharg'd the debt,
Which this day's favour did beget?
I ran; but all I brought, was foam.
Thy diet, care, and cost
Do end in bubbles, balls of wind;
Of wind to thee whom I have crost,
But balls of wild-fire to my troubled mind.

Yet still thou goest on.
And now with darkness closest weary eyes,

Saying to man, *It doth suffice:*
Henceforth repose; your work is done.   20
            Thus in thy ebony box
Thou dost enclose us, till the day
Put our amendment in our way,
And give new wheels to our disorder'd clocks.

            I muse, which shows more love,   25
The day or night: that is the gale, this th' harbour;
    That is the walk, and this the arbour;
    Or that the garden, this the grove.
            My God, thou art all love.
    Not one poor minute 'scapes thy breast,   30
    But brings a favour from above;
And in this love, more than in bed, I rest.

Church-monuments.

While that my soul repairs to her devotion,
Here I intomb my flesh, that it betimes
May take acquaintance of this heap of dust;
To which the blast of death's incessant motion,
Fed with the exhalation of our crimes,   5
Drives all at last. Therefore I gladly trust
My body to this school, that it may learn
To spell his elements, and find his birth
Written in dusty heraldry and lines:
Which dissolution sure doth best discern,   10
Comparing dust with dust, and earth with earth.
These laugh at Jet and Marble put for signs,
To sever the good fellowship of dust,
And spoil the meeting. What shall point out them,
When they shall bow, and kneel, and fall down flat   15
To kiss those heaps, which now they have in trust?

Dear flesh, while I do pray, learn here thy stem
And true descent; that when thou shalt grow fat,
And wanton in thy cravings, thou mayst know,
20   That flesh is but the glass, which holds the dust
That measures all our time; which also shall
Be crumbled into dust. Mark here below
How tame these ashes are, how free from lust,
That thou mayst fit thyself against thy fall.

Church-music.

Sweetest of sweets, I thank you: when displeasure
          Did through my body wound my mind,
You took me thence, and in your house of pleasure
          A dainty lodging me assign'd.

5   Now I in you without a body move,
          Rising and falling with your wings:
We both together sweetly live and love,
          Yet say sometimes, *God help poor Kings.*

Comfort, I'll die; for if you post from me,
10   Sure I shall do so, and much more:
But if I travel in your company,
          You know the way to heaven's door.

Church-lock and key.

I know it is my sin, which locks thine ears,
          And binds thy hands,
Out-crying my requests, drowning my tears;
Or else the chillness of my faint demands.

5   But as cold hands are angry with the fire,
          And mend it still;

So I do lay the want of my desire,
Not on my sins, or coldness, but thy will.

Yet hear, O God, only for his blood's sake
                              Which pleads for me: 10
For though sins plead too, yet like stones they make
His blood's sweet current much more loud to be.

The Church-floor.

Mark you the floor? that square and speckled stone,
                    Which looks so firm and strong,
                              Is *Patience*:

And th' other black and grave, wherewith each one
                    Is checkered all along,   5
                              Humility:

The gentle rising, which on either hand
                    Leads to the Choir above,
                              Is *Confidence*:

But the sweet cement, which in one sure band   10
                    Ties the whole frame, is *Love*
                              And *Charity*.

          Hither sometimes Sin steals, and stains
          The marble's neat and curious veins:
But all is cleansed when the marble weeps.   15
          Sometimes Death, puffing at the door,
          Blows all the dust about the floor:
But while he thinks to spoil the room, he sweeps.
          Blest be the *Architect*, whose art
          Could build so strong in a weak heart.   20

The Windows.

Lord, how can man preach thy eternal word?
            He is a brittle crazy glass:
Yet in thy temple thou dost him afford
                This glorious and transcendent place,
5   To be a window, through thy grace.

But when thou dost anneal in glass thy story,
            Making thy life to shine within
The holy Preacher's; then the light and glory
                More rev'rend grows, and more doth win:
10   Which else shows wat'rish, bleak, and thin.

Doctrine and life, colours and light, in one
            When they combine and mingle, bring
A strong regard and awe: but speech alone
                Doth vanish like a flaring thing,
15   And in the ear, not conscience ring.

Trinity Sunday.

Lord, who hast form'd me out of mud,
            And hast redeem'd me through thy blood,
            And sanctifi'd me to do good;

Purge all my sins done heretofore:
5   For I confess my heavy score,
            And I will strive to sin no more.

Enrich my heart, mouth, hands in me,
            With faith, with hope, with charity;
            That I may run, rise, rest with thee.

Content.

Peace mutt'ring thoughts, and do not grudge to keep
    Within the walls of your own breast:
Who cannot on his own bed sweetly sleep,
    Can on another's hardly rest.

Gad not abroad at ev'ry quest and call   5
    Of an untrainèd hope or passion.
To court each place or fortune that doth fall,
    Is wantonness in contemplation.

Mark how the fire in flints doth quiet lie,
    Content and warm t' itself alone: 10
But when it would appear to other's eye,
    Without a knock it never shone.

Give me the pliant mind, whose gentle measure
    Complies and suits with all estates;
Which can let loose to a crown, and yet with pleasure   15
    Take up within a cloister's gates.

This soul doth span the world, and hang content
    From either pole unto the centre:
Where in each room of the well-furnish'd tent
    He lies warm, and without adventure.   20

The brags of life are but a nine days' wonder;
    And after death the fumes that spring
From private bodies make as big a thunder,
    As those which rise from a huge King.

Only thy Chronicle is lost; and yet   25
    Better by worms be all once spent,
Than to have hellish moths still gnaw and fret
    Thy name in books, which may not rent:

When all thy deeds, whose brunt thou feel'st alone,
30   Are chaw'd by others' pens and tongue;
And as their wit is, their digestion,
            Thy nourisht fame is weak or strong.

Then cease discoursing soul, till thine own ground,
            Do not thyself or friends importune.
35 He that by seeking hath himself once found,
            Hath ever found a happy fortune.

The Quiddity.

My God, a verse is not a crown,
No point of honour, or gay suit,
No hawk, or banquet, or renown,
Nor a good sword, nor yet a lute:

5   It cannot vault, or dance, or play;
It never was in *France* or *Spain*;
Nor can it entertain the day
With a great stable or demesne:

It is no office, art, or news,
10 Nor the Exchange, or busy Hall;
    But it is that which while I use
I am with thee, and *most take all.*

Humility.

I saw the Virtues sitting hand in hand
In sev'ral ranks upon an azure throne,
Where all the beasts and fowls by their command
Presented tokens of submission.
5   Humility, who sat the lowest there
                            To execute their call,
When by the beasts the presents tendred were,
                            Gave them about to all.

The angry Lion did present his paw,
Which by consent was giv'n to Mansuetude.   10
The fearful Hare her ears, which by their law
Humility did reach to Fortitude.
The jealous Turkey brought his coral-chain;
                    That went to Temperance.
On Justice was bestow'd the Fox's brain,   15
                    Kill'd in the way by chance.

At length the Crow bringing the Peacock's plume
(For he would not), as they beheld the grace
Of that brave gift, each one began to fume,
And challenge it, as proper to his place,   20
Till they fell out: which when the beasts espied,
                    They leapt upon the throne;
And if the Fox had lived to rule their side,
                    They had depos'd each one.

Humility, who held the plume, at this   25
Did weep so fast, that the tears trickling down
Spoil'd all the train: then saying *Here it is*
For which ye wrangle, made them turn their frown
Against the beasts: so jointly bandying,
                    They drive them soon away;   30
And then amerc'd them, double gifts to bring
                    At the next Session-day.

Frailty.

Lord, in my silence how do I despise
                  What upon trust
Is stylèd *honour*, *riches*, or *fair eyes*;
                  But is *fair dust*!
        I surname them *gilded clay*,   5
            Dear earth, *fine grass*, or *hay*;
In all, I think my foot doth ever tread
                  Upon their head.

But when I view abroad both Regiments;
The world's and thine:
Thine clad with simpleness, and sad events;
The other fine,
Full of glory and gay weeds,
Brave language, braver deeds:
That which was dust before, doth quickly rise,
And prick mine eyes.

O brook not this, lest if what even now
My foot did tread,
Affront those joys, wherewith thou didst endow,
And long since wed
My poor soul, ev'n sick of love:
It may a Babel prove
Commodious to conquer heav'n and thee
Planted in me.

Constancy.

Who is the honest man?
He that doth still and strongly good pursue,
To God, his neighbour, and himself most true:
Whom neither force nor fawning can
Unpin, or wrench from giving all their due.

Whose honesty is not
So loose or easy, that a ruffling wind
Can blow away, or glittering look it blind:
Who rides his sure and even trot,
While the world now rides by, now lags behind.

Who, when great trials come,
Nor seeks, nor shuns them; but doth calmly stay,
Till he the thing and the example weigh:
All being brought into a sum,
What place or person calls for, he doth pay.

10

15

20

5

10

15

Whom none can work or woo
To use in anything a trick or sleight;
For above all things he abhors deceit:
     His words and works and fashion too
All of a piece, and all are clear and straight.   20

     Who never melts or thaws
At close tentations: when the day is done,
His goodness sets not, but in dark can run:
     The sun to others writeth laws,
And is their virtue; Virtue is his Sun.   25

     Who, when he is to treat
With sick folks, women, those whom passions sway,
Allows for that, and keeps his constant way:
     Whom others' faults do not defeat;
But though men fail him, yet his part doth play.   30

     Whom nothing can procure,
When the wide world runs bias from his will,
To writhe his limbs, and share, not mend the ill.
     This is the Mark-man, safe and sure,
Who still is right, and prays to be so still.   35

Affliction (3).

My heart did heave, and there came forth, *O God!*
By that I knew that thou wast in the grief,
To guide and govern it to my relief,
     Making a sceptre of the rod:
        Hadst thou not had thy part,   5
Sure the unruly sigh had broke my heart.

But since thy breath gave me both life and shape,
Thou know'st my tallies; and when there's assigned
So much breath to a sigh, what's then behind?

10   Or if some years with it escape,
          The sigh then only is
A gale to bring me sooner to my bliss.

Thy life on earth was grief, and thou art still
Constant unto it, making it to be
15   A point of honour, now to grieve in me,
          And in thy members suffer ill.
             They who lament one cross,
Thou dying daily, praise thee to thy loss.

The Star.

Bright spark, shot from a brighter place,
     Where beams surround my Saviour's face,
          Canst thou be any where
             So well as there?

5   Yet, if thou wilt from thence depart,
        Take a bad lodging in my heart;
             For thou canst make a debtor,
                And make it better.

First with thy fire-work burn to dust
10   Folly, and worse than folly, lust:
             Then with thy light refine,
                And make it shine:

So disengag'd from sin and sickness,
     Touch it with thy celestial quickness,
15   That it may hang and move
                After thy love.

Then with our trinity of light,
     Motion, and heat, let's take our flight
             Unto the place where thou
20   Before didst bow.

Get me a standing there, and place
    Among the beams, which crown the face
        Of him, who died to part
          Sin and my heart:

That so among the rest I may   25
    Glitter, and curl, and wind as they:
        That winding is their fashion
          Of adoration.

Sure thou wilt joy, by gaining me
    To fly home like a laden bee   30
        Unto that hive of beams
          And garland-streams.

Sunday.

      O day most calm, most bright,
The fruit of this, the next world's bud,
Th' endorsement of supreme delight,
Writ by a friend, and with his blood;
The couch of time; care's balm and bay: 5
The week were dark, but for thy light:
      Thy torch doth show the way.

      The other days and thou
Make up one man; whose face thou art,
Knocking at heaven with thy brow: 10
The worky-days are the back-part;
The burden of the week lies there,
Making the whole to stoop and bow,
      Till thy release appear.

      Man had straight forward gone   15
To endless death: but thou dost pull
And turn us round to look on one,
Whom, if we were not very dull,
We could not choose but look on still;

20   Since there is no place so alone,
         The which he doth not fill.

         Sundays the pillars are,
      On which heav'n's palace archèd lies:
       The other days fill up the spare
25   And hollow room with vanities.
       They are the fruitful beds and borders
       In God's rich garden: that is bare,
         Which parts their ranks and orders.

         The Sundays of man's life,
30   Threaded together on time's string,
       Make bracelets to adorn the wife
       Of the eternal glorious King.
       On Sunday heaven's gate stands ope;
       Blessings are plentiful and rife,
35   More plentiful than hope.

         This day my Saviour rose,
      And did inclose this light for his:
       That, as each beast his manger knows,
       Man might not of his fodder miss.
40   Christ hath took in this piece of ground,
       And made a garden there for those
         Who want herbs for their wound.

         The rest of our Creation
      Our great Redeemer did remove
45   With the same shake, which at his passion
       Did th' earth and all things with it move.
       As Samson bore the doors away,
       Christ's hands, though nail'd, wrought our salvation,
         And did unhinge that day.

50   The brightness of that day
      We sullied by our foul offence:
       Wherefore that robe we cast away,
       Having a new at his expense,

Whose drops of blood paid the full price,
That was required to make us gay,   55
    And fit for Paradise.

    Thou art a day of mirth:
And where the week-days trail on ground,
Thy flight is higher, as thy birth.
O let me take thee at the bound,   60
Leaping with thee from sev'n to sev'n,
Till that we both, being toss'd from earth,
    Fly hand in hand to heav'n!

Avarice.

Money, thou bane of bliss, and source of woe,
    Whence com'st thou, that thou art so fresh and fine?
    I know thy parentage is base and low:
Man found thee poor and dirty in a mine.
Surely thou didst so little contribute   5
    To this great kingdom, which thou now hast got,
    That he was fain, when thou wert destitute,
To dig thee out of thy dark cave and grot:
Then forcing thee, by fire he made thee bright:
    Nay, thou hast got the face of man; for we   10
    Have with our stamp and seal transferr'd our right:
Thou art the man, and man but dross to thee.
    Man calleth thee his wealth, who made thee rich;
    And while he digs out thee, falls in the ditch.

Ana-$\begin{Bmatrix} \text{MARY} \\ \text{ARMY} \end{Bmatrix}$gram.

How well her name an *Army* doth present,
In whom the *Lord of Hosts* did pitch his tent!

To all Angels and Saints.

O glorious spirits, who after all your bands
See the smooth face of God, without a frown
   Or strict commands;
Where ev'ry one is king, and hath his crown,
If not upon his head, yet in his hands:

Not out of envy or maliciousness
Do I forbear to crave your special aid:
   I would address
My vows to thee most gladly, blessèd Maid,
And Mother of my God, in my distress.

Thou art the holy mine, whence came the gold,
The great restorative for all decay
   In young and old;
Thou art the cabinet where the jewel lay:
Chiefly to thee would I my soul unfold:

But now (alas!) I dare not; for our King,
Whom we do all jointly adore and praise,
   Bids no such thing:
And where his pleasure no injunction lays,
('Tis your own case) ye never move a wing.

All worship is prerogative, and a flower
Of his rich crown, from whom lies no appeal
            At the last hour:
Therefore we dare not from his garland steal,
To make a posy for inferior power.   25

Although then others court you, if ye know
What's done on earth, we shall not fare the worse,
            Who do not so;
Since we are ever ready to disburse,
If any one our Master's hand can show.   30

Employment (2).

He that is weary, let him sit.
            My soul would stir
And trade in courtesies and wit,
            Quitting the fur
To cold complexions needing it.   5

Man is no star, but a quick coal
            Of mortal fire:
Who blows it not, nor doth control
            A faint desire,
Lets his own ashes choke his soul.   10

When th' elements did for place contest
            With him, whose will
Ordain'd the highest to be best;
            The earth sat still,
And by the others is opprest.   15

Life is a business, not good cheer;
            Ever in wars.
The sun still shineth there or here,
            Whereas the stars
Watch an advantage to appear.   20

O that I were an Orange-tree,
                    That busy plant!
Then should I ever laden be,
                    And never want
Some fruit for him that dressèd me.

But we are still too young or old;
                    The man is gone,
Before we do our wares unfold:
                    So we freeze on,
Until the grave increase our cold.

Denial.

When my devotions could not pierce
                    Thy silent ears;
Then was my heart broken, as was my verse:
                    My breast was full of fears
                    And disorder:

My bent thoughts, like a brittle bow,
                    Did fly asunder:
Each took his way; some would to pleasures go,
                    Some to the wars and thunder
                    Of alarms.

As good go anywhere, they say,
                    As to benumb
Both knees and heart, in crying night and day,
                    Come, come my God, O come,
                    But no hearing.

O that thou shouldst give dust a tongue
                    To cry to thee,
And then not hear it crying! all day long
                    My heart was in my knee,
                    But no hearing.

Therefore my soul lay out of sight,
        Untuned, unstrung:
My feeble spirit, unable to look right,
        Like a nipt blossom, hung
                Discontented.   25

        O cheer and tune my heartless breast,
                Defer no time;
That so thy favours granting my request,
        They and my mind may chime,
                And mend my rhyme.   30

Christmas.

All after pleasures as I rid one day,
    My horse and I, both tir'd, body and mind,
    With full cry of affections, quite astray;
I took up in the next inn I could find.
There when I came, whom found I but my dear,   5
    My dearest Lord, expecting till the grief
    Of pleasures brought me to him, ready there
To be all passengers' most sweet relief?
O Thou, whose glorious, yet contracted light,
    Wrapt in night's mantle, stole into a manger;   10
    Since my dark soul and brutish is thy right,
To Man of all beasts be not thou a stranger:
    Furnish and deck my soul, that thou mayst have
    A better lodging, than a rack, or grave.

The shepherds sing; and shall I silent be?   15
                My God, no hymn for thee?
My soul's a shepherd too; a flock it feeds
                Of thoughts, and words, and deeds.
The pasture is thy word: the streams, thy grace
                Enriching all the place.   20

Shepherd and flock shall sing, and all my powers
             Out-sing the day-light hours.
Then we will chide the sun for letting night
             Take up his place and right:
25   We sing one common Lord; wherefore he should
             Himself the candle hold.
I will go searching, till I find a sun
             Shall stay, till we have done;
A willing shiner, that shall shine as gladly,
30   As frost-nipt suns look sadly.
Then we will sing, and shine all our own day,
             And one another pay:
His beams shall cheer my breast, and both so twine,
Till ev'n his beams sing, and my music shine.

Ungratefulness.

Lord, with what bounty and rare clemency
             Hast thou redeem'd us from the grave!
             If thou hadst let us run,
             Gladly had man adored the sun,
5   And thought his god most brave;
Where now we shall be better gods than he.

Thou hast but two rare cabinets full of treasure,
             The *Trinity*, and *Incarnation*:
             Thou hast unlocked them both,
10   And made them jewels to betroth
             The work of thy creation
Unto thyself in everlasting pleasure.

The statelier cabinet is the *Trinity*,
             Whose sparkling light access denies:
15   Therefore thou dost not show
             This fully to us, till death blow
             The dust into our eyes:
For by that powder thou wilt make us see.

But all thy sweets are packt up in the other;
          Thy mercies thither flock and flow: 20
            That as the first affrights,
        This may allure us with delights;
            Because this box we know;
For we have all of us just such another.

But man is close, reserv'd, and dark to thee: 25
          When thou demandest but a heart,
            He cavils instantly.
         In his poor cabinet of bone
            Sins have their box apart,
Defrauding thee, who gavest two for one.   30

Sighs and Groans.

               O do not use me
After my sins! look not on my desert,
But on thy glory! then thou wilt reform
And not refuse me: for thou only art
The mighty God, but I a silly worm;   5
               O do not bruise me!

               O do not urge me!
For what account can thy ill steward make?
I have abus'd thy stock, destroy'd thy woods,
Suck'd all thy magazines: my head did ache,   10
Till it found out how to consume thy goods:
               O do not scourge me!

               O do not blind me!
I have deserved that an Egyptian night
Should thicken all my powers; because my lust   15
Hath still sew'd fig-leaves to exclude thy light:
But I am frailty, and already dust;
               O do not grind me!

                                    O do not fill me
20   With the turn'd vial of thy bitter wrath!
        For thou hast other vessels full of blood,
        A part whereof my Saviour emptied hath,
        Ev'n unto death: since he died for my good,
                                    O do not kill me!

                                    But O reprieve me!
25   For thou hast *life* and *death* at thy command;
        Thou art both *Judge* and *Saviour*, *feast* and *rod*,
        Cordial and *Corrosive*: put not thy hand
        Into the bitter box; but O my God,
30   My God, relieve me!

The World.

        Love built a stately house; where *Fortune* came,
        And spinning fancies, she was heard to say,
        That her fine cobwebs did support the frame,
        Whereas they were supported by the same:
5   But *Wisdom* quickly swept them all away.

        Then *Pleasure* came, who liking not the fashion,
        Began to make *Balconies*, *Terraces*,
        Till she had weak'ned all by alteration:
        But rev'rend *laws*, and many a *proclamation*
10   Reformèd all at length with menaces.

        Then enter'd *Sin*, and with that Sycamore,
        Whose leaves first sheltered man from drought and dew,
        Working and winding slyly evermore,
        The inward walls and sommers cleft and tore:
15   But *Grace* shor'd these, and cut that as it grew.

        Then *Sin* combin'd with *Death* in a firm band
        To raze the building to the very floor:
        Which they effected, none could them withstand.
        But *Love* and *Grace* took *Glory* by the hand,
20   And built a braver Palace than before.

Coloss. 3:3
Our life is hid with Christ in God.

My words and thoughts do both express this notion,
That *Life* hath with the sun a double motion.
The first *Is* straight, and our diurnal friend,
    The other *Hid* and doth obliquely bend.
One life is wrapt *In* flesh, and tends to earth: 5
The other winds towards *Him*, whose happy birth
Taught me to live here so, *That* still one eye
Should aim and shoot at that which *Is* on high:
        Quitting with daily labour all *My* pleasure,
          To gain at harvest an eternal *Treasure*.   10

Vanity (1).

      The fleet Astronomer can bore,
And thread the spheres with his quick-piercing mind:
He views their stations, walks from door to door,
      Surveys, as if he had design'd
To make a purchase there: he sees their dances,   5
      And knoweth long before,
Both their full-ey'd aspects, and secret glances.

      The nimble Diver with his side
Cuts through the working waves, that he may fetch
His dearly-earnèd pearl, which God did hide   10
      On purpose from the vent'rous wretch;
That he might save his life, and also hers,
      Who with excessive pride
Her own destruction and his danger wears.

15   The subtle Chymick can divest
And strip the creature naked, till he find
The callow principles within their nest:
     There he imparts to them his mind,
Admitted to their bed-chamber, before
20   They appear trim and drest
To ordinary suitors at the door.

     What hath not man sought out and found,
But his dear God? who yet his glorious law
Embosoms in us, mellowing the ground
25   With show'rs and frosts, with love and awe,
So that we need not say, Where's this command?
     Poor man, thou searchest round
To find out *death*, but missest *life* at hand.

Lent.

Welcome dear feast of Lent: who loves not thee,
He loves not Temperance, or Authority,
     But is compos'd of passion.
The Scriptures bid us *fast*; the Church says, *now*:
5 Give to thy Mother, what thou wouldst allow
     To ev'ry Corporation.

The humble soul compos'd of love and fear
Begins at home, and lays the burden there,
     When doctrines disagree.
10 He says, in things which use hath justly got,
I am a scandal to the Church, and not
     The Church is so to me.

True Christians should be glad of an occasion
To use their temperance, seeking no evasion,
     When good is seasonable;
15 Unless Authority, which should increase
The obligation in us, make it less,
     And Power itself disable.

Besides the cleanness of sweet abstinence,
Quick thoughts and motions at a small expense,   20
          A face not fearing light:
Whereas in fullness there are sluttish fumes,
Sour exhalations, and dishonest rheums,
          Revenging the delight.

Then those same pendant profits, which the spring   25
And Easter intimate, enlarge the thing,
          And goodness of the deed.
Neither ought other men's abuse of Lent
Spoil the good use; lest by that argument
          We forfeit all our Creed.   30

It's true, we cannot reach Christ's forti'th day;
Yet to go part of that religious way,
          Is better than to rest:
We cannot reach our Saviour's purity;
Yet are we bid, *Be holy ev'n as he.*   35
          In both let's do our best.

Who goeth in the way which Christ hath gone,
Is much more sure to meet with him, than one
          That travelleth by-ways:
Perhaps my God, though he be far before,   40
May turn, and take me by the hand, and more
          May strengthen my decays.

Yet Lord instruct us to improve our fast
By starving sin and taking such repast
          As may our faults control: 45
That ev'ry man may revel at his door,
Not in his parlour; banqueting the poor,
          And among those his soul.

Virtue.

Sweet day, so cool, so calm, so bright,
The bridal of the earth and sky:

The dew shall weep thy fall tonight;
             For thou must die.

5   Sweet rose, whose hue angry and brave
Bids the rash gazer wipe his eye:
Thy root is ever in its grave,
             And thou must die.

Sweet spring, full of sweet days and roses,
10   A box where sweets compacted lie;
My music shows ye have your closes,
             And all must die.

Only a sweet and virtuous soul,
Like season'd timber, never gives;
15   But though the whole world turn to coal,
             Then chiefly lives.

The Pearl (Matt. 13:45)

I know the ways of learning; both the head
And pipes that feed the press, and make it run;
What reason hath from nature borrowèd,
Or of itself, like a good housewife, spun
5   In laws and policy; what the stars conspire,
What willing nature speaks, what forc'd by fire;
Both th' old discoveries, and the new-found seas,
The stock and surplus, cause and history:
All these stand open, or I have the keys:
10   Yet I love thee.

I know the ways of honour, what maintains
The quick returns of courtesy and wit:
In vies of favours whether party gains,
When glory swells the heart, and mouldeth it
15   To all expressions both of hand and eye,
Which on the world a true-love-knot may tie,
And bear the bundle, wheresoe'er it goes:

How many drams of spirit there must be
To sell my life unto my friends or foes:
                    Yet I love thee.   20

I know the ways of pleasure, the sweet strains,
The lullings and the relishes of it;
The propositions of hot blood and brains;
What mirth and music mean; what love and wit
Have done these twenty hundred years, and more: 25
I know the projects of unbridled store:
My stuff is flesh, not brass; my senses live,
And grumble oft, that they have more in me
Than he that curbs them, being but one to five:
                    Yet I love thee.   30

I know all these, and have them in my hand:
Therefore not sealèd, but with open eyes
I fly to thee, and fully understand
Both the main sale, and the commodities;
And at what rate and price I have thy love;   35
With all the circumstances that may move:
Yet through these labyrinths, not my grovelling wit,
But thy silk twist let down from heav'n to me;
Did both conduct, and teach me, how by it
                    To climb to thee.   40

Affliction (4).

Broken in pieces all asunder,
                    Lord, hunt me not,
                    A thing forgot,
Once a poor creature, now a wonder,
            A wonder tortur'd in the space   5
Betwixt this world and that of grace.

My thoughts are all a case of knives,
           Wounding my heart
           With scatter'd smart,
10   As wat'ring pots give flowers their lives.
           Nothing their fury can control,
           While they do wound and prick my soul.

All my attendants are at strife,
           Quitting their place
15   Unto my face:
Nothing performs the task of life:
           The elements are let loose to fight,
           And while I live, try out their right.

O help, my God! let not their plot
           Kill them and me,
20   And also thee,
Who art my life: dissolve the knot,
           As the sun scatters by his light
           All the rebellions of the night.

Then shall those powers, which work for grief,
           Enter thy pay,
25   And day by day
Labour thy praise, and my relief:
           With care and courage building me,
30   Till I reach heav'n, and much more, thee.

Man.

My God, I heard this day,
That none doth build a stately habitation,
    But he that means to dwell therein.
    What house more stately hath there been,
5   Or can be, than is Man? to whose creation
    All things are in decay.

For Man is ev'ry thing,
And more: He is a tree, yet bears no fruit;
A beast, yet is, or should be more:
Reason and speech we only bring.   10
Parrots may thank us, if they are not mute,
They go upon the score.

Man is all symmetry,
Full of proportions, one limb to another,
And all to all the world besides: 15
Each part may call the farthest, brother:
For head with foot hath private amity,
And both with moons and tides.

Nothing hath got so far,
But Man hath caught and kept it, as his prey.   20
His eyes dismount the highest star:
He is in little all the sphere.
Herbs gladly cure our flesh; because that they
Find their acquaintance there.

For us the winds do blow,   25
The earth doth rest, heav'n move, and fountains flow.
Nothing we see, but means our good,
As our delight, or as our treasure:
The whole is, either our cupboard of food,
Or cabinet of pleasure.   30

The stars have us to bed;
Night draws the curtain, which the sun withdraws;
Music and light attend our head.
All things unto our flesh are kind
In their descent and being; to our mind   35
In their ascent and cause.

Each thing is full of duty:
Waters united are our navigation;
Distinguishèd, our habitation;
Below, our drink; above, our meat;   40
Both are our cleanliness. Hath one such beauty?
Then how are all things neat?

More servants wait on Man,
Than he'll take notice of: in ev'ry path
He treads down that which doth befriend him,
When sickness makes him pale and wan.
O mighty love! Man is one world, and hath
Another to attend him.

Since then, my God, thou hast
So brave a Palace built; O dwell in it,
That it may dwell with thee at last!
Till then, afford us so much wit;
That, as the world serves us, we may serve thee,
And both thy servants be.

Antiphon (2).

Chor. Praisèd be the God of love,
           Men.   Here below,
           Ang.   And here above:
Cho. Who hath dealt his mercies so,
           Ang.   To his friend,
           Men.   And to his foe;

Cho. That both grace and glory tend
           Ang.   Us of old,
           Men.   And us in th' end.
Cho. The great shepherd of the fold
           Ang.   Us did make,
           Men.   For us was sold.

Cho. He our foes in pieces brake;
           Ang.   Him we touch;
           Men.   And him we take.
Cho. Wherefore since that he is such,
           Ang.   We adore,
           Men.   And we do crouch.

Cho.   Lord, thy praises should be more.
                    Men.   We have none,   20
                    Ang.   And we no store.
Cho.   Praisèd be the God alone,
          Who hath made of two folds one.

Unkindness.

Lord, make me coy and tender to offend:
In friendship, first I think, if that agree,
                    Which I intend,
                Unto my friend's intent and end.
I would not use a friend, as I use Thee.   5

If any touch my friend, or his good name;
It is my honour and my love to free
                    His blasted fame
                From the least spot or thought of blame.
I could not use a friend, as I use Thee.   10

My friend may spit upon my curious floor:
Would he have gold? I lend it instantly;
                    But let the poor,
                And thou within them, starve at door.
I cannot use a friend, as I use Thee.   15

When that my friend pretendeth to a place,
I quit my interest, and leave it free:
                    But when thy grace
                Sues for my heart, I thee displace,
Nor would I use a friend, as I use Thee.   20

Yet can a friend what thou hast done fulfil?
O write in brass, *My God upon a tree*
                    His blood did spill
                Only to purchase my good-will:
Yet use I not my foes, as I use Thee.   25

Life.

I made a posy, while the day ran by;
Here will I smell my remnant out, and tie
          My life within this band.
But time did beckon to the flowers, and they
5 By noon most cunningly did steal away,
          And wither'd in my hand.

My hand was next to them, and then my heart:
I took, without more thinking, in good part
          Time's gentle admonition:
10 Who did so sweetly death's sad taste convey,
Making my mind to smell my fatal day;
          Yet sug'ring the suspicion.

Farewell dear flowers, sweetly your time ye spent,
Fit, while ye lived, for smell or ornament,
15   And after death for cures.
I follow straight without complaints or grief,
Since if my scent be good, I care not, if
          It be, as short as yours.

Submission.

But that thou art my wisdom, Lord,
    And both mine eyes are thine,
My mind would be extremely stirr'd
    For missing my design.

5 Were it not better to bestow
    Some place and power on me?
Then should thy praises with me grow,
    And share in my degree.

But when I thus dispute and grieve,
    I do resume my sight,   10
And pilf'ring what I once did give,
    Disseise thee of thy right.

How know I, if thou shouldst me raise,
    That I should then raise thee?
Perhaps great places and thy praise   15
    Do not so well agree.

Wherefore unto my gift I stand;
    I will no more advise:
Only do thou lend me a hand,
    Since thou hast both mine eyes.   20

Justice (1).

    I cannot skill of these thy ways.
Lord, thou didst make me, yet thou woundest me;
Lord, thou dost wound me, yet thou dost relieve me:
Lord, thou relievest, yet I die by thee:
Lord, thou dost kill me, yet thou dost reprieve me.   5
    But when I mark my life and praise,
    Thy justice me most fitly pays:
For, *I do praise thee, yet I praise thee not:*
My prayers mean thee, yet my prayers stray:
I would do well, yet sin the hand hath got: 10
My soul doth love thee, yet it loves delay.
    I cannot skill of these my ways.

Charms and Knots.

Who read a chapter when they rise,
Shall ne'er be troubled with ill eyes.

A poor man's rod, when thou dost ride,
Is both a weapon and a guide.

5 Who shuts his hand, hath lost his gold:
Who opens it, hath it twice told.

Who goes to bed and doth not pray,
Maketh two nights to ev'ry day.

Who by aspersions throws a stone
10 At th' head of others, hit their own.

Who looks on ground with humble eyes,
Finds himself there, and seeks to rise.

When th' hair is sweet through pride or lust,
The powder doth forget the dust.

15 Take one from ten, and what remains?
Ten still, if sermons go for gains.

In shallow water heav'n doth show;
But who drinks on, to hell may go.

Affliction (5).

My God, I read this day,
That planted Paradise was not so firm,
As was and is thy floating Ark; whose stay
And anchor thou art only, to confirm
5   And strengthen it in ev'ry age,
          When waves do rise, and tempests rage.

At first we liv'd in pleasure;
Thine own delights thou didst to us impart:
When we grew wanton, thou didst use displeasure
10 To make us thine: yet that we might not part,
          As we at first did board with thee,
          Now thou wouldst taste our misery.

There is but joy and grief;
If either will convert us, we are thine:
Some Angels us'd the first; if our relief   15
Take up the second, then thy double line
      And sev'ral baits in either kind
      Furnish thy table to thy mind.

      Affliction then is ours;
We are the trees, whom shaking fastens more,   20
While blust'ring winds destroy the wanton bow'rs,
And ruffle all their curious knots and store.
      My God, so temper joy and woe,
      That thy bright beams may tame thy bow.

Mortification.

      How soon doth man decay!
When clothes are taken from a chest of sweets
      To swaddle infants, whose young breath
      Scarce knows the way;
      Those clouts are little winding sheets,   5
Which do consign and send them unto death.

      When boys go first to bed,
They step into their voluntary graves,
      Sleep binds them fast; only their breath
      Makes them not dead: 10
      Successive nights, like rolling waves,
Convey them quickly, who are bound for death.

      When youth is frank and free,
And calls for music, while his veins do swell,
      All day exchanging mirth and breath   15
      In company;
      That music summons to the knell,
Which shall befriend him at the house of death.

      When man grows staid and wise,
Getting a house and home, where he may move   20

Within the circle of his breath,
   Schooling his eyes;
  That dumb inclosure maketh love
Unto the coffin, that attends his death.

25   When age grows low and weak,
Marking his grave, and thawing ev'ry year,
   Till all do melt, and drown his breath
    When he would speak;
  A chair or litter shows the bier,
30Which shall convey him to the house of death.

   Man, ere he is aware,
Hath put together a solemnity,
   And dressed his hearse, while he has breath
    As yet to spare:
   Yet Lord, instruct us so to die,
35That all these dyings may be life in death.

Decay.

Sweet were the days, when thou didst lodge with Lot,
Struggle with Jacob, sit with Gideon,
Advise with Abraham, when thy power could not
Encounter Moses' strong complaints and moan:
   Thy words were then, *Let me alone*.

One might have sought and found thee presently
At some fair oak, or bush, or cave, or well:
Is my God this way? No, they would reply:
He is to Sinai gone, as we heard tell:
   List, ye may hear great Aaron's bell.

But now thou dost thyself immure and close
In some one corner of a feeble heart:
Where yet both Sin and Satan, thy old foes,
Do pinch and straiten thee, and use much art
   To gain thy thirds and little part.

I see the world grows old, when as the heat
Of thy great love once spread, as in an urn
Doth closet up itself, and still retreat,
Cold sin still forcing it, till it return,
     And calling *Justice*, all things burn.   20

Misery.

    Lord, let the Angels praise thy name.
Man is a foolish thing, a foolish thing,
    Folly and Sin play all his game.
His house still burns, and yet he still doth sing,
      Man is but grass,   5
      He knows it, fill the glass.

    How canst thou brook his foolishness?
Why, he'll not lose a cup of drink for thee:
    Bid him but temper his excess;
Not he: he knows, where he can better be,   10
      As he will swear,
      Than to serve thee in fear.

    What strange pollutions doth he wed,
And make his own? as if none knew, but he.
    No man shall beat into his head,
That thou within his curtains drawn canst see: 15
      They are of cloth,
      Where never yet came moth.

    The best of men, turn but thy hand
For one poor minute, stumble at a pin: 20
    They would not have their actions scann'd,
Nor any sorrow tell them that they sin,
      Though it be small,
      And measure not their fall.

25   They quarrel thee, and would give over
The bargain made to serve thee: but thy love
        Holds them unto it, and doth cover
Their follies with the wing of thy mild Dove,
                    Not suff'ring those
30   Who would, to be thy foes.

        My God, Man cannot praise thy name:
Thou art all brightness, perfect purity;
        The sun holds down his head for shame,
Dead with eclipses, when we speak of thee:
35   How shall infection
                Presume on thy perfection?

        As dirty hands foul all they touch,
And those things most, which are most pure and fine:
        So our clay hearts, ev'n when we crouch
40 To sing thy praises, make them less divine.
                    Yet either this,
                Or none, thy portion is.

        Man cannot serve thee; let him go,
And serve the swine: there, there is his delight:
45   He doth not like this virtue, no;
Give him his dirt to wallow in all night:
                These Preachers make
                His head to shoot and ache.

        O foolish man! where are thine eyes?
50 How hast thou lost them in a crowd of cares?
        Thou pull'st the rug, and wilt not rise,
No, not to purchase the whole pack of stars:
                    There let them shine,
                Thou must go sleep, or dine.

55   The bird that sees a dainty bow'r
Made in the tree, where she was wont to sit,
        Wonders and sings, but not his power
Who made the arbour: this exceeds her wit.

                But Man doth know
         The spring, whence all things flow: 60

    And yet as though he knew it not,
His knowledge winks, and lets his humours reign;
    They make his life a constant blot,
And all the blood of God to run in vain.
              Ah wretch! what verse   65
          Can thy strange ways rehearse?

    Indeed at first Man was a treasure,
A box of jewels, shop of rarities,
    A ring, whose posy was, *My pleasure*:
He was a garden in a Paradise: 70
            Glory and grace
         Did crown his heart and face.

    But sin hath fool'd him. Now he is
A lump of flesh, without a foot or wing
    To raise him to the glimpse of bliss: 75
A sick toss'd vessel, dashing on each thing;
           Nay, his own shelf:
         My God, I mean myself.

Jordan (2).

When first my lines of heav'nly joys made mention,
Such was their lustre, they did so excel,
That I sought out quaint words, and trim invention;
My thoughts began to burnish, sprout, and swell,
Curling with metaphors a plain intention,   5
Decking the sense, as if it were to sell.

Thousands of notions in my brain did run,
Off'ring their service, if I were not sped:
I often blotted what I had begun;
This was not quick enough, and that was dead.   10
Nothing could seem too rich to clothe the sun,
Much less those joys which trample on his head.

As flames do work and wind, when they ascend,
So did I weave my self into the sense.
But while I bustled, I might hear a friend
Whisper, *How wide is all this long pretence!*
There is in love a sweetness ready penned:
Copy out only that, and save expense.

Prayer (2).

Of what an easy quick access,
My blessed Lord, art thou! how suddenly
    May our requests thine ear invade!
To show that state dislikes not easiness,
    If I but lift mine eyes, my suit is made:
Thou canst no more not hear, than thou canst die.

Of what supreme almighty power
Is thy great arm which spans the east and west,
    And tacks the centre to the sphere!
By it do all things live their measured hour:
We cannot ask the thing, which is not there,
    Blaming the shallowness of our request.

Of what unmeasurable love
Art thou possessed, who, when thou couldst not die,
    Wert fain to take our flesh and curse,
And for our sakes in person sin reprove,
That by destroying that which ti'd thy purse,
    Thou mightst make way for liberality!

Since then these three wait on thy throne,
Ease, Power, and *Love*; I value prayer so,
    That were I to leave all but one,
Wealth, fame, endowments, virtues, all should go;
I and dear prayer would together dwell,
    And quickly gain, for each inch lost, an ell.

Obedience.

My God, if writings may
Convey a Lordship any way
Whither the buyer and the seller please;
Let it not thee displease,
If this poor paper do as much as they.									5

On it my heart doth bleed
As many lines as there doth need
To pass itself and all it hath to thee.
To which I do agree,
And here present it as my special deed.								10

If that hereafter Pleasure
Cavil, and claim her part and measure,
As if this passèd with a reservation,
Or some such words in fashion;
I here exclude the wrangler from thy treasure.							15

O let thy sacred will
All thy delight in me fulfil!
Let me not think an action mine own way,
But as thy love shall sway,
Resigning up the rudder to thy skill.								20

Lord, what is man to thee,
That thou shouldst mind a rotten tree?
Yet since thou canst not choose but see my actions;
So great are thy perfections,
Thou mayst as well my actions guide, as see.							25

Besides, thy death and blood
Showed a strange love to all our good:
Thy sorrows were in earnest, no faint proffer,
Or superficial offer
Of what we might not take, or be withstood.							30

Wherefore I all forgo:
To one word only I say, No:
Where in the deed there was an intimation
Of a gift or donation,
Lord, let it now by way of purchase go.

He that will pass his land,
As I have mine, may set his hand
And heart unto this deed, when he hath read;
And make the purchase spread
To both our goods, if he to it will stand.

How happy were my part,
If some kind man would thrust his heart
Into these lines; till in heav'n's Court of Rolls
They were by winged souls
Ent'red for both, far above their desert!

Conscience.

Peace prattler, do not lour:
Not a fair look, but thou dost call it foul:
Not a sweet dish, but thou dost call it sour:
Music to thee doth howl.
By list'ning to thy chatting fears
I have both lost mine eyes and ears.

Prattler, no more, I say:
My thoughts must work, but like a noiseless sphere;
Harmonious peace must rock them all the day:
No room for prattlers there.
If thou persistest, I will tell thee,
That I have physic to expel thee.

And the receipt shall be
My Saviour's blood: whenever at his board
I do but taste it, straight it cleanseth me,
And leaves thee not a word;

No, not a tooth or nail to scratch,
And at my actions carp, or catch.

Yet if thou talkest still,
Besides my physic, know there's some for thee: 20
Some wood and nails to make a staff or bill
For those that trouble me:
The bloody cross of my dear Lord
Is both my physic and my sword.

Sion.

Lord, with what glory wast thou serv'd of old,
When Solomon's temple stood and flourished!
    Where most things were of purest gold;
    The wood was all embellished
With flowers and carvings, mystical and rare: 5
All showed the builder's, craved the seer's care.

Yet all this glory, all this pomp and state
Did not affect thee much, was not thy aim;
    Something there was, that sow'd debate:
    Wherefore thou quitt'st thy ancient claim: 10
And now thy Architecture meets with sin;
For all thy frame and fabric is within.

There thou art struggling with a peevish heart,
Which sometimes crosseth thee, thou sometimes it:
    The fight is hard on either part.   15
    Great God doth fight, he doth submit.
All Solomon's sea of brass and world of stone
Is not so dear to thee as one good groan.

And truly brass and stones are heavy things,
Tombs for the dead, not temples fit for thee: 20
    But groans are quick, and full of wings,
    And all their motions upward be;
And ever as they mount, like larks they sing;
The note is sad, yet music for a king.

Home.

Come Lord, my head doth burn, my heart is sick,
    While thou dost ever, ever stay:
Thy long deferrings wound me to the quick,
    My spirit gaspeth night and day.
        O show thyself to me,
        Or take me up to thee!

How canst thou stay, considering the pace
    The blood did make, which thou didst waste?
When I behold it trickling down thy face,
    I never saw thing make such haste.
        O show thy, & c.

When man was lost, thy pity looked about
    To see what help in th' earth or sky:
But there was none; at least no help without;
    The help did in thy bosom lie.
        O show thy, & c.

There lay thy son: and must he leave that nest,
    That hive of sweetness, to remove
Thraldom from those, who would not at a feast
    Leave one poor apple for thy love?
        O show thy, & c.

He did, he came: O my Redeemer dear,
    After all this canst thou be strange?
So many years baptis'd, and not appear?
    As if thy love could fail or change.
        O show thyself to me,
        Or take me up to thee!

Yet if thou stayest still, why must I stay?
    My God, what is this world to me?
This world of woe? hence all ye clouds, away,
    Away; I must get up and see.
        O show thy, & c.

What is this weary world; this meat and drink,
　That chains us by the teeth so fast?
What is this woman-kind, which I can wink   35
　　Into a blackness and distaste?
　　　O show thy, & c.

With one small sigh thou gav'st me th' other day
　I blasted all the joys about me:
And scowling on them as they pin'd away,   40
　　Now come again, said I, and flout me.
　　　O show thy, & c.

Nothing but drought and dearth, but bush and brake,
　Which way soe'er I look, I see.
Some may dream merrily, but when they wake,   45
　　They dress themselves and come to thee.
　　　O show thy, & c.

We talk of harvests; there are no such things,
　But when we leave our corn and hay:
There is no fruitful year, but that which brings   50
　　The last and lov'd, though dreadful day.
　　　O show thy, & c.

O loose this frame, this knot of man untie!
　That my free soul may use her wing,
Which now is pinioned with mortality,   55
　　As an entangled, hampered thing.
　　　O show thy, & c.

What have I left, that I should stay and groan?
　The most of me to heav'n is fled:
My thoughts and joys are all packt up and gone,   60
　　And for their old acquaintance plead.
　　　O show thy, & c.

Come dearest Lord, pass not this holy season,
　My flesh and bones and joints do pray:
And ev'n my verse, when by the rhyme and reason   65
　　The word is, *Stay*, says ever, *Come*.
　　　O show thy, & c.

The British Church.

I joy, dear Mother, when I view
Thy perfect lineaments, and hue
                    Both sweet and bright.
Beauty in thee takes up her place,
And dates her letters from thy face,
                    When she doth write.

A fine aspect in fit array,
Neither too mean, nor yet too gay,
                    Shows who is best.
Outlandish looks may not compare:
For all they either painted are,
                    Or else undrest.

She on the hills, which wantonly
Allureth all in hope to be
                    By her preferr'd,
Hath kiss'd so long her painted shrines,
That ev'n her face by kissing shines,
                    For her reward.

She in the valley is so shy
Of dressing that her hair doth lie
                    About her ears:
While she avoids her neighbour's pride,
She wholly goes on th' other side,
                    And nothing wears.

But dearest Mother, what those miss,
The mean, thy praise and glory is,
                    And long may be.
Blessed be God, whose love it was
To double-moat thee with his grace,
                    And none but thee.

The Quip.

The merry world did on a day
With his train-bands and mates agree
To meet together, where I lay,
And all in sport to jeer at me.

First, Beauty crept into a rose, 5
Which when I pluckt not, Sir, said she,
Tell me, I pray, Whose hands are those?
But thou shalt answer, Lord, for me.

Then Money came, and chinking still,
What tune is this, poor man? said he: 10
I heard in Music you had skill.
But thou shalt answer, Lord, for me.

Then came brave Glory puffing by
In silks that whistled, who but he?
He scarce allow'd me half an eye. 15
But thou shalt answer, Lord, for me.

Then came quick Wit and Conversation,
And he would needs a comfort be,
And, to be short, make an oration.
But thou shalt answer, Lord, for me. 20

Yet when the hour of thy design
To answer these fine things shall come;
Speak not at large, say, I am thine:
And then they have their answer home.

Vanity (2).

Poor silly soul, whose hope and head lies low;
Whose flat delights on earth do creep and grow:
To whom the stars shine not so fair, as eyes;

Nor solid work, as false embroideries;
5   Hark and beware, lest what you now do measure
And write for sweet, prove a most sour displeasure.

O hear betimes, lest thy relenting
May come too late!
To purchase heaven for repenting,
10   Is no hard rate.
If souls be made of earthly mould,
Let them love gold;
If born on high,
Let them unto their kindred fly:
15   For they can never be at rest,
Till they regain their ancient nest.
Then silly soul take heed; for earthly joy
Is but a bubble, and makes thee a boy.

The Dawning.

Awake sad heart, whom sorrow ever drowns;
Take up thine eyes, which feed on earth;
Unfold thy forehead gathered into frowns:
Thy Saviour comes, and with him mirth:
5   Awake, awake:
And with a thankful heart his comforts take.
But thou dost still lament, and pine, and cry;
And feel his death, but not his victory.

Arise sad heart; if thou dost not withstand,
10   Christ's resurrection thine may be:
Do not by hanging down break from the hand,
Which as it riseth, raiseth thee:
Arise, arise;
And with his burial-linen dry thine eyes:
15   Christ left his grave-clothes, that we might, when grief
Draws tears, or blood, not want a handkerchief.

Iesu.

IESU is in my heart, his sacred name
Is deeply carvèd there: but th' other week
A great affliction broke the little frame,
Ev'n all to pieces: which I went to seek:
And first I found the corner, where was *I*,   5
After, where *ES*, and next where *U* was graved.
When I had got these parcels, instantly
I sat me down to spell them, and perceivèd
That to my broken heart he was *I ease you*,
   And to my whole is *IESU*.   10

Business.

   Canst be idle? canst thou play,
   Foolish soul who sinn'd today?

Rivers run, and springs each one
Know their home, and get them gone:
Hast thou tears, or hast thou none?   5

If, poor soul, thou hast no tears;
Would thou hadst no faults or fears!
Who hath these, those ill forbears.

Winds still work: it is their plot,
Be the season cold, or hot: 10
Hast thou sighs, or hast thou not?

If thou hast no sighs or groans,
Would thou hadst no flesh and bones!
Lesser pains scape greater ones.

   But if yet thou idle be,   15
   Foolish soul, Who died for thee?

Who did leave his Father's throne,
To assume thy flesh and bone;
Had he life, or had he none?

If he had not liv'd for thee,
Thou hadst died most wretchedly;
And two deaths had been thy fee.

He so far thy good did plot,
That his own self he forgot.
Did he die, or did he not?

If he had not died for thee,
Thou hadst lived in misery.
Two lives worse than ten deaths be.

       And hath any space of breath
       'Twixt his sins and Saviour's death?

He that loseth gold, though dross,
Tells to all he meets, his cross:
He that sins, hath he no loss?

He that finds a silver vein,
Thinks on it, and thinks again:
Brings thy Saviour's death no gain?

       Who in heart not ever kneels,
       Neither sin nor Saviour feels.

Dialogue.

Sweetest Saviour, if my soul
    Were but worth the having,
Quickly should I then control
    Any thought of waiving.
But when all my care and pains
Cannot give the name of gains

To thy wretch so full of stains;
What delights or hope remains?

What, Child, is the balance thine,
        Thine the poise and measure?   10
If I say, Thou shalt be mine;
        Finger not my treasure.
What the gains in having thee
Do amount to, only he,
Who for man was sold, can see;   15
That transferr'd th' accounts to me.

But as I can see no merit,
        Leading to this favour:
So the way to fit me for it,
        Is beyond my savour: 20
As the reason then is thine;
So the way is none of mine:
I disclaim the whole design:
Sin disclaims and I resign.

That is all, if that I could   25
        Get without repining;
And my clay my creature would
        Follow my resigning.
That as I did freely part
With my glory and desert,   30
Left all joys to feel all smart --
        Ah! no more: thou break'st my heart.

Dullness.

Why do I languish thus, drooping and dull,
        As if I were all earth?
O give me quickness, that I may with mirth
        Praise thee brimfull!

5   The wanton lover in a curious strain
               Can praise his fairest fair;
     And with quaint metaphors her curlèd hair
               Curl o'er again.

     Thou art my loveliness, my life, my light,
10   Beauty alone to me:
     Thy bloody death and undeserv'd, makes thee
               Pure red and white.

     When all perfections as but one appear,
               That those thy form doth show,
15   The very dust, where thou dost tread and go,
               Makes beauties here;

     Where are my lines then? my approaches? views?
               Where are my window-songs?
     Lovers are still pretending, and ev'n wrongs
20   Sharpen their Muse:

     But I am lost in flesh, whose sug'red lies
               Still mock me, and grow bold:
     Sure thou didst put a mind there, if I could
               Find where it lies.

25   Lord, clear thy gift, that with a constant wit
               I may but look towards thee:
     Look only; for to *love* thee, who can be,
               What angel fit?

Love-joy.

As on a window late I cast mine eye,
I saw a vine drop grapes with *J* and *C*
Anneal'd on every bunch. One standing by
Asked what it meant. I (who am never loath

To spend my judgement) said, It seem'd to me   5
To be the body and the letters both
Of *Joy* and *Charity*. Sir, you have not missed,
The man repli'd; It figures *JESUS CHRIST*.

Providence.

O sacred Providence, who from end to end
Strongly and sweetly movest! shall I write,
And not of thee, through whom my fingers bend
To hold my quill? shall they not do thee right?

Of all the creatures both in sea and land   5
Only to Man thou hast made known thy ways,
And put the pen alone into his hand,
And made him Secretary of thy praise.

Beasts fain would sing; birds ditty to their notes;
Trees would be tuning on their native lute   10
To thy renown: but all their hands and throats
Are brought to Man, while they are lame and mute.

Man is the world's high Priest: he doth present
The sacrifice for all; while they below
Unto the service mutter an assent,   15
Such as springs use that fall, and winds that blow.

He that to praise and laud thee doth refrain,
Doth not refrain unto himself alone,
But robs a thousand who would praise thee fain,
And doth commit a world of sin in one.   20

The beasts say, Eat me: but, if beasts must teach,
The tongue is yours to eat, but mine to praise.
The trees say, Pull me: but the hand you stretch,
Is mine to write, as it is yours to raise.

25   Wherefore, most sacred Spirit, I here present
      For me and all my fellows praise to thee:
      And just it is that I should pay the rent,
      Because the benefit accrues to me.

      We all acknowledge both thy power and love
30   To be exact, transcendent, and divine;
      Who dost so strongly and so sweetly move,
      While all things have their will, yet none but thine.

      For either thy command, or thy permission
      Lay hands on all: they are thy right and left.
35   The first puts on with speed and expedition;
      The other curbs sin's stealing pace and theft.

      Nothing escapes them both; all must appear,
      And be dispos'd, and dress'd, and tun'd by thee,
      Who sweetly temper'st all. If we could hear
40   Thy skill and art, what music would it be!

      Thou art in small things great, not small in any:
      Thy even praise can neither rise, nor fall.
      Thou art in all things one, in each thing many:
      For thou art infinite in one and all.

45   Tempests are calm to thee; they know thy hand,
      And hold it fast, as children do their father's,
      Which cry and follow. Thou hast made poor sand
      Check the proud sea, ev'n when it swells and gathers.

      Thy cupboard serves the world: the meat is set,
50   Where all may reach: no beast but knows his feed.
      Birds teach us hawking; fishes have their net:
      The great prey on the less, they on some weed.

      Nothing engend'red doth prevent his meat:
      Flies have their table spread, ere they appear.
55   Some creatures have in winter what to eat;
      Others do sleep, and envy not their cheer.

      How finely dost thou times and seasons spin,
      And make a twist chequer'd with night and day!

Which as it lengthens winds, and winds us in,
As bowls go on, but turning all the way.   60

Each creature hath a wisdom for his good.
The pigeons feed their tender offspring, crying,
When they are callow; but withdraw their food
When they are fledge, that need may teach them flying.

Bees work for man; and yet they never bruise   65
Their master's flower, but leave it, having done,
As fair as ever, and as fit to use;
So both the flower doth stay, and honey run.

Sheep eat the grass, and dung the ground for more:
Trees after bearing drop their leaves for soil: 70
Springs vent their streams, and by expense get store:
Clouds cool by heat, and baths by cooling boil.

Who hath the virtue to express the rare
And curious virtues both of herbs and stones?
Is there an herb for that? O that thy care   75
Would show a root, that gives expressions!

And if an herb hath power, what have the stars?
A rose, besides his beauty, is a cure.
Doubtless our plagues and plenty, peace and wars
Are there much surer than our art is sure.   80

Thou hast hid metals: man may take them thence;
But at his peril: when he digs the place,
He makes a grave; as if the thing had sense,
And threat'ned man, that he should fill the space.

Ev'n poisons praise thee. Should a thing be lost?   85
Should creatures want for want of heed their due?
Since where are poisons, antidotes are most:
The help stands close, and keeps the fear in view.

The sea, which seems to stop the traveller,
Is by a ship the speedier passage made.   90
The winds, who think they rule the mariner,
Are ruled by him, and taught to serve his trade.

And as thy house is full, so I adore
Thy curious art in marshalling thy goods.
95   The hills with health abound; the vales with store;
The South with marble; North with furs and woods.

Hard things are glorious; easy things good cheap.
The common all men have; that which is rare,
Men therefore seek to have, and care to keep.
100   The healthy frosts with summer-fruits compare.

Light without wind is glass: warm without weight
Is wool and furs: cool without closeness, shade:
Speed without pains, a horse: tall without height,
A servile hawk: low without loss, a spade.

105   All countries have enough to serve their need:
If they seek fine things, thou dost make them run
For their offence; and then dost turn their speed
To be commerce and trade from sun to sun.

Nothing wears clothes, but Man; nothing doth need
110   But he to wear them. Nothing useth fire,
But Man alone, to show his heav'nly breed:
And only he hath fuel in desire.

When th' earth was dry, thou mad'st a sea of wet:
When that lay gather'd, thou didst broach the mountains:
115   When yet some places could no moisture get,
The winds grew gard'ners, and the clouds good fountains.

Rain, do not hurt my flowers; but gently spend
Your honey drops: press not to smell them here:
When they are ripe, their odour will ascend,
120   And at your lodging with their thanks appear.

How harsh are thorns to pears! and yet they make
A better hedge, and need less reparation.
How smooth are silks comparèd with a stake,
Or with a stone! yet make no good foundation.

125   Sometimes thou dost divide thy gifts to man,
Sometimes unite. The Indian nut alone

Is clothing, meat and trencher, drink and can,
Boat, cable, sail and needle, all in one.

Most herbs that grow in brooks, are hot and dry.
Cold fruits warm kernels help against the wind.   130
The lemon's juice and rind cure mutually.
The whey of milk doth loose, the milk doth bind.

Thy creatures leap not, but express a feast,
Where all the guests sit close, and nothing wants.
Frogs marry fish and flesh; bats, bird and beast;   135
Sponges, non-sense and sense; mines, th' earth and plants.

To show thou art not bound, as if thy lot
Were worse than ours; sometimes thou shiftest hands.
Most things move th' under-jaw; the Crocodile not.
Most things sleep lying; th' Elephant leans or stands.   140

But who hath praise enough? nay who hath any?
None can express thy works, but he that knows them:
And none can know thy works, which are so many,
And so complete, but only he that owes them.

All things that are, though they have sev'ral ways,   145
Yet in their being join in one advice
To honour thee: and so I give thee praise
In all my other hymns, but in this twice.

Each thing that is, although in use and name
It go for one, hath many ways in store   150
To honour thee; and so each hymn thy fame
Extolleth many ways, yet this one more.

Hope.

I gave to Hope a watch of mine: but he
            An anchor gave to me.
Then an old prayer-book I did present:
            And he an optic sent.

5   With that I gave a vial full of tears:
                 But he a few green ears:
       Ah Loiterer! I'll no more, no more I'll bring:
                 I did expect a ring.

Sin's round.

       Sorry I am, my God, sorry I am,
       That my offences course it in a ring.
       My thoughts are working like a busy flame,
       Until their cockatrice they hatch and bring:
5   And when they once have perfected their draughts,
       My words take fire from my inflamèd thoughts.

       My words take fire from my inflamèd thoughts,
       Which spit it forth like the Sicilian hill.
       They vent the wares, and pass them with their faults,
10   And by their breathing ventilate the ill.
       But words suffice not, where are lewd intentions:
       My hands do join to finish the inventions.

       My hands do join to finish the inventions:
       And so my sins ascend three stories high,
15   As Babel grew, before there were dissensions.
       Yet ill deeds loiter not: for they supply
       New thoughts of sinning: wherefore, to my shame,
       Sorry I am, my God, sorry I am.

Time.

       Meeting with Time, Slack thing, said I,
       Thy scythe is dull; whet it for shame.
       No marvel Sir, he did reply,
       If it at length deserve some blame:

But where one man would have me grind it,   5
Twenty for one too sharp do find it.

Perhaps some such of old did pass,
Who above all things loved this life;
To whom thy scythe a hatchet was,
Which now is but a pruning-knife.   10
   Christ's coming hath made man thy debtor,
   Since by thy cutting he grows better.

And in his blessing thou art blessed;
For where thou only wert before
An executioner at best;   15
Thou art a gard'ner now, and more,
   An usher to convey our souls
   Beyond the utmost stars and poles.

And this is that makes life so long,
While it detains us from our God.   20
Ev'n pleasures here increase the wrong,
And length of days lengthen the rod.
   Who wants the place, where God doth dwell,
   Partakes already half of hell.

Of what strange length must that needs be,   25
Which ev'n eternity excludes!
Thus far Time heard me patiently:
Then chafing said, This man deludes:
   What do I here before his door?
   He doth not crave less time, but more.   30

Gratefulness.

Thou that hast giv'n so much to me,
Give one thing more, a grateful heart.
See how thy beggar works on thee
                By art.

5   He makes thy gifts occasion more,
              And says, If he in this be crosst
              All thou hast giv'n him heretofore
                        Is lost.

              But thou didst reckon, when at first
10   Thy word our hearts and hands did crave,
              What it would come to at the worst
                        To save.

              Perpetual knockings at thy door,
              Tears sullying thy transparent rooms,
15   Gift upon gift, much would have more,
                        And comes.

              This not withstanding, thou wentst on,
              And didst allow us all our noise:
              Nay thou hast made a sigh and groan
20   Thy joys.

              Not that thou hast not still above
              Much better tunes, than groans can make;
              But that these country-airs thy love
                        Did take.

25   Wherefore I cry, and cry again;
              And in no quiet canst thou be,
              Till I a thankful heart obtain
                        Of thee:

              Not thankful, when it pleaseth me;
30   As if thy blessings had spare days:
              But such a heart, whose pulse may be
                        Thy praise.

Peace.

Sweet Peace, where dost thou dwell? I humbly crave,
   Let me once know.
  I sought thee in a secret cave,
    And ask'd, if Peace were there.
A hollow wind did seem to answer, No: 5
    Go seek elsewhere.

I did; and going did a rainbow note:
    Surely, thought I,
  This is the lace of Peace's coat:
    I will search out the matter.   10
But while I look'd, the clouds immediately
    Did break and scatter.

Then went I to a garden, and did spy
    A gallant flower,
  The Crown Imperial: Sure, said I,   15
    Peace at the root must dwell.
But when I digg'd, I saw a worm devour
    What show'd so well.

At length I met a rev'rend good old man,
    Whom when for Peace   20
  I did demand, he thus began:
    There was a Prince of old
At Salem dwelt, who liv'd with good increase
    Of flock and fold.

He sweetly liv'd; yet sweetness did not save 25
    His life from foes.
  But after death out of his grave
    There sprang twelve stalks of wheat:
Which many wond'ring at, got some of those
    To plant and set.   30

It prosper'd strangely, and did soon disperse
    Through all the earth:
  For they that taste it do rehearse,

That virtue lies therein,
35   A secret virtue bringing peace and mirth
                    By flight of sin.

Take of this grain, which in my garden grows,
                    And grows for you;
           Make bread of it: and that repose
40   And peace which ev'rywhere
With so much earnestness you do pursue,
                    Is only there.

Confession.

O what a cunning guest
Is this same grief! within my heart I made
           Closets; and in them many a chest;
           And like a master in my trade,
5   In those chests, boxes; in each box, a till:
Yet grief knows all, and enters when he will.

No screw, no piercer can
Into a piece of timber work and wind,
           As God's afflictions into man
10   When he a torture hath design'd.
They are too subtle for the subtlest hearts;
And fall, like rheums, upon the tend'rest parts.

We are the earth; and they,
Like moles within us, heave, and cast about:
15   And till they foot and clutch their prey,
           They never cool, much less give out.
No smith can make such locks, but they have keys:
Closets are halls to them; and hearts, high-ways.

Only an open breast
20   Doth shut them out, so that they cannot enter;
           Or, if they enter, cannot rest,
           But quickly seek some new adventure.

Smooth open hearts no fast'ning have; but fiction
Doth give a hold and handle to affliction.

    Wherefore my faults and sins,   25
Lord, I acknowledge; take thy plagues away:
    For since confession pardon wins,
    I challenge here the brightest day,
The clearest diamond: let them do their best,
They shall be thick and cloudy to my breast.   30

Giddiness.

O, what a thing is man! how far from power,
    From settled peace and rest!
He is some twenty sev'ral men at least
    Each sev'ral hour.

One while he counts of heav'n, as of his treasure: 5
    But then a thought creeps in,
And calls him coward, who for fear of sin
    Will lose a pleasure.

Now he will fight it out, and to the wars;
    Now eat his bread in peace,   10
And snudge in quiet: now he scorns increase;
    Now all day spares.

He builds a house, which quickly down must go,
    As if a whirlwind blew
And crusht the building: and it's partly true,   15
    His mind is so.

O what a sight were Man, if his attires
    Did alter with his mind;
And like a Dolphin's skin, his clothes combin'd
    With his desires!   20

Surely if each one saw another's heart,
    There would be no commerce,

No sale or bargain pass: all would disperse,
    And live apart.

25   Lord, mend or rather make us: one creation
    Will not suffice our turn:
Except thou make us daily, we shall spurn
    Our own salvation.

The Bunch of Grapes.

Joy, I did lock thee up: but some bad man
      Hath let thee out again:
And now, methinks, I am where I began
      Sev'n years ago: one vogue and vein,
5   One air of thoughts usurps my brain.
I did toward Canaan draw; but now I am
Brought back to the Red Sea, the sea of shame.

For as the Jews of old by God's command
      Travell'd, and saw no town:
10   So now each Christian hath his journeys spann'd:
      Their story pens and sets us down.
      A single deed is small renown.
God's works are wide, and let in future times;
His ancient justice overflows our crimes.

15   Then have we too our guardian fires and clouds;
      Our Scripture-dew drops fast:
We have our sands and serpents, tents and shrouds;
      Alas! our murmurings come not last.
      But where's the cluster? where's the taste
20   Of mine inheritance? Lord, if I must borrow,
Let me as well take up their joy, as sorrow.

But can he want the grape, who hath the wine?
      I have their fruit and more.
Blessèd be God, who prosper'd *Noah's* vine,
25   And made it bring forth grapes good store.
      But much more him I must adore,

Who of the law's sour juice sweet wine did make,
Ev'n God himself, being pressèd for my sake.

Love unknown.

Dear Friend, sit down, the tale is long and sad:
And in my faintings I presume your love
Will more comply, than help. A Lord I had,
And have, of whom some grounds which may improve,
I hold for two lives, and both lives in me.   5
To him I brought a dish of fruit one day,
And in the middle placed my heart. But he
          (I sigh to say)
Look'd on a servant, who did know his eye
Better than you know me, or (which is one)   10
Than I myself. The servant instantly
Quitting the fruit, seized on my heart alone,
And threw it in a font, wherein did fall
A stream of blood, which issu'd from the side
Of a great rock: I well remember all,   15
And have good cause: there it was dipt and dy'd,
And washt, and wrung: the very wringing yet
Enforceth tears. *Your heart was foul, I fear.*
Indeed 'tis true. I did and do commit
Many a fault more than my lease will bear;   20
Yet still asked pardon, and was not deni'd.
But you shall hear. After my heart was well,
And clean and fair, as I one even-tide
          (I sigh to tell)
Walkt by myself abroad, I saw a large   25
And spacious furnace flaming, and thereon
A boiling cauldron, round about whose verge
Was in great letters set *AFFLICTION.*
The greatness showed the owner. So I went
To fetch a sacrifice out of my fold,   30
Thinking with that, which I did thus present,
To warm his love, which I did fear grew cold.

But as my heart did tender it, the man
Who was to take it from me, slipt his hand,
35   And threw my heart into the scalding pan;
My heart, that brought it (do you understand?)
The offerer's heart. *Your heart was hard, I fear.*
Indeed 'tis true. I found a callous matter
Began to spread and to expatiate there:
40   But with a richer drug than scalding water,
I bath'd it often, ev'n with holy blood,
Which at a board, while many drunk bare wine,
A friend did steal into my cup for good,
Ev'n taken inwardly, and most divine
45   To supple hardnesses. But at the length
Out of the cauldron getting, soon I fled
Unto my house, where to repair the strength
Which I had lost, I hasted to my bed.
But when I thought to sleep out all these faults
50   (I sigh to speak)
I found that some had stuff'd the bed with thoughts,
I would say *thorns.* Dear, could my heart not break,
When with my pleasures ev'n my rest was gone?
Full well I understood, who had been there:
55   For I had giv'n the key to none, but one:
It must be he. *Your heart was dull, I fear.*
Indeed a slack and sleepy state of mind
Did oft possess me, so that when I pray'd,
Though my lips went, my heart did stay behind.
60   But all my scores were by another paid,
Who took the debt upon him. *Truly, Friend,*
For ought I hear, your Master shows to you
More favour than you wot of. Mark the end.
The Font did only, what was old, renew:
65   *The Cauldron suppled, what was grown too hard:*
The Thorns did quicken, what was grown too dull:
All did but strive to mend, what you had marr'd.
Wherefore be cheer'd, and praise him to the full
Each day, each hour, each moment of the week,
70   *Who fain would have you be, new, tender, quick.*

Man's medley.

Hark, how the birds do sing,
   And woods do ring.
All creatures have their joy: and man hath his.
   Yet if we rightly measure,
     Man's joy and pleasure   5
Rather hereafter, than in present, is.

   To this life things of sense
     Make their pretence:
In th' other Angels have a right by birth:
   Man ties them both alone,   10
     And makes them one,
With th' one hand touching heav'n, with th' other earth.

   In soul he mounts and flies,
     In flesh he dies.
He wears a stuff whose thread is coarse and round, 15
   But trimm'd with curious lace,
     And should take place
After the trimming, not the stuff and ground.

   Not that he may not here
     Taste of the cheer,   20
But as birds drink, and straight lift up their head,
   So must he sip and think
     Of better drink
He may attain to, after he is dead.

   But as his joys are double;   25
     So is his trouble.
He hath two winters, other things but one:
   Both frosts and thoughts do nip,
     And bite his lip;
And he of all things fears two deaths alone.   30

   Yet ev'n the greatest griefs
     May be reliefs,

Could he but take them right, and in their ways.
          Happy is he, whose heart
                    Hath found the art
To turn his double pains to double praise.

The Storm.

If as the winds and waters here below
                              Do fly and flow,
My sighs and tears as busy were above;
                              Sure they would move
And much affect thee, as tempestuous times
Amaze poor mortals, and object their crimes.

Stars have their storms, ev'n in a high degree,
                              As well as we.
A throbbing conscience spurrèd by remorse
                              Hath a strange force:
It quits the earth, and mounting more and more,
Dares to assault thee, and besiege thy door.

There it stands knocking, to thy music's wrong,
                              And drowns the song.
Glory and honour are set by till it
                              An answer get.
Poets have wrong'd poor storms: such days are best;
They purge the air without, within the breast.

Paradise.

I bless thee, Lord, because I GROW
Among thy trees, which in a ROW
To thee both fruit and order OW.

What open force, or hidden CHARM
Can blast my fruit, or bring me HARM,

While the inclosure is thine ARM?

Inclose me still for fear I START.
Be to me rather sharp and TART,
Than let me want thy hand and ART.

When thou dost greater judgements SPARE,   10
And with thy knife but prune and PARE,
Ev'n fruitful trees more fruitful ARE.

Such sharpness shows the sweetest FREND:
Such cuttings rather heal than REND:
And such beginnings touch their END.   15

The Method.

Poor heart, lament.
For since thy God refuseth still,
There is some rub, some discontent,
Which cools his will.

Thy Father could   5
Quickly effect, what thou dost move;
For he is *Power*: and sure he would;
For he is *Love*.

Go search this thing,
Tumble thy breast, and turn thy book.   10
If thou hadst lost a glove or ring,
Wouldst thou not look?

What do I see
Written above there? *Yesterday*
I did behave me carelessly,   15
When I did pray.

And should God's ear
To such indifferents chainèd be,
Who do not their own motions hear?
Is God less free?   20

But stay! what's there?
Late when I would have something done,
I had a motion to forbear,
          Yet I went on.

25   And should God's ear,
Which needs not man, be ti'd to those
Who hear not him, but quickly hear
          His utter foes?

               Then once more pray:
30   Down with thy knees, up with thy voice.
Seek pardon first, and God will say,
          Glad heart rejoice.

Divinity.

As men, for fear the stars should sleep and nod,
     And trip at night, have spheres suppli'd;
As if a star were duller than a clod,
     Which knows his way without a guide:

5   Just so the other heav'n they also serve,
       Divinity's transcendent sky:
Which with the edge of wit they cut and carve.
       Reason triumphs, and faith lies by.

Could not that wisdom, which first broach'd the wine,
10   Have thicken'd it with definitions?
And jagg'd his seamless coat, had that been fine,
       With curious questions and divisions?

But all the doctrine, which he taught and gave,
       Was clear as heav'n, from whence it came.
15   At least those beams of truth, which only save,
       Surpass in brightness any flame.

Love God, and love your neighbour. Watch and pray.
Do as ye would be done unto.

O dark instructions; ev'n as dark as day!
Who can these Gordian knots undo?   20

But he doth bid us take his blood for wine.
    Bid what he please; yet I am sure,
To take and taste what he doth there design,
    Is all that saves, and not obscure.

Then burn thy Epicycles, foolish man;   25
    Break all thy spheres, and save thy head.
Faith needs no staff of flesh, but stoutly can
    To heav'n alone both go, and lead.

Ephes. 4:30.
Grieve not the Holy Spirit, & c.

And art thou grievèd, sweet and sacred Dove,
      When I am sour,
      And cross thy love?
Grievèd for me? the God of strength and power
      Griev'd for a worm, which when I tread,   5
      I pass away and leave it dead?

Then weep mine eyes, the God of love doth grieve:
      Weep foolish heart,
      And weeping live:
For death is dry as dust. Yet if ye part,   10
      End as the night, whose sable hue
      Your sins express; melt into dew.

When saucy mirth shall knock or call at door,
      Cry out, Get hence,
      Or cry no more.
Almighty God doth grieve, he puts on sense: 15
      I sin not to my grief alone,
      But to my God's too; he doth groan.

O take thy lute, and tune it to a strain,
              Which may with thee
              All day complain.
There can no discord but in ceasing be.
          Marbles can weep; and surely strings
          More bowels have, than such hard things.

Lord, I adjudge myself to tears and grief,
              Ev'n endless tears
              Without relief.
If a clear spring for me no time forbears,
          But runs, although I be not dry;
          I am no Crystal, what shall I?

Yet if I wail not still, since still to wail
              Nature denies;
              And flesh would fail,
If my deserts were masters of mine eyes:
          Lord, pardon, for thy son makes good
          My want of tears with store of blood.

The Family.

What doth this noise of thoughts within my heart
              As if they had a part?
What do these loud complaints and puling fears,
          As if there were no rule or ears?

But, Lord, the house and family are thine,
              Though some of them repine.
Turn out these wranglers, which defile thy seat:
          For where thou dwellest all is neat.

First Peace and Silence all disputes control,
              Then Order plays the soul;
And giving all things their set forms and hours,
          Makes of wild woods sweet walks and bowers.

Humble Obedience near the door doth stand,
    Expecting a command:
Than whom in waiting nothing seems more slow,   15
    Nothing more quick when she doth go.

Joys oft are there, and griefs as oft as joys;
    But griefs without a noise:
Yet speak they louder than distemper'd fears.
    What is so shrill as silent tears?   20

This is thy house, with these it doth abound:
    And where these are not found,
Perhaps thou com'st sometimes, and for a day;
    But not to make a constant stay.

The Size.

    Content thee, greedy heart.
Modest and moderate joys to those, that have
Title to more hereafter when they part,
    Are passing brave.
    Let th' upper springs into the low   5
    Descend and fall, and thou dost flow.

    What though some have a fraught
Of cloves and nutmegs, and in cinnamon sail;
If thou hast wherewithal to spice a draught,
    When griefs prevail;   10
    And for the future time art heir
    To th' Isle of spices? Is't not fair?

    To be in both worlds full
Is more than God was, who was hungry here.
Wouldst thou his laws of fasting disannul?   15
    Enact good cheer?
    Lay out thy joy, yet hope to save it?
    Wouldst thou both eat thy cake, and have it?

                    Great joys are all at once;
20   But little do reserve themselves for more:
      Those have their hopes; these what they have renounce,
                    And live on score:
          Those are at home; these journey still,
          And meet the rest on Sion's hill.

25   Thy Saviour sentenc'd joy,
      And in the flesh condemn'd it as unfit,
      At least in lump: for such doth oft destroy;
                    Whereas a bit
          Doth 'tice us on to hopes of more,
30   And for the present health restore.

          A Christian's state and case
      Is not a corpulent, but a thin and spare,
      Yet active strength: whose long and bony face
                    Content and care
35   Do seem to equally divide,
          Like a pretender, not a bride.

                  Wherefore sit down, good heart;
      Grasp not at much, for fear thou losest all.
      If comforts fell according to desert,
40   They would great frosts and snows destroy:
          For we should count, since the last joy.

                  Then close again the seam,
      Which thou hast open'd: do not spread thy robe
      In hope of great things. Call to mind thy dream,
45   An earthly globe,
          On whose meridian was engraven,
          These seas are tears, and heav'n the haven.

Artillery.

As I one ev'ning sat before my cell,
Methoughts a star did shoot into my lap.
I rose, and shook my clothes, as knowing well,
That from small fires comes oft no small mishap.
    When suddenly I heard one say,   5
    Do as thou usest, disobey,
    Expel good motions from thy breast,
Which have the face of fire, but end in rest.

I, who had heard of music in the spheres,
But not of speech in stars, began to muse: 10
But turning to my God, whose ministers
The stars and all things are; If I refuse,
    Dread Lord, said I, so oft my good;
    Then I refuse not ev'n with blood
    To wash away my stubborn thought: 15
For I will do, or suffer what I ought.

But I have also stars and shooters too,
Born where thy servants both artilleries use.
My tears and prayers night and day do woo,
And work up to thee; yet thou dost refuse.   20
    Not but I am (I must say still)
    Much more oblig'd to do thy will,
    Than thou to grant mine: but because
Thy promise now hath ev'n set thee thy laws.

Then we are shooters both, and thou dost deign   25
To enter combat with us, and contest
With thine own clay. But I would parley fain:
Shun not my arrows, and behold my breast.
    Yet if thou shunnest, I am thine:
    I must be so, if I am mine.   30
    There is no articling with thee:
I am but finite, yet thine infinitely.

Church-rents and schisms.

Brave rose, (alas!) where art thou? in the chair
Where thou didst lately so triumph and shine,
A worm doth sit, whose many feet and hair
Are the more foul, the more thou wert divine.
This, this hath done it, this did bite the root
And bottom of the leaves: which when the wind
Did once perceive, it blew them under foot,
Where rude unhallow'd steps do crush and grind
     Their beauteous glories. Only shreds of thee,
     And those all bitten, in thy chair I see.

Why doth my Mother blush? is she the rose,
And shows it so? Indeed Christ's precious blood
Gave you a colour once; which when your foes
Thought to let out, the bleeding did you good,
And made you look much fresher than before.
But when debates and fretting jealousies
Did worm and work within you more and more,
Your colour vaded, and calamities
     Turnèd your ruddy into pale and bleak:
     Your health and beauty both began to break.

Then did your sev'ral parts unloose and start:
Which when your neighbours saw, like a north-wind,
They rushèd in, and cast them in the dirt
Where Pagans tread. O Mother dear and kind,
Where shall I get me eyes enough to weep,
As many eyes as stars? since it is night,
And much of Asia and Europe fast asleep,
And ev'n all Afric'; would at least I might
     With these two poor ones lick up all the dew,
     Which falls by night, and pour it out for you!

Justice (2).

O dreadful Justice, what a fright and terror
        Wast thou of old,
        When sin and error
    Did show and shape thy looks to me,
    And through their glass discolour thee!   5
He that did but look up, was proud and bold.

The dishes of thy balance seemed to gape,
        Like two great pits;
        The beam and scape
    Did like some tort'ring engine show: 10
    Thy hand above did burn and glow,
Daunting the stoutest hearts, the proudest wits.

But now that Christ's pure veil presents the sight,
        I see no fears:
        Thy hand is white,   15
    Thy scales like buckets, which attend
    And interchangeably descend,
Lifting to heaven from this well of tears.

For where before thou still didst call on me,
        Now I still touch   20
        And harp on thee.
    God's promises have made thee mine;
    Why should I justice now decline?
Against me there is none, but for me much.

The Pilgrimage.

I travell'd on, seeing the hill, where lay
        My expectation.
    A long it was and weary way.
    The gloomy cave of Desperation

5   I left on th' one, and on the other side
                                    The rock of Pride.

       And so I came to Fancy's meadow strow'd
                             With many a flower:
                    Fain would I here have made abode,
10   But I was quicken'd by my hour.
       So to Care's copse I came, and there got through
                             With much ado.

       That led me to the wild of Passion, which
                             Some call the wold;
15   A wasted place, but sometimes rich.
                    Here I was robb'd of all my gold,
       Save one good Angel, which a friend had ti'd
                             Close to my side.

       At length I got unto the gladsome hill,
20   Where lay my hope,
                    Where lay my heart; and climbing still,
                    When I had gain'd the brow and top,
       A lake of brackish waters on the ground
                             Was all I found.

25   With that abash'd and struck with many a sting
                             Of swarming fears,
                    I fell, and cried, Alas my King;
                    Can both the way and end be tears?
       Yet taking heart I rose, and then perceiv'd
30   I was deceiv'd:

       My hill was further: so I flung away,
                             Yet heard a cry
                    Just as I went, *None goes that way*
                    And lives: If that be all, said I,
35   After so foul a journey death is fair,
                             And but a chair.

The Holdfast.

I threat'ned to observe the strict decree
    Of my dear God with all my power and might.
    But I was told by one, it could not be;
Yet I might trust in God to be my light.
Then will I trust, said I, in him alone.   5
    Nay, ev'n to trust in him, was also his:
    We must confess, that nothing is our own.
Then I confess that he my succour is:
But to have nought is ours, not to confess
    That we have nought. I stood amazed at this,   10
    Much troubled, till I heard a friend express,
That all things were more ours by being his.
    What Adam had, and forfeited for all,
    Christ keepeth now, who cannot fail or fall.

Complaining.

Do not beguile my heart,
    Because thou art
My power and wisdom. Put me not to shame,
    Because I am
Thy clay that weeps, thy dust that calls.   5

Thou art the Lord of glory;
    The deed and story
Are both thy due: but I a silly fly,
    That live or die
According as the weather falls.   10

Art thou all justice, Lord?
    Shows not thy word
More attributes? Am I all throat or eye,
    To weep or cry?
Have I no parts but those of grief?   15

        Let not thy wrathful power
                Afflict my hour,
    My inch of life: or let thy gracious power
                Contract my hour,
20   That I may climb and find relief.

The Discharge.

    Busy inquiring heart, what wouldst thou know?
                Why dost thou pry,
    And turn, and leer, and with a licorous eye
                Look high and low;
5   And in thy lookings stretch and grow?

    Hast thou not made thy counts, and summ'd up all?
                Did not thy heart
    Give up the whole, and with the whole depart?
                Let what will fall:
10   That which is past who can recall?

    Thy life is God's, thy time to come is gone,
                And is his right.
    He is thy night at noon: he is at night
                Thy noon alone.
15   The crop is his, for he hath sown.

    And well it was for thee, when this befell,
                That God did make
    Thy business his, and in thy life partake:
                For thou canst tell,
20   If it be his once, all is well.

    Only the present is thy part and fee.
                And happy thou,
    If, though thou didst not beat thy future brow,
                Thou couldst well see
25   What present things requir'd of thee.

They ask enough; why shouldst thou further go?
                    Raise not the mud
Of future depths, but drink the clear and good.
                    Dig not for woe
          In times to come; for it will grow.   30

Man and the present fit: if he provide,
                    He breaks the square.
This hour is mine: if for the next I care,
                    I grow too wide,
          And do encroach upon death's side.   35

For death each hour environs and surrounds.
                    He that would know
And care for future chances, cannot go
                    Unto those grounds,
          But through a churchyard which them bounds.   40

Things present shrink and die: but they that spend
                    Their thoughts and sense
On future grief, do not remove it thence,
                    But it extend,
          And draw the bottom out an end.   45

God chains the dog till night; wilt loose the chain,
                    And wake thy sorrow?
Wilt thou forestall it, and now grieve tomorrow
                    And then again
          Grieve over freshly all thy pain?   50

Either grief will not come: or if it must,
                    Do not forecast.
And while it cometh, it is almost past.
                    Away distrust:
          My God hath promis'd, he is just.   55

Praise (2).

King of Glory, King of Peace,
           I will love thee;
And that love may never cease,
           I will move thee.

Thou hast granted my request,
           Thou hast heard me:
Thou didst note my working breast,
           Thou hast spar'd me.

Wherefore with my utmost art
           I will sing thee,
And the cream of all my heart
           I will bring thee.

Though my sins against me cried,
           Thou didst clear me;
And alone, when they replied,
           Thou didst hear me.

Sev'n whole days, not one in seven,
           I will praise thee.
In my heart, though not in heaven,
           I can raise thee.

Thou grew'st soft and moist with tears,
           Thou relentedst;
And when Justice called for fears,
           Thou dissentedst.

Small it is, in this poor sort
           To enrol thee:
Ev'n eternity is too short
           To extol thee.

An Offering.

Come, bring thy gift. If blessings were as slow
As men's returns, what would become of fools?
What hast thou there? a heart? but is it pure?
Search well and see; for hearts have many holes.
Yet one pure heart is nothing to bestow: 5
In Christ two natures met to be thy cure.

O that within us hearts had propagation,
Since many gifts do challenge many hearts!
Yet one, if good, may title to a number;
And single things grow fruitful by deserts.   10
In public judgements one may be a nation,
And fence a plague, while others sleep and slumber.

But all I fear is lest thy heart displease,
As neither good, nor one: so oft divisions
Thy lusts have made, and not thy lusts alone;   15
Thy passions also have their set partitions.
These parcel out thy heart: recover these,
And thou mayst offer many gifts in one.

There is a balsam, or indeed a blood,
Dropping from heav'n, which doth both cleanse and close   20
All sorts of wounds; of such strange force it is.
Seek out this All-heal, and seek no repose,
Until thou find and use it to thy good:
Then bring thy gift, and let thy hymn be this;

       Since my sadness   25
       Into gladness
Lord thou dost convert,
        O accept
        What thou hast kept,
As thy due desert.   30

       Had I many,
       Had I any,

(For this heart is none)
                    All were thine
35   And none of mine:
Surely thine alone.

                    Yet thy favour
                    May give savour
To this poor oblation;
40   And it raise
                    To be thy praise,
And be my salvation.

Longing.

                    With sick and famisht eyes,
With doubling knees and weary bones,
                    To thee my cries,
                    To thee my groans,
5   To thee my sighs, my tears ascend:
                                        No end?

                    My throat, my soul is hoarse;
My heart is wither'd like a ground
                            Which thou dost curse.
10   My thoughts turn round,
And make me giddy; Lord, I fall,
                                        Yet call.

                    From thee all pity flows.
Mothers are kind, because thou art,
15   And dost dispose
                            To them a part:
Their infants, them; and they suck thee
                                        More free.

                    Bowels of pity, hear!
20   Lord of my soul, love of my mind,
                            Bow down thine ear!
                            Let not the wind

Scatter my words, and in the same
Thy name!

Look on my sorrows round!   25
Mark well my furnace! O what flames,
What heats abound!
What griefs, what shames!
Consider, Lord; Lord, bow thine ear,
And hear!   30

Lord Jesu, thou didst bow
Thy dying head upon the tree:
O be not now
More dead to me!
Lord hear, *Shall he that made the ear*   35
Not hear?

Behold, thy dust doth stir,
It moves, it creeps, it aims at thee:
Wilt thou defer
To succour me,   40
Thy pile of dust, wherein each crumb
Says, Come?

To thee help appertains.
Hast thou left all things to their course,
And laid the reins   45
Upon the horse?
Is all lockt? hath a sinner's plea
No key?

Indeed the world's thy book,
Where all things have their leaf assign'd: 50
Yet a meek look
Hath interlin'd.
Thy board is full, yet humble guests
Find nests.

Thou tarriest, while I die,   55
And fall to nothing: thou dost reign,
And rule on high,
While I remain

In bitter grief: yet am I styl'd
                                                 Thy child.

                              Lord, didst thou leave thy throne,
Not to relieve? how can it be,
                              That thou art grown
                              Thus hard to me?
Were sin alive, good cause there were
                                                 To bear.

                              But now both sin is dead,
And all thy promises live and bide.
                              That wants his head;
                              These speak and chide,
And in thy bosom pour my tears,
                                                 As theirs.

                              Lord Jesu, hear my heart,
Which hath been broken now so long,
                              That ev'ry part
                              Hath got a tongue!
Thy beggars grow; rid them away
                                                 To day.

                              My love, my sweetness, hear!
By these thy feet, at which my heart
                              Lies all the year,
                              Pluck out thy dart,
And heal my troubled breast which cries,
                                                 Which dies.

The Bag.

Away despair! my gracious Lord doth hear.
            Though winds and waves assault my keel,
            He doth preserve it: he doth steer,
            Ev'n when the boat seems most to reel.
            Storms are the triumph of his art:
Well may he close his eyes, but not his heart.

Hast thou not heard, that my Lord JESUS di'd?
    Then let me tell thee a strange story.
    The God of power, as he did ride
    In his majestic robes of glory,
    Resolv'd to light; and so one day   10
He did descend, undressing all the way.

The stars his tire of light and rings obtain'd,
    The cloud his bow, the fire his spear,
    The sky his azure mantle gain'd.   15
    And when they ask'd, what he would wear;
    He smil'd and said as he did go,
He had new clothes a-making here below.

When he was come, as travellers are wont,
    He did repair unto an inn.   20
    Both then, and after, many a brunt
    He did endure to cancel sin:
    And having given the rest before,
Here he gave up his life to pay our score.

But as he was returning, there came one   25
    That ran upon him with a spear.
    He, who came hither all alone,
    Bringing nor man, nor arms, nor fear,
    Receiv'd the blow upon his side,
And straight he turned, and to his brethren cri'd,   30

If ye have any thing to send or write,
    I have no bag, but here is room
    Unto my father's hands and sight
    Believe me it shall safely come.
    That I shall mind, what you impart;   35
Look, you may put it very near my heart.

Or if hereafter any of my friends
    Will use me in this kind, the door
    Shall still be open; what he sends
    I will present, and somewhat more,   40
    Not to his hurt. Sighs will convey
Any thing to me. Hark, Despair, away.

The Jews.

Poor nation, whose sweet sap, and juice
Our scions have purloin'd, and left you dry:
Whose streams we got by the Apostles' sluice,
And use in baptism, while ye pine and die:
Who by not keeping once, became a debtor;
　　　　And now by keeping lose the letter:

O that my prayers! mine, alas!
O that some Angel might a trumpet sound;
At which the Church falling upon her face
Should cry so loud, until the trump were drown'd,
And by that cry of her dear Lord obtain,
　　　　That your sweet sap might come again!

The Collar.

I struck the board, and cri'd, No more.
　　　　I will abroad.
What? shall I ever sigh and pine?
My lines and life are free; free as the road,
　　　　Loose as the wind, as large as store.
　　　　　　Shall I be still in suit?
Have I no harvest but a thorn
To let me blood, and not restore
What I have lost with cordial fruit?
　　　　　　　　Sure there was wine
Before my sighs did dry it: there was corn
　　　　Before my tears did drown it.
Is the year only lost to me?
　　　　Have I no bays to crown it?
No flowers, no garlands gay? All blasted?
　　　　All wasted?
Not so, my heart: but there is fruit,
　　　　And thou hast hands.

Recover all thy sigh-blown age
On double pleasures: leave thy cold dispute   20
Of what is fit, and not. Forsake thy cage,
    Thy rope of sands,
Which petty thoughts have made, and made to thee
    Good cable, to enforce and draw,
      And be thy law,   25
While thou didst wink and wouldst not see.
      Away; take heed:
      I will abroad.
Call in thy death's head there: tie up thy fears.
      He that forbears   30
    To suit and serve his need,
      Deserves his load.
But as I raved and grew more fierce and wild
    At every word,
Me thoughts I heard one calling, *Child*   35
    And I repli'd, *My Lord.*

The Glimpse.

Whither away delight?
Thou cam'st but now; wilt thou so soon depart,
    And give me up to night?
For many weeks of ling'ring pain and smart
But one half hour of comfort for my heart?   5

Methinks delight should have
More skill in music, and keep better time.
    Wert thou a wind or wave,
They quickly go and come with lesser crime:
Flowers look about, and die not in their prime.   10

Thy short abode and stay
Feeds not, but adds to the desire of meat.
    Lime begg'd of old (they say)
A neighbour spring to cool his inward heat;
Which by the spring's access grew much more great.   15

            In hope of thee my heart
Pickt here and there a crumb, and would not die;
        But constant to his part
Whenas my fears foretold this, did reply,
20   A slender thread a gentle guest will tie.

            Yet if the heart that wept
Must let thee go, return when it doth knock.
        Although thy heap be kept
For future times, the droppings of the stock
25   May oft break forth, and never break the lock.

            If I have more to spin,
The wheel shall go, so that thy stay be short.
        Thou knowst how grief and sin
Disturb the work. O make me not their sport,
30   Who by thy coming may be made a court!

Assurance.

            O spiteful bitter thought!
Bitterly spiteful thought! Couldst thou invent
So high a torture? Is such poison bought?
Doubtless, but in the way of punishment.
5   When wit contrives to meet with thee,
            No such rank poison can there be.

            Thou said'st but even now,
That all was not so fair, as I conceiv'd,
Betwixt my God and me; that I allow
10   And coin large hopes; but, that I was deceiv'd:
            Either the league was broke, or near it;
            And, that I had great cause to fear it.

            And what to this? what more
Could poison, if it had a tongue, express?
15   What is thy aim? wouldst thou unlock the door
To cold despairs, and gnawing pensiveness?

Wouldst thou raise devils? I see, I know,
I writ thy purpose long ago.

    But I will to my Father,
Who heard thee say it. O most gracious Lord,   20
If all the hope and comfort that I gather,
Were from myself, I had not half a word,
    Not half a letter to oppose
    What is objected by my foes.

    But thou art my desert: 25
And in this league, which now my foes invade,
Thou art not only to perform thy part,
But also mine; as when the league was made
    Thou didst at once thyself indite,
    And hold my hand, while I did write.   30

    Wherefore if thou canst fail,
Then can thy truth and I: but while rocks stand,
And rivers stir, thou canst not shrink or quail:
Yea, when both rocks and all things shall disband,
    Then shalt thou be my rock and tower,   35
    And make their ruin praise thy power.

    Now foolish thought go on,
Spin out thy thread, and make thereof a coat
To hide thy shame: for thou hast cast a bone
Which bounds on thee, and will not down thy throat: 40
    What for itself love once began,
    Now love and truth will end in man.

The Call.

Come, my Way, my Truth, my Life:
Such a Way, as gives us breath:
Such a Truth, as ends all strife:
Such a Life, as killeth death.

5   Come, my Light, my Feast, my Strength:
       Such a Light, as shows a feast:
       Such a Feast, as mends in length:
       Such a Strength, as makes his guest.

       Come, my Joy, my Love, my Heart:
10   Such a Joy, as none can move:
       Such a Love, as none can part:
       Such a Heart, as joys in love.

Clasping of hands.

       Lord, thou art mine, and I am thine,
       If mine I am: and thine much more,
       Than I or ought, or can be mine.
       Yet to be thine, doth me restore;
5   So that again I now am mine,
       And with advantage mine the more,
       Since this being mine, brings with it thine,
       And thou with me dost thee restore.
             If I without thee would be mine,
10   I neither should be mine nor thine.

       Lord, I am thine, and thou art mine:
       So mine thou art, that something more
       I may presume thee mine, than thine.
       For thou didst suffer to restore
15   Not thee, but me, and to be mine:
       And with advantage mine the more,
       Since thou in death wast none of thine,
       Yet then as mine didst me restore.
             O be mine still! still make me thine!
20   Or rather make no Thine and Mine!

Praise (3).

Lord, I will mean and speak thy praise,
    Thy praise alone.
My busy heart shall spin it all my days:
    And when it stops for want of store,
Then will I wring it with a sigh or groan,   5
    That thou mayst yet have more.

When thou dost favour any action,
    It runs, it flies:
All things concur to give it a perfection.
    That which had but two legs before,   10
When thou dost bless, hath twelve: one wheel doth rise
    To twenty then, or more.

But when thou dost on business blow,
    It hangs, it clogs:
Not all the teams of Albion in a row   15
    Can hail or draw it out of door.
Legs are but stumps, and Pharaoh's wheels but logs,
    And struggling hinders more.

Thousands of things do thee employ
    In ruling all   20
This spacious globe: Angels must have their joy,
    Devils their rod, the sea his shore,
The winds their stint: and yet when I did call,
    Thou heardst my call, and more.

I have not lost one single tear: 25
    But when mine eyes
Did weep to heav'n, they found a bottle there
    (As we have boxes for the poor)
Ready to take them in; yet of a size
    That would contain much more.   30

But after thou hadst slipt a drop
    From thy right eye,
(Which there did hang like streamers near the top

Of some fair church, to show the sore
35   And bloody battle which thou once didst try)
The glass was full and more.

Wherefore I sing. Yet since my heart,
Though press'd, runs thin;
O that I might some other hearts convert,
40   And so take up at use good store:
That to thy chests there might be coming in
Both all my praise, and more!

Joseph's coat.

Wounded I sing, tormented I indite,
Thrown down I fall into a bed, and rest:
Sorrow hath chang'd its note: such is his will,
Who changeth all things, as him pleaseth best.
5   For well he knows, if but one grief and smart
Among my many had his full career,
Sure it would carry with it ev'n my heart,
And both would run until they found a bier
To fetch the body; both being due to grief.
10 But he hath spoil'd the race; and giv'n to anguish
One of Joy's coats, 'ticing it with relief
To linger in me, and together languish.
I live to show his power, who once did bring
My *joys* to *weep*, and now my *griefs* to *sing*.

The Pulley.

When God at first made man,
Having a glass of blessings standing by,
Let us (said he) pour on him all we can:
Let the world's riches, which dispersèd lie,
5   Contract into a span.

So strength first made a way;
Then beauty flow'd, then wisdom, honour, pleasure:
When almost all was out, God made a stay,
Perceiving that alone of all his treasure
      Rest in the bottom lay.   10

      For if I should (said he)
Bestow this jewel also on my creature,
He would adore my gifts instead of me,
And rest in Nature, not the God of Nature:
      So both should losers be.   15

      Yet let him keep the rest,
But keep them with repining restlessness:
Let him be rich and weary, that at least,
If goodness lead him not, yet weariness
      May toss him to my breast.   20

The Priesthood.

Blest Order, which in power dost so excel,
That with th' one hand thou liftest to the sky,
And with the other throwest down to hell
In thy just censures; fain would I draw nigh,
Fain put thee on, exchanging my lay-sword   5
      For that of th' holy Word.

But thou art fire, sacred and hallow'd fire;
And I but earth and clay: should I presume
To wear thy habit, the severe attire
My slender compositions might consume.   10
I am both foul and brittle; much unfit
      To deal in holy Writ.

Yet have I often seen, by cunning hand
And force of fire, what curious things are made
Of wretched earth. Where once I scorn'd to stand,   15
That earth is fitted by the fire and trade

Of skilful artists, for the boards of those
　　　　Who make the bravest shows.

But since those great ones, be they ne'er so great,
20　Come from the earth, from whence those vessels come;
So that at once both feeder, dish, and meat
Have one beginning and one final sum:
I do not greatly wonder at the sight,
　　　　If earth in earth delight.

25　But th' holy men of God such vessels are,
As serve him up, who all the world commands:
When God vouchsafeth to become our fare,
Their hands convey him, who conveys their hands.
O what pure things, most pure must those things be,
30　　　　Who bring my God to me!

Wherefore I dare not, I, put forth my hand
To hold the Ark, although it seem to shake
Through th' old sins and new doctrines of our land.
Only, since God doth often vessels make
35　Of lowly matter for high uses meet,
　　　　I throw me at his feet.

There will I lie, until my Maker seek
For some mean stuff whereon to show his skill:
Then is my time. The distance of the meek
40　Doth flatter power. Lest good come short of ill
In praising might, the poor do by submission
　　　　What pride by opposition.

The Search.

Whither, O, whither art thou fled,
　　　　My Lord, my Love?
My searches are my daily bread;
　　　　Yet never prove.

My knees pierce th' earth, mine eyes the sky;   5
        And yet the sphere
And centre both to me deny
        That thou art there.

Yet can I mark how herbs below
        Grow green and gay,   10
As if to meet thee they did know,
        While I decay.

Yet can I mark how stars above
        Simper and shine,
As having keys unto thy love,   15
        While poor I pine.

I sent a sigh to seek thee out,
        Deep drawn in pain,
Wing'd like an arrow: but my scout
        Returns in vain.   20

I tun'd another (having store)
        Into a groan;
Because the search was dumb before:
        But all was one.

Lord, dost thou some new fabric mould,   25
        Which favour wins,
And keeps thee present, leaving th' old
        Unto their sins?

Where is my God? what hidden place
        Conceals thee still?   30
What covert dare eclipse thy face?
        Is it thy will?

O let not that of anything;
        Let rather brass,
Or steel, or mountains be thy ring,   35
        And I will pass.

Thy will such an entrenching is,
        As passeth thought:
To it all strength, all subtilties
40   Are things of nought.

Thy will such a strange distance is,
        As that to it
East and West touch, the poles do kiss,
        And parallels meet.

45 Since then my grief must be as large,
        As is thy space,
Thy distance from me; see my charge,
        Lord, see my case.

O take these bars, these lengths away;
50   Turn, and restore me:
Be not Almighty, let me say,
        Against, but for me.

When thou dost turn, and wilt be near;
        What edge so keen,
55 What point so piercing can appear
        To come between?

For as thy absence doth excel
        All distance known:
So doth thy nearness bear the bell,
60   Making two one.

Grief.

O who will give me tears? Come all ye springs,
Dwell in my head and eyes: come clouds, and rain:
My grief hath need of all the wat'ry things,
That nature hath produc'd. Let ev'ry vein
5 Suck up a river to supply mine eyes,
My weary weeping eyes too dry for me,
Unless they get new conduits, new supplies

To bear them out, and with my state agree.
What are two shallow fords, two little spouts
Of a less world? the greater is but small,   10
A narrow cupboard for my griefs and doubts,
Which want provision in the midst of all.
Verses, ye are too fine a thing, too wise
For my rough sorrows: cease, be dumb and mute,
Give up your feet and running to mine eyes,   15
And keep your measures for some lover's lute,
Whose grief allows him music and a rhyme:
For mine excludes both measure, tune, and time.
                                    Alas, my God!

The Cross.

        What is this strange and uncouth thing?
To make me sigh, and seek, and faint, and die,
Until I had some place, where I might sing,
        And serve thee; and not only I,
But all my wealth, and family might combine   5
To set thy honour up, as our design.

        And then when after much delay,
Much wrestling, many a combat, this dear end,
So much desir'd, is giv'n, to take away
        My power to serve thee; to unbend   10
All my abilities, my designs confound,
And lay my threat'nings bleeding on the ground.

        One ague dwelleth in my bones,
Another in my soul (the memory
What I would do for thee, if once my groans   15
        Could be allow'd for harmony):
I am in all a weak disabled thing,
Save in the sight thereof, where strength doth sting.

        Besides, things sort not to my will,
Ev'n when my will doth study thy renown: 20
Thou turnest th' edge of all things on me still,

Taking me up to throw me down:
So that, ev'n when my hopes seem to be sped,
I am to grief alive, to them as dead.

25   To have my aim, and yet to be
Farther from it than when I bent my bow;
To make my hopes my torture, and the fee
        Of all my woes another woe,
    Is in the midst of delicates to need,
30 And ev'n in Paradise to be a weed.

        Ah my dear Father, ease my smart!
These contrarieties crush me: these cross actions
Do wind a rope about, and cut my heart:
        And yet since these thy contradictions
35 Are properly a cross felt by thy Son,
With but four words, my words, *Thy will be done.*

The Flower.

How fresh, O Lord, how sweet and clean
Are thy returns! ev'n as the flowers in spring;
        To which, besides their own demean,
The late-past frosts tributes of pleasure bring.
5   Grief melts away
                Like snow in May,
    As if there were no such cold thing.

Who would have thought my shrivel'd heart
Could have recovered greenness? It was gone
10   Quite underground; as flowers depart
To see their mother-root, when they have blown;
                Where they together
                All the hard weather,
    Dead to the world, keep house unknown.

These are thy wonders, Lord of power,   15
Killing and quick'ning, bringing down to hell
          And up to heaven in an hour;
Making a chiming of a passing-bell.
                    We say amiss,
                    This or that is: 20
          Thy word is all, if we could spell.

          O that I once past changing were,
Fast in thy Paradise, where no flower can wither!
          Many a spring I shoot up fair,
Off'ring at heav'n, growing and groaning thither: 25
                    Nor doth my flower
                    Want a spring-shower,
          My sins and I joining together:

          But while I grow in a straight line,
Still upwards bent, as if heav'n were mine own,   30
          Thy anger comes, and I decline:
What frost to that? what pole is not the zone,
                    Where all things burn,
                    When thou dost turn,
          And the least frown of thine is shown?   35

          And now in age I bud again,
After so many deaths I live and write;
          I once more smell the dew and rain,
And relish versing: O my only light,
                    It cannot be   40
                    That I am he
          On whom thy tempests fell all night.

          These are thy wonders, Lord of love,
To make us see we are but flowers that glide:
          Which when we once can find and prove,   45
Thou hast a garden for us, where to bide.
                    Who would be more,
                    Swelling through store,
          Forfeit their Paradise by their pride.

Dotage.

False glozing pleasures, casks of happiness,
Foolish night-fires, women's and children's wishes,
Chases in arras, gilded emptiness,
Shadows well mounted, dreams in a career,
5   Embroider'd lies, nothing between two dishes;
    These are the pleasures here.

True earnest sorrows, rooted miseries,
Anguish in grain, vexations ripe and blown,
Sure-footed griefs, solid calamities,
10   Plain demonstrations, evident and clear,
Fetching their proofs ev'n from the very bone;
    These are the sorrows here.

But O the folly of distracted men,
Who griefs in earnest, joys in jest pursue;
15   Preferring, like brute beasts, a loathsome den
Before a court, ev'n that above so clear,
Where are no sorrows, but delights more true,
    Than miseries are here!

The Son.

Let foreign nations of their language boast,
What fine variety each tongue affords:
I like our language, as our men and coast:
Who cannot dress it well, want wit, not words.
5   How neatly do we give one only name
To parents' issue and the sun's bright star!
A son is light and fruit; a fruitful flame
Chasing the father's dimness, carri'd far
From the first man in th' East, to fresh and new
10   Western discov'ries of posterity.
So in one word our Lord's humility

We turn upon him in a sense most true:
  For what Christ once in humbleness began,
  We him in glory call, *The Son of Man.*

A true Hymn.

  My joy, my life, my crown!
My heart was meaning all the day,
  Somewhat it fain would say:
And still it runneth mutt'ring up and down
With only this, *My joy, my life, my crown.*   5

  Yet slight not these few words:
If truly said, they may take part
  Among the best in art.
The fineness which a hymn or psalm affords,
Is, when the soul unto the lines accords.   10

  He who craves all the mind,
And all the soul, and strength, and time,
  If the words only rhyme,
Justly complains, that somewhat is behind
To make his verse, or write a hymn in kind.   15

  Whereas if th' heart be moved,
Although the verse be somewhat scant,
  God doth supply the want.
As when th' heart says (sighing to be approved)
O, could I love! and stops: God writeth, *Loved.*   20

The Answer.

My comforts drop and melt away like snow:
I shake my head, and all the thoughts and ends,
Which my fierce youth did bandy, fall and flow
Like leaves about me: or like summer friends,

5   Flies of estates and sunshine. But to all,
     Who think me eager, hot, and undertaking,
     But in my prosecutions slack and small;
     As a young exhalation, newly waking,
     Scorns his first bed of dirt, and means the sky;
10   But cooling by the way, grows pursy and slow,
     And settling to a cloud, doth live and die
     In that dark state of tears: to all, that so
              Show me, and set me, I have one reply,
              Which they that know the rest, know more than I.

A Dialogue-Anthem.

Christian. Death.

Chr.   Alas, poor Death, where is thy glory?
         Where is thy famous force, thy ancient sting?
Dea.   *Alas poor mortal, void of story,*
         Go spell and read how I have kill'd thy King.
5   Chr.   Poor Death! and who was hurt thereby?
         Thy curse being laid on him, makes thee accurst.
Dea.   *Let losers talk: yet thou shalt die;*
         These arms shall crush thee.
Chr.   Spare not, do thy worst. I shall be one day better
         than before:
10   Thou so much worse, that thou shalt be no more.

The Water-course.

     Thou who dost dwell and linger here below,
     Since the condition of this world is frail,
     Where of all plants afflictions soonest grow;
     If troubles overtake thee, do not wail:
5   For who can look for less, that loveth $\begin{cases} \text{Life.} \\ \text{Strife.} \end{cases}$

But rather turn the pipe, and water's course
To serve thy sins, and furnish thee with store
Of sov'reign tears, springing from true remorse:
That so in pureness thou mayst him adore,

Who gives to man, as he sees fit $\begin{cases} \text{Salvation.} \\ \text{Damnation.} \end{cases}$ 10

Self-condemnation.

    Thou who condemnest Jewish hate,
For choosing Barabbas a murderer
      Before the Lord of Glory;
    Look back upon thine own estate,
Call home thine eye (that busy wanderer):   5
      That choice may be thy story.

    He that doth love, and love amiss
This world's delights before true Christian joy,
      Hath made a Jewish choice:
    The world an ancient murderer is;   10
Thousands of souls it hath and doth destroy
      With her enchanting voice.

    He that hath made a sorry wedding
Between his soul and gold, and hath preferr'd
      False gain before the true,   15
    Hath done what he condemns in reading:
For he hath sold for money his dear Lord,
      And is a Judas-Jew.

    Thus we prevent the last great day,
And judge our selves. That light, which sin and passion   20
      Did before dim and choke,
    When once those snuffs are ta'en away,
Shines bright and clear, ev'n unto condemnation,
      Without excuse or cloak.

Bitter-sweet.

Ah my dear angry Lord,
Since thou dost love, yet strike;
Cast down, yet help afford;
Sure I will do the like.

I will complain, yet praise;
I will bewail, approve:
And all my sour-sweet days
I will lament, and love.

The Glance.

When first thy sweet and gracious eye
Vouchsaf'd ev'n in the midst of youth and night
To look upon me, who before did lie
          Welt'ring in sin;
     I felt a sug'red strange delight,
Passing all cordials made by any art,
Bedew, embalm, and overrun my heart,
          And take it in.

     Since that time many a bitter storm
My soul hath felt, ev'n able to destroy,
Had the malicious and ill-meaning harm
          His swing and sway:
     But still thy sweet original joy
Sprung from thine eye, did work within my soul,
And surging griefs, when they grew bold, control,
          And got the day.

If thy first glance so powerful be,
A mirth but open'd and seal'd up again;
What wonders shall we feel, when we shall see
          Thy full-eyed love!

When thou shalt look us out of pain,
And one aspect of thine spend in delight
More than a thousand suns disburse in light,
    In heav'n above.

The 23d Psalm.

The God of love my shepherd is,
    And he that doth me feed:
While he is mine, and I am his,
    What can I want or need?

He leads me to the tender grass,   5
    Where I both feed and rest;
Then to the streams that gently pass:
    In both I have the best.

Or if I stray, he doth convert
    And bring my mind in frame: 10
And all this not for my desert,
    But for his holy name.

Yea, in death's shady black abode
    Well may I walk, not fear:
For thou art with me; and thy rod   15
    To guide, thy staff to bear.

Nay, thou dost make me sit and dine,
    Ev'n in my enemies' sight:
My head with oil, my cup with wine
    Runs over day and night.   20

Surely thy sweet and wondrous love
    Shall measure all my days;
And as it never shall remove,
    So neither shall my praise.

Mary Magdalene.

When blessed Mary wip'd her Saviour's feet,
(Whose precepts she had trampled on before)
And wore them for a jewel on her head,
    Showing his steps should be the street,
5   Wherein she thenceforth evermore
With pensive humbleness would live and tread:

She being stain'd herself, why did she strive
To make him clean, who could not be defil'd?
Why kept she not her tears for her own faults,
10   And not his feet? Though we could dive
    In tears like seas, our sins are pil'd
Deeper than they, in words, and works, and thoughts.

Dear soul, she knew who did vouchsafe and deign
To bear her filth; and that her sins did dash
15 Ev'n God himself: wherefore she was not loth,
      As she had brought wherewith to stain,
      So to bring in wherewith to wash:
And yet in washing one, she washed both.

Aaron.

      Holiness on the head,
    Light and perfections on the breast,
Harmonious bells below, raising the dead
    To lead them unto life and rest.
5   Thus are true Aarons drest.

      Profaneness in my head,
    Defects and darkness in my breast,
A noise of passions ringing me for dead
    Unto a place where is no rest.
10   Poor priest thus am I drest.

            Only another head
        I have, another heart and breast,
Another music, making live not dead,
        Without whom I could have no rest:
            In him I am well drest.   15

            Christ is my only head,
        My alone only heart and breast,
My only music, striking me ev'n dead;
        That to the old man I may rest,
            And be in him new drest.   20

            So holy in my head,
        Perfect and light in my dear breast,
My doctrine tuned by Christ (who is not dead,
        But lives in me while I do rest),
            Come people; Aaron's drest.   25

The Odour. 2 Cor. 2:15

How sweetly doth *My Master* sound! *My Master!*
        As Ambergris leaves a rich scent
            Unto the taster:
        So do these words a sweet content,
An oriental fragrancy, *My Master*.   5

With these all day I do perfume my mind,
        My mind ev'n thrust into them both:
            That I might find
        What cordials make this curious broth,
This broth of smells, that feeds and fats my mind.   10

My Master, shall I speak? O that to thee
        My servant were a little so,
            As flesh may be;
        That these two words might creep and grow
To some degree of spiciness to thee!   15

Then should the Pomander, which was before
        A speaking sweet, mend by reflection,
                And tell me more:
        For pardon of my imperfection
20   Would warm and work it sweeter than before.

For when *My Master*, which alone is sweet,
        And ev'n in my unworthiness pleasing,
                Shall call and meet,
        My servant, as thee not displeasing,
25   That call is but the breathing of the sweet.

This breathing would with gains by sweet'ning me
        (As sweet things traffic when they meet)
                Return to thee.
        And so this new commerce and sweet
30   Should all my life employ and busy me.

The Foil.

        If we could see below
The sphere of virtue, and each shining grace
     As plainly as that above doth show;
This were the better sky, the brighter place.

5   God hath made stars the foil
To set off virtues; griefs to set off sinning:
     Yet in this wretched world we toil,
As if grief were not foul, nor virtue winning.

The Forerunners.

The harbingers are come. See, see their mark;
White is their colour, and behold my head.
But must they have my brain? must they dispark
Those sparkling notions, which therein were bred?

Must dullness turn me to a clod?   5
Yet have they left me, *Thou art still my God*.

Good men ye be, to leave me my best room,
Ev'n all my heart, and what is lodgèd there:
I pass not, I, what of the rest become,
So *Thou art still my God*, be out of fear.   10
   He will be pleasèd with that ditty;
And if I please him, I write fine and witty.

Farewell sweet phrases, lovely metaphors.
But will ye leave me thus? when ye before
Of stews and brothels only knew the doors,   15
Then did I wash you with my tears, and more,
   Brought you to Church well drest and clad:
My God must have my best, ev'n all I had.

Lovely enchanting language, sugar-cane,
Honey of roses, whither wilt thou fly?   20
Hath some fond lover 'tic'd thee to thy bane?
And wilt thou leave the Church, and love a sty?
   Fie, thou wilt soil thy broider'd coat,
And hurt thyself, and him that sings the note.

Let foolish lovers, if they will love dung,   25
With canvas, not with arras clothe their shame:
Let folly speak in her own native tongue.
True beauty dwells on high: ours is a flame
   But borrow'd thence to light us thither.
Beauty and beauteous words should go together.   30

Yet if you go, I pass not; take your way:
For, *Thou art still my God*, is all that ye
Perhaps with more embellishment can say.
Go birds of spring: let winter have his fee,
   Let a bleak paleness chalk the door,   35
So all within be livelier than before.

The Rose.

Press me not to take more pleasure
    In this world of sug'red lies,
And to use a larger measure
    Than my strict, yet welcome size.

5   First, there is no pleasure here:
    Colour'd griefs indeed there are,
Blushing woes, that look as clear
    As if they could beauty spare.

Or if such deceits there be,
10   Such delights I meant to say;
There are no such things to me,
    Who have pass'd my right away.

But I will not much oppose
    Unto what you now advise:
15   Only take this gentle rose,
    And therein my answer lies.

What is fairer than a rose?
    What is sweeter? yet it purgeth.
Purgings enmity disclose,
20   Enmity forbearance urgeth.

If then all that worldlings prize
    Be contracted to a rose;
Sweetly there indeed it lies,
    But it biteth in the close.

25   So this flower doth judge and sentence
    Worldly joys to be a scourge:
For they all produce repentance,
    And repentance is a purge.

But I health, not physic choose:
30   Only though I you oppose,
Say that fairly I refuse,
    For my answer is a rose.

Discipline.

Throw away thy rod,
Throw away thy wrath:
        O my God,
Take the gentle path.

For my heart's desire   5
Unto thine is bent:
        I aspire
To a full consent.

Not a word or look
I affect to own,   10
        But by book,
And thy book alone.

Though I fail, I weep:
Though I halt in pace,
        Yet I creep   15
To the throne of grace.

Then let wrath remove;
Love will do the deed:
        For with love
Stony hearts will bleed.   20

Love is swift of foot;
Love's a man of war,
        And can shoot,
And can hit from far.

Who can scape his bow?   25
That which wrought on thee,
        Brought thee low,
Needs must work on me.

Throw away thy rod;
Though man frailties hath,   30
        Thou art God:
Throw away thy wrath.

The Invitation.

Come ye hither All, whose taste
          Is your waste;
Save your cost, and mend your fare.
God is here prepar'd and drest,
          And the feast,
God, in whom all dainties are.

Come ye hither all, whom wine
          Doth define,
Naming you not to your good:
Weep what ye have drunk amiss,
          And drink this,
Which before ye drink is blood.

Come ye hither all, whom pain
          Doth arraign,
Bringing all your sins to sight:
Taste and fear not: God is here
          In this cheer,
And on sin doth cast the fright.

Come ye hither all, whom joy
          Doth destroy,
While ye graze without your bounds:
Here is joy that drowneth quite
          Your delight,
As a flood the lower grounds.

Come ye hither all, whose love
          Is your dove,
And exalts you to the sky:
Here is love, which having breath
          Ev'n in death,
After death can never die.

Lord I have invited all,
          And I shall

Still invite, still call to thee:
For it seems but just and right
            In my sight,   35
Where is All, there All should be.

The Banquet.

Welcome sweet and sacred cheer,
            Welcome dear;
With me, in me, live and dwell:
For thy neatness passeth sight,
            Thy delight   5
Passeth tongue to taste or tell.

O what sweetness from the bowl
            Fills my soul,
Such as is, and makes divine!
Is some star (fled from the sphere)   10
            Melted there,
As we sugar melt in wine?

Or hath sweetness in the bread
            Made a head
To subdue the smell of sin;   15
Flowers, and gums, and powders giving
            All their living,
Lest the enemy should win?

Doubtless, neither star nor flower
            Hath the power,   20
Such a sweetness to impart:
Only God, who gives perfumes,
            Flesh assumes,
And with it perfumes my heart.

But as Pomanders and wood   25
            Still are good,
Yet being bruis'd are better scented:

God, to show how far his love
                              Could improve,
Here, as broken, is presented.

When I had forgot my birth,
                              And on earth
In delights of earth was drown'd;
God took blood, and needs would be
                              Spilt with me,
And so found me on the ground.

Having rais'd me to look up,
                              In a cup
Sweetly he doth meet my taste.
But I still being low and short,
                              Far from court,
Wine becomes a wing at last.

For with it alone I fly
                              To the sky:
Where I wipe mine eyes, and see
What I seek, for what I sue;
                              Him I view,
Who hath done so much for me.

Let the wonder of this pity
                              Be my ditty,
And take up my lines and life:
Harken under pain of death,
                              Hands and breath;
Strive in this, and love the strife.

The Posy.

Let wits contest,
And with their words and posies windows fill:
Less than the least
Of all thy mercies, is my posy still.

This on my ring,   5
This by my picture, in my book I write:
Whether I sing,
Or say, or dictate, this is my delight.

Invention rest,
Comparisons go play, wit use thy will: 10
Less than the least
Of all God's mercies, is my posy still.

A Parody.

Soul's joy, when thou art gone,
And I alone,
Which cannot be,
Because thou dost abide with me,
And I depend on thee;   5

Yet when thou dost suppress
The cheerfulness
Of thy abode,
And in my powers not stir abroad,
But leave me to my load: 10

O what a damp and shade
Doth me invade!
No stormy night
Can so afflict or so affright,
As thy eclipsed light.   15

Ah Lord! do not withdraw,
Lest want of awe
Make Sin appear;
And when thou dost but shine less clear,
Say, that thou art not here.   20

And then what life I have,
While Sin doth rave,

And falsely boast,
That I may seek, but thou art lost;
25   Thou and alone thou know'st.

O what a deadly cold
Doth me infold!
I half believe,
That Sin says true: but while I grieve,
30   Thou com'st and dost relieve.

The Elixir.

Teach me, my God and King,
In all things thee to see,
And what I do in anything,
To do it as for thee:

5   Not rudely, as a beast,
To run into an action;
But still to make thee prepossess'd,
And give it his perfection.

A man that looks on glass,
10   On it may stay his eye;
Or if he pleaseth, through it pass,
And then the heav'n espy.

All may of thee partake:
Nothing can be so mean,
15   Which with his tincture (for thy sake)
Will not grow bright and clean.

A servant with this clause
Makes drudgery divine:
Who sweeps a room, as for thy laws,
20   Makes that and th' action fine.

This is the famous stone
That turneth all to gold:
For that which God doth touch and own
Cannot for less be told.

A Wreath.

A wreathèd garland of deservèd praise,
Of praise deservèd, unto thee I give,
I give to thee, who knowest all my ways,
My crooked winding ways, wherein I live,
Wherein I die, not live: for life is straight, 5
Straight as a line, and ever tends to thee,
To thee, who art more far above deceit,
Than deceit seems above simplicity.
Give me simplicity, that I may live,
So live and like, that I may know thy ways, 10
Know them and practise them: then shall I give
For this poor wreath, give thee a crown of praise.

Death.

Death, thou wast once an uncouth hideous thing,
Nothing but bones,
The sad effect of sadder groans:
Thy mouth was open, but thou couldst not sing.

For we consider'd thee as at some six 5
Or ten years hence,
After the loss of life and sense,
Flesh being turn'd to dust, and bones to sticks.

We look'd on this side of thee, shooting short;
Where we did find 10
The shells of fledge souls left behind,
Dry dust, which sheds no tears, but may extort.

But since our Saviour's death did put some blood
                    Into thy face;
              Thou art grown fair and full of grace,
Much in request, much sought for, as a good.

For we do now behold thee gay and glad,
                    As at doomsday;
              When souls shall wear their new array,
And all thy bones with beauty shall be clad.

Therefore we can go die as sleep, and trust
                    Half that we have
              Unto an honest faithful grave;
Making our pillows either down, or dust.

Doomsday.

                    Come away,
              Make no delay.
       Summon all the dust to rise,
       Till it stir, and rub the eyes;
       While this member jogs the other,
       Each one whisp'ring, *Live you brother?*

                    Come away,
              Make this the day.
       Dust, alas, no music feels,
       But thy trumpet: then it kneels,
       As peculiar notes and strains
       Cure Tarantula's raging pains.

                    Come away,
              O make no stay!
       Let the graves make their confession,
       Lest at length they plead possession:
       Flesh's stubbornness may have
       Read that lesson to the grave.

Come away,
Thy flock doth stray.
Some to winds their body lend, 20
And in them may drown a friend:
Some in noisome vapours grow
To a plague and public woe.

Come away, 25
Help our decay.
Man is out of order hurl'd,
Parcell'd out to all the world.
Lord, thy broken consort raise,
And the music shall be praise. 30

Judgement.

Almighty Judge, how shall poor wretches brook
          Thy dreadful look,
Able a heart of iron to appal,
            When thou shalt call
      For ev'ry man's peculiar book? 5

What others mean to do, I know not well;
          Yet I hear tell,
That some will turn thee to some leaves therein
          So void of sin,
      That they in merit shall excel. 10

But I resolve, when thou shalt call for mine,
          That to decline,
And thrust a Testament into thy hand:
          Let that be scann'd.
      There thou shalt find my faults are thine. 15

Heaven.

O who will show me those delights on high?
            Echo.   I.
Thou Echo, thou art mortal, all men know.
            Echo.   No.
Wert thou not born among the trees and leaves?
            Echo.   Leaves.
And are there any leaves, that still abide?
            Echo.   Bide.
What leaves are they? impart the matter wholly.
            Echo.   Holy.
Are holy leaves the Echo then of bliss?
            Echo.   Yes.
Then tell me, what is that supreme delight?
            Echo.   Light.
Light to the mind: what shall the will enjoy?
            Echo.   Joy.
But are there cares and business with the pleasure?
            Echo.   Leisure.
Light, joy, and leisure; but shall they persever?
            Echo.   Ever.

Love (3).

Love bade me welcome: yet my soul drew back,
        Guilty of dust and sin.
But quick-ey'd Love, observing me grow slack
        From my first entrance in,
Drew nearer to me, sweetly questioning,
        If I lack'd anything.

A guest, I answer'd, worthy to be here:
        Love said, You shall be he.
I the unkind, ungrateful? Ah my dear,
        I cannot look on thee.

Love took my hand, and smiling did reply,
        Who made the eyes but I?

Truth Lord, but I have marr'd them: let my shame
        Go where it doth deserve.
And know you not, says Love, who bore the blame?   15
        My dear, then I will serve.
You must sit down, says Love, and taste my meat:
        So I did sit and eat.

FINIS.

Glory be to God on high,
And on earth peace,
Good will towards men.

THE CHURCH MILITANT

Almighty Lord, who from thy glorious throne
Seest and rulest all things ev'n as one:
The smallest ant or atom knows thy power,
Known also to each minute of an hour:
5   Much more do Commonweals acknowledge thee,
And wrap their policies in thy decree,
Complying with thy counsels, doing nought
Which doth not meet with an eternal thought.
But above all, thy Church and Spouse doth prove
10   Not the decrees of power, but bands of love.
Early didst thou arise to plant this vine,
Which might the more endear it to be thine.
Spices come from the East; so did thy Spouse,
Trim as the light, sweet as the laden boughs
15   Of *Noah*'s shady vine, chaste as the dove;
Prepar'd and fitted to receive thy love.
The course was westward, that the sun might light
As well our understanding as our sight.
Where th' Ark did rest, there *Abraham* began
20   To bring the other Ark from *Canaan*.
Moses pursu'd this; but King *Solomon*
Finish'd and fixt the old religion.
When it grew loose, the Jews did hope in vain
By nailing Christ to fasten it again.
25   But to the Gentiles he bore cross and all,
Rending with earthquakes the partition-wall:
Only whereas the Ark in glory shone,
Now with the cross, as with a staff, alone,
Religion, like a pilgrim, westward bent,
30   Knocking at all doors, ever as she went.

Yet as the sun, though forward be his flight,
Listens behind him, and allows some light,
Till all depart: so went the Church her way,
Letting, while one foot stept, the other stay
Among the eastern nations for a time,   35
Till both removèd to the western clime.
To *Egypt* first she came, where they did prove
Wonders of anger once, but now of love.
The ten Commandments there did flourish more
Than the ten bitter plagues had done before.   40
Holy *Macarius* and great *Anthony*
Made *Pharaoh Moses*, changing th' history.
Goshen was darkness, Egypt full of lights,
Nilus for monsters brought forth Israelites.
Such power hath mighty Baptism to produce   45
For things misshapen, things of highest use.
How dear to me, O God, thy counsels are!
                    Who may with thee compare?
Religion thence fled into Greece, where arts
Gave her the highest place in all men's hearts.   50
Learning was pos'd, Philosophy was set,
Sophisters taken in a fisher's net.
Plato and *Aristotle* were at a loss,
And wheel'd about again to spell *Christ-Cross.*
Prayers chasèd syllogisms into their den,   55
And *Ergo* was transform'd into *Amen.*
Though *Greece* took horse as soon as *Egypt* did,
And *Rome* as both: yet *Egypt* faster rid,
And spent her period and prefixèd time
Before the other. *Greece* being past her prime,   60
Religion went to *Rome*, subduing those,
Who, that they might subdue, made all their foes.
The Warrior his dear scars no more resounds,
But seems to yield Christ hath the greater wounds,
Wounds willingly endur'd to work his bliss,   65
Who by an ambush lost his Paradise.
The great heart stoops, and taketh from the dust
A sad repentance, not the spoils of lust:

Quitting his spear, lest it should pierce again
70 Him in his members, who for him was slain.
The Shepherd's hook grew to a sceptre here,
Giving new names and numbers to the year.
But th' Empire dwelt in Greece, to comfort them
Who were cut short in Alexander's stem.
75 In both of these Prowess and Arts did tame
And tune men's hearts against the Gospel came:
Which using, and not fearing skill in th' one,
Or strength in th' other, did erect her throne.
Many a rent and struggling th' Empire knew,
80 (As dying things are wont) until it flew
At length to Germany, still westward bending,
And there the Church's festival attending:
That as before Empire and Arts made way,
(For no less harbingers would serve than they)
85 So they might still, and point us out the place
Where first the Church should raise her downcast face.
Strength levels grounds, Art makes a garden there;
Then showers Religion, and makes all to bear.
Spain in the Empire shar'd with Germany,
90 But England in the higher victory:
Giving the Church a crown to keep her state,
And not go less than she had done of late.
Constantine's British line meant this of old,
And did this mystery wrap up and fold
95 Within a sheet of paper, which was rent
From time's great Chronicle, and hither sent.
Thus both the Church and Sun together ran
Unto the farthest old meridian.
How dear to me, O God, thy counsels are!
100   *Who may with thee compare?*
Much about one and the same time and place,
Both where and when the Church began her race,
Sin did set out of Eastern *Babylon*,
And travell'd westward also: journeying on
105 He chid the Church away, where'er he came,

Breaking her peace, and tainting her good name.
At first he got to *Egypt*, and did sow
Gardens of gods, which ev'ry year did grow,
Fresh and fine deities. They were at great cost,
Who for a god clearly a sallet lost.   110
Ah, what a thing is man devoid of grace,
Adoring garlic with an humble face,
Begging his food of that which he may eat,
Starving the while he worshippeth his meat!
Who makes a root his god, how low is he,   115
If God and man be sever'd infinitely!
What wretchedness can give him any room,
Whose house is foul, while he adores his broom?
None will believe this now, though money be
In us the same transplanted foolery.   120
Thus sin in *Egypt* sneaked for a while;
His highest was an ox or crocodile,
And such poor game. Thence he to *Greece* doth pass,
And being craftier much than Goodness was,
He left behind him garrisons of sins   125
To make good that which ev'ry day he wins.
Here Sin took heart, and for a garden-bed
Rich shrines and oracles he purchasèd:
He grew a gallant, and would needs foretell
As well what should befall, as what befell.   130
Nay, he became a poet, and would serve
His pills of sublimate in that conserve.
The world came both with hands and purses full
To this great lottery, and all would pull.
But all was glorious cheating, brave deceit,   135
Where some poor truths were shuffled for a bait
To credit him, and to discredit those
Who after him should braver truths disclose.
From *Greece* he went to *Rome*: and as before
He was a God, now he's an Emperor.   140
Nero and others lodg'd him bravely there,
Put him in trust to rule the Roman sphere.

Glory was his chief instrument of old:
Pleasure succeeded straight, when that grew cold.
145   Which soon was blown to such a mighty flame,
That though our Saviour did destroy the game,
Disparking oracles, and all their treasure,
Setting affliction to encounter pleasure;
Yet did a rogue with hope of carnal joy
150   Cheat the most subtle nations. Who so coy,
So trim, as *Greece* and *Egypt*? yet their hearts
Are given over, for their curious arts,
To such Mahometan stupidities,
As the old heathen would deem prodigies.
155   *How dear to me, O God, thy counsels are!*
                    Who may with thee compare?
Only the West and *Rome* do keep them free
From this contagious infidelity.
And this is all the Rock, whereof they boast,
160   As *Rome* will one day find unto her cost.
Sin being not able to extirpate quite
The Churches here, bravely resolv'd one night
To be a Churchman too, and wear a Mitre:
This old debauchèd ruffian would turn writer.
165   I saw him in his study, where he sat
Busy in controversies sprung of late.
A gown and pen became him wondrous well:
His grave aspect had more of heav'n than hell:
Only there was a handsome picture by,
170   To which he lent a corner of his eye.
As Sin in *Greece* a Prophet was before,
And in old *Rome* a mighty Emperor;
So now being Priest he plainly did profess
To make a jest of Christ's three offices:
175   The rather since his scatter'd jugglings were
United now in one both time and sphere.
From *Egypt* he took petty deities,
From *Greece* oracular infallibilities,
And from old *Rome* the liberty of pleasure,

By free dispensings of the Church's treasure. 180
Then in memorial of his ancient throne
He did surname his palace, *Babylon.*
Yet that he might the better gain all nations,
And make that name good by their transmigrations;
From all these places, but at divers times, 185
He took fine vizards to conceal his crimes:
From *Egypt* anchorism and retir'dness,
Learning from *Greece,* from old *Rome* stateliness:
And blending these he carri'd all men's eyes,
While Truth sat by, counting his victories: 190
Whereby he grew apace and scorn'd to use
Such force as once did captivate the Jews;
But did bewitch, and finely work each nation
Into a voluntary transmigration.
All post to *Rome*: Princes submit their necks 195
Either t' his public foot or private tricks.
It did not fit his gravity to stir,
Nor his long journey, nor his gout and fur.
Therefore he sent out able ministers,
Statesmen within, without doors cloisterers: 200
Who without spear, or sword, or other drum
Than what was in their tongue, did overcome;
And having conquer'd, did so strangely rule,
That the whole world did seem but the Pope's mule.
As new and old *Rome* did one Empire twist; 205
So both together are one Antichrist,
Yet with two faces, as their *Janus* was;
Being in this their old crackt looking-glass.
How dear to me, O God, thy counsels are!
                    Who may with thee compare? 210
Thus Sin triumphs in Western *Babylon*;
Yet not as Sin, but as Religion.
Of his two thrones he made the latter best,
And to defray his journey from the east.
Old and new *Babylon* are to hell and night, 215
As is the moon and sun to heav'n and light.

When th' one did set, the other did take place,
Confronting equally the law and grace.
They are hell's landmarks, Satan's double crest:
220   They are Sin's nipples, feeding th' east and west.
But as in vice the copy still exceeds
The pattern, but not so in virtuous deeds;
So though Sin made his latter seat the better,
The latter Church is to the first a debtor.
225   The second Temple could not reach the first:
And the late reformation never durst
Compare with ancient times and purer years;
But in the Jews and us deserveth tears.
Nay, it shall ev'ry year decrease and fade;
230   Till such a darkness do the world invade
At Christ's last coming, as his first did find:
Yet must there such proportions be assign'd
To these diminishings, as is between
The spacious world and *Jewry* to be seen.
235   Religion stands on tip-toe in our land,
Ready to pass to the *American* strand.
When height of malice, and prodigious lusts,
Impudent sinning, witchcrafts, and distrusts
(The marks of future bane) shall fill our cup
240   Unto the brim, and make our measure up;
When *Seine* shall swallow *Tiber*, and the *Thames*
By letting in them both, pollutes her streams:
When *Italy* of us shall have her will,
And all her calendar of sins fulfil;
245   Whereby one may foretell, what sins next year
Shall both in *France* and *England* domineer:
Then shall Religion to *America* flee:
They have their times of Gospel, ev'n as we.
My God, thou dost prepare for them a way
250   By carrying first their gold from them away:
For gold and grace did never yet agree:
Religion always sides with poverty.
We think we rob them, but we think amiss:
We are more poor, and they more rich by this.

Thou wilt revenge their quarrel, making grace   255
To pay our debts, and leave our ancient place
To go to them, while that which now their nation
But lends to us, shall be our desolation.
Yet as the Church shall thither westward fly,
So Sin shall trace and dog her instantly: 260
They have their period also and set times
Both for their virtuous actions and their crimes.
And where of old the Empire and the Arts
Usher'd the Gospel ever in men's hearts,
Spain hath done one; when Arts perform the other,   265
The Church shall come, and Sin the Church shall smother:
That when they have accomplishèd their round,
And met in th' east their first and ancient sound,
Judgement may meet them both and search them round.
Thus do both lights, as well in Church as Sun,   270
Light one another, and together run.
Thus also Sin and Darkness follow still
The Church and Sun with all their power and skill.
But as the Sun still goes both west and east;
So also did the Church by going west   275
Still eastward go; because it drew more near
To time and place, where judgement shall appear.
How dear to me, O God, thy counsels are!
                    Who may with thee compare?

L'Envoy.

King of Glory, King of Peace,
With the one make war to cease;
With the other bless thy sheep,
Thee to love, in thee to sleep.
Let not Sin devour thy fold,   5
Bragging that thy blood is cold,
That thy death is also dead,
While his conquests daily spread;

That thy flesh hath lost his food,
And thy Cross is common wood.
Choke him, let him say no more,
But reserve his breath in store,
Till thy conquests and his fall
Make his sighs to use it all,
And then bargain with the wind
To discharge what is behind.

Blessèd be God *alone,*
Thrice blessèd Three in One.

FINIS.

ENGLISH POEMS IN THE WILLIAMS MANUSCRIPT NOT INCLUDED IN *THE TEMPLE*

The Holy Communion.

O gracious Lord, how shall I know
Whether in these gifts thou be so
   As thou art ev'rywhere;
Or rather so, as thou alone
Tak'st all the lodging, leaving none   5
   For thy poor creature there?

First I am sure, whether bread stay
Or whether bread do fly away
   Concerneth bread not me.
But that both thou, and all thy train   10
Be there, to thy truth, and my gain
   Concerneth me and Thee.

And if in coming to thy foes
Thou dost come first to them, that shows
   The haste of thy good will.   15
Or if that thou two stations makèst
In Bread and me, the way thou takèst
   Is more, but for me still.

Then of this also I am sure
That thou didst all those pains endure   20
   To'abolish Sin, not Wheat.

Creatures are good, and have their place;
Sin only, which did all deface,
   Thou drivest from his seat.

25   I could believe an Impanation
At the rate of an Incarnation
   If thou hadst died for bread.
But which made my soul to die,
My flesh, and fleshly villainy,
30   That also made thee dead.

That flesh is there, mine eyes deny:
And what should flesh but flesh descry,
   The noblest sense of five.
If glorious bodies pass the sight,
35   Shall they be food and strength, and might
     Even there, where they deceive?

Into my soul this cannot pass;
Flesh (though exalted) keeps his grass
   And cannot turn to soul.
40   Bodies and Minds are different Spheres,
Nor can they change their bounds and meres,
     But keep a constant pole.

This gift of all gifts is the best,
Thy flesh the least that I request.
45   Thou took'st that pledge from me:
Give me not that I had before,
Or give me that, so I have more;
     My God, give me all Thee.

Love.

Thou art too hard for me in Love:
There is no dealing with thee in that Art:
   That is thy Masterpiece I see.
  When I contrive and plot to prove
5 Something that may be conquest on my part

Thou still, O Lord, outstrippest me.

Sometimes, when as I wash, I say,
And shrewdly, as I think, Lord wash my soul
    More spotted than my flesh can be.
    But then there comes into my way   10
Thy ancient baptism, which when I was foul
    And knew it not, yet cleansèd me.

I took a time when thou didst sleep,
Great waves of trouble combating my breast:
    I thought it brave to praise thee then,   15
    Yet then I found, that thou didst creep
Into my heart with joy, giving more rest
    Than flesh did lend thee back again.

Let me but once the conquest have
Upon the matter, 'twill thy conquest prove: 20
    If thou subdue mortality
    Thou do'st no more, than doth the grave:
Whereas if I o'ercome thee and thy Love
    Hell, Death and Devil come short of me.

Trinity Sunday.

He that is one,
    Is none.
Two reacheth thee
In some degree.
Nature and Grace   5
With Glory may attain thy Face.
    Steel and a flint strike fire,
        Wit and desire
    Never to thee aspire,
Except life catch and hold those fast.   10
        That which belief
Did not confess in the first Thief
        His fall can tell,
    From Heaven, through Earth, to Hell.

15

Let two of those alone
To them that fall,
Who God and Saints and Angels lose at last.
He that has one,
Has all.

Even-song.

The Day is spent, and hath his will on me:
  I and the Sun have run our races,
  I went the slower, yet more paces,
    For I decay, not he.

5   Lord make my losses up, and set me free:
  That I who cannot now by day
  Look on his daring brightness, may
    Shine then more bright than he.

If thou defer this light, then shadow me:
10   Lest that the Night, earth's gloomy shade,
  Fouling her nest, my earth invade,
    As if shades knew not Thee.

But Thou art Light and darkness both together:
  If that be dark we cannot see,
15   The sun is darker than a Tree,
    And thou more dark than either.

Yet Thou art not so dark, since I know this,
  But that my darkness may touch thine,
  And hope, that may teach it to shine,
20   Since Light thy Darkness is.

O let my Soul, whose keys I must deliver
  Into the hands of senseless Dreams
  Which know not thee, suck in thy beams
    And wake with thee for ever.

The Knell.

The Bell doth toll:
Lord help thy servant whose perplexèd Soul
    Doth wishly look
    On either hand
And sometimes offers, sometimes makes a stand   5
    Struggling on th' hook.

    Now is the season,
Now the great combat of our flesh and reason:
    O help, my God!
    See, they break in,   10
Disbanded humours, sorrows, troops of Sin,
    Each with his rod.

    Lord make thy Blood
Convert and colour all the other flood
    And streams of grief,   15
    That they may be
Juleps and Cordials when we call on thee
    For some relief.

Perseverance.

My God, the poor expressions of my Love
Which warm these lines, and serve them up to thee
Are so, as for the present I did move,
    Or rather as thou movèdst me.

But what shall issue, whether these my words   5
Shall help another, but my judgement be;
As a burst fowling-piece doth save the birds
    But kill the man, is seal'd with thee.

For who can tell, though thou hast died to win
And wed my soul in glorious paradise;   10

Whether my many crimes and use of sin
  May yet forbid the banns and bliss?

Only my soul hangs on thy promises
With face and hands clinging unto thy breast,
15 Clinging and crying, crying without cease,
  Thou art my rock, thou art my rest.

POEMS FROM IZAAK WALTON'S
THE LIFE OF
MR GEORGE HERBERT

Sonnets.

1.

My God, where is that ancient heat towards thee,
  Wherewith whole shoals of *Martyrs* once did burn,
  Besides their other flames? Doth poetry
Wear *Venus'* livery? only serve her turn?
Why are not *Sonnets* made of thee? and lays   5
  Upon thine altar burnt? Cannot thy love
  Heighten a spirit to sound out thy praise
As well as any she? Cannot thy *Dove*
Outstrip their *Cupid* easily in flight?
  Or, since thy ways are deep, and still the same,   10
  Will not a verse run smooth that bears thy name!
Why doth that fire, which by thy power and might
  Each breast does feel, no braver fuel choose
  Than that, which one day Worms may chance refuse?

2.

Sure Lord, there is enough in thee to dry
  Oceans of *Ink*; for, as the Deluge did
  Cover the Earth, so doth thy Majesty:
Each Cloud distills thy praise, and doth forbid
Poets to turn it to another use.   5
  Roses and *Lilies* speak thee; and to make

A pair of cheeks of them, is thy abuse.
Why should I *Women's eyes* for Crystal take?
Such poor invention burns in their low mind,
10   Whose fire is wild, and doth not upward go
        To praise, and on thee Lord, some *Ink* bestow.
Open the bones, and you shall nothing find
      In the best *face* but *filth*; when Lord, in thee
      The *beauty* lies in the *discovery*.

To my Successor.

If thou chance for to find
A new House to thy mind,
And built without thy Cost:
    Be good to the Poor,
5   As God gives thee store,
And then my Labour's not lost.

ADDITIONAL ENGLISH POEMS

To the Right Hon. the
L. Chancellor (Bacon).

My Lord, a diamond to me you sent
And I to you a Blackamoor present.
Gifts speak their Givers. For as those Refractions,
Shining and sharp, point out your rare Perfections;
So by the Other, you may read in me   5
(Whom Scholar's Habit and Obscurity
Hath soil'd with Black) the colour of my state,
Till your bright gift my darkness did abate.
Only, most noble Lord, shut not the door
Against this mean and humble Blackamoor.   10
    Perhaps some other subject I had tried
    But that my Ink was factious for this side.

A Paradox.
That the Sick are in better
State than the Whole.

You who admire yourselves because
    You neither groan nor weep,
And think it contrary to Nature's laws
    To want one ounce of sleep,
      Your strong belief   5
Acquits yourselves, and gives the sick all grief.

Your state to ours is contrary;
   That makes you think us poor,
So Black'moors think us foul, and we
      Are quit with them, and more.
         Nothing can see,
And judge of things but Mediocrity.

The sick are in themselves a State
   Which health hath nought to do.
How know you that our tears proceed from woe
   And not from better fate,
      Since that mirth hath
Her waters also and desirèd Bath.

How know you that the sighs we send
   From want of breath proceed,
Not from excess? and therefore we do spend
   That which we do not need;
      So trembling may
As well show inward warbling as decay.

Cease then to judge calamities
   By outward form and show,
But view yourselves, and inward turn your eyes,
   Then you shall fully know
      That your estate
Is, of the two, the far more desperate.

You always fear to feel those smarts
   Which we but sometimes prove:
Each little comfort much affects our hearts,
   None but gross joys you move:
      Why then confess
Your fears in number more, your joys are less.

Then for yourselves not us embrace
   Plaints to bad fortune due:
For though you visit us, and wail our case,
   We doubt much whether you
      Come to our bed
To comfort us, or to be comforted.

To *the Lady Elizabeth*
Queen of Bohemia.

Bright soul, of whom if any country known
Had worthy been, thou had'st not lost thine own:
No Earth can be thy Jointure, for the sun
And stars alone unto thy pitch do run
And pace of thy sweet virtues; only they   5
Are thy dominion. Those that rule in clay
Stick fast therein; but thy transcendent soul
Doth for two clods of earth ten spheres control.
And though stars shot from heaven lose their light,
Yet thy brave beams, excluded from their right,   10
Maintain their Lustre still, and shining clear,
Turn wat'rish Holland to a crystal sphere.
Methinks in that Dutch optic I do see
Thy curious virtues much more visibly.
There is thy best Throne. For afflictions are   15
A foil to set off worth, and make it rare.
Through that black tiffany thy virtues shine
Fairer and richer, now we know what's thine
And what is fortune's. Thou hast singled out
Sorrows and griefs, to fight with them a bout   20
At their own weapons, without pomp or state
To second thee against their cunning hate.
O, what a poor thing 'tis to be a Queen
When sceptres, state, Attendants are the screen
Betwixt us and the people; whenas glory   25
Lies round about us, to help out the story,
When all things pull and hale, that they may bring
A slow behaviour to the style of king,
When sense is made by comments! But that face,
Whose native beauty needs not dress or lace   30
To set it forth, and being stript of all,
Is self-sufficient to be the self-thrall
Of thousand hearts; that face doth figure thee
And show thy undivided Majesty,

35 Which misery cannot untwist, but rather
    Adds to the union, as lights do gather
    Splendours from darkness. So close sits the crown
    About thy temples that the furious frown
    Of opposition cannot place thee where
40 Thou should'st not be a Queen, and conquer there.
        Yet hast thou more dominions: God doth give
    Children for kingdoms to thee; they shall live
    To conquer new ones, and shall share the frame
    Of th' universe, like as the winds, and name
45 The world anew. The sun shall never rise
    But it shall spy some of thy victories.
    Their hands shall clip the Eagle's wings and chase
    Those ravening Harpies, which peck at their face,
    At once to Hell, without a baiting-while
50 At Purgatory, their enchanted Isle
    And Paris garden. Then let their perfume
    And Spanish saints, wisely laid up, presume
    To deal with brimstone, that untamèd stench
    Whose fire, like their malice, nought can quench.
55   But joys are stored for thee, thou shalt return
    Laden with comfort thence, where now to mourn
    Is thy chief government, to manage woe,
    To curb some Rebel tears, which fain would flow,
    Making a Head and spring against thy Reason.
60 This is thy empire yet, till better season
    Call thee from out of that surrounded land,
    That habitable sea and brinish strand,
    Thy tears not needing. For that hand Divine,
    Which mingles water with thy Rhenish wine,
65 Will pour full joys to thee, but dregs to those,
    And meet their taste, who are thy bitter foes.

L'Envoy.

Shine on, Majestic soul, abide
Like David's tree, planted beside
The Flemish rivers: in the end,
Thy fruit shall with their drops contend;
Our God will surely dry those tears   5
Which now that moist land to thee bears.
Then shall thy Glory, fresh as flowers
In water kept, maugre the powers
Of Devil, Jesuit, and Spain,
From Holland sail into the Main.   10
Thence, wheeling on, it compass shall
This, our great Sublunary Ball
And with that Ring, thy fame shall wed
Eternity into one Bed.

THE LATIN VERSE

GEORGII HERBERTI ANGLI

MUSAE RESPONSORIAE

AD ANDREAE MELVINI SCOTI
ANTI-TAMI-CAMI-CATEGORIAM

AUGUSTISSIMO POTENTISSIMÓQUE
MONARCHAE IACOBO, D. G.
MAGNAE BRITANNIAE,
FRANCIAE, & HIBERNIAE REGI,
FIDEI DEFENSORI, &C.
GEO. HERBERTUS.

Ecce recedentis foecundo in littore Nili
    Sol generat populum luce fouente nouum.
Antè tui, *CAESAR*, quàm fulserat aura fauoris,
    Nostrae etiam Musae vile fuere lutum:
Nunc adeò per te viuunt, vt repere possint,
    Síntque ausae thalamum solis adire tui.

5

THE MUSES' REPLY

IN RESPONSE TO THE SCOTSMAN ANDREW MELVILLE'S

ANTI-TAMI-CAMI-CATEGORIAM

To the Most Venerable and
Most Mighty Monarch James by
the Grace of God King of Great Britain,
France and Ireland, Defender of the Faith, &c.
George Herbert.

Look how, on the fertile shore of the ebbing Nile
  The sun produces a new people by its nurturing light.
Before the breeze of your favour, Caesar, shone upon me,
  My Muses too were vile mud:
Now, by your power, their life is strong enough to creep,   5
  And bold enough to approach the chamber of your sun.

Illustriss. Celsissimóque
Carolo,
Walliae, & Iuuentutis Principi.

Qvam chartam tibi porrigo recentem,
Humanae decus atque apex iuuentae,
Obtutu placido benignus affles,
Namque aspectibus è tuis vel vnus
Mordaces tineas, nigrásque blattas,
Quas liuor mihi parturit, retundet,
Ceu, quas culta timet seges, pruinas
Nascentes radij fugant, vel acres
Tantùm dulcia leniunt catarrhos.
Sic o te (iuuenem, senémue) credat
Mors semper iuuenem, senem Britanni.

Reuerendissimo in Christo
Patri ac Domino, Episcopo
Vintoniensi, &c.

Sancte Pater, coeli custos, quo doctius vno
    Terra nihil, nec quo sanctius astra vident;
Cùm mea futilibus numeris se verba viderent
    Claudi, penè tuas praeteriêre fores.
Sed properè dextréque reduxit euntia sensus,
    Ista docens soli scripta quadrare tibi.

To His Most Glorious Highness, Charles, Prince of Wales, and Prince of Youth.

This manuscript, brand-new, I hand to you,
You, the glory and apex of human youth,
May you look kindly upon it with a lenient eye.
For a single one of your glances
Will dull the biting bookworms   5
The black moths which envy brings me,
Just as the sunbeams as they are born in the morning
Scatter the frost, fearful to the planted crop,
Or as sweet remedies soothe harsh coughs.
In both your youth and later years, let Death   10
Always consider you young, while the British revere
    your age.

To the Most Reverend Father in Christ and Lord, the Bishop of Winchester, &c.

Holy Father, guardian of heaven; the earth sees nothing
    More learned than you, the stars see nothing
      more sacred;
When my words saw that they were penned up in
      empty numbers,
    They almost passed your door without stopping.
But hurriedly, cleverly, sense caught them as they passed,   5
    Teaching these writings to befit you alone.

Pro Disciplina Ecclesiae Nostrae
Epigrammata Apologetica.

I. Ad Regem
Instituti Epigrammatici ratio.

Cvm millena tuam pulsare negotia mentem
    Constet, & ex illâ pendeat orbis ope;
Ne te productis videar lassare Camoenis,
    Pro solido, CAESAR, carmine frusta dabo.
Cùm tu contundis *Catharos*, vultúque librísque,
    Grata mihi mensae sunt analecta tuae.

II. Ad Melvinum.

Non mea fert aetas, vt te, veterane, lacessam;
    Non vt te superem: res tamen ipsa feret.
Aetatis numerum supplebit causa minorem:
    Sic tu nunc iuuenis factus, egóque senex.
Aspice, dum perstas, vt te tua deserat aetas,
    Et mea sint canis scripta referta tuis.
Ecce tamen quàm suauis ero! cùm, fine duelli,
    Clauserit extremas pugna peracta vices,
Tum tibi, si placeat, fugientia tempora reddam;
    Sufficiet votis ista iuuenta meis.

Epigrams in Defence of the
Discipline of Our Church.

1. *To the King*
The Reason for Writing Epigrams.

Since a thousand matters, it is agreed, beat upon your mind
  And the world hangs upon its work;
And because I am afraid to wear you out with long
    and laboured verses,
   Instead of one large and complete song, CAESAR,
    I shall give you bits and pieces.
While you are beating down the *Cathars*, with
   your bearing and your books,   5
   I am glad of the crumbs from your table.

2. *To Melville.*

It is not my age that allows me to provoke you,
   veteran that you are;
  Nor my age that brings me victory: the case itself does both.
My cause will fill out the lesser number of my age:
  So that you are now made the youth, I the old man.
See how, while you persist, your age deserts you;   5
  And my writings meanwhile are stuffed full with
   your grey hairs.
But see how sweet and gentle I shall be! When the
   fight is finished,
  The struggle ended and the last turns of the battle done,
Then – if you wish – I shall return to you those years
   that now fly away;
  That youth will be a sufficient reward for my prayers.   10

III. Ad eundem.
In Monstrum vocabuli
Anti-Tami-Cami-Categoria.

O quàm bellus homo es! lepido quàm nomine fingis
    Istas *Anti-Tami-Cami-Categorias*!
Sic Catharis noua sola placent; res, verba nouantur:
    Quae sapiunt aeuum, ceu cariosa iacent.
5   Quin liceat nobis aliquas procudere voces:
    Non tibi fingendi sola taberna patet.
Cùm sacra perturbet vester furor omnia, scriptum
    Hoc erit, *Anti-furi-Puri-Categoria*.
Pollubra vel cùm olim damnâris Regiâ in arâ,
10 Est *Anti-pelvi-Melvi-Categoria*.

IV. Partitio
Anti-Tami-Cami-Categoria.

Tres video partes, quò re distinctiùs vtar,
    Anticategoriae, Scoto-Britanne, tuae:
Ritibus vna Sacris opponitur; altera Sanctos
    Praedicat autores; tertia plena Deo est.
5   Postremis ambabus idem sentimus vterque;
    Ipse pios laudo; Numen & ipse colo.
Non nisi prima suas patiuntur praelia lites.
    O bene quòd dubium possideamus agrum!

3. *To the Same.*
On the Monstrosity of
the Phrase Anti-Tami-Cami-Categoria.

Oh what a handsome man you are! With what a
    charming name you craft
      Those *Anti-Oxford-Cambridge-Accusations!*
For only novelties please Puritans; facts and
    words are made new:
      Things which savour of age are set aside as if rotten.
But we can hammer out some words as well: 5
    You're not the only one with access to the
    craftsman's smithy.
Since your fury disturbs all that is sacred, this
    Will be written, *Anti-Raging-Puritan-Accusations.*
And since you once condemned ablutions upon the
    Royal altar,
      It is the *Anti-Basin-Melville-Accusations.*   10

4. *Division of the*
Anti-Tami-Cami-Categoria.

To deal with it more precisely, I discern three
    sections in your work,
    The *Anticategoria*, Anglo-Scot:
One part opposes sacred ritual; the second praises
    Sacred authors; the third is full of God.
In both these latter points we are of the same mind;   5
    I too praise pious men; and I too worship God.
It is only on the first that there is room for
    disagreement.
    The ground on which we fight is not yet won!

V. *In metri genus.*

Cvr, vbi tot ludat numeris antiqua poesis,
   Sola tibi Sappho, femináque vna placet?
Cur tibi tam facilè non arrisêre poetae
   Heroum grandi carmina fulta pede?
5   Cur non lugentes Elegi? non acer Iambus?
   Commotos animos rectiùs ista decent.
Scilicet hoc vobis proprium, qui puriùs itis,
   Et populi spurcas creditis esse vias:
Vos ducibus missis, missis doctoribus, omnes
10   Femineum blandâ fallitis arte genus:
Nunc etiam teneras quò versus gratior aures
   Mulceat, imbelles complacuêre modi.

VI. *De Laruatâ Gorgone.*

Gorgona cur diram laruásque obtrudis inanes,
   Cùm propè sit nobis Musa, Medusa procul?
Si, quia felices olim dixêre poetae
   Pallada gorgoneam, sic tua verba placent.
5   Vel potiùs liceat distinguere. Túque tuíque
   Sumite *gorgoneam,* nostráque *Pallas* erit.

5. *On the Type of Metre.*

Why, when ancient poetry sports with so many
    different metres,
  Does only Sappho, that lady alone please you?
Why have you not been so readily enticed
    By poets' songs propped on heroes' lofty feet?
Why no mournful elegiacs? No sharp iambic?   5
  The former are more fitting for impassioned
    minds,
But the latter of course for you who pass with
    greater purity,
  And believe the ways of the people to be unclean:
Dismiss the leaders, dismiss the teachers, all of you
  Deceive the whole race of women with your
    flattering charm: 10
To make your verse more welcome, soothing to
    delicate ears,
  Unwarlike metres have been your choice.

6. *On the Bewitched Gorgon.*

Why did you put in a dread Gorgon and empty
    ghosts,
  When the Muse is near to us, Medusa far off?
If it is because blessed poets used to say
  That Pallas bears a Gorgon's face, then your
    words may stand.
But let us rather share it out. You, and your friends   5
  Can take the *Gorgon's face*; *Pallas* will be ours.

VII. De Praesulum fastu.

Praesulibus nostris fastus, *Melvine*, tumentes
    Saepiùs aspergis. Siste, pudore vacas.
An quod semotum populo laquearibus altis
    Eminet, id tumidum protinus esse feres?
5   Ergo etiam Solem dicas, ignaue, superbum,
    Qui tam sublimi conspicit orbe viam:
Ille tamen, quamuìs altus, tua crimina ridens
    Assiduo vilem lumine cingit humum.
Sic laudandus erit nactus sublimia Praesul,
10   Qui dulci miseros irradiabit ope.

VIII. De geminâ Academiâ.

Qvis hìc superbit, oro? túne, an Praesules,
    Quos dente nigro corripis?
Tu duplicem solus Camoenarum thronum
    Virtute percellis tuâ;
5   Et vnus impar aestimatur viribus,
    Vtrumque sternis calcitro:
Omnésque stulti audimus, aut hypocritae,
    Te perspicaci atque integro.
An rectiùs nos, si vices vertas, probi,
10   Te contumaci & liuido?
Quisquis tuetur perspicillis Belgicis
    Quâ parte tractari solent,
Res ampliantur, sin per aduersam videt,
    Minora fiunt omnia:

7. *On the Pride of the Bishops.*

Often, *Mr Melville*, you cast aspersions on our
    bishops, saying
  They are puffed up with pride. How shameless you
    are! Stop it!
Would you call puffed up anything that stands out with
    distinction
  Far removed from the people, on high panelled
    ceilings?
If so, you fool, you'd call the Sun proud too,   5
  Since he picks out a path in orbit far from the earth.
But he, although high, laughs down on your charges
  And wreathes the lowly earth with constant light.
So too the Bishop is to be praised as a man who has
    obtained high office,
  And whose sweet skill shall bring light to the wretched.   10

8. *On the Two Universities.*

  Who here is proud? I ask. You, or the Bishops?
    Whom do you tear at with your black tooth?
  You alone with your strength beat down
    The double throne of the Muses;
  A single opponent is reckoned unequal to your
       strength,   5
    With your kicks you send both sprawling:
  We are all called fools, or hypocrites,
    While you are sharp-witted and pure.
  Or could it be the other way round: that we are
      in the right
    While you are stubborn and spiteful?   10
  The man who looks through a Belgian telescope
    – And uses the customary end to do so –
  Sees objects larger; but if he looks the other way
    Everything shrinks:

15   Tu qui superbos caeteros existimas
          (Superbius cùm te nihil)
        Vertas specillum: nam, prout se res habent,
          Vitro minùs rectè vteris.

IX. De S. Baptismi Ritu

Cvm tener ad sacros infans sistatur aquales,
    Quòd puer ignorat, verba profana putas?
Annon sic mercamur agros? quibus ecce Redemptor
    Comparat aeterni regna beata Dei.
5 Scilicet emptorem si res aut parcior aetas
    Impediant, apices legis amicus obit.
Forsitan & prohibes infans portetur ad vndas,
    Et per se Templi limen adire velis:
Sin, *Melvine*, pedes alienos postulet infans,
10   Cur sic displiceat vox aliena tibi?
Rectiùs innocuis lactentibus omnia praestes,
    Quae ratio per se, si sit adulta, facit.
Quid vetat vt pueri vagitus suppleat alter,
    Cùm nequeat claras ipse litare preces?
15 Saeuus es eripiens paruis vadimonia coeli:
    Et tibi sit nemo praes, vbi poscis opem.

You consider everyone else proud   15
  (When in fact nothing is prouder than you).
Turn your lens: for, as things stand,
  You're using the glass the wrong way round.

9. *On the Sacred Rite of Baptism.*

When the tender child is set before the sacred waters,
  Do you think the words are unholy, because the
    child is ignorant?
Don't we trade land under those terms? Land which
    the Redeemer
Compares to the blessed realms of the everlasting God.
Of course if youth or other concerns   5
  Impede the purchaser, a friend performs his legal role.
Perhaps you will forbid the child to be carried to the water,
  And you'd prefer that he makes his own way to the
    door of the Temple:
But, *Melville*, if the child needs to use another's feet,
  Why should the use of another's voice displease
    you so?   10
It would be more correct to provide those innocents,
    still fed on milk,
  With everything that reason would furnish, if he
    grows to adulthood.
Why prevent a second person from assisting the
    wailing child,
  When he himself cannot offer clear prayers?
You are cruel to snatch from small children the
    promise of heaven: 15
  May no-one stand surety for you, when you are
    asking for help.

X. *De Signaculo Crucis.*

Cvr tanta sufflas probra in innocuam Crucem?
Non plùs maligni daemones Christi cruce
Vnquam fugari, quàm tui socij solent.
Apostolorum culpa non leuis fuit
5   Vitâsse Christi spiritum efflantis crucem.
Et Christianus quisque piscis dicitur
Tertulliano, propter vndae pollubrum,
Quo tingimur parui. Ecquis autem brachijs
Natare sine clarissimâ potest cruce?
10   Sed non moramur: namque vestra crux erit,
Vobis fauentibúsue, vel negantibus.

XI. *De iuramento Ecclesiae.*

Articulis sacris quidam subscribere iussus,
    Ah! Cheiragra vetat, quò minùs, inquit, agam.
O verè dictum, & bellè! cùm torqueat omnes
    Ordinis osores articulare malum.

10. *On the Sign of the Cross.*

Why do you blast forth such vile words against
    the blameless Cross?
Wicked demons never fled from the cross of
    Christ
Any more than do your friends.
For the Apostles it was no small sin
To have spurned the cross on which Christ
    breathes out his spirit.   5
And every Christian is called a fish
According to Tertullian, because as children,
We are baptized by washing in the sacred water.
    Moreover, who
Can swim with his arms without making an
    obvious cross?
But let's come to the point: for the cross will be
    yours   10
Whether you approve or deny it.

11. *On the Oath to the Church.*

A certain man was ordered to subscribe to the
    sacred articles.
    Oh! Gout prevents me doing so, he said.
O well said! A fine answer! Since problems of
    articulation
    Torment all those who loathe proper order.

XII. De purificatione post puerperium.

Enixas pueros matres se sistere templis
    Displicet, & laudis tura litare Deo.
Fortè quidem, cùm per vestras Ecclesia turbas
    Fluctibus internis exagitata natet,
5   Vos sine maternis hymnis infantia vidit,
    Vitáque neglectas est satìs vlta preces.
Sed nos, cùm nequeat paruorum lingua, parentem
    Non laudare Deum, credimus esse nefas.
Quotidiana suas poscant si fercula grates,
10   Nostra caro sanctae nescia laudis erit?
Adde pijs animis quaeuis occasio lucro est,
    Quâ possint humili fundere corde preces.
Sic vbi iam mulier decerpti conscia pomi
    Ingemat ob partus, ceu maledicta, suos,
15   Appositè quem commotum subfugerat olim,
    Nunc redit ad mitem, ceu benedicta, Deum.

XIII. De Antichristi decore Pontificali.

Non quia Pontificum sunt olim afflata veneno,
    Omnia sunt temere proijcienda foras.
Tollantur si cuncta malus quae polluit vsus,
    Non remanent nobis corpora, non animae.

12. *On the Purification after*
Childbirth.

That mothers who have given birth should present
    themselves at the temple
  Displeases you, and that they should offer the incense
    of praise to the Lord.
Since the Church is now swimming through mobs
    of your followers,
  Tossed and beaten by waves within,
Perhaps your infancy passed without a mother's hymns,   5
  And your life since has tried to make up for those lost
    prayers.
But since children's tongues cannot do so, we believe
  It is wrong for a parent not to praise God.
If everyday dishes require their own set graces,
  Will our own flesh and blood know nothing of
    holy praise?   10
What's more, devout souls count as a boon any occasion
  On which they can pour forth prayers from a humble
    heart.
So when the wife, guiltily aware of the plucked apple
  Groans as if cursed as she gives birth to her children,
Appropriately enough she now returns, as if blessed,   15
  To God – now mild – whom she once angered and fled
    from.

13. *On the Priestly Beauty of*
the Antichrist.

Just because Priestly things were once blasted with poison,
  They are not all to be cast aside.
If everything were removed which evil usage has
    once polluted,
  Neither our bodies nor our souls would be left to us.

XIV. De Superpelliceo.

Qvid sacrae tandem meruêre vestes,
Quas malus liuor iaculis lacessit
Polluens castum chlamydis colorem
    Dentibus atris?

5   Quicquid ex vrnâ meliore ductum
Luce praelustri, vel honore pollet,
Mens sub insigni specie coloris
    Concipit albi.

Scilicet talem liquet esse solem;
10   Angeli vultu radiante candent;
Incolae coeli melioris albâ
    Veste triumphant.

E creaturis sine mentis vsu
Conditis binas homini sequendas
15   Spiritus proponit, & est vtrique
    Candor amicus.

Ergo ringantur pietatis hostes,
Filij noctis, populus malignus,
Dum suum nomen tenet, & triumphat
20   Albion albo.

XV. De Pileo quadrato.

Qvae dicteria fuderat Britannus
Superpellicei tremendus hostis,
Isthaec pileus audijt propinquus,
Et partem capitis petit supremam;
5   Non sic effugit angulus vel vnus

14. *On the Surplice.*

What then have sacred vestments done to
    deserve this?
That wicked envy goads them with spears
Spoiling the pure colour of the surplice
    With black teeth?

Whatever is drawn from a better urn   5
And shines with a glorious light, or honour,
Is perceived by the mind in the special form
    Of the colour white.

The sun of course is just such an example:
The angels shine brightly from their blazing faces;   10
The residents of higher heaven celebrate their
    triumph
    In white clothing.

From all the creatures created without consciousness
The spirit sets out two for man to follow –
And to both of those   15
    Whiteness is a friend.

So let the enemies of piety, the sons of night
The people of wickedness, chafe and snarl
While Albion, the white country, holds true to
    its name
And triumphs in its whiteness.   20

15. *On the Biretta.*

Those directives poured down
By the dread British enemy of the surplice,
Are heard by the nearby hat,
Which seeks the very top of the head;

Quò dictis minùs acribus notetur.
    Verùm heus! si reputes, tibi tuísque
Longè pileus anteit galerum,
Vt feruor cerebri refrigeretur,
10   Qui vestras edit intimè medullas.
Sed qui tam malè pileos habetis,
Quos Ecclesia comprobat, verendum
Ne tandem caput eius impetatis.

XVI. *In Catharum.*

Cvr Latiam linguam reris nimis esse profanam,
    Quam praemissa probant secula, nostra probant?
Cur teretem Graecam damnas, atque Hellada totam,
    Quâ tamen occisi foedera scripta Dei?
5   Scilicet Hebraeam cantas, & perstrepis vnam:
    Haec facit ad nasum sola loquela tuum.

XVII. *De Episcopis.*

Qvos charos habuit Christus Apostolos,
Testatósque suo tradiderat gregi;
Vt, cùm mors rabidis vnguibus imminens
Doctrinae fluuios clauderet aureae,
5   Mites acciperent Lampada Praesules,
Seruaréntque sacrum clauibus ordinem;

So not even a single corner escapes 5
The notice of harsh words.
But alas! If you give it some thought, for you
    and those of your party
The biretta is much better than a priest's cap:
For in a biretta the brain's fever is cooled –
That fever which eats its way deep into your
    marrow. 10
But you who are so opposed to hats
(Although the Church approves them) should
    take care
That you don't end up attacking the head of
    the Church herself.

16. *Against the Puritan.*

Why do you consider the Latin tongue so profane?
    A language which past ages endorsed, which our
    own endorses?
Why do you condemn smooth Greek, and the whole
    of Hellas,
    The language in which the covenants of the slaughtered
    God were written?
Of course you sing and make a great noise in Hebrew,
    and Hebrew alone: 5
    This is the only language that suits your nose.

17. *On Bishops.*

Those whom Christ held dear as his Apostles,
Who testified to him and to whom he entrusted
    his flock –
So that when death was looming, greedy
    fingernails at the ready,
To seal up the rivers of golden doctrine,

Hos nunc barbaries impia vellicat
Indulgens proprijs ambitionibus,
Et, quos ipsa nequit scandere vertices,
10   Hos ad se trahere et mergere gestiens.
O caecum populum! si bona res siet
Praesul, cur renuis? sin mala, pauculos
Quàm cunctos fieri praestat Episcopos.

XVIII. Ad Melvinum: De ijsdem.

Praesulibus dirum te Musa coarguit hostem,
    An quia Textores Artificésque probas?

XIX. De Textore Catharo.

Cvm piscatores Textor legit esse vocatos,
    Vt sanctum Domini persequerentur opus;
Ille quoque inuadit Diuinam Flaminis artem,
    Subtegmen reti dignius esse putans,
5   Et nunc perlongas Scripturae stamine telas
    Torquet, & in Textu Doctor vtroque cluet.

XX. De Magicis rotatibus.

Qvos tu rotatus, quale murmur auscultas
In ritibus nostris? Ego audio nullum.
Agè, prouocemus vsque ad Angelos ipsos,
Aurésque superas: arbitri ipsi sint litis,

Gentle Bishops might receive the Torch,   5
And preserve with their keys the holy order.
Now impious barbarism plucks at them,
Revelling in its own ambitions;
Unable to scale the heights itself,
It yearns instead to drag them down and drown them.   10
O blind people! If a Bishop is
A good thing, why deny it? If an evil one, better
To make only a few than to give all that office.

18. *To Melville: On the Same.*

Has the Muse made it clear that you are a dread
    enemy of bishops,
  Or is it rather that you endorse weavers and
    craftsmen?

19. *On the Puritan Weaver.*

When the Weaver reads that fishermen were called
  To pursue the holy work of the Lord;
Then he takes upon himself the divine skill of the
    Priest,
  Thinking his warp and woof better than a net,
And now upon the warp of Scripture he weaves   5
  His endless threads, and is hailed as learned in
    both those Texts.

20. *On Magical Whirling.*

What whirling, what kind of murmuring do you hear
In our rites? I hear none.
Come now, let us call upon the Angels themselves,
And the ears of heaven: let them be the judges of our quarrel –

5   Vtrum tenore sacra nostra sint nécne
     Aequabili facta. Ecquid ergo te tanta
     Calumniandi concitauit vrtica,
     Vt, quae Papicolis propria, assuas nobis,
     Falsúmque potiùs quàm crepes [verum] versu?
10   Tu perstrepis tamen; v́tque turgeat carmen
     Tuum tibi, poeta belle, non mystes,
     Magicos rotatus, & perhorridas Striges,
     Dicterijs mordacibus notans, clamas
     Non conuenire precibus ista Diuinis.
15   O saeuus hostis! quàm ferociter pugnas!
     Nihílne respondebimus tibi? Fatemur.

XXI. Ad fratres.

O sec'lum lepidum! circumstant vndique fratres,
    Papicolísque sui sunt, Catharísque sui.
Sic nunc plena boni sunt omnia fratris, amore
    Cùm nil fraterno rarius esse queat.

XXII. De labe maculísque.

Labeculas maculásque nobis obijcis:
Quid? hoccine est mirum? Viatores sumus.
Quò sanguis est Christi, nisi vt maculas lauet,
Quas spargit animae corporis propius lutum?
5   Vos ergo puri! o nomen appositissimum
Quo vulgus ornat vos! At audias parum;
Astronomus olim (vt fama) dum maculas diu,
Quas Luna habet, tuetur, in foueam cadit,
Totúsque caenum Cynthiae ignoscit notis.
10   Ecclesia est mihi Luna; perge in Fabulâ.

Whether our sacred rites have been performed   5
In an even tenor, or not. Have you been stung
By such a nettle of slander
That you ascribe to us what belongs to the Papists,
And rattle on in your verse about what is false rather than
    what is true?
You are really making a racket; and to swell your song   10
Sweet poet (no priest) you make mordant remarks about
Magical whirling and dreadful screech-owls, and shout
That such things do not belong alongside holy prayers.
O savage enemy! How fiercely you fight!
Shall we say nothing in response to you? We admit
    that we shan't.   15

21. *To the Brothers.*

What a delightful age! All around the Brothers stand,
    The Papists and the Puritans both have brothers of
        their own.
So now everything is filled with good brothers,
    although all the same
    Nothing is harder to find than brotherly love.

22. *On Spots and Stains.*

You reproach us for small spots and stains.
But why? Are they so surprising? We are wayfarers.
What is the blood of Christ for, if not to wash off the spots
Which the body's clay spatters too closely upon the soul?
So you are pure! O how appropriate is the name   5
Bestowed upon you by the people! But listen a little;
Once (so they say) an astronomer, as he was observing
At some length the spots on the moon, fell into a ditch,
And immersed in his new knowledge of stains, completely
        forgot the blots upon Cynthia.
For me the Church is like the Moon: take the story from there. 10

XXIII. *De Musicâ Sacrâ.*

Cvr efficaci, Deucalion, manu,
Post restitutos fluctibus obices,
   Mutas in humanam figuram
      Saxa superuacuásque cautes?

5   Quin redde formas, o bone, pristinas,
Et nos reducas ad lapides auos:
   Nam saxa mirantur canentes,
      Saxa lyras citharásque callent.

Rupes tenaces & silices ferunt
10   Potentiori carmine percitas
   Saltus per incultos lacúsque
      Orphea mellifluum secutas.

Et saxa diris hispida montibus
Amphionis testudine nobili
15   Percussa dum currunt ad vrbem
      Moenia contribuêre Thebis.

Tantùm repertum est trux hominum genus,
Qui templa sacris expoliant choris,
   Non erubescentes vel ipsas
20   Duritiâ superare cautes.

O plena centum Musica Gratijs,
Praeclariorum spirituum cibus,
   Quò me vocas tandem, tuúmque
      Vt celebrem decus insusurras?

25   Tu Diua miro pollice spiritum
Caeno profani corporis exuens
   Ter millies coelo reponis:
      Astra rogant, Nouus hic quis hospes?

23. *On Sacred Music.*

Why, Deucalion, did you use your hand's power,
After you had barred the waves once more,
    To transform into human shape
      Rocks and useless crags?

Instead, good man, restore the ancient forms   5
And return us to our ancestral stones:
    For stones admire those who sing,
      Stones understand the lyre and the cithara.

They say that stubborn cliffs and flints
Were roused by a song more powerful than they,   10
    And through the wild groves and lakes
      They followed mellifluous Orpheus.

And jagged rocks on terrible mountains
Were shaken by the noble tortoise-shell
    Of Amphion, and ran tumbling down to the city   15
      Where they formed walls for Thebes.

Only the human race is so savage
As to adorn their temples with sacred choirs,
    But show no shame in outdoing
      The very rocks in their hardness.   20

O Music, filled with a hundred Graces,
The food of more glorious spirits,
    To where do you call me at last, and whisper
      That I should celebrate your beauty?

You, Goddess, releasing with your wonderful thumb   25
The spirit from the unholy filth of the body,
    Return it to the sky three thousand times over:
      And the stars ask: 'Who is this new guest?'

Ardore Moses concitus entheo,
30 Mersis reuertens laetus ab hostibus
    Exuscitat plebem sacratos
        Ad Dominum properare cantus.

Quid hocce? Psalmos audión'? o dapes!
O succulenti balsama spiritûs!
35   Ramenta coeli, guttulaéque
        Deciduae melioris orbis!

Quos David, ipsae deliciae Dei,
Ingens piorum gloria Principum,
    Sionis excelsas ad arces
40   Cum citharis lituísque miscet.

Miratur aequor finitimum sonos,
Et ipse Iordan sistit aquas stupens;
    Prae quo Tibris vultum recondit,
        Eridanúsque pudore fusus.

45 Tún' obdis aures, grex noue, barbaras,
Et nullus audis? cantibus obstrepens,
    Vt, quò fatiges verberésque
        Pulpita, plus spatij lucreris?

At cui videri prodigium potest
50 Mentes, quietis tympana publicae,
    Discordijs plenas sonoris
        Harmoniam tolerare nullam?

XXIV. De eâdem.

Cantus sacros, profane, mugitus vocas?
    Mugire multò mauelim quàm rudere.

Moses, in the grip of divine inspiration,
Returning joyously from the drowning of the enemy   30
    Roused the people to quicken
      A holy song to the Lord.

What is this? Don't I hear Psalms? O banquets!
O balm for the vigorous spirit!
    Flakes of heaven, and the falling   35
      Droplets of a better world!

The Psalms which David, God's darling,
The great glory of holy Kings,
    In the lofty citadels of Sion,
      Mingles with the cithara and the trumpet.   40

The nearby sea marvels at the sound,
And Jordan itself halts its waters in amazement;
    Before it the Tiber hides its face,
      And so does the Po, suffused with shame.

Do you block your crude ears, new flock,   45
And fail to hear? Clamouring against the songs
    To make more space
      For wearing out your pulpits?

But who can find it surprising
That minds which are drums disturbing the public peace,   50
    Filled with resounding discord,
      Should tolerate no harmony?

24. *On the Same.*

    So, blasphemous man, you call sacred songs
      lowing, do you?
     I would rather low than bray.

XXV. *De rituum vsu.*

Cvm primùm ratibus suis
nostram Caesar ad insulam
olim appelleret, intuens
omnes indigenas loci
5   viuentes sine vestibus,
O victoria, clamitat,
certa, ac perfacilis mihi!
   Non alio Cathari modo
dum sponsam Domini pijs
10 orbam ritibus expetunt,
atque ad barbariem patrum
vellent omnia regredi,
illam tegminis insciam
prorsus Daemoni & hostibus
15 exponunt superabilem.
   Atqui vos secus, o boni,
sentire ac sapere addecet,
si vestros animos regant
Scripturae canones sacrae:
20 Namque haec, iure, cuipiam
vestem non adimi suam,
sed nudis & egentibus
non suam tribui iubet.

XXVI. *De annulo coniugali.*

Sed nec coniugij signum, Melvine, probabis?
   Nec vel tantillum pignus habebit amor?
Nulla tibi si signa placent, è nubibus arcum
   Eripe coelesti qui moderatur aquae.
5   Illa quidem à nostro non multùm abludit imago,
   Annulus & plenus tempore forsan erit.

25. *On the Use of Rites.*

When Caesar first
Set foot from his ships
Upon our island,
Seeing all the natives of the place
Living without clothes: 5
'O victory', he cried,
'Is assured me, and an easy one at that!'

In the same way the Puritans
While they long for a bride for the Lord
Naked of pious rituals,   10
And wish for everything to be stripped back
To the barbarity of their ancestors,
They lay her out, all ignorant of clothing,
An easy conquest for the Devil and her enemies.

But for you, good men,   15
It's proper to feel differently, and be wise,
If the canons of sacred Scripture
Govern your hearts:
For scripture does not demand that a man
Be stripped of his own clothing,   20
But only that he offer what is not his
To those who are poor and naked.

26. *On the Wedding Ring.*

Won't you endorse even the sign of marriage, Melville?
   Shall love not have even so small a token as this?
If you disapprove of all signs, tear the rainbow
   From the clouds, since it marks the constraint of
      heaven's water.
For that image is not so far different from ours,   5
   And in time, perhaps, it will form a complete ring.

Sin nebulis parcas, & nostro parcito signo,
    Cui non absimilis sensus inesse solet.
Scilicet, vt quos ante suas cum coniuge tedas
10   Merserat in lustris perniciosa venus,
Annulus hos reuocet, sistátque libidinis vndas
    Legitimi signum connubiale tori.

XXVII. De Mundis & mundanis.

Ex praelio vndae ignísque (si Physicis fides)
    Tranquillus aer nascitur:
Sic ex profano Cosmico & Catharo potest
    Christianus extundi bonus.

XXVIII. De oratione Dominicâ.

Qvam Christus immortalis innocuo gregi
    voce suâ dederat,
        quis crederet mortalibus
orationem reijci septemplicem,
5   quae miseris clypeo
        Aiacis est praestantior?
Haec verba superos aduolaturus thronos
    Christus, vt auxilij
        nos haud inanes linqueret,
10 (cùm dignius nil posset aut melius dare)
    pignora chara sui
        fruenda nobis tradidit.
Quis sic amicum excipiet, vt Cathari Deum,
    qui renouare sacri

But if you spare the clouds, then spare our sign too,
   In which there is often a similar meaning:
Namely, that those whom, before their marriage,
   Dread lust had drowned in its muddy depths,   10
The ring retrieves, and the marriage bond
   Of a legitimate union stills the waters of desire.

27. *On the Pure and the Worldly.*

From the battle of water and of fire (if we trust the
    doctors)
   Is born the tranquil air:
So from an irreligious worldly man and the Puritan
   A good Christian can be hammered out.

28. *On the Lord's Prayer.*

As for the prayer which immortal Christ gave to his
    innocent flock
   With his own voice –
      Who would have thought that this
Sevenfold prayer would be rejected by mortal men?
   A prayer which is a more powerful help   5
      For the wretched even than the shield of Ajax?
On the verge of flight to his throne in heaven
   Christ handed to us these words,
      In order not to leave us empty of all assistance
(Since nothing could be a better or more worthy gift)   10
   Words for us to enjoy
      As dear pledges of himself.
Who will welcome a friend in the way that the Puritans
    welcome their God?
   These men who dare to retouch

audent amoris Symbolum?
        Tu verò quisquis es, caue ne, dum neges,
          improbe, verba Dei,
          te deneget VERBVM Deus.

XXIX. *In Catharum quendam.*

Cvm templis effare, madent sudaria, mappae,
    Trux caper alarum, suppara, laena, sagum.
Quin populo, clemens, aliquid largire caloris:
    Nunc sudas solus; caetera turba riget.

XXX. *De lupâ lustri*
Vaticani.

Calumniarum nec pudor quis nec modus?
Nec *Vaticanae* desines vnquam *Lupae*
Metus inanes? Nos pari praeteruehi
Illam Charybdim cautione nouimus
5   Vestrámque Scyllam, aequis parati spiculis
Britannicam in Vulpem, ínque Romanam Lupam.
Dicti fidem firmabimus Anagrammate.

The very Symbol of divine love?   15
You, whoever you are, beware, in case, while you deny
   (Wicked man!) the words of God
      God denies you his WORD.

29. *On a Certain Puritan.*

When you preach in the temples, handkerchiefs are
      soaked, as are napkins,
   The savage armpit goat, shirts, cloaks, even a
      woollen overcoat.
Why don't you, kind man, lavish some of your
      heat upon the people:
   Now you are sweating alone; the rest of the mob
      has the chills.

30. *On the She-Wolf of the Vatican Brothel.*

Is there no shame in slander, and no limit to it?
Will you never set aside your vain fears
Of the *Vatican She-Wolf*? We have learnt to steer
      with equal care
Around that Charybdis, and your Scylla, armed
      with stakes against both:
The British Fox, and the Roman Wolf.   5
I shall demonstrate the truth of this with an
      Anagram.

XXXI. *De impositione manuum.*

Nec dextra te fugit, almi Amoris emblema?
Atqui manus imponere integras praestat,
Quàm (more vestro) imponere inscio vulgo.
Quantò Impositio melior est Imposturâ!

XXXII. *Supplicum Ministrorum raptus.*

κωμῳδούμενος

Ambitio Cathari quinque constat Actibus.
I.   Primò, vnus aut alter parum ritus placet:
      Iam repit impietas volatura illico.
II.   Mox displicent omnes. Vbi hoc permanserit
5 III.   Paulò, secretis mussitans in angulis
      Quaerit recessus. Incalescit fabula:
IV.   Erumpit inde, & contineri nescius
V.   Syluas pererrat. Fibulis dein omnibus
      Prae spiritu ruptis, quò eas resarciat
10   Amstellodamum corripit se. *Plaudite.*

XXXIII. *De Autorum*
enumeratione.

Qvò magìs inuidiam nobis & crimina confles,
   Pertrahis in partes nomina magna tuas;
Martyra, Calvinum, Bezam, doctúmque *Bucerum,*
   Qui tamen in nostros fortiter ire negant.

31. *On the Laying on of Hands.*

Does the right hand, an emblem of healing love, not flee
    from you?
The laying on of pure hands is more effective,
Than (as is your custom) to trick the ignorant crowd.
How much better is imposition than imposture!

32. *The Frenzy of the*
Petitioning Ministers
in the Comic Mode.

    The ambition of the Puritan consists of five Acts:
I.   First, one rite or another dissatisfies him.
    Next sacrilege crawls on: it'll take flight at any
       moment now.
II. Soon all rituals displease him. When this has lasted
III. For a little while, muttering in private corners   5
    He looks for a way out. The play hots up:
IV. Then he breaks out, and being beyond control
V. Roams the woods. Then once all the clasps
    Around the soul are broken, he dashes off
    To Amsterdam to sew them back on again. *Applause!* 10

33. *On the Enumeration*
of Authors.

That you may better rouse envy and accusations against us,
    You drag in great names on your side;
Martyr, *Calvin*, *Beza*, and learned *Bucer*,
    Men who nevertheless refuse to march against us.

5   *Whitaker,* erranti quem praefers carmine, miles
           Assiduus nostri papilionis erat.
       Nos quoque possemus longas conscribere turmas,
           Si numero starent praelia, non animis.
       Primus adest nobis, Pharisaeis omnibus hostis,
10   Christus Apostolici cinctus amore gregis.
       Tu geminas belli portas, o *Petre,* repandis,
           Dum gladium stringens *Paulus* ad arma vocat.
       Inde Patres pergunt quadrati, & tota Vetustas.
           Nempe Nouatores quis Veteranus amat?
15   Iam *Constantinus* multo se milite miscet;
           Inuisámque tuis erigit hasta Crucem.
       Hipponensis adest properans, & torquet in hostes
           Lampada, quâ studijs inuigilare solet.
       Téque Deum alternis cantans *Ambrosius* iram,
20   Immemor antiqui mellis, eundo coquit.
       Haec etiam ad pugnam praesens, quâ viuimus, aetas
           Innumeram nostris partibus addit opem.
       Quos inter plenúsque Deo genióque Iacobus
           Defendit veram mente manúque *fidem.*
25   Interea ad sacrum stimulat sacra Musica bellum,
           Quâ sine vos miseri lentiùs itis ope.
       Militat & nobis, quem vos contemnitis, Ordo;
           Ordine discerni maxima bella solent.
       O vos inualidos! Audi quem talibus armis
30   Euentum Naso vidit et admonuit;
       Vna dies Catharos ad bellum miserat omnes:
           Ad bellum missos perdidit vna dies.

Whitaker, whom you endorse in misguided song, was a
    devoted   5
  Soldier of our pavilion.
We too could make out a long list of squadrons
  If battles depended upon numbers, not on hearts.
The first on our side, an enemy to every Pharisee,
  Christ himself, girt with the love of the Apostolic flock.   10
Then you, O *Peter*, spread open the twin gates of war,
  While *Paul* unsheathes his sword and makes the call to arms.
Then proceed the Fathers drawn up in order, and the whole
    Early Church.
  What Veteran, indeed, loves fresh new recruits?
Now *Constantine* with his great soldiery joins forces;   15
  His spear raises aloft the Cross so hated by your men.
The man from Hippo comes hurrying to join us, and hurls
  Against the enemy the lamp which lights his long studies.
And *Ambrose* comes singing the *Te Deum* in antiphon,
  Forgetful of classical sweetness, brewing his anger as he goes. 20
This present age, in which we live,
  Adds too a countless host to our side.
Among them James, filled with God and with inspiration,
  He guards the true *faith* with hand and mind.
Meanwhile sacred Music rouses us to sacred battle –   25
  Without her help you wretched people proceed more
    slowly.
The Apostolic Succession you despise also fights for us;
  The greatest of battles are generally determined by their
    ordered procession.
O you feeble men! Hear the outcome of such array
  Which Ovid saw and warned of: 30
One day sent all the Puritans to war:
  Once sent to war, one day destroyed them all.

XXXIV. *De auri sacrâ fame.*

Claudis auaritiâ Satyram; statuísque sacrorum
    Esse recidendas, Aeace noster, opes.
Caetera condonabo tibi, scombrísque remittam:
    Sacrilegum carmen, censeo, flamma voret.

XXXV. *Ad Scotiam. Protrepticon ad Pacem.*

Scotia quae frigente iaces porrecta sub Arcto,
    Cur adeò immodicâ relligione cales?
Anne tuas flammas ipsa Antiperistasis auget,
    Vt niue torpentes incaluêre manus?
5 Aut vt pruna gelu summo mordaciùs vrit,
    Sic acuunt zelum frigora tanta tuum?
Quin nocuas extingue faces, precor: vnda propinqua est,
    Et tibi vicinas porrigit aequor aquas:
Aut potiùs Christi sanguis demissus ab alto,
10 Vicinúsque magìs nobiliórque fluit:
Ne, si flamma nouis adolescat mota flabellis,
    Ante diem vestro mundus ab igne ruat.

XXXVI. *Ad seductos*
innocentes.

Innocuae mentes, quibus inter flumina mundi
    Ducitur illimi candida vita fide,
Absit vt ingenuum pungant mea verba pudorem;
    Perstringunt vestros carmina sola duces.
5 O vtinam aut illorum oculi (quod comprecor vnum)
    Vobis, aut illis pectora vestra forent.

34. *On the Holy Greed for Gold*

You round off your Satire with greed; and you decide,
    Our Aeacus, that the sacred rites must be shorn of
      all wealth.
I shall return all your writings to you, release them to mackerel:
    Flame should devour, I think, your sacrilegious song.

35. *To Scotland. An Exhortation to Peace*

Scotland, which lies stretched out beneath the Arctic chill,
    Why do you blaze so hotly with radical religion?
Does the Antiperistasis itself augment your flames,
    When hands, once numbed by snow, grow warm?
Or, as a live coal burns more keenly in the deepest ice,   5
    Does such cold sharpen your zeal?
I beg you, put out the deadly torches: the water is near,
    And its surface extends your neighbouring waters:
Or rather, Christ's blood sent down from on high,
    Flows more closely and is a nobler thing: 10
Beware, lest the flame of your torches be fanned by fresh blasts,
    And the world consumed in fire before the appointed day.

36. *To the Innocent Who Have been Led Astray*

Innocent minds, whose pure life is led
    Among the waters of the world with a clear, shining faith,
Far be it that my words should wound your natural chastity;
    These songs censure your leaders alone.
My only plea is this: would that you had   5
    Their eyes, and they your hearts.

XXXVII. Ad Melvinum.

Atqui te precor vnicè per ipsam,
Quae scripsit numeros, manum; per omnes
Musarum calices, per & beatos
Sarcasmos quibus artifex triumphas;
Quin per Presbyteros tuos; per vrbem
Quam curto nequeo referre versu;
Per charas tibi nobilésque dextras,
Quas subscriptio neutiquam inquinauit;
Per quicquid tibi suauiter probatur;
Ne me carminibus nimis dicacem,
Aut saeuum reputes. Amica nostra est
Atque edentula Musa, nec veneno
Splenis perlita contumeliosi.
　　Nam si te cuperem secare versu,
Totámque euomerem potenter iram
Quam aut Ecclesia despicata vobis,
Aut laesae mihi suggerunt Athenae,
(Et quem non stimularet haec simultas?)
Iam te funditus igneis Camoenis,
Et Musâ crepitante subruissem:
Omnis linea sepiam recusans
Plumbo ducta fuisset aestuanti,
Centum stigmatibus tuos inurens
Profanos fremitus bonásque sannas:
Plùs charta haec mea delibuta dictis
Haesisset tibi, quàm suprema vestis
Olim accreuerit *Herculi* furenti:
Quin hoc carmine Lexicon probrorum
Extruxissem, vbi, cùm moneret vsus,
Haurirent tibi tota plaustra Musae.
　　Nunc haec omnia sustuli, tonantes
Affectus socijs tuis remittens.
Non te carmine turbidum vocaui,
Non deridiculúmue, siue ineptum,
Non striges, magiámue, vel rotatus,

37. To Melville.

But I beseech you especially by that very hand,
Which wrote the poems; by all
The cups of the Muses, and by the blessed
Wit by which you triumph as an artist;
Even by your Presbyters; by the city   5
Which I can't survey in a brief verse;
By the noble right hands you hold dear,
Which no signature debased;
By whatever you condone with sweetness;
So that you should not think me too glib   10
Or cruel in my verse: my Muse is friendly
And toothless, not smeared all over with
The poison of an abusive spleen.
    For if I wished to cut you with my verse,
And to vomit forcefully all the anger   15
That has been stored up in me by the disdain your friends
Showed for the Church, and by their abuse of Athens
(And who would not be roused by this quarrel?)
I would by now have thoroughly destroyed you
With fiery Latin Muses, or the crackling Greek one: 20
Every single line, refusing ink,
Would have been drawn in seething lead,
Branding with a hundred scars
Your ungodly groans and your fine grimaces:
This paper of mine, smeared all over with words,   25
Would have stuck to you more than his last cloak
Once clung to raging *Hercules*:
Indeed by this song I could have built
A whole Lexicon of insults from which, when necessary,
The Muses could drain off whole barrels for you.   30
    But I have held off from all these things,
Leaving thundering bombast for your friends.
I have not used a poem to call you mad,
Nor ridiculous, nor silly,

Non fastus tibi turgidos repono;
Errores, maculas, superbiámque,
Labes, somniáque, ambitúsque diros,
Tinnitus *Berecynthios* omittens
40   Nil horum regero tibi merenti.
        Quin te laudibus orno: quippe dico,
Caesar sobrius ad rei Latinae
Vnus dicitur aduenire cladem:
Et tu solus ad *Angliae* procellas
45   (Cùm plerumque tuâ sodalitate
Nil sit crassius, impolitiúsue)
Accedis bene doctus, et poeta.

XXXVIII. *Ad Eundem.*

Incipis irridens; stomachans in carmine pergis;
    Desinis exclamans: tota figura, vale.

XXXIX. *Ad Seren. Regem.*

Ecce pererratas, Regum doctissime, nugas,
Quas gens inconsulta, suis vexata procellis,
Libandas nobis absorbendásque propinat!
O caecos animi fratres! quis vestra fatigat
5   Corda furor, spissâque afflat caligine sensus?
Cernite, quàm formosa suas Ecclesia pennas
Explicat, & radijs ipsum pertingit Olympum!
Vicini populi passim mirantur, & aequos
Mentibus attonitis cupiunt addiscere ritus:
10   Angelicae turmae nostris se coetibus addunt:
Ipse etiam Christus coelo speculatus ab alto,
Intuitúque vno stringens habitacula mundi,
Sola mihi plenos, ait, exhibet *Anglia* cultus.

Nor do I pay you back with screech owls, or sorcery,
   or whirling wheels,   35
Nor puffed up pretension;
As for errors, stains and pride,
Sins, and dreams and dreadful ostentation,
I cast none of these back on you
– Aside from *Berecynthian* tinkling of cymbals –   40
Although you deserve it.
   Instead I adorn you with praise: for I say
Caesar is known as the only sober man
To approach the ruin of the Latin state;
And although, in general, nothing is more crass and inelegant 45
Than your sect, nevertheless you on your own incite
English storms, learned man that you are, and a poet.

38. *To the Same.*

You begin with a jeer; in your anger you carry on in poetry;
   You end by shouting: farewell, all of it.

39. *To His Most Serene Majesty.*

Behold, most learned of Kings, the wrong-headed trifles
Which a thoughtless people, troubled by their own petty strife,
Offer us to taste and to drink down!
O brothers, blind in spirit! What insanity
Wears down your hearts, and blasts your senses with a
     swirling fog?   5
Look, see how the lovely Church spreads out its wings
And touches even Olympus with her rays!
Everywhere the neighbouring peoples stand in awe, and
With marvelling minds long to learn the same rituals:
Angelic hosts join our forces: 10
Christ himself watches from the height of heaven,
Sweeping the little dwellings of the world with a single glance,

Scilicet has olim diuisas aequore terras
15   Seposuit Diuina sibi, cùm conderet orbem,
        Progenies, gemmámque suâ quasi pyxide clausit.
            O qui *Defensor Fidei* meritissimus audis,
        Responde aeternùm titulo; quóque ordine felix
        Coepisti, pergas simili res texere filo.
20   Obrue feruentes, ruptis conatibus, hostes:
        Quásque habet aut patulas, aut caeco tramite, moles
        Haeresis, euertas. Quid enim te fallere possit?
        Tu venas laticésque omnes, quos sacra recludit
        Pagina, gustâsti, multóque interprete gaudes:
25   Tu Synodósque, Patrésque, & quod dedit alta vetustas
        Haud per te moritura, Scholámque introspicis omnem.
        Nec transire licet quo mentis acumine findis
        Viscera naturae, commistúsque omnibus astris
        Ante tuum tempus coelum gratissimus ambis.
30   Hâc ope munitus securior excipis vndas,
        Quas Latij Catharíque mouent, atque inter vtrasque
        Pastor agis proprios, medio tutissimus, agnos.
            Perge, decus Regum; sic, Augustissime, plures
        Sint tibi vel stellis laudes, & laudibus anni:
35   Sic pulsare tuas, exclusis luctibus, ausint
        Gaudia sola fores: sic quicquid somnia mentis
        Intus agunt, habeat certum meditatio finem:
        Sic positis nugis, quibus irretita libido
        Innumeros mergit vitiatâ mente poetas,
40   Sola *Iacobaeum* decantent carmina nomen.

And says: '*England* alone offers me worship in its fullest form.'
Of course the Divine Offspring, when he shaped the world
Set these lands, divided by the sea, apart,   15
And shut them like a jewel in a box.
  O you who most deservedly hear yourself called *Defender
    of the Faith*,
Always answer to your title; and in the same propitious
Way in which you have begun, continue to weave matters
    with the same thread.
Overcome the furious foe, his attempts disrupted,   20
May you overturn whatever projects heresy
Is fostering, either openly or in a dark and secret path. For
    what can deceive you?
You have tasted all the veins and liquids which sacred scripture
Reveals, and you rejoice in many commentators:
You consider the Synods, the Fathers, and all that far-off
    antiquity –   25
No longer soon to die, because of you – offers, and the entire
    School.
Nor could we overlook the sharpness of mind with which
    you prise open
The inner workings of nature; and, mingled with all the stars,
You approach heaven before your time, most welcome there.
Confident in these gifts, you calmly face the waves   30
Which Roman Catholics and Puritans stir up, and between
    them both
As a shepherd, safest in the middle path, you drive your lambs.
  Keep on, glory of Kings; so, your Excellence, may your
    praises
Outnumber the stars, and your years outnumber your praises:
With grief driven out, joys alone will dare   35
To beat upon your doors: thus whatever one's private dreams
May be, let meditation have a fixed aim and end:
All trifles set aside – for passion entangled in such trifles
Has drowned innumerable poets in madness –
May songs sing out alone the name of *James*.   40

XL. *Ad Deum.*

Qvem tu, summe Deus, semel
Scribentem placido rore beaueris,
    Illum non labor irritus
Exercet miserum; non dolor vnguium
    Morsus increpat anxios;
Non maeret calamus; non queritur caput:
    Sed faecunda poëseως
Vis, & vena sacris regnat in artubus;
    Qualis nescius aggerum
Exundat fluuio Nilus amabili.
    O dulcissime Spiritus,
Sanctos qui gemitus mentibus inseris
    A Te Turture defluos,
Quòd scribo, & placeo, si placeo, tuum est.

FINIS

40. *To God.*

He whom you, great God, have once
Blessed with gentle dew as he writes,
  No pointless toil makes him
A wretched man; no painful fingers
  Reproach him for his anxious biting;   5
No pen droops; no head complains:
  But the eloquent force and vein
Of *poesy* reigns in the sacred limbs;
  As the Nile, thinking nothing of its banks,
Spills over in its tender flood.   10
  O sweetest Spirit,
You who sow the seeds of holy groans in
    men's mind,
  Groans that pour down from you, the
    Turtle-Dove –
What I write, and the pleasure I give, if I do
    so, is all yours.

FINIS

Lucus

I. Homo, Statua.

Svm, quis nescit, Imago Dei, sed saxea certè:
  Hanc mihi duritiem contulit improbitas.
Durescunt proprijs euulsa corallia fundis,
  Haud secus ingenitis dotibus orbus Adam.
5 Tu, qui cuncta creans docuisti marmora flere,
  Haud mihi cor saxo durius esse sinas.

II. Patria.

Vt tenuis flammae species caelum vsque minatur,
  Igniculos legans, manserit ipsa licet;
Sic mucronatam reddunt suspiria mentem,
  Votáque scintillae sunt animosa meae.
5 Assiduo stimulo carnem Mens vlta lacessit,
  Sedula si fuerit, perterebrare potest.

III. In Stephanum lapidatum.

Qvi silicem tundit, (mirum tamen) elicit ignem:
  At Caelum è saxis elicuit Stephanus.

The Sacred Grove

1. *Man, a Statue.*

I am – in case you didn't realize – the Image of God;
    but one made of stone, that's for sure:
    It was sin that brought this hardness upon me.
Coral flowers torn from their proper bases grow hard;
    So too Adam, once deprived of his natural inheritance.
You who, creating all things, taught marble to weep,   5
    Do not allow my heart to be harder than stone.

2. *Homeland.*

As the slender shape of a flame reaches up to heaven,
   Sending off little fires, although it remains behind;
So sighs sharpen my mind to a point,
   And heartfelt prayers are my sparks.
The avenging Mind goads and harries the flesh with
     constant assault: 5
   If it is truly persistent, it can bore its way right through.

3. *On Stephen, Stoned.*

He who pounds flint (how remarkable!) brings forth fire:
   But Stephen brought forth Heaven from rocks.

IV. In Simonem Magum.

Ecquid emes Christum? pro nobis scilicet olim
    Venditus est Agnus, non tamen emptus erit.
Quin nos Ipse emit, precioso faenora soluens
    Sanguine: nec precium merx emit vlla suum.
5   Ecquid emes Caelum? quin stellam rectiùs vnam
    Quo precio venit, fac, liceare priùs.
Nempe graui fertur scelerata pecunia motu,
    Si sursum iacias, in caput ipsa ruit.
Vnicus est nummus, caelo Christóque petitus,
10 Nempe in quo clarè lucet Imago Dei.

V. In S. Scripturas.

Heu, quis spiritus, igneúsque turbo
Regnat visceribus, meásque versat
Imo pectore cogitationes?
Nunquid pro foribus sedendo nuper
5   Stellam vespere suxerim volantem,
Haec autem hospitio latere turpi
Prorsùs nescia, cogitat recessum?
Nunquid mel comedens, apem comedi
Ipsâ cum dominâ domum vorando?
10 Imò, me nec apes, nec astra pungunt:
Sacratissima Charta, tu fuisti
Quae cordis latebras sinúsque caecos
Atque omnes peragrata es angiportus
Et flexus fugientis appetitûs.
15 Ah, quàm docta perambulare calles
Maeandrósque plicásque, quàm perita es!
Quae vis condidit, ipsa nouit aedes.

4. *On Simon Magus.*

And so will you buy Christ? Of course it's true that once
   The Lamb was sold for us, but all the same he
     won't be bought.
Rather, He bought us, clearing our debts with his precious
   Blood: no goods have ever bought their own price.
And so will you buy Heaven? No, better you bid for
     a single star   5
   At the price at which it comes, do that first.
Surely ill-gotten gains are slow and heavy to carry:
   If you cast them up, they fall back upon your head.
There is only one coin that is sought by heaven and by Christ,
   Namely the one in which the Image of God clearly shines. 10

5. *On Sacred Scripture.*

  Alas, what spirit, what fiery whirlwind
  Rules in my insides, and stirs my
  Thoughts deep in my breast?
  Could it be that recently as I was sitting by the door
  In the evening I sucked in a falling star;   5
  And this star, unsuited to lurking concealed
  In a disreputable lodging, is trying to find a way out?
  Have I eaten the bee, while eating the honey –
  Consuming its mistress along with the house?
  No – neither bee nor star has wounded me: 10
  Most holy scriptures, it's you who have,
  You who have travelled through the hiding places of
     the heart,
  Its blind alleys, all its narrow lanes
  And the byways of desire even as it flees.
  Oh, how skilled you are at making your way through   15
  These intricate meandering paths, how crafty!
  The power that built a dwelling knows it best.

VI. *In pacem Britannicam.*

Anglia cur solùm fuso sine sanguine sicca est,
    Cùm natet in tantis caetera terra malis?
Sit licet in pelago semper, sine fluctibus illa est,
    Cùm qui plus terrae, plus habuere maris.
5 Naufragij causa est alijs mare, roboris Anglo,
    Et quae corrumpit moenia, murus aqua est.
Nempe hìc Religio floret, regina quietis,
    Túque super nostras, Christe, moueris aquas.

VII. *Auaritia.*

Avrum nocte videns, vidisse insomnia dicit:
    Aurum luce videns, nulla videre putat.
O falsos homines! Vigilat, qui somniat aurum,
    Plúsque habet hic laetus, quàm vel Auarus habet.

VIII. *In Lotionem pedum Apostolorum.*

Solem ex Oceano Veteres exurgere fingunt
    Postquam se gelidis nocte refecit aquis:
Veriùs hoc olim factum est, vbi, Christe, lauares
    Illos, qui mundum circumiere, pedes.

6. *On the British Peace.*

Why is England alone dry, with no blood spilt,
    While the rest of the earth is swimming in wickedness?
Although always in the sea, she is a land without waves,
    While those who have more land, have more sea.
For others, the sea brings shipwreck, but for England
        strength,   5
    And that which topples walls, is her wall of water.
Surely Religion blossoms here, Queen of Peace,
    And you, Christ, move upon our waters.

7. *Avarice.*

Seeing gold by night, he says what he saw was a dream:
    Seeing gold by daylight, he thinks what he sees is no
        dream at all.
O deluded men! It's the man who dreams of gold who is
        awake;
    He has more, happy man that he is, than the greedy
        man ever possesses.

8. *On the Washing of the Apostles' Feet.*

The sun, the ancients believed, rises from the Ocean
    After he has refreshed himself at night in the icy waters:
This was made more true when, Christ, you bathed
    Those feet which went on round the world.

IX. *In D. Lucam.*

Cvr Deus elegit Medicum, qui numine plenus
　　Diuinâ Christi scriberet acta manu?
Vt discat sibi quisque, quid vtile: nempe nocebat
　　Crudum olim pomum, tristis Adame, tibi.

X. *Papae titulus*
Nec Deus Nec Homo.

Qvisnam Antichristus cessemus quaerere; Papa
　　Nec Deus est nec Homo: Christus vterque fuit.

XI. *Tributi solutio.*

Piscis tributum soluit; & tu Caesari:
　　Vtrumque mirum est: hoc tamen mirum magìs,
Quòd omnibus tute imperes, nemo tibi.

XII. *Tempestas Christo*
dormiente.

Cvm dormis, surgit pelagus: cùm, Christe, resurgis,
　　Dormitat pelagus: Quàm bene fraena tenes!

9. *On Luke the Doctor.*

Why did God choose a Doctor in order that he, filled
    with the spirit,
  Might write the deeds of Christ with his holy hand?
It was so each man might learn what helps for himself:
    of course
  That unripe apple of old, sad Adam, was harmful for you.

10. *The Title of the Pope*

We should cease asking 'who is the Antichrist?'; the Pope
  Is neither God nor Man: Christ was both.

11. *Payment of Tribute.*

The fish pays its tribute; as do you to Caesar:
Both are strange: but the second is stranger,
Since you govern all, but no-one governs you.

12. *The Storm while
Christ Sleeps.*

While you slumber, the storm rises: when, Christ, you
    wake again,
  Then the storm sleeps: How well you hold the reins!

XIII. Bonus Ciuis.

Sagax Humilitas, eligens viros bonos
Atque euehens, bonum facit faecundius,
Quàm si ipse solus omnia interuerteret,
Suámque in alijs possidet prudentiam.

XIV. In Vmbram Petri.

Produxit Vmbram corpus, Vmbra corpori
Vitam reduxit: ecce gratitudinem.

XV. Martha: Maria.

Christus adest: crebris aedes percurrite scopis,
    Excutite aulaea, & luceat igne focus.
Omnia purgentur, niteat mihi tota supellex,
    Parcite luminibus, sítque lucerna domus:
5   O cessatrices! eccum puluisculus illìc!
    Corde tuo forsan, caetera munda, SOROR.

XVI. Amor.

Qvid metuant homines infrà, supráue minentur
    Sydera, pendenti sedulus aure bibis:
Vtque ouis in dumis, haeres in crine Cometae,
    Sollicitus, ne te stella perita notet:
5   Omnia quaerendo, sed te, super omnia, vexas:
    Et quid tu tandem desidiosus? AMO.

13. *The Good Citizen.*

Shrewd Humility, who picks out the good men
And raises them up, creates that way a greater good
Than if one man alone purloined it all:
Her good sense is invested in that of others.

14. *On Peter's Shadow.*

The body brought forth a Shadow, the Shadow
    to the body
  Brought back life: an act of thanks.

15. *Martha: Mary.*

'Christ is here! Dash through the house with broom after broom,
  Shake out the curtains, light a fire in the hearth.
Everything must be cleaned, all my furniture must shine,
  Spare the torches – the house itself shall be a lamp:
You sluggards! Look – here's a speck of dust!'   5
  'In your heart, perhaps, SISTER: all the rest is clean.'

16. *Love.*

What men fear below, or what the stars threaten above,
  You drink in avidly with flapping ears:
Like a sheep among brambles, you are trapped in a
    comet's hair,
  Worried that a cunning star might notice you there:
By questioning everything, you make everything
    troublesome – especially yourself: 5
  But why so idle? I AM IN LOVE.

XVII. *In Superbum.*

Magnas es; esto. Bulla si vocaberis,
Largiar & istud: scilicet Magnatibus
Difficilis esse haud soleo: nam, pol, si forem,
Ipsi sibi sunt nequiter facillimi.
5   Quin, mitte nugas; téque carnem & sanguinem
Communem habere crede cum Cerdonibus:
Illum volo, qui calceat lixam tuum.

XVIII. *In eundem.*

Vnusquisque hominum Terra est & filius arui.
   Dic mihi, mons sterilis, vallis an vber eris?

XIX. *Afflictio.*

Qvos tu calcasti fluctus, me, Christe, lacessunt,
   Transiliúntque caput, qui subiere pedes.
Christe, super fluctus si non discurrere detur:
   Per fluctus saltem, fac, precor, ipse vadem.

XX. *In κενοδοξίαν.*

Qvi sugit auido spiritu rumusculos
Et flatulentas aucupatur glorias,
Foelicitatis culmen extra se locat,
Spargítque per tot capita, quot vulgus gerit.

17. *On a Proud Man.*

You're an important man: that's how it is. If you go
    by the name 'Bubble',
I'll flatter you and call you that. With important men
It's not my style to be awkward: and even if I were, there's
    no question –
They're still shamelessly easy on themselves.
But come on, forget this nonsense; your flesh and blood   5
Is shared – believe it! – with cobblers:
The man, I mean, who fits your servant's shoes.

18. *On the Same.*

Every man is Earth and the son of the field.
Tell me, what will you be – sterile mountain, or a fertile
    valley?

19. *Affliction.*

Those waves you trod upon, Christ, strike upon me
    And leap over my head, though they run beneath your feet.
Christ, if I lack the gift to run across the waves:
    Through them at least, I beg you, grant that I might pass.

20. *On Vainglory.*

He who sucks with a greedy spirit upon common gossip
And chases exaggerated empty glories,
Puts beyond his reach the peak of happiness,
And scatters it among a group as large as the common herd.

5   Tu verò collige te, tibíque insistito,
Breuiore nodo stringe vitae sarcinas,
Rotundus in te: namque si ansatus sies,
Te mille rixae, mille prensabunt doli,
Ducéntque, donec incidentem in cassidem
10   Te mille nasi, mille rideant sinus.
Quare, peritus nauta, vela contrahas,
Famámque nec difflaueris, nec suxeris:
Tuásque librans actiones, gloriam
Si ducat agmen, reprime; sin claudat, sinas.
15   Morosus, oxygala est: leuis, coagulum.

XXI. *In Gulosum.*

Dvm prono rapis ore cibos, & fercula verris,
    Intra extráque graui plenus es illuuie.
Non iam ventriculus, verùm spelunca vocetur
    Illa cauerna, in quâ tot coiere ferae.
5   Ipse fruare, licet, solus graueolente sepulcro;
    Te petet, ante diem quisquis obire cupit.

XXII. *In Improbum disertum.*

Sericus es dictis, factis pannusia Baucis:
    Os & lingua tibi diues, egena manus:
Ni facias, vt opes linguae per brachia serpant,
    Aurea pro naulo lingua Charontis erit.

Gather yourself together, work for it yourself,   5
And bind the load of life with a tighter knot,
Round and firm in yourself: for if you let yourself
    stick out, like a handle,
A thousand troubles, and thousand toils will fall upon you,
And drag you, stumbling into the trap, until
A thousand noses, a thousand breasts laugh heartily at you.   10
For that reason, skilled sailor that you are, draw in your sails,
Don't puff up your fame, don't suck it in:
Balance your actions, and if glory
Leads the column, rein it in; if it stumbles, loosen the rein.
The dull and fastidious man is curd: the fickle man,
    mere rennet.   15

21. *On the Glutton.*

While you lower your mouth to swoop upon food,
    and sweep in serving-dishes,
      Inside and out you are heavy with filth.
It's not called a little stomach now, but a cave,
      That cavern, thronging with wild beasts.
It's only you, of course, who can enjoy the heavy
    odour of the tomb;   5
Anyone who longs to die before his time – he'll
    seek you out.

22. *On the Wicked but Eloquent Man.*

There is silk in your words, but in your deeds the rags of Baucis:
    Your mouth and tongue – they're rich; your hand is poor:
Unless you can make your tongue's wealth creep down
    your arms,
    Your golden tongue will only be good for paying Charon.

XXIII. Consolatio.

Cvr lacrymas & tarda trahis suspiria, tanquam
  Nunc primùm socij mors foret atra tui?
Nos autem, à cunis, omnes sententia Mortis
  Quotidie iugulat, nec semel vllus obit.
5 Viuimus in praesens: hesternam viuere vitam
  Nemo potest: hodie vita sepulta prior.
Trecentos obijt Nestor, non transijt annos,
  Vel quia tot moritur, tot viguisse probes.
Dum lacrymas, it vita: tuus tibi clepsydra fletus,
10 Et numerat mortes singula gutta pares;
Frustra itaque in tot funeribus miraberis vnum,
  Sera nimis lacryma haec, si lacrymabis, erit.
Siste tuum fletum & gemitus: namque imbribus istis
  Ac zephyris, carnis flos remeare nequit.
15 Nec tu pro socio doleas, qui fugit ad illud
  Culmen, vbi pro te nemo dolere potest.

XXIV. In Angelos.

Intellectus adultus Angelorum
Haud nostro similis, cui necesse,
Vt dentur species, rogare sensum:
Et ni lumina ianuam resignent,
5 Et nostrae tribuant molae farinam,
Saepe ex se nihil otiosa cudit.
A nobis etenim procul remoti
Labuntur fluuij scientiarum:
Si non per species, nequimus ipsi,
10 Quid ipsi sumus, assequi putando.
Non tantum est iter Angelis ad vndas,

23. *Consolation.*

Why do you weep and draw long slow sighs, as if
   Your friend's dark death was a new thing?
From our very cradles, the sentence of Death
   Strangles us all every day, and nobody dies just once.
We live for the present moment: to live yesterday's life –   5
   That no one can do: that past life today is dead and buried.
It was three hundred years that Nestor died, not lived for,
   Or because he died so much, you could claim that he lived
      that often as well.
While you weep, life passes: your weeping is your water clock,
   And each drop counts a single death;   10
Amidst all those deaths it's pointless to be surprised at one,
   And those tears, if you weep them, will come too late.
Stop your tears and groans: even among those showers
   And gales, the flower of flesh cannot return.
And do not lament for a companion, who flees to that   15
   Peak, where no one can lament for you.

24. *On Angels.*

The perfect understanding of the Angels
Is not like ours, which must
Ask the senses to provide images:
And if eyes do not unseal the door,
And bring grist to our mill,   5
From itself the idle mind often grinds out nothing.
For they are set far off from us indeed,
The flowing streams of knowledge:
Without images, we could not
Work out what we are ourselves.   10
For the Angels it's not such a journey to those waters,

Nullo circuitu scienda pungunt,
Illis perpetuae patent fenestrae,
Se per se facili modo scientes,
15   Atque ipsi sibi sunt mola & farina.

$$XXV.\ Roma.\ Anagr. \begin{cases} Oram.\ Maro. \\ Ramo.\ Armo. \\ Mora.\ Amor. \end{cases}$$

ROMA, tuum nomen quam non pertransijt ORAM,
   Cùm Latium ferrent secula prisca iugum?
Non deerat vel fama tibi, vel carmina famae,
   Vnde MARO laudes duxit ad astra tuas.
5   At nunc exucco similis tua gloria RAMO
   A veteri trunco & nobilitate cadit.
Laus antiqua & honor perijt: quasi scilicet ARMO
   Te deiecissent tempora longa suo.
Quin tibi tam desperatae MORA nulla medetur,
10   Quâ Fabio quondam sub duce nata salus.
Hinc te olim gentes miratae odere vicissim;
   Et cum sublatâ laude recedit AMOR.

XXVI. Vrbani VIII Pont. Respons.

Cvm Romam nequeas, quod aues, euertere, nomen
   Inuertis, mores carpis & obloqueris:
Te Germana tamen pubes, te Graecus & Anglus
   Arguit, exceptos quos pia Roma fouet:
5   Hostibus haec etiam parcens imitatur Iesum.
   Inuertis nomen. Quid tibi dicit? AMOR.

They feel the touch of direct knowledge.
For them eternal windows stand open,
Readily by their own nature they know themselves
And to themselves they are both grist and mill.   15

25. *Rome.* $\left\{ \begin{array}{l} \textit{Frontier. \quad Maro.} \\ \textit{Branch. \quad Shoulder.} \\ \textit{Delay. \quad Love.} \end{array} \right.$
Anagram

ROME, what FRONTIER has your name not crossed,
    Since the ancient times bore the yoke of Latium?
You did not lack fame, or the songs of fame,
    By which MARO bore your praises to the stars.
And now your glory, like a withered BRANCH   5
    Falls from an aged trunk and from nobility.
Ancient praise and honour have perished: as if from
        their SHOULDER
    Distant times had cast you down.
Indeed no DELAY can cure you in your despair,
    Although once, when Fabius ruled, delay brought
        salvation.   10
Hence the nations who once admired you now hate you
        in their turn;
    And when praise has subsided, LOVE withdraws.

26. *Response of Pope Urban VIII.*

Since you cannot do what you crave and overturn Rome, you
        jumble
    Her name instead, you attack and abuse her customs:
The youth of Germany, of Greece and England all
    Censure you, all of whom Rome has welcomed and cherishes:
In sparing her enemies she imitates Jesus.   5
    You jumble her name. What does it tell you? LOVE.

XXVII. Respons. ad Vrb. VIII.

Non placet vrbanus noster de nomine lusus
    Romano, sed res seria Roma tibi est:
Nempe Caput Romae es, cuius mysteria velles
    Esse iocum soli, plebe stupente, tibi:
5   Attamen VRBANI delecto nomine, constat
    Quàm satur & suauis sit tibi Roma iocus.

XXVIII. Ad Vrbanum VIII Pont.

Pontificem tandem nacta est sibi Roma poetam:
    Res redit ad vates, Pieriósque duces:
Quod Bellarminus nequijt, fortasse poetae
    Suauiter efficient, absque rigore Scholae.
5   Cedito Barbaries: Helicon iam litibus instat,
    Squalorémque togae candida Musa fugat.

XXIX. Λογικὴ θυσία.

Ararúmque Hominúmque ortum si mente pererres,
    Cespes viuus, Homo; mortuus, Ara fuit:
Quae diuisa nocent, Christi per foedus, in vnum
    Conueniunt; & Homo viua fit Ara Dei.

27. *Response to Urban VIII.*

Our *urbane* game on the name of Rome does not please
    you,
  But for you the business of Rome is a serious matter:
Indeed you are Rome's Head, whose mysteries you'd like
    To make a joke for you alone, as the common people
    gape in wonder:
But with your chosen name of URBAN, it's clear   5
  How sweet and satisfying a joke Rome is for you.

28. *To Pope Urban VIII.*

At last Rome has found herself a poet-pope:
  Government returns to bards, to Pierian lords:
What Bellarmine could not do, perhaps the poets
  Will manage sweetly, without the severity of scholarship.
Give way, barbarity! Already Helicon looms over the
    lawsuits,   5
  And the gleaming Muse puts to flight the toga's
  grime.

29. *Reasonable Sacrifice.*

If you survey in your mind the rise of Altars and of Men,
  The living turf was Man; the dead, the Altar:
Divided, these do harm; but now are joined by Christ's pledge
  Into one; and Man becomes the living Altar of God.

XXX. *In Thomam Didymum.*

Dvm te vel digitis minister vrget,
Et hoc indicium subis, Redemptor?
Nempe es totus amor, medulla amoris,
Qui spissae fidei breuíque menti
Paras hospitium torúmque dulcem,
Quô se condat & implicet volutans
Ceu fidâ statione & arce certâ,
Ne perdat Leo rugiens vagantem.

5

XXXI. *In Solarium.*

Coniugium Caeli Terraéque haec machina praestat;
    Debetur Caelo lumen, & vmbra solo:
Sic Hominis moles animâque & corpore constat,
    Cuius ab oppositis fluxit origo locis.
Contemplare, miser, quantum terroris haberet
    Vel sine luce solum, vel sine mente caro.

5

XXXII. *Triumphus Mortis.*

O mea suspicienda manus, ventérque perennis!
Quem non Emathius torrens, non sanguine pinguis
Daunia, non satiat bis ter millesima caedis
Progenies, mundíque aetas abdomine nostro
Ingluuiésque minor. Quercus habitare feruntur
Prisci, crescentésque vnà cum prole cauernas:
Nec tamen excludor: namque vnâ ex arbore vitam
Glans dedit, & truncus tectum, & ramalia mortem.
    Confluere intereà passim ad Floralia pubes
Coeperat, agricolis mentémque & aratra solutis:

5

10

30. *On Thomas Didymus.*

While your servant probes you with his fingers,
Do you submit even to this test, Redeemer?
For sure you are pure love, the marrow of love,
For the hard of faith and the shallow mind
You prepare a welcome and a sweet resting-place,   5
Where they may hide and turn and wrap themselves
As in a sure lodging or a certain citadel,
So that no roaring lion will destroy them as they wander.

31. *On the Sundial.*

This machine demonstrates the marriage of Heaven and Earth;
   Its light is owed to Heaven, its shadow to the ground:
Thus the mass of man is fixed between soul and body,
   His source flows from opposite places.
Consider, wretched man, how much terror there would be   5
   For the ground without the light, or the flesh without
      the mind.

32. *The Triumph of Death.*

O my admirable hand, and my everlasting belly!
A stomach that neither the seething Emathian river,
      nor Daunia
Fat with blood, nor even the twice three thousand-fold
      offspring of slaughter satisfies,
The world is younger than our stomach
And its voracious maw. The men of old dwelt, they say,
      in oak trees,
And as they and their children grew, in caverns: 5
But I am not shut out: for from a single tree the acorn
Gave life, its trunk a shelter, its branches – Death.

Compita feruescunt pedibus, clamoribus aether.
Hìc vbi discumbunt per gramina, salsior vnus
Omnia suspendit naso, sociósque lacessit:
Non fert Vcalegon, atque amentata retorquet
15 Dicta ferox: haerent lateri conuitia fixo.
Scinditur in partes vulgus ceu compita: telum
Ira facit, mundúsque ipse est apotheca furoris.
Liber alit rixas: potantibus omnia bina
Sunt, praeter vitam: saxis hic sternitur, alter
20 Ambustis sudibus: pars vitam in pocula fundunt,
In patinas alij: furit inconstantia vini
Sanguine, quem dederat, spolians. Primordia Mortis
Haec fuerant: sic Tisiphone virguncula lusit.
    Non placuit rudis atque ignara occisio: Morti
25 Quaeritur ingenium, doctúsque homicida probatur.
Hinc tyrocinium, paruóque assueta iuuentus,
Fictáque Bellona & verae ludibria pugnae,
Instructaéque acies, hyemésque in pellibus actae,
Omniáque haec vt transadigant sine crimine costas,
30 Artificésque necis clueant, & mortis alumni.
Nempe & millenos ad palum interficit hostes
Assiduus tyro, si sit spectanda voluntas.
Heu miseri! Quis tantùm ipsis virtutibus instat
Quantùm caedi? adeón' vnam vos pascere vitam,
35 Perdere sexcentas? crescit tamen hydra nocendi
Tristis, vbi ac ferrum tellure reciditur imâ,
Faecundúsque chalybs sceleris, iam sanguine tinctus,
Expleri nequit, & totum depascitur Orbem.
Quid memorem tormenta, quibus prius horruit aeuum;
40 Balistásque Onagrósque & quicquid Scorpio saeuus
Vel Catapulta potest, Siculíque inuenta magistri,
Anglorúmque arcus gaudentes sanguine Galli,
Fustibalos fundásque, quibus, cum Numine, fretus
Strauit Idumaeum diuinus Tityrus hostem?
45 Adde etiam currus, & cum temone Britanno
Aruiragum, falcésque obstantia quaeque metentes.
Quin Aries ruit, & multâ Demetrius arte:

Meanwhile from all directions to the feast of Flora flowed the
    young men,
Farmers who had set aside their worries along with the
    ploughshares: 10
The crossroads grew warm with feet, the air with cries.
As they lie around on the grass, one mocking fellow
Turns up his nose, and dares his friends:
Ucalegon can't bear it, and hurls back words
Like slingshots, fierce man that he is: his insults pierce
    and stick deep in his opponent's side.   15
Like the crossroads, the crowd divides into factions: anger
Makes a weapon, and the world itself is a store-house of rage.
Bacchus nourishes brawls: for men in their cups
Everything is doubled – except their life: one man is felled by
    rocks, another
By stakes burnt hard in the fire: some pour out their lives like
    wine into goblets,   20
Others empty it over serving dishes. Treacherous wine
    rages wildly,
Plundering the blood it had itself provided. These were the first
Beginnings of Death: thus Tisiphone amused herself as
    a little girl.

Killing, crude and simple, wasn't enough: they looked for
A flair for Death. The learned killer was the thing.   25
From this flowed raw recruits, young men accustomed to little,
A makeshift Bellona, real warfare treated as a game,
Battle lines drawn up, and winters endured only in skins –
All this so men might pierce ribs without blame,
And be famed as craftsmen of slaughter and foster children
    of death.   30
For sure, the dedicated new recruit finishes off
A thousand opponents at the tilt, if his desire counts for
    anything.
Alas you wretched men! Who pursues the virtues
As keenly as slaughter? Surely for you to feed a single life
You needn't waste six hundred? Yet still the hydra of violence
    grows ever stronger   35

Sic olim cecidere.
　　Deerat adhuc vitijs hominum dignissima mundo
50　Machina, quam nullum satìs execrabitur aeuum;
　　Liquitur ardenti candens fornace metallum,
　　Fusáque decurrit notis aqua ferrea sulcis:
　　Exoritur tubus, atque instar Cyclopis Homeri
　　Luscum prodigium, medióque foramine gaudens.
55　Inde rotae atque axes subeunt, quasi sella curulis
　　Quâ Mors ipsa sedens hominum de gente triumphat.
　　Accedit Pyrius puluis, laquearibus Orci
　　Erutus, infernae pretiosa tragemata mensae,
　　Sulphureóque lacu, totâque imbuta Mephiti.
60　Huic Glans adijcitur (non quam ructare vetustas
　　Creditur, ante satas prono cum numine fruges)
　　Plumbea glans, liuensque suae quasi conscia noxae,
　　Purpureus lictor Plutonis, epistola Fati
　　Plumbis obsignata, colósque & stamina vitae
65　Perrumpens, Atropi vetulae marcentibus vlnis.
　　　　Haec vbi iuncta, subit viuo cum fune minister,
　　Fatalémque leuans dextram, quâ stupeus ignis
　　Mulcetur vento, accendit cum fomite partem
　　Pulueris inferni; properat datus ignis, & omnem
70　Materiam vexat: nec iam se continet antro
　　Tisiphone; flammâ & fallaci fulmine cincta
　　Euolat, horrendúmque ciet bacchata fragorem.
　　It stridor, caelósque omnes & Tartara findit.
　　Non iam exaudiri quicquam vel Musica caeli
75　Vel gemitus Erebi: piceo se turbine voluens
　　Totámque eructans nubem, Glans proruit imo
　　Praecipitata; cadunt vrbes, formidine muri
　　Diffugiunt, fragilísque crepant coenacula mundi.
　　Strata iacent toto millena cadauera campo
80　Vno ictu: non sic pestis, non stella maligno
　　Afflatu perimunt: en, Cymba Cocytia turbis
　　Ingemit, & defessus opem iam Portitor orat.
　　Nec Glans sola nocet; mortem quandoque susurrat
　　Aura volans, vitámque aer, quam pauerat, aufert.
85　　Dicite, vos Furiae, quâ gaudet origine Monstrum.

Grim as she is; when iron is torn from deep in the earth,
And the fertile steel of wickedness, already dyed with blood,
Cannot be satisfied, and devours the entire World.
Why should I recall siege engines, the dread of former times;
And the ballistas, and onagres, and whatever savage Scorpio   40
Or the Catapult could do, and the inventions of the
    Sicilian master
The bows of the English that rejoice in the blood of the French,
The sling-staffs and the sling-stones, on which, with God's help
Holy Tityrus relied, and laid low the Idumaean enemy?
Add to these the chariot, and Arviragus with his British wagon,   45
And the sickles harvesting whatever stands in their way.
Yes and also the attack of the battering ram, and Demetrius
    with all his craft:
So they fell in times gone by.

But still the engine most worthy of the sins of man
Was missing from the world: a device no age shall curse enough;   50
Metal shining with heat melts in the blazing kiln,
And the water of iron runs down freely in the familiar grooves:
The tube appears, and like Homer's Cyclops,
A one-eyed monster, rejoices in its central hole.
Then wheels and axles support it, like a curule's chair,   55
In which sits Death herself, triumphing over the race of men.
Next is the dust of fire, the gunpowder, bursting out
From the coffered ceilings of Orcus – precious sweetmeats for
    Hell's table –
And from the lake of sulphur, stained with all of Mephis.
To this is added an Acorn (but *not* the one belched by
    primitive man,   60
So it's said, before crops were sown with heaven's help)–
No, the acorn of lead, blue-black, as if aware of its guilt,
The purple lictor of Pluto, Fate's letter
Sealed with lead, tearing through
The distaffs and the threads of life, now that the arms   65
Of elderly Atropos are withering away.

Nox Aetnam, noctémque Chaos genuere priores.
Aetna Cacum igniuomum dedit, hic Ixiona multis
Cantatum; deinde Ixion cum nubibus atris
Congrediens genuit Monachum, qui limen opacae
90   Triste colens cellae, noctúque & Daemone plenum,
Protulit horrendum hoc primus cum puluere monstrum.
Quis Monachos mortem meditari, & puluere tristi
Versatos neget, atque humiles, queîs talia cordi
Tam demissa, ipsámque adeò subeuntia terram?
95   Nec tamen hìc noster stetit impetus: exilit omni
Tormento peior Iesuita, & fulminat Orbem,
Ridens Bombardas miseras, quae corpora perdunt
Non animas, raróque ornantur sanguine regum
Obstreperae stulto sonitu, criménque fatentes.
100   Imperij hìc culmen figo: mortalibus actum est
Corporéque atque animo. Totus mihi seruiat Orbis.

Once these parts are assembled, a servant approaches with
    a lighted fuse,
Lifts his deadly hand, in which the hemp fire
Is coaxed by the wind, and with a touch-wood sets aflame a
    sliver
Of the dust of hell. Once set, the fire rushes on, attacks   70
All the fuel: no longer does Tisiphone
Contain herself within her cave; girded with flame and
    treacherous lightning
She flies forth, and raging madly stirs a dreadful clamour.
The shrieking din surges out, and splits the whole heavens,
    and even Hell.
Nothing can be heard – not the Music of Heaven   75
Nor the groaning of Erebus: spinning in a pitchy whirlwind
And vomiting forth an entire cloud, the Acorn shoots forth
    from deep below
Hurled quickly; cities fall, with dread walls
Fly apart, and the upper regions of the brittle world resound.
A thousand corpses are scattered across the plain   80
With a single blow. Neither plague, nor the stars with their ill
Wind destroy like this: look, the skiff of Cocytus groans
With the crowd aboard, and, exhausted, the Pilot begs for aid.
Nor is it the Acorn alone that harms; since the breeze as it flies
Now whispers death, the very air now steals away the life
    which it had fed.   85

Tell me, Furies, what origin the Monster rejoices in.
Night begat Aetna, and Chaos first gave rise to Night.
Aetna produced Cacus, who vomits fire, and Cacus Ixion,
The subject of so many songs; then Ixion, mingling with
    black clouds,
Conceived a Monk, who, dwelling on the gloomy threshold   90
Of a shadowy cell, filled with Night and Demons,
First produced with powder this dreadful prodigy.
Who denies that Monks meditate on death? And that,
    grovelling in filthy dust,
And lowly themselves, they give rise to such grim things,
Objects even from beneath the earth?   95

XXXIII. *Triumphus Christiani. In Mortem.*

Ain' verò? quanta praedicas? hercle aedepol,
Magnificus es screator, homicida inclytus.
Quid ipse faciam? qui nec arboreas sudes
In te, nec arcus, scorpionésue, aut rotas,
5   Gladiósue, Catapultásue teneam, quin neque
Alapas nec Arietes? Quid ergo? Agnum & Crucem.

XXXIV. *In Iohannem ἐπιστήθιον*

Ah nunc, helluo, fac, vt ipse sugam:
Num totum tibi pectus imputabis?
Fontem intercipis omnibus patentem?
Quin pro me quoque sanguinem profudit,
5   Et ius pectoris inde consecutus
Lac cum sanguine posco deuolutum;
Vt, si gratia tanta copuletur
Peccati veniae mei, vel ipsos
Occumbens humero Thronos lacessam.

And yet our strength is not yet at an end: there leaps up, worse
Than any siege-engine, a Jesuit who threatens the World,
Laughing at the pitiful Cannons, which destroy merely bodies
Not souls, adorned occasionally by the blood of kings,
Clamorous with their stupid sound, confessing their own guilt. 100

Here I fix the summit of my power: for mortal men I am
The certain end of body and of soul. All the world should
    serve me.

33. *The Triumph of the Christian.*
Against Death.

Truly? What predictions do you make? There's no
    doubt whatsoever –
You are the marvellous splutterer, famous murderer.
What can I do? I who bear no wooden stakes
Against you, nor bows, nor catapults, nor wheels,
Or swords, or siege engines, not even   5
Palms or battering rams? What indeed? The Lamb
    and the Cross.

34. *To John, Leaning on the*
Breast of the Lord.

Ah now, you glutton, come on, let me suck too:
Surely you won't claim the whole breast for yourself?
Do you snatch away that spring that lies open to all?
For he shed his blood for me as well,
And I too have a claim upon the breast: 5
I demand the milk mingled with blood.
Then, if enough grace comes with it
To cleanse my sin, then I'll strike with my shoulder
Even those thrones as I fall and die.

XXXV. *Ad Dominum.*

Christe, decus, dulcedo, & centum circiter Hyblae,
    Cordis apex, animae pugnáque páxque meae,
Quin, sine, te cernam; quoties iam dixero, cernam;
    Immoriárque oculis, o mea vita, tuis.
5 Si licet, immoriar: vel si tua visio vita est,
    Cur sine te, votis immoriturus, ago?
Ah, cernam; Tu, qui caecos sanare solebas,
    Cùm te non videam, méne videre putas?
Non video, certum est iurare; aut si hoc vetuisti,
10   Praeuenias vultu non facienda tuo.

FINIS

35. *To the Lord.*

Christ, fine, sweet, like a hundred Hyblas, famed for honey,
   Peak of the heart, the strife of my soul, and its peace.
O, grant that I should see you; as often as I have
      said it, I shall see you;
   And I shall die in your eyes, o my life.
If I can, I shall die: or if the sight of you proves life to me,   5
   Why do I go on without you, on the verge of death
      in my prayers?
Ah, I shall see; You who would always heal the blind,
   When I do not see you, do you think that I can see at all?
I swear it, I do not see; or, if you have forbidden
      such oaths,
   Prevent my swearing with your countenance.

FINIS

Passio Discerpta

I. *Ad Dominum morientem.*

Cvm lacrymas oculósque duos tot vulnera vincant,
   Impar, & in fletum vel resolutus, ero;
Sepia concurrat, peccatis aptior humor,
   Et mea iam lacrymet culpa colore suo.

II. *In sudorem sanguineum.*

Qvò fugies, sudor? quamuìs pars altera Christi
   Nescia sit metae; venula, cella tua est.
Si tibi non illud placeat mirabile corpus,
   Caetera displiceat turba, necesse, tibi:
Ni me fortè petas; nam quantò indignior ipse,
   Tu mihi subueniens dignior esse potes.

III. *In eundem.*

Sic tuus effundi gestit pro crimine sanguis,
   Vt nequeat paulò se cohibere domi.

The Passion in Pieces

1. *To the Dying Lord.*

Since my tears, my two eyes, are overwhelmed by such
    wounding,
  I shall be unequal to the task, dissolved in weeping;
May ink come to my aid, a liquid better suited to sins,
  And may my guilt now weep in its proper colour.

2. *On the Sweat of Blood.*

Where will you flee, sweat? Although the other aspect
    of Christ
  Knows no limit, the narrow vein is your chamber.
If you are not satisfied with that marvellous body,
  You certainly won't be by the rest of this mob:
Unless, perhaps, it's me you're seeking: for the more
    undeserving I am,   5
  The more deserving you may be in coming to my aid.

3. *On the Same.*

Your blood so longs to be poured out for sin,
  That it is unable to keep even a little of itself at home.

IV. In latus perfossum.

Christe, vbi tam duro patet in te semita ferro,
Spero meo cordi posse patere viam.

V. In Sputum & Conuicia.

O barbaros! sic os rependitis sanctum,
Visum quod vni praebet, omnibus vitam,
Sputando, praedicando? sic Aquas vitae
Contaminatis alueósque caelestes
Sputando, blasphemando? nempe ne hoc fiat
In posterum, maledicta Ficus arescens
Gens tota fiet, atque vtrinque plectetur.
Parate situlas, Ethnici, lagenásque,
Graues lagenas, Vester est Aquae-ductus.

VI. In Coronam spineam.

Christe, dolor tibi supplicio, mihi blanda voluptas;
Tu spinâ miserè pungeris, ipse Rosâ.
Spicula mutemus: capias Tu serta Rosarum,
Qui Caput es, spinas & tua Membra tuas.

4. *On the Pierced Side.*

Christ, when remorseless steel has laid open a path
    inside you,
  I hope that road may lie open for my heart.

5. *On the Spitting and the Mockery.*

O barbaric men! Is this how you recompense the
    holy face
Which offers sight to one man, life to all –
By spitting, and swearing? Is this how you defile
The Waters of life and its sacred course
By spitting, by blaspheming? To prevent this ever
    happening   5
In the future, the whole people shall become
A Fig Tree, cursed and withering,
Assaulted from all sides.
Prepare your jars, Gentiles, and your flasks –
Large and heavy flasks, for this aqueduct is yours.   10

6. *On the Crown of Thorns.*

Christ, your torment is pain for you, for me delightful
    pleasure;
  You are pricked wretchedly with a thorn, I by a Rose.
Let us exchange darts: you should take the garland of
    Roses,
  For you are the Head, while we, your limbs, should
    bear the thorns.

VII. In Arund. Spin. Genuflex. Purpur.

Qvàm nihil illudis, Gens improba! quàm malè cedunt
   Scommata! Pastorem semper Arundo decet.
Quàm nihil illudis! cùm quò magìs angar acuto
   Munere, Rex tantò verior inde prober.
5   Quàm nihil illudis flectens! namque integra posthâc
   Posteritas flectet córque genúque mihi.
Quàm nihil illudis! si, quae tua purpura fingit,
   Purpureo meliùs sanguine Regna probem.
At non lusus erit, si quem tu laeta necasti
10   Viuat, & in mortem vita sit illa tuam.

VIII. In Alapas.

Ah! quàm caederis hinc & inde palmis!
   Sic vnguenta solent manu fricari:
Sic toti medicaris ipse mundo.

IX. In Flagellum.

Christe, flagellati spes & victoria mundi,
   Crimina cùm turgent, & mea poena prope est,
Suauiter admoueas notum tibi carne flagellum,
   Sufficiat virgae saepiùs vmbra tuae.
5   Mitis agas: tenerae duplicant sibi verbera mentes,
   Ipsáque sunt ferulae mollia corda suae.

7. *On the Reed, the Thorns, the Bowing Down and the Scarlet.*

How empty are your games, you wicked People! How
   badly your taunts
  Work out! The Reed will always belong to the
  Shepherd.
How empty are your games! The more I am tormented
   by a barbed
  Gift, the more truly I am proven King.
How empty are your games as you bow down! For
   after this a pure   5
  Posterity shall bend heart and knee to me.
How empty are your games! If, with my purple blood,
  I shall better claim the realms that *your* purple apes.
But it will be no game, if he whom you have gladly
   slaughtered
  Should live, and that life prove to be your death.   10

8. *On the Slaps.*

Ah! How they beat you on all sides with their palms!
  Ointments, too, are rubbed in by hand.
Thus you yourself heal all the world.

9. *On the Whip.*

Christ, the hope and victory of a world beneath the lash,
  When accusations rise, and my punishment is near at hand,
May you wield sweetly the lash your flesh has known,
  And may the shadow of your staff be all that is required.
Be gentle: tender minds double the blows they receive,   5
  And soft hearts are their own rods.

X. *In vestes diuisas.*

Si, Christe, dum suffigeris, tuae vestes
   Sunt hostium legata, non amicorum,
Vt postulat mos; quid tuis dabis? Teipsum.

XI. *In pium Latronem.*

O nimium Latro! reliquis furatus abundè,
   Nunc etiam Christum callidus aggrederis.

XII. *In Christum crucem ascensurum.*

Zacchaeus, vt Te cernat, arborem scandit:
Nunc ipse scandis, vt labore mutato
Nobis facilitas cedat & tibi sudor.
Sic omnibus videris ad modum visûs.
5   Fides gigantem sola, vel facit nanum.

XIII. *Christus in cruce.*

Hic, vbi sanati stillant opobalsama mundi,
   Aduoluor madidae laetus hiánsque Cruci:
Pro lapsu stillarum abeunt peccata; nec acres
   Sanguinis insultus exanimata ferunt.
5   Christe, fluas semper; ne, si tua flumina cessent,
   Culpa redux iugem te neget esse Deum.

10. *On the Divided Garments.*

If, Christ, while you are fixed to the cross, your clothes
    Are left to enemies, not friends,
As custom demands; what will you give to your own?
       Yourself.

11. *On the Good Thief.*

O too much a Thief! You have stolen lavishly from
    everyone else,
    Now in your cunning you approach even Christ.

12. *On Christ about to*
Ascend the Cross.

To see you, Zacchaeus climbed a tree:
Now, your tasks switched round, it's you who climb,
To bring ease for us and sweat for you.
Each man sees you from his own perspective:
Faith alone makes a giant, or a dwarf.   5

13. *Christ on the Cross.*

Here, where drips the balm for the healed world,
    I am driven, joyful and mouth agape to the dripping
      Cross:
Those drips as they fall make sins depart; soulless sins
    Cannot bear the sharp assaults of blood.
Christ, may you always flow; for if your flow should
    cease,   5
    Sin shall revive, and deny that you are God that
    flows for ever.

XIV. In Clauos.

Qvalis eras, qui, ne melior natura minorem
    Eriperet nobis, in Cruce fixus eras;
Iam meus es: nunc Te teneo: Pastórque prehensus
    Hoc ligno, his clauis est, quasi Falce suâ.

XV. Inclinato capite. Joh. 19.

Vvlpibus antra feris, nidíque volucribus adsunt,
    Quodque suum nouit strôma, cubile suum.
Qui tamen excipiat, Christus caret hospite: tantùm
    In cruce suspendens, vnde reclinet, habet.

XVI. Ad Solem deficientem.

Qvid hoc? & ipse deficis, Caeli gigas,
    Almi choragus luminis?
Tu promis Orbem manè, condis vesperi,
    Mundi fidelis clauiger:
5   At nunc fatiscis. Nempe Dominus aedium
    Prodegit integrum penu,
Quámque ipse lucis tesseram sibi negat,
    Negat familiae suae.
Carere discat verna, quo summus caret
10   Paterfamilias lumine.
Tu verò mentem neutiquam despondeas,
    Resurget occumbens Herus:
Tunc instruetur lautiùs radijs penu,
    Tibi supererunt & mihi.

14. *On the Nails.*

How great you were, to be nailed upon the Cross
  So that your better nature would not deprive us of the
    lesser.
Now you are mine: I hold you now: the Shepherd is seized
  By this wood, by these nails – as if by his own crook.

15. *On the Bowed Head, John 19.*

Wild foxes have their caves, bird their nests,
  Each thing knows its own shelter, its own resting-place.
But He is the exception, for Christ has no host: or only
  As he hangs upon the cross: there he may lay his head.

16. *On the Sun in Eclipse.*

What's this? Are you too failing, Giant of heaven
  Chorus leader of the nurturing light?
You draw forth your Orb in the morning, you hide it
   in the evening,
  A loyal torchbearer for the world:
But now you are growing weak. Surely the Master of
   the house   5
  Has spent the whole of his store,
And the chink of light he denies himself,
  He denies his own family.
Let the household slave learn to do without that light which
  The head of the household lacks.   10
But do not lose heart in any way:
  The Master as he dies shall rise again;
Then the store shall be more lavishly stocked with sunbeams,
  More than enough for you and for me.

XVII. *Monumenta aperta.*

Dvm moreris, Mea Vita, ipsi vixere sepulti,
  Próque vno vincto turba soluta fuit.
Tu tamen, haud tibi tam moreris, quàm viuis in illis,
  Asserit & vitam Mors animata tuam.
5   Scilicet in tumulis Crucifixum quaerite, viuit:
  Conuincunt vnam multa sepulcra Crucem.
Sic, pro Maiestate, Deum, non perdere vitam
  Quam tribuit, verùm multiplicare decet.

XVIII. *Terrae-motus.*

Te fixo vel Terra mouet: nam, cum Cruce, totam
  Circumferre potes; Sampson vt antè fores.
Heu stolidi, primùm fugientem figite Terram,
  Tunc Dominus clauis aggrediendus erit.

XIX. *Velum scissum.*

Frustra, Verpe, tumes, propola cultûs,
Et Templi parasite; namque velum
Diffissum reserat Deum latentem,
Et pomoeria terminósque sanctos
5   Non vrbem facit vnicam, sed Orbem.
Et pro pectoribus recenset aras,
Dum cor omne suum sibi requirat
Structorem, & Solomon vbique regnet.

17. *The Opened Tombs.*

As you were dying, My Life, the buried dead came
    to life,
    The binding of one man has freed the rest.
And yet, you do not so much die in yourself as you
    live in them,
    And Death takes on and animates your life.
Go seek the Crucified one among the tombs, he lives: 5
    Together many sepulchers defeat this single Cross.
Thus, because of his Majesty, it is right for God
    Not to waste the life he gave, but to multiply it.

18. *The Earthquake.*

Once you are nailed up, the Earth moves: for, with
    the Cross, you can
    Carry the whole world around; as Samson moved
    the pillars in the past.
Foolish men! first nail down the Earth as it flees,
    Only then can you tackle the Lord of the earth
    with nails.

19. *The Torn Veil.*

In vain, Circumcised Man, you swell with pride, you
    huckster of worship
And parasite of the Temple; for the veil
Once torn reveals the hidden God,
And makes the bounds and holy limits
Not a single city, but a World.   5
He counts every heart an altar,
Until every heart seeks its own
Maker, and Solomon rules everywhere.

Nunc Arcana patent, nec inuolutam
10 Phylacteria complicant latrîam.
Excessit tener Orbis ex Ephebis,
Maturúsque suos coquens amores
Praeflorat sibi nuptias futuras.
Vbique est Deus, Agnus, Ara, Flamen.

XX. *Petrae scissae.*

Sanus Homo factus, vitiorum purus vterque;
    At sibi collisit fictile Daemon opus.
Post vbi Mosaicae repararent fragmina Leges,
    Infectas tabulas facta iuuenca scidit.
5 Haud aliter cùm Christus obit, prae funere tanto
    Constat inaccessas dissiluisse petras.
Omnia, praeter corda, scelus confregit & error,
    Quae contrita tamen caetera damna leuant.

XXI. *In Mundi sympathiam*
cum Christo.

Non moreris solus: Mundus simul interit in te,
    Agnoscítque tuam Machina tota Crucem.
Hunc ponas animam mundi, Plato: vel tua mundum
    Ne nimium vexet quaestio, pone meam.

Now mysteries lie open, and phylacteries no longer
Enfold secretive worship.   10
The young World has emerged from puberty,
In its maturity it inclines towards love
And savours in advance its own future marriage.
Everywhere is God, the Lamb, the Altar and the Priest.

20. *The Cleft Rocks.*

Humanity was made whole, man and woman alike
    flawless;
  But the Devil smashed the clay for his own sake.
When later the Laws of Moses repaired the pieces,
  A heifer made by man split the tablets that no man had
    made.
So too when Christ died: in the face of such destruction   5
  Rocks that had never been scaled were forced to break
    apart.
Sin and wickedness have broken everything – except for
    hearts;
  But grind those hearts, and they lighten all losses.

21. *On the Harmony of the World with Christ.*

You are not dying alone: inside you, the World is dying too,
  And the whole mechanism of the earth recognizes your
    Cross.
Take this man, Plato, as your 'World-Soul': and should your
    theory
  Trouble the world too much, take mine instead.

Memoriae Matris Sacrum

I

Ah Mater, quo te deplorem fonte? Dolores
  Quae guttae poterunt enumerare meos?
Sicca meis lacrymis Thamesis vicina videtur,
  Virtutúmque choro siccior ipse tuo.
In flumen moerore nigrum si funderer ardens,
  Laudibus haud fierem sepia iusta tuis.
Tantùm istaec scribo gratus, ne tu mihi tantùm
  Mater: & ista Dolor nunc tibi Metra parit.

II

Corneliae sanctae, graues Semproniae,
Et quicquid vspiam est seuerae foeminae,
Conferte lacrymas: Illa, quae vos miscuit
Vestrásque laudes, poscit & mixtas genas.
Namque hanc ruinam salua Grauitas defleat,
Pudórque constet vel solutis crinibus;
Quandoque vultûs sola maiestas, Dolor.
  Decus mulierum perijt: & metuunt viri
Vtrumque sexum dote ne mulctauerit.
Non illa soles terere comptu lubricos,
Struices superbas atque turritum caput
Molita, reliquum deinde garriens diem

A Sacred Gift in Memory
of My Mother

I

Ah mother, from what spring might I weep for you?
    What drops could count out my griefs?
Next to my tears, the neighbouring Thames seems dry
    And I dryer than your chorus of virtues.
If I were poured, still burning, into a river black with
        grief
    I could not make ink enough for your praises.   5
For this alone I write in thanks: that you are for me
        not only
    Mother: now Sorrow delivers these Metres.

2

Holy Cornelias, serious Sempronias,
And sober women wherever they may be,
Combine your tears: this woman, who combined in her person
All of you and your praises, demands that you join your cheeks.
For Solemnity, still intact, should weep at this ruin,   5
And Modesty stand firm, even with hair loosed around
        her shoulders;
At such times the only majesty of expression is Sorrow.

The glory of women is dead: and men are afraid
That her talents have diminished both sexes.
She did not waste the quickly-passing days in dressing her hair,   10
Struggling to lift a proud edifice of turrets on her head

(Nam post Babelem linguae adest confusio)
Quin post modestam, qualis integras decet,
Substructionem capitis & nimbum breuem,
Animam recentem rite curauit sacris
Adorta numen acri & igneâ prece.

   Dein familiam lustrat, & res prandij,
Horti, colíque distributim pensitat.
Suum cuique tempus & locus datur.
Inde exiguntur pensa crudo vespere.
Ratione certâ vita constat & domus,
Prudenter inito quot-diebus calculo.
Totâ renident aede decus & suauitas
Animo renidentes priùs. Sin rarior
Magnatis appulsu extulit se occasio,
Surrexit vnà & illa, seséque extulit:
Occasione certat, imò & obtinet.
Proh! quantus imber, quanta labri comitas,
Lepos seuerus, Pallas mixta Gratijs;
Loquitur numellas, compedes & retia:
Aut si negotio hora sumenda est, rei
Per angiportus & maeandros labitur,
Ipsos Catones prouocans oraculis.
Tum quanta tabulis artifex? quae scriptio?
Bellum putamen, nucleus bellissimus,
Sententiae cum voce mirè conuenit,
Volant per orbem literae notissimae:
O blanda dextra, neutiquam istoc pulueris,
Quò nunc recumbis, scriptio merita est tua,
Pactoli arena tibi tumulus est vnicus.

   Adde his trientem Musices, quae molliens
Mulcénsque dotes caeteras visa est quasi
Caelestis harmoniae breue praeludium.
Quàm mira tandem Subleuatrix pauperum!
Languentium baculus, teges iacentium,
Commune cordis palpitantis balsamum:
Benedictiones publicae cingunt caput,
Caelíque referunt & praeoccupant modum.

Then passing the rest of the day in idle conversation
(For after Babel came the confusion of tongues);
But instead she dressed her head modestly and low,
Fitting for noble women, with only a shallow cloud of hair,   15
Then tended to her awakened soul with the proper rites
And assailed God with keen and fiery prayers.

Then she surveys her household, and carefully distributes
    the tasks:
Of meals, the garden, and the day's spinning.
To each its proper time and place is given,   20
So that the tasks allotted for the day are completed early in
    the evening.
Under her steady attention both life and the home are stable
    and well-managed,
Benefiting from her daily care in accounts.
The sweetness and grace that shine throughout the building
Shine first in her soul. But if, from time to time –   25
With the sudden arrival of an important guest – an occasion
    arose,
She rose to meet it, and drew herself up:
Does battle with the event, and of course prevails.
Oh! What a shower of speech, what a courteous tongue,
Charm – though severe, Pallas mixed with the Graces;   30
Her words are fetters, shackles and nets.
Or if an hour must be spent on business, she glides at once
Through the winding alleys and byways of the matter,
Rivalling the Catos themselves with her oracular remarks.
How great a craftswoman was she on paper? What of her
    writing?   35
A fine shell, and a kernel of the most beautiful kind,
With a wonderful harmony of sense and expression.
Her famed letters fly around the globe:
O charming hand, for sure your writing has not deserved
In any sense that patch of dust in which you now lie: 40
For you the sands of Pactolus are the only proper tomb.

To these add a third attribute: Music, which tempering

50 Fatisco referens tanta quae numerant mei
    Solùm dolores, & dolores, stellulae.
        At tu qui ineptè haec dicta censes filio,
    Nato parentis auferens Encomium,
    Abito, trunce, cum tuis pudoribus.
55 Ergo ipse solùm mutus atque excors ero
    Strepente mundo tinnulis praeconijs?
    Mihíne matris vrna clausa est vnico,
    Herbae exoletae, ros-marinus aridus?
    Matríne linguam refero, solùm vt mordeam?
60 Abito, barde. Quàm piè istic sum impudens!
    Tu verò mater perpetim laudabere
    Nato dolenti: literae hoc debent tibi
    Queîs me educasti; sponte chartas illinunt
    Fructum laborum consecutae maximum
65 Laudando Matrem, cùm repugnant inscij.

III

    Cvr splendes, O Phoebe? ecquid demittere matrem
        Ad nos cum radio tam rutilante potes?
    At superat caput illa tuum, quantum ipsa cadauer
        Mens superat; corpus solùm Elementa tenent.
5   Scilicet id splendes: haec est tibi causa micandi,
        Et lucro apponis gaudia sancta tuo.

And soothing her other gifts seemed to be
A brief foretaste of the harmony of heaven.
And finally – how wonderful a Reliever of the poor!   45
For those who stumble, a staff, a cover for those who fall,
A general balm for the anxious heart:
Public blessings wreathe her head;
The heavens echo them, and even anticipate the measure.
I grow weak relating so many points that only my sorrows   50
Can number; my sorrows, the lesser stars.

But you, who consider these unfitting words for a son,
Depriving a child of the praise of his parent,
Be gone, cripple, along with your scruples.
Should I alone then be mute and stupid   55
While the world resounds with tinkling proclamations?
Is my mother's urn closed only to me?
The grasses gone, the rosemary withered?
Do I bring back my tongue for her, only to bite it?
Be gone, you fool. How devoutly shameless I am in this
    matter!   60
For as a mother you shall be praised for ever more
By your grieving son: this my letters owe to you –
The letters you taught me; gladly they smear the pages
Having pursued the greatest fruit of their toils
In praising my Mother, although the ignorant resist it.   65

3

Why do you shine, O Phoebus? Do you have any power to
    send down
    My mother to us, with your beams that glow so red?
But her head overtops your own, just as Mind itself
    Outdoes the corpse; the Elements claim only the body.
Of course that's why you shine, this is the cause of your
    glittering: 5
    You've claimed for yourself the benefit of her sacred joys.

Verùm heus, si nequeas caelo demittere matrem,
    Sítque omnis motûs nescia tanta quies,
Fac radios saltem ingemines, vt dextera tortos
10   Implicet, & matrem, matre manente, petam.

IV

    Qvid nugor calamo fauens?
Mater perpetuis vuida gaudijs,
    Horto pro tenui colit
Edenem Boreae flatibus inuium.
5   Quin caeli mihi sunt mei,
Materni decus, & debita nominis,
    Dúmque his inuigilo frequens
Stellarum socius, pellibus exuor.
    Quare Sphaeram egomet meam
10   Connixus, digitis impiger vrgeo:
    Te, Mater, celebrans diu,
Noctu te celebrans luminis aemulo.
    Per te nascor in hunc globum
Exemplóque tuo nascor in alterum:
15   Bis tu mater eras mihi,
Vt currat paribus gloria tibijs.

V

Horti, deliciae *Dominae*, marcescite tandem;
    Ornâstis capulum, nec superesse licet.
Ecce decus vestrum spinis horrescit, acutâ
    Cultricem reuocans anxietate manum:
5 Terram & funus olent flores: Dominaéque cadauer
    Contiguas stirpes afflat, eaéque rosas.

Oh but still, even if you have no power to send her down
   from heaven, my mother,
  And if such repose knows nothing of any motion,
At least redouble your rays, so that my right hand might
  Weave and twist them together and reach her, my mother,
    even as she stays where she is.   10

4

  Why do I trifle my time on a reed?
My mother, now bedewed with endless joy,
  Instead of a narrow garden, tends
An Eden closed to the North Wind's blasts.

  But my heaven is this: 5
The glory of my mother's name, and all that is owed to it,
  And while I keep watch over these things, a frequent
Companion of the stars, I shed my skin.

  For this reason, binding my sphere
Firmly together, I press on tirelessly with my fingers: 10
  Celebrating you, Mother, all the time,
Singing of you by night, the rival of the light.

  By you born into this world,
By your example I am born into another:
  Twice were you mother to me,   15
So your glory should run with paired flutes.

5

Gardens, the darling of their Mistress, begin to wither at last;
  You have adorned the bier, and cannot live for longer.
See how your glory is bristling with thorns, sharp
  With sorrow calling back the hand that tended you:
Flowers smell of earth and death: the body of their mistress   5
  Breathes upon the root stocks nearby, and they upon the roses.

In terram violae capite inclinantur opaco,
    Quaéque domus Dominae sit, grauitate docent.
Quare haud vos hortos, sed coemeteria dico,
10   Dum torus absentem quisque reponit heram.
Eugè, perite omnes; nec posthâc exeat vlla
    Quaesitum Dominam gemma vel herba suam.
Cuncta ad radices redeant, tumulósque paternos;
    (Nempe sepulcra satis numen inempta dedit.)
15 Occidite; aut sanè tantisper viuite, donec
    Vespere ros maestis funus honestet aquis.

VI

Galene, frustra es, cur miserum premens
Tot quaestionum fluctibus obruis,
    Arterias tractans micantes
        Corporeae fluidaéque molis?
5 Aegroto mentis: quam neque pixides
Nec tarda possunt pharmaca consequi,
    Vtrumque si praederis Indum,
        Vltrà animus spatiatur exlex.
Impos medendi, occidere si potes,
10 Nec sic parentem ducar ad optimam:
    Ni sanctè, vtì mater, recedam,
        Morte magìs viduabor illâ.
Quin cerne vt erres, inscie, brachium
Tentando sanum: si calet, aestuans,
15   Ardore scribendi calescit,
        Mater inest saliente venâ.
Si totus infler, si tumeam crepax,
Ne membra culpes, causa animo latet
    Qui parturit laudes parentis:
20   Nec grauidis medicina tuta est.

Violets bow towards the earth with their shady heads
   Indicating by their weight where their Mistress now resides.
So now I call you not gardens but burial grounds,
   As each bed sets to rest its missing mistress.   10
Yes, perish, all of you; from now on let nothing shoot up
   In search of its mistress, no herb or bud.
Let everything return to its roots and ancestral mounds;
   (Without doubt God has given enough sepulchres without
      price.)
Die then; or live in health only until   15
   In the evening dew honours the corpse with sorrowful waters.

6

Galen, you are wasting your time, why harass me in my
      misery
And overwhelm me with wave upon wave of questions,
   Handling the quivering arteries
      Of this bodily, liquid mass?

I am sick in mind: and neither ointment boxes   5
Nor slow working drugs can reach that,
   Even if you plunder both Indies,
      The mind wanders of its own accord, beyond the law.

You have no power to heal, even if you can kill,
But that won't work either to bring me to the best of parents: 10
   If I don't depart from life, like my mother, in a holy fashion
      Then death will only deprive me of her all the more.

But see how you err, ignorant man,
By touching my arm, which is quite healthy: if it's warm,
      burning even,
   It is growing hot with the ardour of writing,   15
      My mother is inside my leaping vein.

If I should be all swollen, creaking and distended,
Don't blame my limbs: the reason lurks in my mind

Irregularis nunc habitus mihi est:
Non exigatur crasis ad alterum.
   Quod tu febrem censes, salubre est
   Atque animo medicatur vnum.

VII

    Pallida materni Genij atque exanguis imago,
In nebulas similésque tui res gaudia nunquid
Mutata? & pro matre mihi phantasma dolosum
Vberáque aerea hiscentem fallentia natum?
5   Vae nubi pluuiâ grauidae, non lacte, meásque
Ridenti lacrymas quibus vnis concolor vnda est.
Quin fugias? mea non fuerat tam nubila Iuno,
Tam segnis facies aurorae nescia vernae,
Tam languens genitrix cineri supposta fugaci:
10 Verùm augusta parens, sanctum os caelóque locandum,
Quale paludosos iamiam lictura recessus
Praetulit Astraea, aut solio Themis alma vetusto
Pensilis, atque acri dirimens Examine lites.
Hunc vultum ostendas, & tecum, nobile spectrum,
15 Quod superest vitae, insumam: Solíque iugales
Ipse tuae solùm adnectam, sine murmure, thensae.
Nec querar ingratos, studijs dum tabidus insto,
Effluxisse dies, suffocatámue Mineruam,
Aut spes productas, barbatáque somnia vertam
20 In vicium mundo sterili, cui cedo cometas
Ipse suos tanquam digno pallentiáque astra.
    Est mihi bis quinis laqueata domuncula tignis
Rure; breuísque hortus, cuius cum vellere florum
Luctatur spacium, qualem tamen eligit aequi
25 Iudicij dominus, flores vt iunctiùs halent
Stipati, rudibúsque volis imperuius hortus

Which is giving birth to a parent's praises:
    And for those who are pregnant, medicines are not safe. 20

My condition is unusual, I admit:
Such a combination shouldn't be enforced on anyone else.
    What you consider a fever, is a healthy condition
       And it alone can heal my heart.

7

Pale and bloodless semblance of a maternal Guardian Spirit,
Surely joy has not been transformed into such mists and
    clouds as yours?
Replacing my mother with a deceptive phantom
With breasts made of air to trick the child as he gapes?
Curses upon you, you cloud heavy with rain, not milk,
    mocking   5
My tears, tears the same colour as your waters.
Why don't you leave? My Juno was never so cloud-like,
So dull of face, knowing nothing of a spring dawn,
So lifeless a mother mocked up by mere fugitive ash:
But a revered parent, a holy face and one to be found in
    heaven,   10
Of the sort that Astraea displayed, as she was about
    to leave
Her marshy retreats, or like kind Themis leaning down
From her venerable throne, and settling all suits with the
    keen tongue of her Balance.
Show that face, and with you, noble ghost,
I'll pass what remains of my life: and for my part
    I'd attach   15
The Sun's team to your sacred car, without a murmur.
And I would not complain that days had flown past without
    acknowledgment, while I
Languished away over my studies, or that Minerva was
    suffocated,

Sit quasi fasciculus crescens, & nidus odorum.
Hìc ego túque erimus, variae suffitibus herbae
Quotidie pasti: tantùm verum indue vultum
30   Affectûsque mei similem; nec languida misce
Ora meae memori menti: ne dispare cultu
Pugnaces, teneros florum turbemus odores,
Atque inter reliquos horti crescentia foetus
Nostra etiam paribus marcescant gaudia fatis.

VIII

Paruam piámque dum lubenter semitam
    Grandi reaéque praefero,
Carpsit malignum sydus hanc modestiam
    Vinúmque felle miscuit.
5   Hinc fremere totus & minari gestio
    Ipsis seuerus orbibus;
Tandem prehensâ comiter lacernulâ
    Susurrat aure quispiam,
Haec fuerat olim potio Domini tui.
10   Gusto probóque Dolium.

Or that I should consign long cherished hopes and bearded
    dreams
To the sterile world of chance and change – and concede to
    that world   20
As befits it, its comets and its paling stars.

I have a little cottage coffered with ten beams
In the country; and a small garden, whose space contends
With a fleece of flowers – such a garden as a lord of good
    judgement
Chooses, so that the flowers breathe more closely   25
Packed together, and the garden, impervious to
    clumsy feet
Might be as it were a flourishing nosegay, and a nest of
    spices.
Here we shall be, you and I, fed daily on the smoke of
    various herbs:
Only don a true likeness and one that suits my temper; don't
    contaminate
My memory with your listless appearance; for fear that we   30
Should enter battle over this difference
And disturb the delicate fragrance of the flowers;
And lest, among the remaining children of the garden, our
Growing joys might wilt in a similar fate.

8

While I was happily choosing a small and pious path
    Rather than a wide and guilty one,
An unlucky star stole even this modest aspiration
    And mingled my wine with gall.
Hence I long to roar with all my being and threaten   5
    Harshly the very planets;
At length someone tugged my little cloak
    And whispered in my ear:
'This was once the cup of your Lord.'
    I taste and I approve the Vintage.   10

IX

Hoc, Genitrix, scriptum proles tibi sedula mittit.
    Siste parum cantus, dum legis ista, tuos.
Nôsse sui quid agant, quaedam est quoque musica sanctis,
    Quaéque olim fuerat cura, manere potest.
5 Nos miserè flemus, solésque obducimus almos
    Occiduis, tanquam duplice nube, genis.
Interea classem magnis Rex instruit ausis:
    Nos autem flemus: res ea sola tuis.
Ecce solutura est, ventos causata morantes:
10   Sin pluuiam, fletus suppeditâsset aquas.
Tillius incumbit Dano, Gallúsque marinis,
    Nos flendo: haec nostrûm tessera sola ducum.
Sic aeuum exigitur tardum, dum praepetis anni
    Mille rotae nimijs impediuntur aquis.
15 Plura tibi missurus eram (nam quae mihi laurus,
    Quod nectar, nisi cum te celebrare diem?)
Sed partem in scriptis etiam dum lacryma poscit,
    Diluit oppositas candidus humor aquas.

X

Nempe huc vsque notos tenebricosos
Et maestum nimio madore Caelum
Tellurísque Britannicae saliuam
Iniustè satìs arguit viator.
5 At te commoriente, Magna Mater,
Rectè, quem trahit, aerem repellit

9

Your zealous child sends you, Mother, this writing.
  Stop your songs for a while, while you read these.
For the saints, it is itself a kind of music to hear what their
    dear ones are doing,
  And if what was once their concern, can remain so.
We weep wretchedly, we obscure the kindly suns   5
  With dimming eyes, as if with a double layer of cloud.
Meanwhile the King draws up a fleet for great deeds of
    daring:
  But we are weeping: for your people that is all that
    matters.
Look, now the fleet is about to set out, its delay blamed on
    the winds,
  Not the rain: but our weeping could have supplied the
    water.   10
Tillius harries the Dane: France heads for the sea,
  We for weeping: this is the only watchword for our lords.
So the ages roll slowly past, while the thousand wheels
  Of the rapid year are blocked by the excess of water.
I was on the point of sending you more (for what is the
    laurel to me,   15
  What nectar, unless I spend the day with you?)
But as a tear demands a role in my writing,
  The bright liquid dissolves the waters in its way.

10

Surely up to now the gloomy south winds
And the Sky sad and heavy with rain
And British earth reduced to mud
  – All these the traveller has stressed unfairly.
But now at your death, Great Mother,   5
He quite rightly rejects the damp air he breathes in

Cum probro madidum, reúmque difflat.
Nam te nunc Ager, Vrbs, & Aula plorant:
Te nunc Anglia, Scotiaéque binae,
10   Quin te Cambria peruetusta deflet,
Deducens lacrymas prioris aeui
Ne serae meritis tuis venirent.
Non est angulus vspiam serenus,
Nec cingit mare, nunc inundat omnes.

XI

Dvm librata suis haeret radicibus ilex
  Nescia vulturnis cedere, firma manet.
Post vbi crudelem sentit diuisa securem,
  Quò placet oblato, mortua fertur, hero:
5   Arbor & ipse inuersa vocer: dúmque insitus almae
  Assideo Matri, robore vinco cedros.
Nunc sorti pateo, expositus sine matre procellis,
  Lubricus, & superans mobilitate salum.
Tu radix, tu petra mihi firmissima, Mater,
10   Ceu Polypus, chelis saxa prehendo tenax:
Non tibi nunc soli filum abrupere sorores,
  Dissutus videor funere & ipse tuo.
Vnde vagans passim rectè vocer alter Vlysses,
  Alteráque haec tua mors, Ilias esto mihi.

Resentfully, and blows out the offending mouthful.
For now Country, City and Court weep for you:
For you now England, and the two Gaelic lands,
Yes, even ancient Wales weeps,   10
All three drawing down the tears of an earlier age
For fear they should come too late for your virtues.
There is no clear corner anywhere,
The sea no longer girts us round, but floods us all.

II

As long as the holm-oak is balanced and clings with its own
    roots
    Not knowing how to yield to the southeast winds, firm it
      remains.
But afterwards it's split and feels the cruel axe,
    Carried off dead for the pleasure of the lord to whom it's
      offered:
I too am called a felled tree: as long as I am grafted to my
    nurturing   5
    Mother, and sit alongside her, I outdo the cedars in
      strength.
But now I lie open to my fate, exposed without my mother
    to the blasts of the wind,
    Unsteady, my motion surpassing even the salt sea.
You are my root, my firmest base, Mother,
    Like a Polypus, I grasp the rocks tightly with my arms: 10
It is not your thread alone that the sisters have cut,
    By your death I too have come apart at the seams.
For my ceaseless wandering I should be called a second
    Ulysses,
    And let this your death be a second Iliad for me.

XII

Facesse, Stoica plebs, obambulans cautes,
Exuta strato carnis, ossibus constans,
Iísque siccis adeò vt os Molossorum
Haud glubat inde tres teruncios escae.
5   Dolere prohibes? aut dolere me gentis
Adeò inficetae, plumbeae, Meduseae,
Ad saxa speciem retrahentis humanam,
Tantóque nequioris optimâ Pirrhâ?
At fortè matrem perdere haud soles demens:
10   Quin nec potes; cui praebuit Tigris partum.
Proinde parco belluis, nec irascor.

XIII

EPITAPHIUM

Hic sita foeminei laus & victoria sexus:
   Virgo pudens, vxor fida, seuera parens:
Magnatúmque inopúmque aequum certamen & ardor:
   Nobilitate illos, hos pietate rapit.
5   Sic excelsa humilísque simul loca dissita iunxit,
   Quicquid habet tellus, quicquid & astra, fruens.

12

Be gone, you mob of Stoics, prowling crag,
Stripped of the covering of flesh, standing in bones,
And those bones so dry that the mouth of Molossian
    hounds
Scarcely peels from them three farthings of scraps.
Do you forbid grief? Or just my grief, of such   5
Coarse sort, leaden, like Medusa,
Returning the human race to rock,
Unworthy compared to the peerless Pyrrha?
But perhaps, mad as you are, you know nothing of a
    mother's loss:
You really couldn't: since a Tiger bore you.   10
So I shall be merciful to wild beasts, and not grow
    angry.

13

EPITAPH

Here lies the praise and victory of the female sex:
   As a girl, chaste; as wife, faithful; stern as a parent:
Of the powerful and the poor equally the prize and passion:
   By her nobility she wins over the former, the latter by her
    piety.
She, both high and low at once, joined far distant regions,   5
   Delighting in all that the earth, all that the stars contain.

XIV

Ψυχῆς ἀσθενὲς ἔρκος, ἀμαυρὸν πνεύματος ἄγγος
Τῷδε παρὰ τύμβῳ δίζεο, φίλε, μόνον.
Νοῦ δ᾽ αὐτοῦ τάφος ἐστ᾽ ἀστήρ· φέγγος γὰρ ἐκείνου
Φεγγώδη μόνον, ὡς εἰκὸς, ἔπαυλιν ἔχει.
5 Νῦν ὁράας, ὅτι κάλλος ἀπείριτον ὠπὸς ἀπαυγοῦς
Οὐ σαθρόν, οὐδὲ μελῶν ἔπλετο, ἀλλὰ νόος.
Ὅς διὰ σωματίου πρότερον καὶ νῦν δι᾽ Ὀλύμπου
Ἀστράπτων, θυρίδων ὡς δῖα, νεῖμε σέλας.

XV

Μῆτερ, γυναικῶν αἴγλη, ἀνθρώπων ἔρις,
Ὄδυρμα δαιμόνων, Θεοῦ γεώργιον,
Πῶς νῦν ἀφίπτασαι, γόου καὶ κινδύνου
Ἡμᾶς λιποῦσα κυκλόθεν μεταιχμίους;
5 Μενοῦνγε σοφίην, εἰ σ᾽ ἀπηλλάχθαι χρεών,
Ζωῆς ξυνεργὸν τήνδε διαθεῖναι τέκνοις
Ἐχρῆν φυγοῦσα, τήν τ᾽ ἐπιστήμην βίου.
Μενοῦν τὸ γλαφυρόν, καί μελίρροον τρόπων,
Λόγων τε φίλτρον, ὥσθ᾽ ὑπεξελθεῖν λεών.
10 Νῦν δ᾽ ᾤχου ἔνθεν δ᾽ ὡς στρατὸς νικηφόρος
Φέρων τὸ πᾶν, κἄγων· ἢ ὡς Ἀπαρκτίας
Κήπου συνωθῶν ἀνθινὴν εὐωδίαν,
Μίαν τ᾽ ἀταρπον συμπορεύεσθαι δράσας.
Ἐγὼ δὲ ῥινὶ ξυμβαλὼν ἰχνηλατῶ
15 Εἴ που τύχοιμι τῆσδ᾽ ἀρίστης ἀτραποῦ,
Θανεῖν συνειδὼς κρεῖττον, ἢ ἄλλως βιοῦν.

14

The weak defence of the soul, the blind vessel of the spirit –
    At this tomb seek, friend, only that.
The mind's own tomb is a star: for the light of that tomb
    Has its only fit dwelling in light like itself.
Now you see that the unlimited beauty of her radiant face   5
    Could not decay, and was of the mind, not the body –
That mind, gleaming first in her small body, and now
        throughout Olympus,
    Spread forth her radiance, like sunlight through windows.

15

Mother, a glorious light for women, a spur to strife for men,
Lament of the Demons, the cultivated field of God,
Why do you fly away now, leaving us surrounded
On all sides by grief and danger?
But if you had to go, you ought to have granted   5
To your children as you left,
Wisdom to help them live, an understanding of existence,
Polished charm, the sweet flow of good manners,
And the spell of words, to bring to those you meet.
But now like a victorious army you are gone from here   10
Bearing everything with you, and taking it away; or like the
        North Wind
Gathering together all the flowery scents of the garden,
Creating a single path for all to travel.
I am tracking the scent, nose to the ground
Hoping to hit upon this best path of all,   15

XVI

Χαλεπὸν δοκεῖ δακρῦσαι,
Χαλεπὸν μὲν οὐ δακρῦσαι·
Χαλεπώτερον δὲ πάντων
Δακρύοντας ἀμπαύεσθαι
5   Γενέτειραν οὔ τις ἀνδρῶν
Διδύμαις κόραις τοιαύτην
Ἐποδύρεται πρεπόντως.
Τάλας, εἴθε γ᾽ Ἄργος εἴην
Πολυόμματος, πολύτλας,
10   Ἵνα μητρὸς εὐθενούσης
Ἀρετὰς διακριθείσας
Ἰδίαις κόραισι κλαύσω.

XVII

Αἰάζω γενέτειραν, ἐπαιάζουσι καί ἄλλοι,
Οὐκ ἔτ᾽ ἐμὴν ἰδίας φυλῆς γράψαντες ἀρωγὸν,
Προυνομίῳ δ᾽ ἀρετῆς κοινὴν γενέτειραν ἑλόντες.
Οὐκ ἔνι θαῦμα τόσον σφετερίζειν· οὐδὲ γὰρ ὕδωρ,
5   Οὐ φέγγος, κοινόν τ᾽ ἀγαθὸν, μίαν εἰς θύραν εἴργειν
Ἡ θέμις, ἢ δυνατόν. σεμνώματος ἔπλετο στάθμη,
Δημόσιον τ᾽ ἴνδαλμα καλοῦ, θεῖόν τε κάτοπτρον.
     Αἰάζω γενέτειραν, ἐπαιάζουσι γυναῖκες,
Οὐκ ἔτι βαλλομένης χάρισιν βεβολημέναι ἦτορ,
10   Αὐτὰρ ἄχει μεγάλῳ κεντούμεναι· εὖτε γὰρ αὗται
Τῆς περὶ συλλαλέουσιν, ἑοῦ ποικίλματος ἄρδην
Λήσμονες, ἡ βελόνη σφαλερῷ κῆρ τραύματι νύττει
Ἔργου ἁμαρτηκυῖα, νέον πέπλον αἵματι στικτὸν
Μητέρι τεκταίνουσα, γόῳ καὶ πένθεσι σύγχρουν.
15   Αἰάζω γενέτειραν, ἐπαιάζουσιν ὀπῶραι,
Οὐκ ἔτι δεσποίνης γλυκερᾷ μελεδῶνι τραφεῖσαι·
Ἧς βίος ἠελίοιο δίκην, ἀκτῖνας ἱέντος
Πραεῖς εἰαρινούς τε χαραῖς ἐπικίδνατο κῆπον·

16

It seems it's hard to weep,
Hard not to weep;
But hardest of all
For those who are weeping to cease.
No man weeps fittingly   5
For such a mother
With his two eyes.
Wretched as I am, would I were Argos
Many-eyed, enduring much,
To lament the virtues   10
Of my mother as she lived
With an eye for each of her attributes.

17

I mourn my mother, and other men mourn for her as well –
Describing her no longer as the guardian of my own
    particular family,
In their song of her virtue they have chosen her as their shared
    ancestress.
There is nothing remarkable in this appropriation: for it is
    not just
To shut up behind a single door water, nor light, nor the
    common good –   5
Neither just nor possible. She was the principle of holiness,
The people's image of goodness, and mirror of the divine.

I mourn my mother, and women mourn for her as well,
Their hearts no longer struck by the graces of her who is now
    struck down,
But pierced with a terrible grief; for when they   10
Talk about her together, quite heedless of their embroidery,
The needle pricks them with a wound that endangers their
    heart,

Αὐτὰρ ὅδ᾽ αὖ θάνατος κυρίης ὡς ἥλιος αὖος
20   Σειρίου ἡττηθεὶς βουλήμασι, πάντα μαραίνει.
Ζῶ δ᾽ αὐτός βραχύ τι πνείων, ὥστ᾽ ἔμπαλιν αὐτῆς
Αἶνον ὁμοῦ ζώειν καὶ πνεύματος ἄλλο γενέσθαι
Πνεῦμα, βίου πάροδον μούνοις ἐπέεσσι μετρῆσαν.

XVIII

Κύματ᾽ ἐπαφριοῶντα Θαμήσεος, αἴκε σελήνης
   Φωτὸς ἀπαυραμένης ὄγκου ἐφεῖσθε πλέον,
Νῦν θέμις ὀρφναίῃ μεγάλης ἐπὶ γείτονος αἴσῃ
   Οὐλυμπόνδε βιβᾶν ὕμμιν ἀνισταμένοις.
5   Ἀλλὰ μενεῖτ᾽, οὐ γὰρ τάραχος ποτὶ μητέρα βαίνῃ,
   Καὶ πρέπον ὧδε παρὰ δακρυόεσσι ῥέειν.

Missing its proper mark, and fashions a dress for my mother
Stippled with blood, coloured by lamentation and by pain.

I mourn my mother, and the fruits and flowers mourn for her
    as well, 15
No longer nurtured by their mistress' sweet care;
Her life, like the sun, sent forth the gentle rays of spring
And scattered the garden with joys.
But her death, like a dried-up sun,
Defeated by scheming Sirius, withers everything. 20
And yet I live, though short of breath, so that once again
Her praise lives on with me and from my breath comes
    another
Breath, measuring out the path of her life with words alone.

18

Foam-flecked waves of the Thames, if you wish to claim
    A greater portion of the moon's pride for yourself, robbed
    as she has been of her light,
You now have the right to enter the dark realm of your
    powerful neighbour,
    Bursting your banks to step towards Olympus.
But wait! No chaos should approach my mother: 5
    It is proper to flow like this alongside those who weep.

XIX

Excussos manibus calamos, falcémque resumptam
    Rure, sibi dixit Musa fuisse probro.
Aggreditur Matrem (conductis carmine Parcis)
    Funeréque hoc cultum vindicat aegra suum.
5   Non potui non ire acri stimulante flagello:
    Quin Matris superans carmina poscit honos.
Eia, agedum scribo: vicisti, Musa; sed audi,
    Stulta semel scribo, perpetuò vt sileam.

19

I had shaken the reed pipes from my hand, and taken
    up once more the scythe
  In the fields: the Muse said that this was an insult
    to her.
She confronts my Mother (having bribed the Fates with
    a song)
  And, sickened by her death, claims worship in
    compensation.
I could not but go on, under the harsh lash of her whip: 5
  And indeed my Mother's overwhelming honour
    demands such songs.
All right, come on then, I'm writing: you've won, Muse.
    But listen:
  I'm writing these trivial poems just once, to be silent
    ever after.

Alia Poemata Latina

In Obitum Henrici Principis Walliae.

Ite leues (inquam), Parnassia numina, Musae,
Non ego vos posthâc hederae velatus amictu
Somnis (nescio queîs) nocturna ad vota vocabo:
Sed nec Cyrrhaei saltus Libethriáue arua
5 In mea dicta ruant; non tam mihi pendula mens est,
Sic quasi Dijs certem, magnos accersere montes:
Nec vaga de summo deducam flumina monte,
Qualia parturiente colunt sub rupe sorores:
Si-quas mens agitet moles (dum pectora saeuo
10 Tota stupent luctu) lachrymísque exaestuet aequis
Spiritus, hi mihi iam montes, haec flumina sunto.
Musa, vale, & tu Phoebe; dolor mea carmina dictet;
Hinc mihi principium: vos o labentia mentis
Lumina, nutantes paulatim acquirite vires,
15 Viuite, dum mortem ostendam: sic tempora vestram
Non comedant famam, sic nulla obliuia potent.
Quare age, Mens, effare, precor, quo numine laeso?
Quae suberant causae? quid nos committere tantum,
Quod non Lanigerae pecudes, non Agmina lustrent?
20 Annon longa fames miseraéque iniuria pestis
Poena minor fuerat, quàm fatum Principis aegrum?
Iam foelix Philomela, & menti conscia Dido!
Foelices, quos bella premunt, & plurimus ensis!
Non metuunt vltrà; nostra infortunia tantùm

Other Latin Poems

On the Death of Henry, Prince of Wales.

Begone then (I say) fickle Parnassian powers, Muses,
I shall not henceforth, veiled in a cloak of ivy,
Call you from dreams (of any sort) to midnight rites:
But neither the groves of Cyrrha nor the fields of Libethra
Need rush upon my words; it is not my intention   5
To summon mighty mountains, as if I were warring with
    the Gods themselves:
Nor shall I draw down from the peak of the mountain
    wandering waters,
Such waters as the sisters tend beneath rock that gave
    them birth:
If my mind must grapple with such burdens (while all
    my heart
Is stupefied with savage grief) and if my spirit must
    boil over   10
With tears equal to that task, let those burdens be my
    mountains, those tears my rivers.
Farewell, Muse, and you too, Apollo; may grief dictate
    my songs;
I'll start with this: O you fading lights
Of the mind, grow slowly stronger even as you falter,
Live on, while I depict death: thus time   15
Shall not consume your fame, no forgetfulness shall have
    that power.

25   Fatáque Fortunásque & spem laesêre futuram.
      Quòd si fata illi longam invidêre salutem
      Et patrio regno (sub quo iam Principe nobis
      Quid sperare, imò quid non sperare licebat?)
      Debuit ista pati prima & non nobilis aetas:
30   Aut cita mors est danda bonis aut longa senectus:
      Sic lactare animos & sic ostendere gemmam
      Excitat optatus auidos, & ventilat ignem.
      Quare etiam nuper Pyrij de pulueris ictu
      Principis innocuam seruastis numina Vitam,
35   Vt morbi perimant, alióque in puluere prostet?
      Phoebe, tui puduit quum summo manè redires
      Sol sine sole tuo! quàm te tum nubibus atris
      Totum offuscari peteres, vt nocte silenti
      Humana aeternos agerent praecordia questus:
40   Tantùm etenim vestras (Parcae) non flectit habenas
      Tempus edax rerum, túque o mors improba sola es,
      Cui caecas tribuit vires annosa vetustas.
      Quid non mutatum est? requiêrunt flumina cursus;
      Plus etiam veteres coelum videre remotum:
45   Cur ideo verbis tristes effundere curas
      Expeto, tanquam haec sit nostri medicina doloris?
      Immodicus luctus tacito vorat igne medullas,
      Vt, fluuio currente, vadum sonat, alta quiescunt.

Why then, Muse, come on, speak out, I beg you, was the
    divinity offended?
What were the hidden reasons? What sin so great have we
    committed
That neither the wool-bearing beasts, nor the herds could
    atone for it?
Wouldn't a long famine or the destruction of a grim plague   20
Have been a lesser punishment, than the Prince's wretched
    fate?
Now is Philomela blessed, and Dido, too, aware of her
    intention!
Lucky those whom war oppresses, and many a sword!
They fear nothing more; our misfortune has only
Wounded Fate, Fortune and our hope for the future.   25
But if the fates begrudged enduring health to him
And to his father's realm (for that Prince's rule
For what could we have hoped? – no, rather for
    what could we not?)
Then they ought to have struck the very earliest and least
    noble stage of life:
Either a swift death or a lengthy old age is what the good
    deserve: 30
To delude the soul in this way, and display the jewel
Rouses greedy wishes, and fans the flame.
Why too did you, divine powers, so recently preserve
    from the blast of gunpowder
The life of the Prince, unharmed,
Only for disease to destroy it, and he set out for sale in dust
    of a different order?   35

Apollo, how ashamed you were to return at dawn
You, the sun, alone, without your sun! How you
    might then have begged
To be covered completely with black clouds, so that in the
    silence of night
Human hearts might keep up an everlasting lamentation:
To your reins only (Fates) does time   40

Innupta Pallas, nata Diespitre,
Aeterna summae gloria regiae,
    Cui dulcis arrident Camoenae
        Pieridis Latiaéque Musae,

5   Cur tela Mortis vel tibi vel tuis
Quâcunque guttâ temporis imminent?
    Tantâque propendet staterâ
        Regula sanguinolenta fati?

Númne Hydra talis, tantáne bellua est
10 Mors tot virorum sordida sanguine,
    Vt mucro rumpatur Mineruae,
        Vtque minax superetur Aegis?

Tu flectis amnes, tu mare caerulum
Vssisse prono fulmine diceris,
15   Aiacis exesas triremes
        Praecipitans grauiore casu.

Tu discidisti Gorgoneas manus
Nexas, capillos anguibus oblitos,
    Furuósque vicisti Gigantes,
20   Enceladum pharetrámque Rhoeci.

Not bend, Time the glutton of matter, and you O wicked
    Death are the only one
To whom gnarled old age had offered unlimited power.

What has not been changed? The rivers rest in their course;
Men of old saw heaven even farther off:
Why then am I so eager to pour forth in words   45
Gloomy cares, as if this were the remedy for our pain?
Immoderate grief devours the marrow in silent fire,
Just as, in a running river, the shallows resound, while the
    deeps are silent.

[Ode Appended to the
Previous Poem]

Virgin Pallas, daughter of Zeus,
Eternal glory of the highest palace,
    Upon whom smile the Camoenae of sweet
        Pieria and the Muses of Latium,

Why do the shafts of Death loom   5
Over you and yours at every drop of time?
    Why does Fate's bloody rule
        Hover heavy with its balance?

Surely the Hydra is not so dreadful, nor Death
Begrimed with the blood of so many men,   10
    Such a beast that Minerva's sword-tip is broken,
        That even the dread Aegis is overwhelmed?

You re-route rivers, you are said
To have scorched the green sea itself with a plummeting
    thunderbolt;
    Ajax's ruined triremes   15
        You cast headlong for a more serious reason.

Ceu victa, Musis porrigit herbulas
Pennata caeci dextra Cupidinis,
 Non vlla Bellonae furentis
  Arma tui metuunt alumni.

25 Pallas retortis caesia vocibus
Respondit: Eia, ne metuas, precor,
 Nam fata non iustis repugnant
  Principibus, sed amica fiunt.

Vt si recisis arboribus meis
30 Nudetur illic lucus amabilis,
 Fructúsque post mortem recusent
  Perpetuos mihi ferre rami,

Dulcem rependent tum mihi tibiam
Pulchrè renatam ex arbore mortuâ,
35 Dignámque coelesti coronâ
  Harmoniam dabit inter astra.

G. Herbert Coll. Trin.

In Natales et Pascha Concurrentes.

Cvm tu, Christe, cadis, nascor; mentémque ligauit
 Vna meam membris horula, téque cruci.
O me disparibus natum cum numine fatis!
 Cur mihi das vitam, quam tibi, Christe, negas?
5 Quin moriar tecum: vitam, quam negligis ipse,
 Accipe; ni talem des, tibi qualis erat.

You have cut off the hands of the Gorgon
Bound as they were, her hair smeared with snakes,
   You have conquered the swarthy Giants,
     Enceladus and the bow of Rhoecus.   20

As if he too is conquered, Cupid's feathered hand
Offers to the Muses a posy of herbs,
   Your followers have no fear
     Of any of the weapons of raging Bellona.

Grey-eyed Pallas replies with swift words: 25
Come now, have no fear, I beg you,
   For the fates do not contend against
     Just princes, but are friendly towards them.

So if, my trees are cut down,
The lovely grove stripped bare,   30
   And after death the branches there
     Refuse to bear for me perpetual fruit,

They shall repay me then with the sweet tibia
Beautifully reborn from the dead tree,
   And it shall grant, fit for a heavenly crown,   35
     A harmony among the stars.

            G. Herbert, Trinity College

On His Birthday and Good Friday Falling on the Same Day.

As you die, Christ, I am born; one little hour bound
  My mind to my limbs, you to the Cross.
Me, born with a fate quite unlike that of God!
  Why give me that life which, Christ, you deny to yourself?
But surely I shall die with you: that life, for which
    you care so little,
  Take it up! As long as the life you give is not like
  the one you had.   5

Hoc mihi legatum tristi si funere praestes,
    Christe, duplex fiet mors tua vita mihi:
Atque vbi per te sanctificer natalibus ipsis,
10   In vitam & neruos Pascha coaeua fluet.

In Obitum Serenissimae
Reginae Annae.

Qvo Te, foelix Anna, modo deflere licebit?
    Cui magnum imperium, gloria maior erat:
Ecce meus torpens animus succumbit vtrique,
    Cui tenuis fama est, ingeniúmque minus.
5 Quis, nisi qui manibus Briareus, oculísque sit Argus,
    Scribere, Te dignùm, vel lachrymare queat!
Frustra igitur sudo: superest mihi sola voluptas,
    Quòd calamum excusent Pontus & Astra meum:
Namque Annae laudes coelo scribuntur aperto,
10   Sed luctus noster scribitur Oceano.

                 G. Herbert Coll. Trin. Soc.

Ad Autorem Instaurationis Magnae.

Per strages licet autorum veterúmque ruinam
    Ad famae properes vera Tropaea tuae,
Tam nitidè tamen occidis, tam suauiter, hostes,
    Se quasi donatum funere quisque putat.
5 Scilicet apponit pretium tua dextera fato,
    Vulneréque emanat sanguis, vt intret honos.
O quàm felices sunt, qui tua castra sequuntur,
    Cùm per te sit res ambitiosa mori.

If by your sorrowful death you offer this as a legacy for me,
    Christ, then your death will become for me a double life:
And when I am sanctified by you on my own natal day,
    The Passion, brother, shall flow into my life and my very
        fibre.   10

On the Death of the Fairest
Queen Anne.

How, blessed Anna, will it be possible to mourn you?
    You who possessed great authority, and greater glory:
See how my failing spirit droops at both,
    I who possess only slender renown, and less ability.
What man, unless he had the hands of Briareus, and the eyes
      of Argus,   5
    Could write something worthy of you – or even weep it.
Therefore I sweat in vain: only this pleasure remains for me,
    That the Sea and the Stars excuse my pen:
For the praises of Anne are written on the expanses of heaven,
    But our grief is inscribed upon the Ocean.   10

G. Herbert, Fellow of Trinity College

To the Author of INSTAURATIO MAGNA.

Although through the wreckage and ruin of ancient authors
    You are hastening to your fame's true rewards,
Still you slay your enemies so charmingly, so sweetly,
    That each one thinks his death a gift.
I've no doubt that your right hand adds value to fate,   5
    And blood drips from the wound, so that honour can enter.
O how lucky are they, who follow your camp,
    Since a man could aspire to die in your service.

Comparatio inter Munus Summi
Cancellariatus et Librum.

Mvnere dum nobis prodes, Libróque futuris,
　　In laudes abeunt secula quaeque tuas;
Munere dum nobis prodes, Libróque remotis,
　　In laudes abeunt iam loca quaeque tuas:
5　Hae tibi sunt alae laudum. Cui contigit vnquam
　　Longius aeterno, latius orbe decus?

In Honorem Illustr. D. D. Verulamij,
S^{ti} Albani, Mag. Sigilli Custodis
post Editam ab eo Instaurationem Magnam.

Qvis iste tandem? non enim vultu ambulat
Quotidiano! Nescis, ignare? Audies!
Dux Notionum; veritatis Pontifex;
Inductionis Dominus, & Verulamij;
5　Rerum magister vnicus, at non Artium;
Profunditatis pinus, atque Elegantiae;
Naturae Aruspex intimus; Philosophiae
Aerarium; sequester expèrientiae,
Speculationísque; Aequitatis signifer;
10　Scientiarum, sub pupillari statu
Degentium olim, Emancipator; Luminis
Promus; Fugator Idolûm, atque nubium;
Collega Solis; Quadra Certitudinis;
Sophismatomastix; Brutus Literarius,
15　Authoritatis exuens tyrannidem;

Comparison between the Office and the Book of the High Chancellor.

While you assist us with your office, and men of the future
  with your book,
    Each age turns to your praises;
While you assist us with your office, and far off men with
  your book,
    Each place turns to your praise:
These are the wings of your praise. Who before has ever
  enjoyed   5
    A glory longer than eternity, broader than the earth?

In Honour of the Illustrious Lord Verulam, Viscount St Alban, Keeper of the Great Seal, After the Publication of His Instauratio Magna.

'Who then is this man? For he doesn't walk around
With an ordinary expression!' Don't you know, you idiot?
  Listen then!
The Commander of Ideas; Archpriest of truth;
Lord of the Inductive Method, and of Verulam;
As master of matter (though not of Arts) unique.   5
The Pine of Profundity, and of Elegance;
A deep diviner of Nature's inner workings; of Philosphy
The treasury; the agent of experimentation,
And of speculation; the standard-bearer of Impartiality;
The Saviour of the sciences, which have long been   10
Living as orphans; of Light
The Steward; Router of Idols, and of clouds;
Colleague of the Sun; the measure of Certainty;

Rationis & sensûs stupendus Arbiter;
Repumicator mentis; Atlas Physicus,
Alcide succumbente Stagiritico;
Columba Noae, quae in vetustis artibus
20   Nullum locum requiémue cernens perstitit
Ad se suaéque matris Arcam regredi:
Subtilitatis Terebra; Temporis Nepos
Ex Veritate matre; Mellis alueus;
Mundíque & Animarum sacerdos vnicus;
25   Securis errorum; ínque Naturalibus
Granum Sinapis, acre Alijs, crescens sibi:
    O me probè lassum! Iuuate, Posteri!

                    G. HERBERT ORAT. Pub. in
                         Acad. Cantab.

Aethiopissa ambit Cestum
Diuersi Coloris Virum.

Qvid mihi si facies nigra est? hoc, Ceste, colore
    Sunt etiam tenebrae, quas tamen optat amor.
Cernis vt exustâ semper sit fronte viator;
    Ah longum, quae te deperit, errat iter.
5   Si nigro sit terra solo, quis despicit aruum?
    Claude oculos, & erunt omnia nigra tibi:
Aut aperi, & cernes corpus quas proijcit vmbras;
    Hoc saltem officio fungar amore tui.
Cùm mihi sit facies fumus, quas pectore flammas
10   Iamdudum tacitè delituisse putes?
Dure, negas? O fata mihi praesaga doloris,
    Quae mihi lugubres contribuere genas!

Scourge of Sophistry; a literary Brutus,
Shedding the tyranny of authority; 15
A wonderful Judge of Sense and Reason;
The Polisher of the Mind; Atlas of Natural Philosophy,
Even as the Herculean Stagirite falls reeling;
Noah's Dove, who could not find
Any place of rest amongst the arts of old, and so determined 20
To return to herself and to her mother's Ark:
Gimlet of Subtlety; Grandson of Time
Descended from mother Truth; hive of Honey;
The only priest of the World and of Souls;
The axe of error; and in matters of Nature 25
The mustard-seed, sour to others, flourishing in itself:
    O I am truly worn out! Help me, Posterity!

                G. HERBERT, Public Orator at the
                        University of Cambridge.

An Ethiopian Girl Woos Cestus, a Man of a Different Colour.

What matters it to me if my face is black? Of the same
    colour, Cestus,
  Is the dark, and love longs for the dark all the same.
You know that travellers always have a brow burnt by the sun;
  Ah a long road indeed must she wander, the girl who dies
    for love of you.
If earth of the land is black, who despises the furrow? 5
  Shut your eyes, and everything is black to you:
Or open them, and you'll see the shadows cast by the body;
  This service at least I'll perform for love of you.
Since my face is smoke, what flames do you think
  Have lurked all this time within my breast in silence? 10
Hard-hearted, do you refuse? O the fates were foresightful
    of my grief
  When they gave me these mournful cheeks!

Dum petit Infantem.

Dvm petit Infantem Princeps, Grantámque Iacobus,
    Quisnam horum maior sit, dubitatur, amor.
Vincit more suo Noster: nam millibus Infans
    Non tot abest, quot nos Regis ab ingenio.

In obitum incomparabilis Francisci Vicecomitis Sancti Albani, Baronis Verulamij.

Dvm longi lentíque gemis sub pondere morbi
    Atque haeret dubio tabida vita pede,
Quid voluit prudens Fatum, iam sentio tandem:
    Constat, *Aprile* vno te potuisse mori:
5 Vt *Flos* hinc lacrymis, illinc *Philomela* querelis,
    Deducant *linguae* funera sola tuae.

GEORGIVS HERBERT

In Sacram Anchoram Piscatoris, G. Herbert.

Qvod Crux nequibat fixa, Clauíque additi,
(Tenere Christum scilicet, ne ascenderet)
Tuíue Christum deuocans facundia
Vltra loquendi tempus; addit Anchora:
5 Nec hoc abundè est tibi, nisi certae Anchorae
Addas sigillum: nempe Symbolum suae
Tibi debet Unda & Terra certitudinis.

    Quondam fessus Amor loquens Amato,
    Tot & tanta loquens amica, scripsit:
10 Tandem & fessa manus, dedit sigillum.

While He Seeks the Infanta. *

While Prince to Spain, and King to Cambridge goes,
The question is, whose love the greater shows:
Ours (like himself) o'ercomes; for his wit's more
Remote from ours, than Spain from Britain's shore.

On the Death of the Incomparable
Francis, Viscount St Alban,
Baron Verulam.

While you groan beneath the weight of a long, slow illness,
  And your fading life clings on, with a trembling gait,
Now at last I see what careful Fate has planned:
  It is obvious that you could only have died in *April*:
So that *Flora* weeping here, and *Philomela* lamenting there,   5
  May conduct the funeral – the funeral only of your *tongue*.

GEORGE HERBERT

On the Sacred Anchor of the
Fisherman, G. Herbert.†

Although the Crosse could not Christ here detain,
Though nail'd unto't, but he ascends again,
Nor yet thy eloquence here keep him still,
But onely while thou speak'st; This Anchor will.
Nor canst thou be content, unlesse thou to   5
This certain Anchor adde a Seal, and so
The Water, and the Earth both unto thee
Doe owe the symbole of their certainty.

* Herbert's translation
† Herbert's translation

Suauis erat, qui scripta dolens lacerando recludi,
Sanctius in Regno Magni credebat Amoris
(In quo fas nihil est rumpi) donare sigillum.

Munde, fluas fugiásque licet, nos nostráque fixi:
Deridet motus sancta catena tuos.

15

When Love being weary made an end
Of kinde Expressions to his friend,   10
He writ; when's hand could write no more,
He gave the Seale, and so left o're.

How sweet a friend was he, who being griev'd
His letters were broke rudely up, believ'd
'Twas more secure in great Loves Common-weal   15
(Where nothing should be broke) to adde a Seal.

Let the world reel, we and all ours stand sure,
This holy Cable's of all storms secure.

[Another version] *

When my dear Friend, could write no more,
He gave this *Seal*, and, so gave ore.
When winds and waves rise highest, I am sure,
This *Anchor* keeps my *faith*, that, me secure.

* Also by Herbert

Appendix:
Latin Poetry and Latin Metre

Latin is a highly inflected language. This means that it changes the grammatical function of words by changing their endings, as in English 'walk' is a present tense verb, but 'walked' is a past tense, and 'cat' indicates one animal, but 'cats' tells us that there are two or more. In Latin this capacity of words to indicate their grammatical function by changes to their form is much greater than in English and applies to almost all parts of speech with many possible forms. One of the most significant differences is that Latin uses these changes of ending to indicate the difference between the grammatical subject of a sentence (the person or thing who is performing the action of the verb) and the object (the person or thing to whom that action is done). For instance, in English, we indicate the difference between 'the dog bit Joseph' and 'Joseph bit the dog' by changing the order of words in the sentence – accordingly, that order is essential to the meaning: the noun that comes before the verb is the subject (the person or thing 'doing' the verb, in this case the person biting) and the noun that comes after the verb is the object (in this case, the one who is bitten). Latin, on the other hand, uses different forms of the words for 'dog' and 'Joseph' to indicate which is the subject and which the object. (We see a remnant in English of this sort of change in the difference between 'I' and 'me', 'they' and 'them', 'she' and 'her'.) The result – which is particularly significant for poetry – is that Latin has much greater flexibility of word order, allowing a poet to choose the order of words for poetic effect – for instance, to place two nouns or two adjectives together – rather than principally for sense.

In addition, and partly as a result of this feature of Latin, Latin has fewer of the 'little' words that English has: words like 'the', 'a', 'of', 'for', 'to' are mostly unnecessary in Latin, since changes to the endings of words often indicate these meanings. This adds to the compression that can be achieved, especially in poetry. For instance, the very last word of Herbert's Latin verse collection *Passio Discerpta* is *meam*, a Latin adjective which means 'my', but which also indicates by its form that it is referring to something that is grammatically feminine (all nouns in Latin have a gender, as in French) and which is the object of the sentence, not its subject. In this instance it refers to the (feminine) noun *quaestio*, meaning the subject of an enquiry or debate. Herbert is here addressing Plato and urging him to recognize Christ as the 'soul of the world'. The poem is about the choice between classical philosophy and Christianity, and the superiority of the latter. But the flexibility of Latin word order allows Herbert to end the poem – and with it, the whole collection – with a single word, *meam*, which suggests his own adherence to, and representation of, the Christian world view ('my theory', that is, the Christian understanding of the world) but also refers strongly to *himself* and his work: me, the poet, *my* words. The much greater limitations on English word order make it impossible to recreate this kind of effect.

The conventions governing the composition of Latin verse in the classical (rather than medieval) tradition were well understood in early modern England, but they are quite different to the principles of scansion in English verse. English poetry is usually described in terms of beats or stresses, and the patterns of, for instance, an iambic pentameter, are created by the juxtaposition of stressed and unstressed syllables. The patterns of Latin poetry, by contrast, are constructed not primarily according to whether or not a syllable is stressed in speech, but whether it is long or short.

This is not the place to offer a detailed account of the distinctions between long and short syllables in Latin, but the basic principles are easy to grasp. The syllables of words have a natural length (for instance, the common word *dominus* ('lord' or 'master') is three short syllables). A cluster of two or more consonants tends to make the preceding vowel long, and this is true whether the consonant cluster is part of the same word or starts a new one. For instance, in the word *Christus* ('Christ' in Latin), the cluster of *s* and *t* makes the *i* long, so the first syllable of that word is a long not a short syllable. In the phrase *Christum callidum* the combination of the *m* at the end of the *Christum* and the *c* at the beginning of *callidum* make the final syllable of *Christum* long. Many 'quantities' – that is, whether a syllable is long or short – can be deduced from applying a small set of rules of this sort, while some others have to be learnt alongside vocabulary on an individual basis. The final syllable of each line is lengthened by its position – because it is natural to pause at the end of a line of poetry. For this reason a syllable which is naturally short can stand in this position, where it 'counts' as a long syllable.

In addition, where one word ends with a vowel and the next word begins with a vowel – as we find twice in the phrase *ex praelio undae ignisque* (*Musae Responsoriae* 27) – the two words are 'elided', that is the *o* of *praelio* and the *u* of *undae* are merged to form a single syllable, and the same thing happens in this line between *undae* and *ignis*. Conventionally, this effect is not represented in written Latin (though it is pronounced in reading poetry aloud), unlike in Greek poetry, and indeed in English: the poetic form *'Twas* (for 'it was') is an example of a similar phenomenon.

In order to describe the patterns of long and short syllables in Latin metres, we use a conventional notation: – denotes a long syllable, and ⌣ a short syllable. So two longs is shown as: – –, two shorts as ⌣ ⌣, and so on. The following notes use these symbols to indicate the patterns of longs and shorts in each of the Latin metres that Herbert uses. Where the poet has a choice – for instance between a long and a short syllable or a long and two shorts – this is represented by printing both options, with the 'standard' or 'basic' pattern in the main line and the possible alternative option above. Latin verse lines are conventionally divided into 'feet', internal divisions marked here by | .

In these notes I have avoided as much as possible the technical

terms used by scholars of Latin metre; and in some of the more
flexible forms I have also simplified to a small degree the range
of options available in order to reflect most straightforwardly
what we actually find in Herbert's poetry. Almost every thor-
ough Latin grammar offers more detailed explanation of the
principles of Latin metre for interested readers. Freis, Freis and
Miller includes a full guide to the metres of *Memoriae Matris
Sacrum*, which includes many but not all of those described
here.

DACTYLIC HEXAMETER

The hexameter line is the metrical form used in both Greek and
Latin epic poems, but also in other long and medium-length
forms such as didactic and pastoral. Occasionally, epigrams or
other short pieces are found in hexameters: usually this sug-
gests some association between the subject or tone of the poem
and the typical themes and subjects of hexameter verse (such as
glory, heroism or religious or mythological themes). The hex-
ameter line is also used as the first line in each elegiac couplet
(see below). The word 'dactylic' refers to the basic pattern of a
long followed by two shorts (– ◡ ◡, also called a dactyl).

The basic pattern of a hexameter line in Latin is as follows:

This is a flexible metre. In each of the first four feet the poet can
choose between the basic pattern of the metre – ◡ ◡ or two
longs – –. For an example of Herbert's Latin hexameters, see
for example *Lucus* 32 ('The Triumph of Death'). By far the
longest poem in *Lucus*, the hexameter has been chosen to suit
the mock-epic subject and tone of that poem. By contrast, it is
also used, to solemn effect, for *Musae Responsoriae* 39, a seri-
ous poem in praise of the king, and the penultimate piece in the
collection.

ELEGIAC COUPLETS

Elegiac couplets are composed of a hexameter line (see above) followed by a pentameter (that is, a shorter line of five feet). In this second shorter line, there is a strong break half way through (indicated by ‖):

$$
\bar{–}\; \smile\smile \mid \bar{–}\; \smile\smile \mid \bar{–}\; \smile\smile \mid \bar{–}\; \smile\smile \mid \bar{–}\; \smile\smile \mid \smile\,\bar{–}
$$

$$
–\; \text{uu} \mid \bar{–}\; \text{uu} \mid \bar{–}\; \| \bar{–}\; \text{uu} \mid \bar{–}\; \text{uu} \mid –\; \overset{u}{–}
$$

The second line of each couplet (the pentameter) is less flexible than the first (the hexameter), since the poet may choose between – ⌣ ⌣ and – – only in the first two feet of the line. Accordingly, in a poem composed in elegiac couplets each even-numbered line (the pentameters) sounds more alike than the odd-numbered lines. Conventionally, there is also often a distinction in sense or tone between the hexameter and the pentameter lines. In epigrams, this can be used to point a contrast or present alternative perspectives.

A very large number of Herbert's Latin poems use elegiac couplets: it is the metre that he uses most frequently. The first poem of *Lucus* is an example.

IAMBIC TRIMETERS

After elegiac couplets, this is the second most-commonly used metrical form for early modern Latin epigrams, and it is one that Herbert used often. The basic pattern is as follows:

$$
\smile\,–\,\smile\,– \mid \smile\,–\,\smile\,– \mid \smile\,–\,\smile\,\bar{–}
$$

The iambic metres (iambic trimeters, iambic distichs and choliambics) also allow 'resolution': this is where any syllable that is long (–) in the basic pattern may be replaced by two shorts (⌣⌣). In combination with the existing short syllables in the metrical pattern, this allows for runs of several short syllables in a row. This makes iambic forms some of the most flexible in Latin poetry, leading to a large range of possible rhythmic effects. Herbert uses iambic trimeters fairly frequently: an example is *Lucus* 11.

IAMBIC DISTICHS

A less common form, this creates couplets from an iambic trimeter (see above) followed by an iambic dimeter – that is, a short two-foot version of the iambic line.

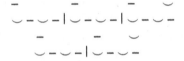

The resulting couplets – of a longer followed by a slightly shorter line – gives a similar effect to the elegiac couplet, but iambic distichs are conventionally associated more with critical, satiric or invective poems. Like iambic trimeters, 'resolution' is allowed (see **iambic trimeter** above). A good example is *Musae Responsoriae* 8. *Memoriae Matris Sacrum* 8 is also in this metre.

CHOLIAMBIC

A variant of the iambic trimeter which is associated strongly with satirical and invective poetry. Herbert uses this form just once at *Memoriae Matris Sacrum* 12, in which he attacks those who (apparently) criticize the extent of his grief.

⌣–⌣–|⌣–⌣–|⌣– –⌣

Like iambic trimeters and the iambic distich, the choliambic allows 'resolution' of long syllables (see **iambic trimeter** above).

HENDECASYLLABLES

This eleven-syllable line is associated particularly with Catullus and the neo-Latin imitators of Catullus (from Pontano onwards). It is also often used for epigrams. Herbert uses the metre fairly often: examples are *Lucus* 5, *Passio Discerpta* 19 and *Memoriae Matris Sacrum* 10.

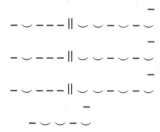

SAPPHICS

This is a Latin adaptation of a Greek lyric metre used (among others) by Sappho. The form in which is it most commonly written in Latin lyric verse of Herbert's time is modelled upon Horace's Sapphic stanza. A poem in Sapphics is composed of four-line stanzas or verses, and each stanza follows a rigid metrical scheme. The first three lines of each stanza follow an identical pattern, with a different form in the shorter final line (sometimes understood as an extension of line three):

As the poet has very few options in this metrical form, Sapphics – like the other lyric metres – are particularly challenging to compose. For an example in Herbert, see *Musae Responso-riae* 14.

ALCAICS

Like Sapphics, these four-line stanzas use a form inherited from Greek poets (the name refers to the archaic Greek poet Alcaeus), but adapted for Latin by Horace. This is the most common metrical form in Horace's *Odes*, and it is associated in particular with fairly serious, and often public poetry. This form was widely used in early modern Europe for grand public odes or odes on serious political themes.

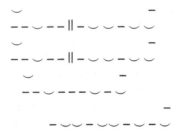

As most of the quantities in this metre are fixed, each stanza sounds rhythmically similar. In particular, the metre is marked by the 'slower' third line (with three long syllables in a row in the middle) and the 'quicker' final line (with a large proportion of short syllables). For an example in Herbert, see the major ode on music *Musae Responsoriae* 23.

GLYCONICS

The 'glyconic' line is the basis of many more complex metres, including the various asclepiad metres (see below). Neither Horace nor Catullus used a sequence of pure glyconics in a poem, but we do find the line used in this way in some of Seneca's tragic choruses, and also in neo-Latin verse. Herbert uses this form – as a single repeated line, though arranged into verses – in *Musae Responsoriae* 25.

'LESSER' ASCLEPIAD

This fairly unusual form is simply a repeated 'asclepiad' line, an expanded form of the glyconic. For an example in Herbert, see *Musae Responsoriae* 17. This is a challenging verse form: only the second syllable of each line may be either long or short.

'THIRD' ASCLEPIAD

Another asclepiad metre formed by alternating in couplets a gly-conic line and a 'lesser' asclepiad line (see above for both). Herbert uses this metre in *Musae Responsoriae* 40, an ode addressed to God himself, and the final poem of the collection, and again in *Memoriae Matris Sacrum* 4. This relatively unusual metre is also found at Horace, *Odes* 4.3, in praise of Horace's Muse. Herbert's poem echoes the language as well as the metre of the Horatian ode.

Confusingly, different reference works number the asclepiad metres differently, and some books refer to this as the 'second' or 'fourth' rather than 'third' asclepiad.

'THIRD' ARCHILOCHIAN

Used just once by Herbert, at *Musae Responsoriae* 28, this unusual metre is normally printed in classical texts as two lines, but in Herbert's text it is arranged as three: a longer first line and two shorter lines of slightly different metrical form. The first line of this pattern is in fact an iambic trimeter and the last line an iambic dimeter (see **iambic distichs** above); the middle line is the same as the second half of the iambic pentameter (used as the second line in an **elegiac couplet**). This metre is used by Horace in *Epodes* 11.

ANACREONTICS

A light metre of short eight-syllable lines, this metre is found in the *Anacreontea*, a collection of Greek lyric poetry fashionable in Herbert's day. Early modern Latin poets also used this metre, but in Herbert's verse it is found only in a Greek poem, *Memoriae Matris Sacrum* 16.

Like most lyric metres, the quantities in each line are largely fixed. It is only the final syllable which may be either long or short.

Notes

Biblical quotations are from the King James Bible, except for the Psalms. These were more familiar to Herbert in Coverdale's version of 1535, which was included in the Book of Common Prayer, according to which they were to be recited at Morning and Evening Prayer daily over every month.

Abbreviations Used in the Notes

Andrewes	*Lancelot Andrewes: Sermons*, ed. G. M. Story (Oxford: Clarendon Press, 1967)
B	The Bodleian Library Manuscript (Tanner 307) of *The Temple* copied by the scribes at Little Gidding, the community headed by H's friend Nicholas Ferrar, from a 'little book' (Walton, now lost) entrusted to them by H on his deathbed. A diplomatic edition of it, ed. Mario A. di Cesare, was published by Medieval and Renaissance Texts and Studies (Binghampton, NY, 1995)
BCP	The Book of Common Prayer
Blair	Rhonda L. Blair, 'George Herbert's Greek Poetry', *Philological Quarterly* 64 (1984), 573–84
Bloch	Chana Bloch, *Spelling the Word: George Herbert and the Bible* (Berkeley: University of California Press, 1985)
CP	George Herbert, *A Priest to the Temple, or, the Country Parson* (1652)
FFM	*Memoriae Matris Sacrum*, ed. Catherine Freis, Richard Freis and Greg Miller (Fairfield, Conn.: George Herbert Journal, Special Studies and Monographs, 2012)
Geneva	The Geneva Bible (1560)
Gilmore	John I. Gilmore, 'Aethiopissoe: the classical tradition, Neo-Latin verse and images of race in George Herbert and Vincent Bourne', *Classical Reception Journal* 1 (2009), 73–86

H	George Herbert
HC	Holy Communion
Heaney	Seamus Heaney, *The Redress of Poetry* (London: Faber and Faber, 1995)
Hutchinson	*The Works of George Herbert*, ed. F. E. Hutchinson (Oxford: Clarendon Press, 1941 and 1945)
KJB	The King James Bible (1611)
Knights	L. C. Knights, *Explorations* (London: Chatto & Windus, 1946)
Laws	Richard Hooker, *Of the Laws of Ecclesiastical Polity* in *Works*, ed. Keble (Oxford, 1836)
NT	The New Testament
OED	Oxford English Dictionary
OT	The Old Testament
Puttenham	George Puttenham, *The Art of English Poesy* (1589); Critical Edition by Whigham and Rebhorn (Ithaca, NY: Cornell University Press, 2007)
Summers	Joseph H. Summers, *George Herbert: His Religion and Art* (London: Chatto & Windus, 1954)
Tuve	Rosamund Tuve, *A Reading of George Herbert* (London: Faber and Faber, 1952)
W	The manuscript of H's poems in Dr Williams's Library, London
Walton	Izaak Walton, *The Life of Mr George Herbert* (1675), as reprinted in *George Herbert: The Complete English Works*, ed. Ann Pasternak Slater (London: Everyman's Library, 1995)
Wilcox	Helen Wilcox, *The English Poems of George Herbert* (Cambridge: Cambridge University Press, 2007)
1633	George Herbert, *The Temple, Sacred Poems and Private Ejaculations* (Cambridge: T. Buck and R. Daniel, 1633)

THE TEMPLE: SACRED POEMS AND PRIVATE EJACULATIONS

The title page of 1633 is based on that of B, where 'The Dedication' is in the middle of the page and written by one of the Little Gidding scribes who also worked on the main text. Above it is written

The Temple
Psal: 29:8.

In his Temple doth every man
speake of his honour.

in Nicholas Ferrar's hand. H's own title, inscribed at the top of every page from 'The Altar' to the final 'Love (3)' in W, B and 1633, is 'The Church'. So *The Temple* seems to be Ferrar's invention. And his addition of the quotation from Psalm 29 is not particularly apt to the continual mood swings of H's poetry. The subtitle 'Sacred Poems and Private Ejaculations' (apparently the printers' contribution in capital letters) is nearer the mark – an ejaculation being an outburst of feeling into words. The printers also moved 'The Dedication' to follow 'The Printers to the Reader'.

The Printers to the Reader

The Printers . . . Reader: the first biography of H, by Nicholas Ferrar (not 'the printers') and a source for Walton's much longer *Life* of 1670.

4–6   *the Muses . . . Helicon*: nine deities who inspired writers and were based on Mount Helicon in Boeotia – thus the sponsors of pagan and secular literature.

36   *his Word*: the Bible.

47   *the Ecclesiastical dignity*: Bishop Williams of Lincoln granted H the prebend (income) of the church at Leighton Bromswold near Little Gidding in 1626. H and the Ferrars worked together on its restoration and furnishing (which survives). H offered to resign the income to Ferrar, who took on the practicalities but refused the offer.

65   *Less than the least of God's mercies*: H's motto adapted from Ephesians 3:8 and the refrain of his poem 'The Posy'.

The Dedication

The first poem in W. Its last two lines show that, while H kept his English poems in manuscript all his life, he did expect them to be read by others – as the following poem *The Church-Porch* bears out.

1   *first fruits*: Deuteronomy 26.

The Church-porch

Church porches, furnished with benches, sheltered informal gatherings and conversations – and often a little village school, such as John Evelyn attended as a child. Accordingly, this long poem is both didactic and chatty: seventy-seven stanzas in iambic pentameters with much enjambement. There is a topic to each stanza with the moral in the final couplet. If H here fails to take his own advice to 'give men turns of speech' (line 303), he rewards patient readers by his wit and vivid pictures from life. Its topics range through sex, drink, lying, idleness, education, table manners, money, dress, gaming, conversation, jokes, friendship, cleanliness, almsgiving and churchgoing. Experience and observation of the secular world are its main source, with advice about churchgoing (particularly how to govern oneself during poor sermons) in the last ten stanzas. The biblical Book of Proverbs is a model: see Bloch, pp. 179–187. See also H's own collections of proverbs, *Outlandish* [i.e., foreign] *Proverbs* and *Jacula Prudentum*.

PERIRRHANTERIUM

A pagan (Greek) instrument for sprinkling purifying water on participants before a religious ceremony, especially sacrifice. As 'SUPERLIMINARE', which follow *The Church-Porch*, makes clear, taking the good advice in *The Church-Porch* would be a kind of moral purification, being sprinkled before a sacrifice. Psalm 51:7: 'Purge me with hyssop and I shall be clean: wash me and I shall be whiter than snow.'

7–24 Beware of lust . . . pollute and foul: W has three stanzas:

> Beware of lust (startle not) O beware
> It makes the soul a blot: it is a rod
> Whose twigs are pleasures, and they whip thee bare,
> It spoils an Angel: robs thee of thy God.
>> How dare those eyes upon a bible look
>> Much less towards God, whose Lust is all their book?

> Abstain or wed: if thou canst not abstain
> Yet wedding mars thy fortune, fast and pray:
> If this seems monkish; think which brings most pain
> Need or incontinency: the first way
>> If thou choose bravely and rely on God
>> He'll make thy wife a blessing not a rod.

> Let not each fancy make thee to detest
> A virgin-bed, which hath a special crown
> If it concur with virtue: do thy best
> And God will show thee how to take the town,

> And win thy self: compare the joys and so
> If rottenness have more, let heaven go.

19 *If God had laid all common*: Lines 19–22 refer to the enclosing or impaling of open common land by fencing for arable use (ploughing: a metaphor for sex).

24 *cross*: perverse, contradictory.

30 *round*: of drinks.

31–2 *He that is drunken . . . lost the reins*: See St Augustine, *Sermon* 33, where a drunkard 'wickedly smothered his pregnant mother, tried to rape his sister, almost killed his father and fatally wounded two other sisters'. Quoted in Robert Burton, *The Anatomy of Melancholy* (1632), Pt.1. Sect.2. Memb.3. Subs.13.

36 *All worldly . . . by beast*: W has instead:

> He that has all ill, and can have no good
> Because no knowledge, is not earth but mud.

39 *can*: drinking vessel.

48 *God's stamp*: 'God created man in his own image,' Genesis 1:7. The same Greek word *ikon* is used for Caesar's stamp on a coin in Matthew 22:20.

50 *nor make thy shame thy glory*: 'whose glory is in their shame', Phillippians 3:19.

60 *Epicure*: an irreligious sybarite; *bate*: abstain from.

64 *pares*: peels.

71 *broad*: 'broad is the way, that leadeth to destruction,' Matthew 7:13.

76 *working*: agitated.

80 *dressing, mistressing, and compliment*: Word for word the same as line 30 of Donne's 'To Mr Tilman after he had taken orders'. Tilman was ordained priest in 1620 when Donne and H had known one another for twenty years.

87 *Redeem truth from his jaws*: an excellent metaphor of the scholar's duty.

90 *If they dare . . . or grave*: W has an additional stanza next:

> If thou art nothing, think what thou wouldst be
> He that desires is more than half the way.
> But if thou cool, then take some shame to thee
> Desire and shame, will make thy labour, play:
> > This is earth's language, for if heaven come in,
> > Thou hast run all thy race, ere thou begin.

94   *sheepishness*: mean-spirited, withdrawn.
96   *gone to grass*: grazing, merely consuming like sheep.
99   *mark*: take aim at.
100   *ship them over*: send them abroad.
102   *And if God's . . . let thine*: If not moved by having a child in God's image, at least consider your own image in society.
106   *leave*: in the sense of lack.
110   *rest*: contentment.
117   *stour*: sturdy.
120   *shelf*: submerged sand bank or rock as dangers to navigation.
123   *Simp'ring*: affected, complicitous smiling.
124   *corner*: the least room; *clue*: a ball of thread or yarn.
128   *sconces*: small, defensive lodges or guardhouses at a gateway (here, the mouth).
133   *sickly healths*: unhealthy toasts (oxymoronic).
137   *Ecliptic*: orbital.
141   *shop*: in the sense of a workshop.
143   *humours*: passions.
153   *scraper*: skinflint.
157   *Never exceed . . . may make*: spend income (but no more) when young, but less in old age when you have dependants.
163   *Yet in thy . . . some evil*: W has instead:

> Yet in thy pursing still thyself distrust
> Lest gaining gain on thee, and fill thy heart
> Which if it cleave to coin, one common rust
> Will canker both, yet thou alone shalt smart:
> > One common weight will press down both, yet so
> > As that thy self alone to hell shalt go.

165   *conjurer's devil*: A conjurer is a magician or juggler, his devil (with Faustian ambiguity) his subordinate assistant (as one who does work for a senior lawyer) or the Devil himself.
168   *the quick*: sensitive, living tissue.
171   *Take stars for money*: cf. 'Affliction (1)', lines 11–12: 'Such stars I counted mine: both heav'n and earth / Paid me my wages in a world of mirth'; and Traherne (1637–4), *The Third Century* 3: 'The skies were mine, and so were the sun and moon and stars.'
179   *curious*: fastidious.
181   *They that by pleading clothes*: this stanza is a confused mixture of metaphors amounting to advice against promising more than you can actually manage.

187 *bear the bell*: take the lead.
198 *Finds his . . . church glass*: a startlingly actual image of ruin and oblivion. Heralds made their official visitations every thirty years. Note the 'at length': it was hard to find at all.
212 *Allay*: means of tempering or refining.
217 *Catch not . . . not speak*: a jumble amounting to Kipling's advice in 'If' to 'keep your head when all about you / Are losing theirs and blaming it on you.'
223–8 *If that thy . . . with the best*: H had been reading his friend Bacon's *Speech against Duels* (1614) with its example of Gonzalo Hernandez de Cordova, surnamed the Great Captain:

> But for this apprehension of a disgrace, that a fillip to the person should be a mortal wound to the reputation, it were good that men would hearken unto the saying of *Consalvo* the great and famous commander, that was wont to say: a gentleman's honour should be *de tela crassiore*, of a good, strong warp or web that everything should not catch in it, when as now it seems they are but of cobweb or lawn, or such light stuff, which certainly is weakness, and not true greatness of mind, but like a sick man's body, that is so tender that it feels everything.

228 *toy*: a trifle.
241 *engine*: of warfare (an excellent metaphor).
258 *parcel-devil*: part/participant-devil.
261 *Be not thine own worm*: Don't be down on yourself (the worm a common metaphor for envy).
265 *bate*: downgrade.
268 *And not the . . . on his back*: refers to Aesop's fable of the ass carrying a sacred image who supposed that the reverence of the bystanders was towards him, not the image.
269 *cloth of state*: a rich fabric hung behind a throne or as a canopy over it.
270 *arras*: the finest, as distinct from *mean* (ordinary) *tapestry*.
274 *pay down all his fear*: redeem him from it.
276 *David . . . Jonathan, Christ . . . John*: the biblical exemplars of friendship of a quality now gone.
277 *surety*: one who makes himself liable for the debts of another. Proverbs 6:1–2: 'if thou be surety for thy friend . . . thou art snared.'
283–8 *If thou be . . . weakness score*: 48 is an almost incomprehensible stanza. Its general drift is towards caution and moderation.

289 *In thy discourse . . . desire to please*: the beginning of a section of six stanzas about conversation, which show H's love of, and deep interest in, reciprocity.

293 *draw*: play.

297 *lose his rest*: In the card game of Primero the 'rest' were reserve stakes agreed at the outset, the loss of which lost you the game. The skill was to know when to show your hand.

301 *Master-gunner*: the leader in a conversation.

309 *feel*: (for).

317 *the bow*: the rainbow, which never hits the heavenly sphere.

341 *live alone*: alone are really alive.

347 *I care not*: read as if in quotation marks.

360 *scores*: debts; *clear*: obvious.

365 *fit*: mood.

367–70 W has instead:

> Leave not thine own dear-country-cleanliness
> For this French sluttery which so current goes
> As if none could be brave, but who profess
> First to be slovens, and forsake their nose.

368 *board*: approach.

369 *noisomeness*: offensive smelliness.

375 *single market-money*: small change.

378 *names*: places.

380 *stamp*: image.

383 *Let thy . . . heav'n's gate*: 'Thine alms are come up for a memorial before God,' Acts 10:4.

384 *both*: alms and you.

385 *tithe*: the tenth of agricultural income due to the Church.

386 *purloin'd*: stolen.

391 *Twice*: Morning and Evening Prayer were the Church of England's daily services.

392 *so oft*: i.e., twice. See Tobias Venner, *Via recta ad vitam longam or A plaine philosophical discourse* (1620), p. 177–8: '*Whether the ordinary use of two meales a day, be best for the preservation of health?* I answer, omitting the precise observation of the time, countrey and custome, that the use of two competent meales in the day, *viz.* of Dinner and Supper, is generally best for those within the limits of 25, & 60 years, leading a studious, or sedentary kinde of life, if they desire to avoid crudity [indigestion], the originall of most diseases. But such as use much exercise, or are of an hot or cholericke temperature, may use it oftener, as three

times a day ... Our usual time for dinner, in all places, is about eleven of the clocke, and for supper, in most places, about six.' I am grateful to Keith Thomas for this reference.

393 *cheer is mended*: your fare and wellbeing are enhanced (by Sunday services); the *food* is metaphorical of church worship, not necessarily the eucharist (see 'Superliminare').

397 *brave design*: fine intention.

399 *love's a weight to hearts*: see St Augustine, *Confessions* xiii 10: 'my weight is my love. Wherever I am carried, my love is carrying me.'

403 *be bare*: take off your hat.

409 H agrees with James I against the radical puritans who preferred preaching. At the Hampton Court Conference of 1604, called to settle religion, Bishop Bancroft complained of there being too much emphasis on preaching, 'which motion his majesty liked very well, very acutely taxing the hypocrisy of our times, which placeth all religion in the ear, through which there is an easy passage; but prayer, which expresseth the heart's affection, and is the true devotion of the mind, as a matter putting us to overmuch trouble.' William Barlowe, *The Summe and Substance of the Conference at Hampton Court* (1605), pp. 198–9. Walton relates that at Leighton Bromswold H made the reading pew, whence the prayers were led, and the pulpit (usually much higher) 'of an equal height' because prayer and preaching were 'equally useful'. This unusually balanced arrangement survives there.

425 *cozen*: cheat.

428 *conceiv'st*: understand.

429 *God calleth preaching folly*: 'it pleased God by the foolishness of preaching to save them that believe,' 1 Corinthians 1:21.

449 *The Jews ... we, folly*: The law was given to Israel on Mount Sinai with thunder (Exodus 19:16), but the Jews disobeyed it. 1 Corinthians 1:18: 'the preaching of the cross is to them that perish foolishness; but unto us which are saved it is the power of God.'

450 *hedge us in*: punitively, as in Lamentations 3:7: 'He hath hedged me about, that I cannot get out.'

460 *an ell*: an arm's length.

SUPERLIMINARE

Superliminare is an abstruse Latin word denoting an inscription on the lintel above a threshold. In W it is the title of the second quatrain (four-line poem of two couplets), with 'Perirrhanterium' as the title of the first. In B and 1633 it is at the top of the page over both quatrains,

'Perirrhanterium' having been transferred to the head of *The Church-Porch*, thus enhancing the architectural design. This latter rearrangement could be Ferrar's, bolstering his choice of *The Temple* for the whole book.

4   *The church's mystical repast*: This line has a wider application than to Holy Communion alone.
5   *Avoid*: Withdraw, give place (intransitive).
7   *Or that ... to be so*: an important qualification. H believed in the religious efficacy of groaning/longing (see esp. 'Sion').

The Altar

Neither for H nor for his BCP did 'altar' denote the 'table' (the BCP's word, also 'God's board') used for Holy Communion. This is made abundantly and spectacularly clear by the shape of the poem: that of an Old Testament altar, as shown in woodcuts in the Geneva Bible at Exodus 30 and 1 Kings 6. The latter is particularly important because it shows an altar standing before the doors of the temple proper or Holy of Holies: positioned, like this poem in the book, at the entrance. In the elaborate frontispiece to the NT in the KJB another such altar with the lamb sacrificed on it is central. From now on, in B and 1633, pages are headed *The Church*.

This is the first of H's shaped or figure poems. Puttenham describes the form at pp. 179–90: 'Your last proportion is that of a figure, so called for that it yields an ocular representation, your metres being by good symmetry reduced into certain geometrical figures, whereby the maker is restrained to keep him within his bounds, and showeth not only more art, but serveth also much better for briefness and subtlety of device.' H's 'good symmetry' is vertical, like the pillar in Puttenham, p. 186. The first eight lines consist of two pentameters, two tetrameters and four dimeters. This is reversed or mirrored in the last eight lines. All rhyming in couplets. Despite the restrictions of the form and the plethora of biblical references, H's poem comes across as transparently heartfelt and reads aloud easily.

1   *broken*: 'The sacrifice of God is a broken spirit: a broken and a contrite heart, O God, shalt thou not despise,' Psalm 51:17.
2   *cemented*: The accent is on the first syllable.
4   *No workman's ... the same*: The poem's place just after the threshold ('Superliminare') reflects the momentous crossing of Deuteronomy 27:2–5: 'And it shall be on the day when ye pass over Jordan unto the land which the Lord thy God giveth thee,

that thou shalt set thee up great stones, and plaister them with plaister: and thou shalt write upon them all the words of this law ... and there shalt thou build an altar unto the Lord thy God, an altar of stones: thou shalt not lift up any iron tool upon them.'

5   *A HEART alone*: 'ye are manifestly declared to be the epistle of Christ ministered by us, written not with ink, but with the Spirit of the living God; not in tables of stone, but in fleshy tables of the heart,' 2 Corinthians 3:3; and 'I will put my law in their inward parts, and write it in their hearts,' Jeremiah 31:33; *stone*: 'I will take the stony heart out of their flesh, and will give them an heart of flesh,' Ezekiel 11:19. These texts were very important to H. See 'The Sinner', lines 13–14, and 'Sepulchre', lines 17–20.

11   *frame*: the shape of this poem as a meeting place of thought and feeling, God and man.

14   *stones*: Luke 19:37–40: When the crowd of his disciples acclaim Jesus's entry to Jerusalem 'some of the Pharisees from among the multitude said unto him, Master, rebuke thy disciples. And he answered and said unto them, I tell you, that, if these should hold their peace, the stones would immediately cry out.' H's poem will speak when he has fallen silent.

15   *SACRIFICE*: Note the visual pun of SACRIFICE being placed on/ above ALTAR – the capital letters (of 1633, not in B) drawing attention to it.

The Sacrifice

Carefully arranging his poems to fit his biblical template, H moves from the altar in the frontispiece of the KJB NT to the lamb sacrificed upon it. Because Jesus was killed at Passover (the festival of the foundation of the Jewish nation when lambs were sacrificed), he was understood as the ultimate Passover lamb (and so the foundation of the Christian Church). Sacrifice works by moral displacement. It is inherently ambiguous: 'My woe, man's weal [welfare],' as Christ says in the last stanza. Christ's self-offering is understood as an act of a love so absolute – an offering of his human-divine self rather than a substitute – as to set aside fairness for the sake of the beloved. 'And know you not, says Love, who bore the blame?' is the turning point of H's supreme and final poem 'Love (3)'. William Empson, in *Seven Types of Ambiguity* (London: Chatto & Windus, 1930), prized this poem as an example of the creative force of ambiguity at its most extreme: 'Herbert deals, in this poem, on the scale and by the methods necessary to it, with the most deeply rooted notion of the human mind' (p. 295). He praised its 'unassuming grandeur ... achieved by successive fireworks of contradiction' (pp. 268 f.).

The idea of casting the poem in the form of a monologue by Christ, the ultimate sacrificial victim, was suggested to H by the Bible: Lamentations 1:12: 'Is it nothing to you, all ye that pass by? behold, and see if there be any sorrow like unto my sorrow.' In line with ancient tradition and passiontide ritual, H imputes these words to Christ in his first line and in the refrain which concludes each of the sixty-three stanzas – hence the first-person singular throughout. Lancelot Andrewes preached on the same text, similarly reverting to it throughout his sermon, on Good Friday 1604 at Whitehall, five minutes from H's home at Charing Cross. H very probably knew it; he was then thirteen. The sermon was widely read and thrice reprinted.

The 'strange monotony of accent, simplicity of purpose, and rarefied intensity of feeling' (Empson p. 287) of H's epic (not his usual style) are achieved in rhyming pentameter triplets, always followed by the unrhymed trimeter refrain, changed from a question to a statement only at the very end. The *Passio Discerpta* sequence covers very similar ground, though as an epigram sequence, rather than the dramatic monologue here.

1   *O, all ye, who pass by*: Lamentations 1:12: 'Is it nothing to you, *all ye that pass by*? behold, and see if there be any sorrow like unto my sorrow.' H uses only the italicized words, but implies (thus engaging the Bible-familiar reader) the next sentence, particularly 'see', which he explores with prompt irony.

3   *To me ... you find*: by being God incarnate.

5   *make a head*: gather for action. Matthew 26:3-4: 'Then assembled together the chief priests, and the scribes, and the elders of the people, unto the palace of the high priest, who was called Caiaphas, and consulted that they might take Jesus by subtilty, and kill him.'

10   *Had to ... Egyptian slave*: Exodus.

13   *Mine own ... bag did bear*: Matthew 26:14-15: 'Then one of the twelve, called Judas Iscariot, went unto the chief priests, and said unto them, What will ye give me, and I will deliver him unto you? And they covenanted with him for thirty pieces of silver.' John 12:4-6: after Jesus was anointed by Mary, 'Then saith one of his disciples, Judas Iscariot, Simon's son, which should betray him, Why was not this ointment sold for three hundred pence,

and given to the poor? This he said, not that he cared for the poor; but because he was a thief, and had the bag [purse], and bare what was put therein.'

21 *melts*: Andrewes, p. 151: 'the estimate thereof (anguish) we may take from the second word (the Hebrew Gholel) . . ., of *melting*.' Luke 22:41–44: on the Mount of Olives Jesus 'kneeled down, and prayed, saying, Father, if thou be willing, remove this cup from me . . . And being in an agony, he prayed more earnestly: and his sweat was as it were great drops of blood falling down to the ground.'

29 *Yet my Disciples sleep*: Luke 22:45: 'And when he rose up from prayer, and was come to his disciples, he found them sleeping for sorrow.'

31 *my doctrine*: Matthew 26:38 and 41: 'watch with me', 'watch and pray'; *stain*: disdain.

35 *How with . . . seek the sun*: John 18:3: 'Judas then, having received a band of men and officers from the chief priests and Pharisees, cometh thither with lanterns and torches and weapons.'

38 *Who am . . . true relief*: John 14:6: 'I am the way, the truth, and the life.'

41 *Judas . . . with a kiss*: Matthew 26:48–9: 'Now he that betrayed him gave them a sign, saying, Whomsoever I shall kiss, that same is he: hold him fast. And forthwith he came to Jesus and said, Hail, master; and kissed him.'

43 *gates*: his lips.

45 *See, they . . . with the hands*: Matthew 26:50: 'they . . . laid hands on Jesus, and took him.'

47 *I suffer . . . their bands*: John 18:12: 'and bound him'.

49 *All my Disciples fly*: Matthew 26:56: 'Then all the disciples forsook him, and fled.'

49–50 *a bar / Betwixt my friends and me*: Andrewes, p. 153: 'between the passioned powers of his soul, and whatsoever might anyways refresh him, there was a traverse drawn, and he left in the estate of a weather beaten tree, all desolate and forlorn.'

51 *That brought . . . East from far*: Matthew 2.

53 *Then from . . . to another bound*: John 18:12–13: 'Then the band and the captain and officers of the Jews took Jesus, and bound him, and led him away to Annas first . . .'

55 *Comments*: which misinterpret (confound) Jesus's teaching.

57 *The Priest . . . witness seek*: Matthew 26:59: 'Now the chief priests, and elders, and all the council, sought false witness against Jesus, to put him to death.'

58–9 *meek / And ... great week*: Isaiah 53:7: 'he is brought as a lamb to the slaughter, and as a sheep before her shearers is dumb, so he openeth not his mouth'; *Paschal*: Passover (the great Jewish national feast: see Exodus 12 and Deuteronomy 16 – the latter insisting that it be in Jerusalem), during which lambs were sacrificed and Jesus also died, making it the 'great' or 'holy' week of the Christian year.

61   *accuse me of great blasphemy*: Matthew 26:63–5: 'The high priest answered and said unto him, I adjure thee by the living God, that thou tell us whether thou be the Christ, the Son of God. Jesus saith unto him, Thou hast said ... Then the high priest rent his clothes, saying, He hath spoken blasphemy.'

63   *robbery*: Philippians 2:6–7: 'Who, being in the form of God, thought it not robbery to be equal with God (The Greek means "thought not equality with God something to be seized or snatched"), but made himself of no reputation ... and became obedient unto death, even the death of the cross.'

65–6 *Temple ... raisèd as before*: Matthew 26:60–61: 'At the last came two false witnesses, and said, This fellow said, I am able to destroy the temple of God, and to build it in three days.' Cf. also John 2:21.

67   *built the world*: John 1:3: 'All things were made by him.'

69–71 *breath ... breathing*: Genesis 2:7: 'And the Lord God formed man of the dust of the ground, and breathed into his nostrils the breath of life; and man became a living soul.' Christ being the divine creator, as in John1:3 above; *rendereth*: gives back.

73   *lead me unto Herod*: Luke 23:7–12, in which Pilate sends Jesus to Herod, who had jurisdiction in Galilee. Herod examined and mocked him and sent him back to Pilate 'and the same day Pilate and Herod were made friends together: for before they were at enmity between themselves.' An example of St Paul's doctrine of Jew and Gentile reconciled by Christ's death (Ephesians 2:14).

78   *Who teach ... fingers to fight*: Psalm 144:1: 'Blessed be the Lord my strength: who teaches my hands to war and my fingers to fight.'

79   *Hosts*: armies.

89   *I answer nothing*: Matthew 27:14: 'And he answered him [Pilate] to never a word.'

90   *If stony hearts ... gentle love*: Andrewes, p. 150: 'his very sight so pitiful, as it would have moved the hardest heart of them all to have relented.'

91   *But who ... with a dove*: H's own (aristocratic) riddle.

95   *Because . . . still are high*: Genesis 8:8–9: Noah, surviving the flood
      in his ark, 'sent forth a dove from him, to see if the waters were
      abated from off the face of the ground; but the dove found no rest
      for the sole of her foot, and she returned unto him into the ark.'

98   *It is not fit he live a day*: Acts 22:22, where the hostile mob
      shouts at St Paul that 'it is not fit that he should live.' H's mistake
      suggests that he is not looking things up in his Bible but relying
      on his memory.

101   *a stranger*: a gentile; *holdeth off*: Matthew 27:24: Pilate 'took
      water, and washed his hands before the multitude, saying, I am
      innocent of the blood of this just person: see ye to it.'

102   *Away, away*: John 19:15.

107   *wish my blood on them and theirs*: Matthew 27:25: 'Then
      answered all the people, and said, His blood be on us, and on
      our children.'

111   *But honey . . . their night*: that is, if they had taken his blood
      upon themselves rightly and devoutly they would have been
      redeemed by it, but they are ignorantly perverse (H's own com-
      mentary on line 107).

113   *They choose . . . all agree*: Matthew 27:15–22: 'Now at that
      feast the governor was wont to release unto the people a pris-
      oner, whom they would.' Pilate offers them a choice between
      Jesus and Barabbas (Luke 23:19: 'who for a certain sedition
      made in the city, and for murder, was cast into prison'). In Mat-
      thew this all comes before Pilate's hand-washing. H's mistake in
      order is a further indication that he is relying on memory,
      absorbed in his own commentary and collation (scripture linked
      to scripture), which is thicker around here than previously.

114   *courtesy*: a good turn (they being murderers, too).

118   *Prince of peace*: Isaiah 9:6; *peace that doth pass*: Philippians 4:7:
      'the peace of God, which passeth all understanding'. Used as a
      blessing in BCP.

119   *glass*: reflect.

121   *Why, Caesar . . . not I*: sarcastic, but scriptural. John 19:15:
      'Pilate saith unto them, Shall I crucify your King? The chief priests
      answered, We have no king but Caesar.' A (fictional?) betrayal of
      their whole history and tradition, particularly the great Moses's
      miracle at Exodus 17:6, cleaving the rock to release water.

123   *try*: ascertain.

127   *grief*: pain; *mysteriousness*: Andrewes, p. 151: 'what his feelings
      were, it is dangerous to define, we may be too bold to determine
      them.'

129 *They buffet me . . . as they list*: Mark 14:65: 'And some began to
       spit on him, and to cover his face, and to buffet him, and to say
       unto him, Prophesy [at line 142].' Matthew 26:68 adds 'Who is
       he that smote thee?'

134 *Who by my . . . man eyes*: Mark 8:23, the healing of a blind man:
       'and when he had spit on his eyes, and put his hands upon him,
       he asked him if he saw ought.'

137 *My face . . . be divine*: a collation of Jesus's blindfolding with
       Exodus 34:33, where 'Moses put a veil on his face' because it
       shone from encounter with God, and Jesus's face, which 'did
       shine as the sun' at his transfiguration at Matthew 17:2.

146 *utmost*: ambiguous: both loudest and last.

147 *he*: ('each one') nearly dies before me.

151 *Your tears . . . be kept*: Luke 23:28: on the way to the Cross
       'Jesus turning unto them said, 'Daughters of Jerusalem, weep not
       for me, but for yourselves [in view of the coming destruction of
       Jerusalem in CE 70].'

154 *There they . . . abuse me all*: Matthew 27:27-30: 'Then the sol-
       diers of the governor took Jesus into the common hall . . . and
       they stripped him, and put on him a scarlet robe. And when they
       had platted a crown of thorns, they put it upon his head, and a
       reed in his right hand: and they bowed the knee before him, and
       mocked him, saying, Hail, King of the Jews! And they did spit
       upon him, and took the reed, and smote him on the head.' H
       takes no less than eight stanzas to expound the symbolic irony
       latent in each item of torture and mockery.

155 *Yet for twelve . . . I could call*: Matthew 26:53, when Peter drew
       his sword to defend Jesus at his arrest, Jesus rebuked him with
       'Thinkest thou that I cannot now pray to my Father, and he shall
       presently give me more than twelve legions of angels?'

162 *For these . . . doth bear*: Isaiah 5:1-7: 'the vineyard of the Lord
       of hosts is the house of Israel' but it only brings forth wild grapes,
       so God cursed and laid it waste: 'there shall come up briars and
       thorns.'

165 *So sits . . . Adam's fall*: Genesis 3:18: God punished Adam's diso-
       bedience by cursing the ground he had to cultivate: 'Thorns also
       and thistles shall it bring forth to thee.'

166 *Upon my . . . remove it all*: H has Jesus himself do what, in Mat-
       thew, the soldiers do to him.

167 *thrall*: bondage.

170. *They strike . . . all store*: Exodus 17:6 again, as at line 122, shad-
       owed by 1 Corinthians 10:4: 'that rock was Christ.'

178 *weeds*: clothes.
182 *Which Angels ... the grace*: 1 Peter 1:10–12: the sufferings of
     Christ, foretold by prophets, 'which things the angels desire to
     look into'.
186 *Who Crucify ... strong shout*: Matthew 27:23: 'they cried out
     the more, saying, Let him be crucified.'
189 *They lead ... putting then*: Matthew 27:31.
191 *Whom devils ... of men*: refers to Jesus's casting out devils, as in
     Matthew 8.
193 *engross*: concentrate.
197 *My cross ... I faint*: Matthew 27:32: 'And as they came out,
     they found a man of Cyrene, Simon by name: him they com-
     pelled to bear his cross.'
199 *The decreed ... mortal Saint*: Matthew 16:24: 'Then said Jesus
     unto his disciples, If any man will come after me, let him deny
     himself, and take up his cross, and follow me.'
201 *O all ye ... behold and see*: a reprise of the opening line.
202 *tree*: has three successive connotations, deftly handled by H: the
     tree of the knowledge of good and evil in the Garden of Eden
     (Genesis 2:17) with its forbidden fruit; the gallows-tree of the
     Cross; the tree of life in the Garden of Eden (Genesis 2:9 and
     3:22), whose fruit would have given Adam and Eve everlasting
     life had they not been expelled. Empson liked the homely picture
     of Christ as a boy 'stealing from his father's orchard' or a 'Jack
     and the Beanstalk' climbing to heaven (p. 232): a reading dis-
     missed by Tuve as fanciful (p. 88).
205 *world*: in the quasi-adjectival sense of a vast quantity, an infinity.
207 *By words ... I must win*: The two *worlds* are the original crea-
     tion by God's *words* of Genesis 1 and the subsequent sinful
     world after Adam's disobedience.
213 *O my God ... leav'st thou me*: Matthew 27:46: 'Jesus cried with
     a loud voice, saying, ... My God, my God, why hast thou for-
     saken me?' The shock to theology and human feeling of this cry
     is conveyed with economy by H repeating it (to reinforce it)
     without completing it.
218 *this*: my body; *that*: my soul. Andrewes, p. 150: 'In this one,
     peradventure some *sicut* (similarity) may be found, in the pains
     of the body: but in the second, the sorrow of the soul, I am sure,
     none. And indeed the pain of the body is but the body of pain:
     the very soul of sorrow and pain is the soul's sorrow and pain.'
219 *Reproaches*: Matthew 27:39–40: 'And they that passed by reviled
     him, wagging their heads, and saying, Thou that destroyest the

temple, and buildest it in three days, save thyself. If thou be the
Son of God, come down from the cross.'

221 *Now heal thyself, Physician*: Luke 4:23: 'Ye will surely say unto
me this proverb, Physician, heal thyself.' Transposed by H to the
passion and expounded in the next verse – another sign that he
works from memory.

231 *death*: Romans 8:2: 'the law of the Spirit of life in Christ Jesus hath
made me free from the law of sin and death,' and St Paul passim.

233 *A king ... on high*: Matthew 27:37: 'And set up over his head
his accusation written, THIS IS JESUS THE KING OF THE JEWS.'

237 *vinegar minglèd with gall*: Matthew 27:34: 'They gave him vin-
egar to drink mingled with gall' – out of its original order.

239 *With Manna ... them all*: Exodus 16, when the Israelites in the
wilderness called for bread, God rained down 'small round'
things, which they ate and called 'manna' (verse 15): 'angels'
food', according to Psalm 78:25.

241 *They part ... lot dispose*: Matthew 27:35: 'and parted his gar-
ments, casting lots.' Cf. *Passio Discerpta* 10.

242 *type*: image or exemplar – of love because it had healed all who
touched it (Matthew 14:26), but not these 'malicious foes'.

245–7 *Nay, after ... might flow*: John 19:34: 'one of the soldiers
with a spear pierced his side, and forthwith came there out
blood and water' understood sacramentally as the wine/blood of
Holy Communion and the water of Baptism. Cf. *Passio Dis-
cerpta* 4.

249 *But now ... is finishèd*: John 19:30: 'When Jesus therefore had
received the vinegar, he said, It is finished: and he bowed his
head, and gave up the ghost.' *Passio Discerpta* 15 (which is titled
'On the bowed head, John 19').

252 *Never was grief like mine*: Note the change to the refrain, as at
line 216.

The Thanksgiving

The poet's vain attempt at an adequate response to Christ's monologue
in 'The Sacrifice' (which should be read first), in rhyming couplets of
five and four feet, accumulating frantically and climaxing in his col-
lapse at the last line. There is abundant irony by means of puns. Hence
an element of self-satire, even comedy, to provide relief after the unre-
mitting seriousness of 'The Sacrifice'. This is the monologue of a
well-intentioned Pharisee, proposing abundant good works, brought
up short by love.

After consecration and communion in the BCP Holy Communion service the priest prays God 'to accept this our sacrifice of praise and thanksgiving', later reflecting that 'although we be unworthy, through our manifold sins, to offer unto thee any sacrifice, yet we beseech thee to accept this, our bounden duty and service.' Whether human beings could properly or appropriately respond to Christ's sacrifice was a matter of radical doubt. H reflects St Paul's doctrine, insistently enforced by the protestant reformers, of the total depravity and impotence of humanity as opposed to the total goodness and power of God. Christ's sacrifice had swung this extreme situation through 180 degrees by the omnipotent divine victim willingly taking the guilt and impotence upon himself. There was nothing, the poet concludes, to match such a turnaround.

4   *preventest*: go before, surpass.
9   *My God . . . from me*: echo of 'The Sacrifice', line 215, now with the text completed.
11   *skipping*: a pun: both moving with light and jumping feet (like this poem) and omitting. B has the comma after this word, 1633 before it. W has *neglecting* instead, with a comma before it.
14   *posy*: pun: both a bunch of flowers and a line of verse (poesy).
16   *hand*: pun: both Christ's wounded hand and his handwriting.
17   *revenge*: pun: pay back and fight back.
18   *try*: test.
30   *When with . . . have done*: postponement until line 49.
31   *predestination*: God's prerogative to determine human lives, cheekily usurped by the poet: a wittily flippant reference to the most disputed doctrine of his day.
33   *spittle*: hospital; *mend common ways*: pun: both repair roads and improve public morals.
36   *for fashion*: for appearance's sake.
47   *Thy art . . . on thee*: a crescendo of concerns particularly valued by H: music, wit, bible-reading, love – all collapsing in the face of Christ's Passion.

The Reprisal

The title denotes an attack in revenge, a retaliation, taking up the military references in 'The Thanksgiving' (lines 17 and 48) and showing that we are in a deliberate set or sequence of poems. In W, less interestingly but showing the connection, entitled 'The Second Thanksgiving'. Lines of four, five, five and four feet, mirroring five

and four in 'The Thanksgiving' and, instead of couplets, four-line
verses rhyming *abab*. All this slows down the headlong impetus of
'The Thanksgiving' and makes for cohesion.

6   *a disentanglèd state*: an estate uncomplicated by debt.
8   *For by thy ... die for thee*: I can only die for you (Christ),
     because your death (delivering me from moral impotence) ena-
     bled me to.
13   *confession*: of sin (total inadequacy).
16   *The man*: me (as participating in the old Adam). Philippians 4:13:
     'I can do all things through Christ which strengtheneth me.'

The Agony

The title is from Luke 22:44: 'And being in an agony he [Christ on the
Mount of Olives] prayed more earnestly: and his sweat was as it were
great drops of blood falling down to the ground.' The meditative, mildly
satirical, first verse, is a further rallentando in the series of poems. But it
ends with a jolt on the two great monosyllables at the end. Then the
poem opens onto an extraordinary juxtaposition of pain (in its second
verse, described with wincing actuality) and pleasure (in its third verse,
described deliciously). This poem is more elaborate in form than 'The
Reprisal', which in turn was more elaborate than 'The Thanksgiving'.
There are three verses, the first four lines of each rhyming *abab*, the last
two lines clinching the argument with a rhyming pentameter couplet. Cf.
Passio Discerpta 2 ('On the sweat of blood', addressing the blood itself).

1   *Philosophers*: intellectuals, whether 'natural' (scientific) or
     'moral' philosophers.
3   *staff*: walking stick and measuring rod.
6   *Sin and Love*: cf. 'Affliction (5)', line 13: 'There is but joy and
     grief.'
10   *His skin ... bloody be*: Isaiah 63:2-3: 'Wherefore art thou red in
     thine apparel, and thy garments like him that treadeth in the
     winefat? I have trodden the winepress alone; and of the people
     there was none with me.' A hint to the biblically learned of the
     wine to come in the next verse.
11   *Sin*: all the sin in the world bearing down on Christ.
13   *assay*: assess the quality of.
14   *on the cross a pike*: John 19:34 (recalled from 'The Sacrifice',
     lines 246-7): 'one of the soldiers with a spear pierced his side,
     and forthwith came there out blood and water,' interpreted
     sacramentally.

17   *Love*: the terminus of H's thought, the simple motive and effect of the complex antinomies of sacrifice, so for H ultimately – God.

18   *Which my . . . as wine*: Note the terse wit expressing sensuous mysticism.

The Sinner

A confession and the most elaborate poem of the series so far. It is a sonnet of two quatrains rhyming *abab*, followed by a third rhyming *cddc* and closing with a rhyming couplet. The *cddc* rhyming of the third quatrain (lines 9–13: 'small', 'heart', 'part', 'call') is unusual generally, but occasionally used by Sidney, Donne and Jonson – interesting because Sidney was H's relation, Donne his friend, Jonson his contemporary and a former Westminster boy like H. The effect is graceful: variety, tightening things up and slowing them down a little, leading towards the closing rhyming couplet. H used this scheme also in his sonnets 'Holy Baptism' (1), 'Redemption' and 'Prayer'. Here the topic is repentance and the day is Sunday, as line 4 indicates. Repentance was much emphasized in the BCP services, Morning and Evening Prayer and Holy Communion.

2   *treasur'd*: stored up.

4   *seventh note*: Sunday (*note* in the sense of a mark, as in music).

5   *quarries*: heaps made of the deer killed at a hunt (see 'Christmas', line 1).

7   *cross*: contradictory.

8   *the circumference . . . the centre*: a contrast between the immense *circumference* and the tiny *centre*.

9   *quintessence*: 'The spirit and good extract' of the next line: accent on the first syllable.

12   *image*: Genesis 1:27: 'God created man in his own image.'

14   *Remember . . . in stone*: a return to the imagery of 'The Altar'.

Good Friday

Good Friday: The day of the year on which Christ's death was commemorated. In W the two poems here were separated by an intervening poem, there entitled 'The Passion', but in B and 1633 'Redemption'. To make this later double poem (as in B and 1633) H edited the poem beginning *Since* thoroughly, reversed their order in W and joined them up. Thus he achieved the double-poem form, which he preferred for the great days of the Church's year (see 'Easter' and 'Christmas') and allowed the masterly intervening sonnet, retitled 'Redemption', to follow it as the fitting climax of the penitential series. H's reversal of W's order to make 'Good Friday' made for narrative development: a first poem in an active, restless mood, then a second which is more serene. The first poem explores the meaning of the day, ending in prayer – which the second poem fulfils by interiorizing it. So the first poem is busy: each verse a quatrain of dimeter (2 feet), tetrameter (4), tetrameter (4), dimeter (2), rhyming *aabb*. Every sentence in the first three stanzas is a question, an aspiration or prayer in the last two. The second poem is also in quatrains, rhyming *aabb*, but all tetrameters and no questions – so it is more even and settled. 'The abandonment of conceits for a plainer truth represents that leaning towards sobriety which always seemed to [H], in the end, finer and wittier than fine wit' (Vendler, pp. 149–50). The whole poem is subjective, insistently concerned with the business of writing poetry and its difficulties in the face of its transcendent subject: difficulties to be triumphantly overcome in the objectivity of 'Redemption'. Cf. *Passio Discerpta* 1.

2   *measure*: pun: musical-poetical/arithmetical.
4   *tell*: count.
7   *since one . . . first breath*: Matthew 2:2: 'we have seen his star in the east.'
9   *leaf*: pun: of a tree/of a book.
12   *Of the true vine*: John 15:1: 'I am the true vine.'
18   *several*: separate; *get*: beget.
21–2   *Since blood . . . bloody fight*: W had

>   Since nothing Lord can be so good
>   To write thy sorrows in, as blood

24   *box*: pun: his heart and his writing box. Boxes are a favourite metaphor of H's (see 'Evensong', 'Virtue', 'Confession').
26   *Thy whips . . . thy woes*: instruments of Christ's Passion.
29–32 *Sin being . . . blot or burn*: W had

>   Sin being gone o do thou fill
>   The Place, & keep possession still.
>   For by the writings all may see
>   Thou hast an ancient claim on me.

32   *writings*: the scriptures and his poetry.

Redemption

The crown of the series developed out of 'The Sacrifice', still seen from the point of view of the beneficiary, but now in an allegory with wonderfully fresh narrative actuality, rather than tortuous self-examination. Thus objectified, Christ's loving sacrifice is made all the more impressive, not least by his four italicized (by the 1633 printer) words (H's boldly creative substitute for Christ's last words in the Gospels) in the last line. The title, substituted for 'The Passion' in W, is a pun: 'buying back' both in religious/salvation and in legal/contractual terms. Both are in play throughout the poem. This is a sonnet in the same form as the previous 'The Sinner', with lines 10 and 11 rhyming. The octet (lines 1–8) is set in the country, the sestet (lines 9–14) in the town: both realistically. The content is allegorical, not problematic but easy to decode from the start with the help of the title and the first line. H's allegories are not crowded with grandly personified abstract entities, but modestly attuned to everyday realities (see 'The Family', 'Time', 'The Quip' and, supremely, 'Love (3)'). This one is based on Leviticus 25: 23–25, where God says 'the land is mine . . . and in all the land . . . ye shall grant a redemption for the land, if thy brother be waxen poor,' and Ephesians 1:7 and Colossians 1:14, which both say that in Christ 'we have redemption through his blood'. Two parables in Matthew's gospel are in the background. In Matthew 25:14–30 a man deals out various sums of money to his three servants. The first two increase theirs while he is away, but the third hides his rather than growing it and is condemned on his lord's return. Matthew 21:33–43 tells of a man who made a vineyard and let it out to tenants and went away. The tenants beat or killed the servants whom the man sent to collect the 'fruits' or rent due to him, climaxing in the murder of his son and heir. These parables surface at the beginning and the heart-stopping end. H's own parable-poem is at least the equal of its biblical precedents.

7   *land*: the Promised Land covenanted to Israel in the Old Testament (see Exodus 19:5), to which Christ had 'lately' descended from heaven by incarnation.

9   *his great birth*: as heir and Lord of King David (Mark 12:35–7).

10–11   *Sought him . . . and courts*: W had:

> Sought him in cities, theatres, resorts
> In grottos, gardens, palaces and courts.

H then omitted the grottos (covered by gardens), put in parks and got it all to scan and read better by confining the various places to one line under the general category of 'resorts' in the line before.

Sepulchre

An elegiac poem, not in W, it laments not only Christ's dead body, which Joseph of Arimathea laid 'in a sepulchre which was hewn out of the rock, and rolled a stone unto the door of the sepulchre' (Mark 15:46), but also humanity's failure to accept him. Sadness is actualized by the metre: tercets of three solemn, rhyming pentameters, followed by one-foot lines going short-long-short, called amphibrachs. There are six of these amphibrachs, carefully arranged in three pairs which rhyme and, at the same time, balance opposites: *receive/leave, murder/order, hold/withhold*. Stone has provided H with a favourite metaphor for the human heart since 'The Altar'. Here he explores it to beautifully cool, quiet and recollected effect.

13   *Where our ... brain thee*: John 10:31: 'Then the Jews took up stones again to stone him.'
17   *the law by heav'nly art*: Exodus 31:18 again.
19   *letter of the word*: Christ as the incarnation of the divine Word (John 1:14); *letter*: inscription, imprint.

Easter

Two poems for the day of Christ's resurrection in W, each with this title, though in the same order. In B and 1633 the title is dropped from the head of the second poem, thus making one double poem like 'Good Friday'. The double form grew on H as he revised – and the second poem here is a radical revision of its previous version in W (see below). As in 'Good Friday', the first poem is full of active aspiration, the second of fulfilled serenity. But this is altogether a greater achievement – one of H's greatest in feeling as in form. The first poem has three six-line stanzas, their first two lines rhyming: a pentameter, followed by a brisk little iambic dimeter, which puts a spring in its step. This is repeated in the next two lines and followed by a rhyming pentameter couplet. So the rhyme scheme is a simple *aabbcc* – no waiting about for rhymes. There is much enjambement, one line following another with no break or breath, to keep it all on the go. The second poem is lyrically relaxed. The music prepared for in the first poem now breaks out into song. Christ is the active early riser. The poet can only wonder and enjoy. So its three verses are all in tetrameters rhyming *abab*: a simpler scheme than the first poem's, with only one enjambement rather than six.

3   *likewise*: Colossians 3:1: 'If ye then be risen with Christ, seek those things which are above.'
5   *calcinèd*: in alchemy the reducing of base ore to ashes by fire in order to get *gold*.
9   *wood to resound*: the hollow, wooden 'body' of the lute or viol.
11   *key*: Sacred music was set a minor third higher than secular. So *taught* puns with *taut*.
13   *Consort*: play together.
15–16 *three parts vied And multiplied*: The triad or common chord was the basis and spring of harmony. Here its three parts are for heart, lute and Spirit.
19–30 *I got me . . . one ever*: The earlier (lame in comparison) version in W was:

> I had prepared many a flow'r
> To strow thy way and Victory,
> But thou wast up before mine hour
> Bringing thy sweets along with thee.
>
> The sun arising in the east
> Though he bring light and th'other scents:
> Can not make up so brave a feast
> As thy discovery presents.
>
> Yet though my flow'rs be lost, they say
> A heart can never come too late.
> Teach it to sing thy praise this day,
> And then this day, my life shall date.

20   *boughs*: Matthew 21:8, when Jesus entered Jerusalem people 'cut down branches from the trees, and strewed them in the way'. CP XIII: the church 'at great festivals [should be] stuck with boughs and perfumed with incense [the *perfume* of line 24]'.
22   *sweets*: fragrances as well as tastes (the *liquor sweet* of the Communion wine in 'The Agony', line 17. Everybody was expected to take communion on Easter Day.)
29   *three hundred*: a round figure.

Easter-wings

A miraculous marriage of form and content. The constraints of the
figure form, as in 'The Altar', not only allow but inspire a fluent and
heartfelt poem. It consists of two palindromes in both metre and
rhyme. The lines reduce from five feet to four, to three, to two, to one,
rhyming *ababa*, and then do the same in reverse, rhyming *cdcdc*. In W
the lines are justified to the right-hand margin; the same in B but with
a slight inward curve (possibly an accidental effect of the elaborate
sloping calligraphy, rather than deliberate). They take a page each and
face each other on a double-spread. So we have two birds flying along:
Christ and the poet. Unfortunately in 1633 the printer decided to turn
them upwards through ninety degrees and shape the lines into sym-
metrical triangles. He seems to have thought that the flight should be
vertical rather than horizontal (perhaps taking his cue from 'rise / As
larks' – but larks are still horizontal as they rise!). Since each of the
stanzas is narrative, horizontal is better. The manuscripts show that
this is how H first wrote (W) and then left (B) it.

   Easter-Wings: Malachi 4:2: 'the Sun of righteousness [shall] arise
with healing in his wings,' and Isaiah 40:31: 'they that wait upon the
Lord shall renew their strength; they shall mount up with wings as
eagles.' There were wing-shaped figure poems in *The Greek Anthol-
ogy* (by Simmias of Rhodes) and in Puttenham, pp. 183–5.

10   *Then shall ... in me*: Note the onomatopoeic force of the
     alliteration.
19   *imp*: implant: in falconry, restoratively implanting or grafting
     healthy feathers into damaged ones.

Holy Baptism (1)

The preface to baptism in the BCP recommended that the ancient cus-
tom of baptizing at Easter be followed 'as near as may conveniently
be'. Hence the placing here. Baptism, the water-sacrament of cleans-
ing from sin and initiation into the Church, was administered to
infants with sponsors. So the poem is retrospective. W, B and 1633 all
have two separate poems, one after the other, with this title. H did not
make them into one double poem, although the first is discursive, the
second lyrical, as in 'Good Friday', 'Easter', 'The Holy Communion'
and 'Christmas'. The first poem is a sonnet with lines 10 and 11 rhym-
ing. The argument depends on the permanence and indissolubility of

the sacrament, triumphant (in a typically familiar way) in the final couplet. W had the earlier form:

> When backward on my sins I turn mine eyes
> > And then beyond them all my Baptism view
> > As he that heaven beyond much thicket spies
> I pass the shades, and fix upon the true
> Waters above the heavens. O sweet streams
> > You do prevent most sins and for the rest
> > You give us tears to wash them: let those beams
> Which then joined with you still meet in my breast
> And mend as rising stars and rivers do.

6   *piercèd side*: John 19:34 again: 'one of the soldiers with a spear pierced his side, and forthwith came there out blood and water.'

Holy Baptism (2)

Each stanza is a palindrome. In 'Easter-Wings' the metrical shaping of the two palindromes went from fat to thin, then back to fat. Here they go from from thin to fat, then back to thin: two, four, five, four, two feet. The palindromic rhyme scheme *ababa* is the same. Once again, the scheme is custom-built for the content: we may grow, but first and last we are, and should be, 'as little children' (Matthew 18:3). This suited H's personal psychology. In the BCP baptism service Mark 10: 13–16 was read out: 'and they brought young children to him [Jesus], that he should touch them: and his disciples rebuked those that brought them. But when Jesus saw it, he was much displeased, and said unto them, Suffer the little children to come unto me, and forbid them not: for of such is the kingdom of God. Verily I say unto you, Whosoever shall not receive the kingdom of God as a little child, he shall not enter therein. And he took them up in his arms, put his hands upon them, and blessed them.'

2   *narrow way and little gate*: Matthew 7:14: 'strait is the gate, and narrow is the way, which leadeth unto life.'
4   *antedate*: 'The habit of faith which afterward doth come with years, is but a further building up of the same edifice, the first foundation of which was laid by the sacrament of baptism,' Richard Hooker, *The Laws of Ecclesiastical Polity* (1597), Book V Ch. lxiv s. 2.
10   *Behither*: short of, barring/except.

Nature

Theologically, nature is understood as opposed to grace – in the first
stanza here, actively. Grace has dominated *The Temple* from 'The Sac-
rifice' onwards. Now nature threatens its revenge. The movement of
the poem is restless and bumpy: three tetrameters are followed by a
dimeter and a trimeter which rhyme, then a tetrameter again. Cf. 'The
Collar'.

2   *deny*: like St Peter in Matthew 26:69–75.
7   *this venom lurk*: The poison causes extreme flatulence.
10 *by kind*: following its nature.
14 *Engrave . . . law and fear*: Exodus 25:12, the law engraved in
    stone, yet again.

Sin (1)

'Equally admirable for the weight, number and expression of the
thoughts, and for the simple dignity of the language', Coleridge,
Biographia Literaria, xix. A regular Shakespearean sonnet, which,
like 'Prayer (1)', is a list: here of well-intentioned things (with subtle
but important hints of repression in lines 3, 6 and 7) – all dramatically
exploded in the final couplet. This poem can be read as an overture to
the next one, 'Affliction (1)'.

2   *season*: mature.
6   *sorted*: assorted.
13 *array*: arrangement, usually military.
13–14 *Yet all . . . quite away*: W had:

> Yet all these fences with one bosom sin
> Are blown away, as if they ne'er had been.

Affliction (1)

'One of the most remarkable records in the language of the achieve-
ment of maturity and of the inevitable pains of the process' (Knights, p.
124). 'There is a remarkable lack of censorship; even with the Psalms
as precedent, H shows his absolute willingness to say how things are,
to choose the accurate verb, to follow the truth of feeling' (Vendler, p.
43). This is the first of no less than five poems with this title. H

understands his sorrows as visited upon him by God: not God incarnate and redeeming in Christ – no sign of Him here, in contrast to previous poems – but God the omnipotent creator and director of all historical events, the senior member of the divine Trinity, whom H noticeably refrains from calling Father (though 'dear' in the penultimate line) – and accuses of enticement and entrapment. As a result of his belief, he takes his troubles not just personally, but as personally meant; and is thus in agreement with the Old Testament writers who complained bitterly of God's treatment of them, especially Job (his past happiness in Chapter 29, present misery in Chapter 7, and dogged truthfulness) and the Psalms (e.g., 102:10–11: 'thou hast taken me up, and cast me down. My days are gone like a shadow: and I am withered like grass.' Also Psalms 22 and 38, etc.).

Iambic pentameters are the obvious vehicle for autobiographical narrative. H intersperses them with iambic trimeters to keep up the pace, while the concluding pentameter couplets to each verse mark very temporary pauses or apparent resolutions, only to be left behind by the next verse. The very last couplet is forcefully ambiguous and realistically unresolved. It all has yet to make the sense which only sincere mutual trust could provide. But for the time being there is a lot getting in the way of that.

5   *natural*: as distinct from supernatural.
9   *household-stuff*: the contents of the universe. H in CP X 'admires and imitates the wonderful providence and thrift of the great householder of the world'. This agrees with 'stars' and 'heav'n and earth' in line 11.
17   *sudden*: impetuous; see 'The Answer', lines 5–6: 'all, / Who think me eager, hot, and undertaking.'
25   *began*: (to say).
29–30 *I scarce ... I liv'd*: W had:

> I did not know
> That I did live, but by a pang of woe.

32   *friends die*: Friends included family and supporters. In 1617 H's brothers William and Charles died; his brother Richard died in 1622, and his sister Margaret Vaughan in 1623 – all while he was at Cambridge, where 'thou didst betray me to a ling'ring book, / And wrap me in a gown.' After the success of his oration in 1623 (see Introduction) H withdrew from Cambridge. In 1624–7 he was footloose, often ill and indecisive. So this poem seems to belong to 1623/4.

45   *academic praise*: H was admired in Cambridge, particularly as the University Orator. People were sorry that he left.

53   *cross-bias*: from bowling, the weighted bias swerving the wood (bowl) from the direction set by the bowler. See the last stanza of 'Constancy'.

57   *wish I were a tree*: cf. 'O that I were an orange-tree, / That busy plant!' ('Employment (2)').

60   *just*: justified (in my existence).

65   *I am clean forgot*: Psalm 31:14: 'I am clean forgotten as a dead man out of mind.'

66   *Let me . . . love thee not*: Romans 12:9: 'Let love be without dissimulation.' Also I Corinthians 13:6: charity/love 'rejoiceth in the truth'.

Repentance

The form is similar to that of 'Nature', i.e., six stanzas consisting of three tetrameters and a pentameter followed by two dimeters and a final tetrameter. Rhyme scheme *aabccb*. Psalm-like in its emotional register, and with many specific allusions to the Psalms and other biblical material, it is spiced with references to medicine, the weather and music.

1   *Lord, I . . . sin is great*: Psalm 32:5: 'I will acknowledge my sin unto thee.'

3   *With thy . . . momentary bloom*: Job 14:1–2 (quoted in the BCP Burial Service): 'Man that is born of a woman hath but a short time to live, and is full of misery. He cometh up, and is cut down, like a flower; he fleeth as it were a shadow, and never continueth in one stay.' Psalm 103:15–16: 'The days of man are but as grass; for he flourisheth as a flower of the field. / For as soon as the wind goeth over it, it is gone: and the place thereof shall know it no more.'

4   *pressing*: (forward).

7   *Man's age . . . three*: Psalm 39:6: 'mine age is even as nothing in respect of thee.'

8   *Each day . . . us see*: as every day shows (?).

9–10 *Thus are we . . . sorrows old*: W had:

> Looking on this side, and beyond us all:
> We are born old.

11   *told*: accounted/explained.
21   *wormwood*: a bitter herb, once used medicinally.
22   *stay*: delay.
25–6 *When thou ... woe and wan*: Psalm 39:12: 'When thou with rebukes chasteneth man for sin, thou makest his beauty to consume away.'
27–8 *Bitterness fills ... and decay*: Psalm 22:14: 'my heart also in the midst of my body is even like melting wax.'
28–30 *Pine, and decay ... other parts*: W had:

> Melt and consume
> To smoke and fume
> Fretting to death our other parts.

31   *But thou ... grief destroy*: Revelation 21:4: 'There shall be no more death, neither sorrow, nor crying, neither shall there be any more pain.'
32   *That so ... may joy*: Psalm 51:8: 'that the bones which thou hast broken may rejoice.'

Faith

H treats the most solemn and integral topic of Reformation theology as a kind of fairy-tale magic. This idiosyncratic poem is enjoyable as it scrapes along the perilous edge of treating faith as fantasy or 'conceit' (a fanciful or witty notion), an exercise of the imagination available to everybody. The title derives from Hebrews 11:1: 'Now faith is the substance of things hoped for, the evidence of things not seen' ('evidence' means manifestation/showing). The list of instances of faith which follows in Hebrews is of heroes of faith in the biblical tradition, from Abel to the prophets. H, in contrast and characteristically, lists various everyday things – a feast, a medicinal root, money, a manger, a peasant, the sun, bushes, his body – rather than taking on the epic historical sweep of Hebrews. Several of the things in H's list conceal or advertise biblical precedents, such as Adam, Christ's birth and the Bible itself. There are eleven stanzas, each a couple of pentameters flanked on either side by tetrameters, rhyming *abab*: simple, as suits H's ingenuous tone of voice.

4   *And bring ... things to him*: The God of the previous two poems – hostile in 'Affliction', bitter in 'Repentance' – here shows his kindlier side and cares for man's ease and comfort.

6   *feast*: the Holy Communion?

7   *straight*: (away).

8   *a welcome guest*: cf. 'Love (3)'.

9   *outlandish root*: foreign, so possibly the snake-root of Virginia.

11   *foot*: Adam's heel bruised by the serpent in Genesis 3:15?

13   *owèd thousands and much more*: Matthew 18:24–7: 'one was brought unto him which owed him ten thousand talents ... Then the lord of that servant was moved with compassion, and loosed him, and forgave him the debt.'

15–16   *And liv'd ... lets me go*: W had:

> And liv'd accordingly with no new score,
> My Creditor believ'd so too.

21   *lower*: further down or on.

22   *lower*: pun; *the common manger*: Luke 2:7: Mary laid the new-born Jesus in a manger.

25–8   *If bliss ... conditions fit*: In faith all are equal.

30   *clerk*: cleric or scholar.

31   *Thus dost ... bend and crouch*: Luke 1:52: 'He hath put down the mighty from their seats, and exalted them of low degree [BCP 'the humble and meek']': a verse of the *Magnificat* that was recited daily at Evening Prayer.

36   *And in this ... hath done*: Genesis 1:9–17: God created earth, seas and plants on the third day of creation, the sun and moon after that on the fourth day. John 1:9: Jesus 'the true Light, which lighteth every man that cometh into the world'.

38   *groves*: a metaphor for sins in 'Holy Baptism (1)'.

44   *flesh again*: the Creed said at Morning and Evening Prayer: 'I believe in ... the resurrection of the body.' Job 19:26: 'though after my skin worms destroy this body, yet in my flesh shall I see God.'

Prayer (1)

A sonnet with H's preferred rhyme scheme of a couplet in lines 10 and 11. A string of nouns without a verb was a recognized rhetorical trope, such as H would have dealt with as Praelector in Rhetoric at Cambridge. Often anthologized, this poem keeps its readers' attention by its vivid variety – both of items and of the length they occupy from one whole line (line 4) to five in a line (line 9). There is much reversal, turning things downside-up, suitable to the power of lowly prayer over the heavenly realm. H's masterstroke is those last two words, bringing the reader home and down to earth after a string of exotic metaphors. H often makes brilliantly positive use of bathos.

1   *banquet*: Hooker called the Holy Communion a 'heavenly banquet' (*Laws* V. lxvii. 11). But H probably intends the contemporary meaning of a light repast between meals ('running banquets') or the supplementary dessert enjoyed in banqueting houses set in gardens or towers, or in college common rooms. Prayer is not a sacrament; *Angels' age*: limitless, unlike man's short span.

2   *God's breath ... birth*: Genesis 2:7: 'God ... breathed into his nostrils the breath of life' – here reversed.

3   *in paraphrase*: expressing itself in words.

4   *plummet sounding*: the lead at the end of a line let down by a sailor to fathom (sound) the depth of the sea beneath him. Here reversed to go upwards.

5   *Engine*: of war.

6   *Reversèd*: from earth to heaven, like the plummet; *spear*: John 19:34: 'one of the soldiers with a spear pierced his side.'

7   *The six-days ... in an hour*: weekdays transposed into another key, as in music, by a daily hour of prayer. The musical reference is wonderfully taken up in the next line.

8   *fear*: respect.

10 *Exalted Manna*: manna, the food dropped down by God on the Israelites in Exodus 16, here thrown into reverse and shot upwards.

11 *ordinary*: everyday.

12 *The milky way*: Ovid, *Metamorphoses* I, lines 168–173: the shining way or road of the gods to Jupiter's palace; *the bird of Paradise*: legless, so always in flight.

13 *Church-bells*: calling to prayer.

14 *land of spices*: Revelation 5:8: 'golden vials full of odours, which are the prayers of the saints'. Song of Solomon 4:14: the beloved's garden contains 'Spikenard and saffron; calamus and cinnamon, with all trees of frankincense; myrrh and aloes, with all the chief spices'.

The Holy Communion

In the BCP Lord's Supper or Holy Communion the faithful received bread and wine as the body and blood of Christ. The title of this service is from 1 Corinthians 10:16: 'The cup of blessing which we bless, is it not the communion of the blood of Christ? The bread which we break, is it not the communion of the body of Christ?' This was preferred to the old title of 'Mass', because scriptural and communal. Just in what sense Christ was present in the bread and wine was the subject of endless and divisive debate, ranging from the symbolic to the real, with the Church of England somewhere in the middle. Hooker concluded his discussion of it in *Laws* (V. lxvii) with 'why should any cogitation possess the mind of a faithful communicant but this, O my God thou art true, O my soul thou art happy!' – pretty much H's pattern and mind here. H made this double poem out of a poem in W entitled 'Prayer', revised and preceded by a new poem of four six-line stanzas, using a pentameter followed by a trimeter rhyming couplet, then a tetrameter, a pentameter and a final trimeter; rhyming scheme *abbacc*. All this conveys a sense of syncopated argument hither and thither. The second poem is much simpler with its four stanzas alternating tetrameters and trimeters rhyming *abab*. Cogitation over and done with, it is happy, light and lyrical: H's usual way in his double poems.

3   *sold*: Matthew 26:15: Judas betrayed Jesus 'for thirty pieces of silver'.

5   *without*: outside and/or lacking.

9   *rest*: passive ease.

10   *length*: of my body.

16   *outworks*: front line of an army's defences.

19   *grace*: as distinct from nature and matter (*elements*).

21   *privy*: private.

22   *subtle*: elusive, delicate.

23   *those*: the material elements. *Attend*: watch out for.

24   *Dispatches*: messages.

25   *captive*: in the body.

27   *Another lift*: refers to the taking up of the body and soul together to heaven in the general resurrection of the dead.

30   *lump to leaven*: dough raised by yeast.

33   *not know*: because he had not yet eaten the forbidden fruit of the tree of moral knowledge (Genesis 2:17).

37–40 *Thou hast . . . their food*: W had:

> But we are strangers grown, O Lord,
>   Let prayer help our losses,
> Since thou hast taught us by thy word,
>   That we may gain by crosses.

Antiphon (1)

A cheerful poem, celebrating the fulfilling reciprocity which H loved and longed for, both in form and content (earth and heaven in the first stanza, community and individual in the second). The title means a church song for alternating voices: a form in BCP Morning and Evening Prayer, even when only said. The two-line choral refrain of hexameter and dimeter opens, centres and closes the poem. The versicles which come between are rhyming couplets of trimeters: simple thoughts in an unforced complexity of form. The sources are Psalm 95 (the 'Venite' in BCP Morning Prayer), 'O come, let us sing unto the Lord', and Psalm 1 (the 'Jubilate' in Morning Prayer), 'O be joyful in the Lord, all ye lands: serve the Lord with gladness, and come before his presence with a song.'

9   *shout*: the inelegant sound of a rustic congregation bellowing the metrical Psalms in the barbarous Sternhold and Hopkins translation often included in copies of the BCP.

Love (1) and (2)

A pair of sonnets, the first being invective against profane love, the second aspiring to sacred love. They are very much in the tradition of Sidney, especially his sonnet 'Leave me, O love which reacheth but to dust.' But their tone – disgruntled and priggish in the first sonnet, domineering in the second – is at variance with the subject, which H treats so wonderfully in 'Love (3)'. The title is only over the first sonnet in W, B and 1633. Both sonnets have H's favoured variant of lines 10 and 11 rhyming.

1   *great frame*: the universe.
3   *parcell'd*: divided up.
6   *invention*: imaginative creativity.
10   *game*: of tennis?
13   *scarf or glove*: often love tokens (gloves one of the 'fine knacks for ladies' in Dowland's song).

Love (2)

1   *Heat*: taking up the last lines of the previous sonnet.
6   *pant*: (for).
11   *in kind*: as distinct from in cash.

12   *disseisèd*: wrongly dispossessed.
13   *All knees . . . shall rise*: Philippians 2:10: 'at the name of Jesus
      every knee should bow.'

The Temper (1)

H is bewildered by his own extreme mood swings. Understanding
them to be the Almighty's working on him, a plausible understanding
of them needs to have a wide – even universal – scope. So extreme
spatial metaphors dominate the earlier stanzas, the fifth being a des-
perate plea to get it all over with. The poem might end there. But the
sixth stanza is an abrupt change of mood. It is resigned and uses the
more mundane or everyday metaphors of debt and music. Again, it
might stop there. Yet none of this will quite do. The problem remains:
how to settle matters with a God or destiny at once so overwhelming
and so contradictory. The last stanza is, finally, a genuine resolution.
The precise placing of nouns in the penultimate line fixes it. God's
power at the beginning of it and the poet's trust at the end of it are
united by love: that word repeated, once for God and once for the
poet, shows love to be what they have in common. Reciprocity, always
so desired by H, at last! So the final line disposes of the previous anx-
ious spatial metaphors. All in all, there are seven four-line stanzas, the
lines of diminishing length: pentameter, two tetrameters and a trime-
ter. So experience is pondered, narrowing towards an exclamation, a
question or a resolution (temporary or final).
    The Temper: In W 'The Christian Temper'. The meaning includes
the tempering of metals and musical instruments, but more impor-
tantly mental balance or composure, especially under provocation,
and the associated balance of 'humours' in the body. As elsewhere,
H's title achieves aptness and fit only at the close.

2   *steel*: the most hard-tempered metal.
5   *heav'ns*: one on top of the other (St Paul got to the third of seven
      in 2 Corinthians 12:2).
9   *rack*: torture by stretching.
11   *tent*: tabernacle such as served as a proto-temple for the Jews in
      the wilderness, but here clearly the heavens, as in Psalm 19:5: 'In
      them hath he set a tabernacle for the sun.'
13   *meet arms*: pun: measure up for combat.
16   *spell*: reckon.
17   *roof*: Psalm 84:3: 'the sparrow hath found here an house, and
      the swallow a nest where she may lay her young: even thy altars,

O Lord of hosts, my king and my God.' The verse implies a life
after death, so also refers to Revelation 6:9: the altar in heaven
with the souls of martyrs under it.

22–4 *Stretch or ... music better*: The poet being a *debtor*, *stretch*
means torment and/or extend the time for payment (with recol-
lection of *stretch* in line 13 and the racking in line 9); *or contract*:
either to agree terms or to shorten. The musical metaphor of
lines 23–4 is without such ambiguity.

25–8 *Whether I fly ... ev'ry where*: Psalm 139:6–7: 'Whither shall I
go then from thy Spirit: or whither shall I go then from thy
presence? / If I climb up into heaven, thou art there: if I go down
to hell, thou art there also.'

The Temper (2)

In spite of the resolution concluding the previous poem with the same
title (is this, in effect, a double poem?) things have gone wrong again –
an instance of H's candid realism. The poem consists of four verses of
two tetrameters sandwiched between two pentameters; rhyme scheme
abba – making for a steadier effect than the previous poem's.

3   *dart*: Psalm 38:2: 'thine arrows stick fast in me', among many
     instances in the Psalms of God shooting at people.
4   *Save*: spare.
5   *grosser world*: of nature as opposed to grace.
7   *race*: raze.
9   *O fix thy chair of grace*: Hebrews 4:16: 'Let us therefore come
     boldly unto the throne of grace, that we may obtain mercy, and
     find grace to help in time of need'; the Jacobean royal court, like
     the Elizabethan, was continually on the move between palaces
     and great houses, making it difficult for suitors to know where
     to go with their solicitations.
12   *bowers*: inner rooms, bedrooms (from French 'boudoirs').
14   *elements*: of the material, *grosser* world: earth, air, fire and water.

Jordan (1)

A polemic, starting with ten lines of aggressive attack. H wrote two
poems with this title, the second more honest than this one, which is
marred by a certain priggishness. They are about poetry and truth, art
and simplicity. It is an inevitable and immortal topic for writers and
readers alike, putting H with Wordsworth's championing of the

utmost simplicity of subject and diction in *Lyrical Ballads* and with his great predecessors, Shakespeare and Sidney. Sidney in his *Apology* condemned 'that honey-flowing matron eloquence, apparelled, or rather disguised, in a courtesan-like painted affectation'; and in the first sonnet of *Astrophil and Stella* began with 'Loving in truth, and fain in verse my love to show' and ended with ' "Fool," said my Muse to me; "look in thy heart, and write." '

Jordan: Refers enigmatically to 2 Kings 5. Naaman, a Syrian General, seeking a cure for his leprosy, resorted to the Israelite prophet Elisha, who refused to see him, but sent an underling to tell him to wash seven times in Israel's River Jordan. Naaman, offended by this off-hand treatment, protested that he had greater rivers at home. Persuaded by his servants to give it a go, he bathed in the Jordan and 'his flesh came again like unto the flesh of a little child, and he was clean.' The story appealed to H, with his belief that 'Childhood is health' ('Holy Baptism 2') and his obsession with cleanliness. The river imagery implied by the title is also important because it is repeatedly associated with poetic inspiration – both by the ancient poets (Callimachus and Horace in particular), but also by H in his Latin verse – cf., e.g., *Memoriae Matris Sacrum* 1. Jordan is mentioned specifically (in combination with classical rivers) at *Musae Responsoriae* 23.42 – a major Latin poem on his poetic vocation. There are three stanzas of four pentameters followed by a tetrameter to ram things home, rhyming *ababa*. The last stanza abandons rhetorical questions and enjambements for plain assertion.

1   *fictions*: poetic inventions, here viewed as false.

5   *true*: real, suggesting God's throne; *painted*: depicted.

7   *sudden*: visually surprising; *shadow*: obscure.

9   *divines*: guesses.

11   *Shepherds*: prominent in Spenser's *Shepherds Calendar* and Sidney's *Old Arcadia*, also featuring in Shakespeare's *As You Like It*. More generally, shepherds are the singers of pastoral poetry – an enormous classical and post-classical tradition.

12   *list*: like to; *pull for Prime*: draw the winning card in the game of Primero.

13   *nightingale or spring*: topoi of poetic inspiration.

14   *Nor let . . . loss of rhyme*: H can rhyme like the best of them.

15   *My God, My King*: Psalms, passim. The first and conclusive biblical allusion after so much from secular poetry.

Employment (1)

H had the famous protestant work ethic. In CP XXXII he put 'to everybody the need of a vocation ... taken from the nature of man, wherein God hath placed two great Instruments, Reason in the soul, and a hand in the Body, as engagements of working: so that even in Paradise man had a calling'. Lack of work other than poetry worried H a great deal. It is reflected in this agitated poem: six restless little stanzas of two tetrameters, a pentameter and a dimeter, rhyming *abab*.

1   *If as a flower ... and die*: Psalm 103:15–16: 'The days of man are but as grass: for he flourisheth as a flower of the field / For as soon as the wind goeth over it, it is gone: and the place thereof shall know it no more.' H substitutes *frost* for wind.

6   *room*: space.

8   *doom*: Day of Judgement.

11   *this place*: on earth.

12   *stuff*: content.

19   *that*: (honey).

20   *these*: (flowers).

21   *thy great chain*: the Great Chain of Being, the linked hierarchy of the universe from dust to God.

23   *consort*: (of musicians).

23–4 *Lord place me ... poor reed*: W had:

> Lord that I may the sun's perfection gain
> Give me his speed.

24   *reed*: a rustic panpipe or a reed pen.

The Holy Scriptures 1 and 2

The Bible had become increasingly available and affordable in the later sixteenth century. The Geneva translation of 1560, in roman type, quarto and octavo format, with illustrations and copious notes, enjoyed widespread sales and popularity. In 1611 it was joined by the Authorized or King James translation, which gradually overtook it. In H's time English bibles were common reading, new enough to be exciting: anyone who could read had the oracles of God for himself.

H's naive enthusiasm for what Blake called 'the most entertaining of books' is directly religious with, of course, no sign of a modern critical approach. The first sonnet of the pair is an encomium on the Bible, with the poet as its lively salesman; the second an exuberantly practical description of its use. 'Ladies, look here' at line 8 of the first sonnet is a cheery and welcome interruption of the list of virtues, implying some social occasion, perhaps a fair. Articles VI and VII of the BCP's 39 Articles of Religion 1562 asserted that: 'Holy Scripture containeth all things necessary to salvation ... both in the Old and New Testament everlasting life is offered to Mankind by Christ.' The translators of the KJB in their 'Epistle Dedicatory' called it 'God's holy Truth'. The BCP Collect for Advent II went in for some detailed guidance, followed by H here: 'Blessed Lord, who hast called all holy Scriptures to be written for our learning; grant that we may in such wise hear them, read, mark, learn, and inwardly digest them, that by patience, and comfort of thy holy Word, we may embrace, and ever hold fast the blessed hope of everlasting life, which thou hast given us in our Saviour Jesus Christ.'

2. *Suck*: CP IIII : '... the storehouse and magazine of life and comfort, the Holy Scriptures. There he sucks and lives.' Psalm 119:103: 'O how sweet are thy words unto my throat: yea, sweeter than honey to my mouth.'

8 *thankful glass*: mirror for which you'll be grateful. James 1: 23–5 contrasts a man who looks at himself 'in a glass ... and straightway forgetteth what manner of man he was', and someone who 'looketh into the perfect law of liberty' and is 'a doer of the work ... blessed in his deed'.

9 *well*: John 4:5–15: Jesus meets a woman at Jacob's well and tells her that 'Whosoever drinketh of this water shall thirst again: but whosoever drinketh of the water that I shall give him shall never thirst; but the water that I shall give him shall be in him a well of water springing up into everlasting life.'

11 *lidger*: ambassador.

13 *handsel*: first instalment

14 *Subject to ... bended knee*: a *jeu d'esprit* – as is the whole poem. The open Bible is like a map in an atlas in which the heavenly sphere is represented as flat. The final words 'bended knee' combine the posture of prayer with that of a horseman mounting his steed: a startling paradox that represents the combination of attentive subjection and being on top of the subject, which makes for good if knotty reading.

4   *the constellations of the story*: Resumes the figure of the astro-
     nomical map at the end of the previous sonnet – which is to be
     taken up again at the end of this poem.
6   *Unto a third . . . doth lie*: In CP IIII H recommends 'diligent Col-
     lation of Scripture. For all Truth being consonant to it self, and all
     being penned by one and the same Spirit, it cannot be, but that an
     industrious and judicious comparing of place with place must be
     a singular help for the right understanding of the Scriptures.' Col-
     lation was how reformed theologians made sense of the diversities
     and contradictions so abundant in the Bible, while sticking to the
     belief that 'one and the same Spirit' was the author of it all.
7   *dispersèd*: from here and there; *watch*: make up.
8   *These three . . . Christian's destiny*: For an example of this, see
     'The Bunch of Grapes'.
9   *Such are . . . makes good*: In CP III the first and best commen-
     tary on Scripture is 'a holy Life'.
11   *find me out*: Hebrews 4:12: 'the word of God . . . is a discerner
     of the thoughts and intents of the heart.'
13   *Stars are . . . do miss*: Astrology and horoscopes are fallible.
14   *stars*: In the KJB asterisks (typographical symbols like little
     stars) abound in the margins to direct the reader to another, rel-
     evant passage or instance: thus a great help to collation and the
     making of H's 'constellations'.

Whitsunday

Another happy poem with plenty of witty 'invention'. It is addressed
to the Holy Spirit in a prayer of seven stanzas of three tetrameters fol-
lowed by a pentameter, rhyming *abab*: a simple scheme, mellifluously
tripping along. Whitsun (aka Pentecost) is the seventh Sunday after
Easter (which H has written about earlier in the collection) celebrating
the coming of the Holy Spirit promised by Jesus after his departure. It
was called Whitsun after the white robes worn by those baptized on
that day in the early Church.

1   *Dove*: Matthew 3:16: at his baptism by John the Baptist he 'saw
     the spirit of God descending like a dove'.
2   *golden wings*: Psalm 68:13: 'the wings of a dove: that is covered
     with silver wings, and her feathers like gold'.
5   *fire*: Acts 2:3: 'And there appeared unto them [the apostles of
     Jesus] cloven tongues like as of fire, and it sat upon each of them.
     And they were all filled with the Holy Ghost.'

7   *open house*: H's mother and grandparents were famously hospitable. The old custom of the Whitsun ale, a fundraising parish party arranged for everybody by the churchwardens, seems to inform these lines and the appeal for restoration of the festival at the end. Puritans disliked it, but H was 'a lover of old customs ... because country people are much addicted to them' (CP XXXV).

8   *Feasting*: (spiritually, by preaching).

11 *stars*: Acts 2:3: the 'cloven tongues like as of fire' which descended on the apostles.

12 *mend*: improve.

13 *The sun*: St Peter's Pentecost sermon at Acts 2:20, quoting Joel 2:31: 'The sun shall be turned into darkness.'

13–28 *The sun ... miraculous right*: W had instead of these four stanzas the following muddled lines, referring to Lucifer/Satan in the first stanza and a maternal God (cf. *Memoriae Matris Sacrum* VII) in the third:

> But we are fall'n from heaven to earth,
> And if we can stay there, it's well.
> He that first fell from his great birth
> Without thy help, leads us his way to hell.

> Lord once more shake the heaven and earth
> Lest want of graces seem thy thrift:
> For sin would fain remove the dearth
> And lay it on thy husbandry, for shift.

> Show that thy breasts cannot be dry
> But that from them joys purl forever
> Melt into blessings all the sky,
> So we may suck: to praise thee, never.

16 *Going about the world*: the worldwide mission of the apostles fired off by Pentecost.

17 *pipes of gold*: Echoes Zechariah 4:12, where they conduct oil for anointing.

20 *Of those ... side wound*: Refers to the martyrdoms of the apostles and schisms (splits) in the Church.

23 *braves*: challenges.

Grace

An unexpectedly gloomy poem considering its title: six stanzas, each of three tetrameters, followed by a dimeter refrain. Simple enough metrically, but the rhyme scheme is a tour de force: every stanza has a second line which rhymes with the refrain. This dramatizes the stubborn absence of the title's 'Grace'. It is the one thing needful for salvation and human fulfilment, but it never comes and H is stuck in a world without it. He gets nowhere: same old refrain, same old rhymes. If God keeps on like this, H will only be able to stop repeating his refrain (finally italicized as a self-quotation) when he is dead.

Grace: Romans, passim, e.g., 3:24: 'Being justified freely by his grace through the redemption that is in Christ Jesus'. The refrain is derived from James 1:17: 'Every good gift ... is from above', and Isaiah 45:8: 'Drop down, ye heavens, from above, and let the skies pour down righteousness.'

1   *stock*: Of the fifty-nine meanings of this versatile noun in the OED, most commentators prefer the first: the stump or trunk of a tree. But this does not quite fit, and pun-loving H should be allowed more than one meaning. I prefer two: 1. collective, for the animals on a farm (figurative, agreeing with 'husbandry' in the next line); 2. a capital sum to trade with, as distinct from revenue (H's 'increase' in this line), which H used figuratively in 'Affliction (1)' ('Besides what I might have / Out of my stock of natural delights, augmented with thy gracious benefits'). John Smith (1618–52) of Queens' College, Cambridge, seems to have read this poem, published in Cambridge in six editions in his lifetime, when he wrote in his *Select Discourses* (1652): 'to prepare our souls more and more to receive of his liberality ... that the stock which he is pleased to impart to us may not lie dead within us'.

6   *Thy house*: the world (agreeing with the next line).

10 *thy Dove*: the Holy Spirit of the previous poem.

14 *remove*: step or stage, also the mole removing earth as it burrows away.

19 *cross*: oppose.

21 *O come! ... know the way*: Between stanzas 5 and 6 W had (crossed out):

> What if I say thou seek'st delays
> Wilt thou not then my fault reprove?

> Prevent my sin to thine own praise:
> Drop from above.

23   *where*: to heaven (by death).

Praise (1)

There is a difficulty with praise. It is required in public worship. But if
it is not personal, spontaneous and sincere it is not itself. H owns up
to this candidly in a poem of frustration, like the preceding 'Grace'. It
is complex, both metrically and rhyme-wise. Five stanzas, each with a
pentameter, a dimeter, a tetrameter and a dimeter refrain; rhyme
scheme of *aaab*, with the refrains (*b*) always ending with 'more'. H
may have got the idea from Donne's 'A Hymn to God the Father' with
its dimeter refrains ending with 'more'. But Donne rhymes his refrains
with his second and fourth lines, achieving a stately and integrated
effect. H is modest in thought and skilfully hesitant in form.

3   *Mend*: improve; *estate*: condition.
12   *He may do more*: 1 Samuel 17: young David killed the giant Gol-
     iath with a stone from his shepherd's sling.
15   *To a brave soul*: Herbal medicine, once in the body, is near the
     soul and cheers it.
17   *Poor bees*: Bees were an image of industry (and also of poetic
     composition – see Horace *Odes*, 4.2). See also *Lucus*, 5.
17–20 *O raise me . . . much more*: W had:

> O raise me then: for if a spider may
>   Spin all the day:
>   Not flies but I shall be his prey
>   Who do no more.

Affliction (2)

After its strong opening 'attack' it gets rather too cerebral for anguish
as previously evoked in 'Affliction (1)'. The imagery of the second
stanza is gruesome, if surreal enough to make it look like a source for
the sea of tears in *Alice's Adventures in Wonderland* (cf. *Memoriae
Matris Sacrum*, 1, 9 and 10). The form is metrically and rhyme-wise

complex again: trimeter, pentameter, tetrameter, trimeter, pentameter; rhyming *abbaa*. The effect is knotty, like the content.

1 *Kill me not ev'ry day*: 1 Corinthians 15:31: 'I die daily.'
2 *one death for me*: 1 Thessalonians 5:9–10: 'Jesus Christ, who died for us', and St Paul, passim.
4 *in broken pay*: in instalments.
5 *Methusalem's stay*: Genesis 5:27: 'all the days of Methuselah were nine hundred sixty and nine years: and he died.' H multiplies this already huge sum by the number of hours in a year, which would total about eight and a half million instalments.
10 *bloody sweat*: Luke 22:44: Jesus's 'sweat was as it were great drops of blood falling down to the ground'.
11 *Thou art my grief alone*: in two senses: cause and bearer (Isaiah 53:4: 'Surely he hath borne our griefs, and carried our sorrows').
15 *imprest*: payment in advance.

Matins

An aptly bright and chirpy poem, the second and third stanzas putting witty riddles to God, the fourth and fifth anticipating a happy day. In the first BCP (1549) Matins and Evensong were the traditional titles of the morning and evening liturgies. But this was short-lived and in the second BCP (1552) these were changed to Morning and Evening Prayer. It remained so in 1559 and ever after. This is important because it shows that H's two poems are neither alternatives to, nor commentaries upon, his BCP's Morning and Evening Prayer. Those were public liturgies. This is a supplementary act of personal devotion, such as his friend Lancelot Andrewes devised for his private use. It is very much in the first person singular. The titles show H's respect for the Pre-Reformation Church. The lines grow in length – trimeter, two tetrameters, final pentameter – as the poet bestirs himself. Simple *abab* rhyme scheme.

3 *My morning-soul and sacrifice*: Psalm 5:3: 'My voice shalt thou hear betimes, O Lord: early in the morning will I direct my prayer unto thee, and will look up.'
4 *make a match*: come to terms.
11 *art*: skill.
13 *estate*: condition.
19 *work and workman*: creation and Creator.
20 *sunbeam*: Pun on 'beam': of wood and of light.

Sin (2)

This poem comes aptly between the bright hopes of 'Matins' and the penitence of 'Evensong'. 'Sin' is a happy surprise after its forbidding title. Its argument is from St Augustine, H's favourite theologian, *Confessions* 7:18, where he asserts that everything in the world God made is good: 'Evil, then, of which I sought whence it was, is not any substance because, if it were a substance, it would be good.' It is nothing, the abyss which would drive us mad if steadfastly contemplated. The devil (God's prosecuting angel in The Book of Job) serves us as an image, dream or 'apparition' of sin, seen in 'perspective': a lens or a picture seen askew (like Holbein's *Ambassadors*, and referring to *paint* in line 2). So H explores appearance and reality and gives the devil his due. Three rhyming tetrameters followed by a pentameter couplet make for a thoughtful effect. The second stanza resolves the problems of the first by a change of viewpoint.

5   *wants*: lacks.
9   *foul*: echoes line 2.

Evensong (1)

The form is elaborate on the page, dreamily discursive when read aloud. Metrically, each stanza moves through lines of 3, 5, 4, 4, 3, 4, 4 and finally 5 feet. Rhyme-wise it goes *abbacddc* in the first and third stanzas, but ending *cdcd* in the second and *acac* in the last. So metre and rhyme do not coincide but rather play along with the loose association of thoughts of someone retiring for the night and finally dropping off. (1633 wrongly split the four eight-line stanzas of B into eight four-line ones, spoiling the effect.) The first half of the first verse is childlike, the second half artificial, with its thoughts that God cannot see him (or he would die on the spot) and has no son (because he has surrendered him to humanity): all rather contrived. Then things loosen up. The second verse expresses guilt for a misspent day and the third God's relaxed patience. The last verse has the beauty of what Vendler (p. 161) calls 'final self-acceptance', and H 'love'. That word 'love' occurs three times in the last stanza: in its first line, as a rhyme with that at line 29 (altering the previous rhyme scheme to *abbaacac* for this verse), and in the last line. For H, no word is more transformative – hence the unprecedented *acac* rhyming of the last four lines.

Evensong: see note on 'Matins'.

13   *diet*: allowance of food and expenses of living.
15   *crosst*: contradicted.
16   *wild-fire*: uncontrolled conflagration.
28   *that*: the day; *this*: the night.
32   *And in this . . . in bed, I rest*: Psalm 4:9: 'I will lay me down in peace, and take my rest: for it is thou, Lord, only that makest me dwell in safety.'

Church-monuments

The first of a group of five poems, three gathered together from here and there in W and two new ones ('The Church-Floor' and 'The Windows'). They ponder features of the church as building and place of worship. This gives a refreshing objectivity and locality to the poems, H usually being so subjective and internal. The monuments of H's day, such as that to his father and mother at Montgomery, were particularly elaborate, grandiose and boastful – and thus a sitting target for H's soberly pessimistic critique. The manuscripts, both W and B, have it as one continuous poem. The printer of 1633 broke it into four stanzas, perspicaciously noticing that the rhyme scheme, *abcabc*, suggests that. But the punctuation does not. So the manuscripts are followed here as closer to H himself and his metre: all pentameters which flow into one another with minimal interruption in a quietly relentless progress to the grave. Summers (p. 134) comments: 'the sentences sift down through the rhyme scheme skeleton like the sand through the glass.' Internal rhymes are hidden in lines 4 and 6 ('blast'/'last') and lines 15–18 ('bow'/'now'; 'they'/'pray'; and 'flat'/'that'/'fat'). They weigh things down. The word 'dust' appears over and over – at lines 3, 11 (twice), 13, 20 and 23, with 'dusty' at line 9 – like a muffled bell accompanying the sad procession. There is not the slightest reference to resurrection or immortality. The words at the actual burial in the BCP Burial of the Dead – 'we therefore commit his body to the ground; earth to earth, ashes to ashes, dust to dust' – are quoted in line 11, but without the subsequent 'in sure and certain hope of the Resurrection to eternal life'.

2   *betimes*: in good time, early.
3   *dust*: Genesis 3:19: God says to man: 'dust thou art, and unto dust shalt thou return'; Psalm 22:15: 'thou shalt bring me into the dust of death'; Ecclesiastes 3:20: 'all go unto one place; all are of the dust, and all turn to dust again.'

8   *spell*: understand, get by heart.
9   *lines*: of descent, pedigrees – as often on Jacobean monuments, along with heraldry.
17   *stem*: genealogy
20   *glass*: hourglass.
23   *How tame . . . free from lust*: an astonishing line.

Church-music

According to Walton and Aubrey, H was an expert musician, the former relating that in his final years at Bemerton (being in W, 'Church-Music' is probably earlier than that) he attended Sung Evensong in Salisbury Cathedral twice a week, which, he said, 'elevated his soul and was his heaven upon earth'. In his school days the fine choral music at Westminster Abbey under Orlando Gibbons was available to him, and William Byrd dined occasionally at his home in Charing Cross. His enthusiasm carries this happy poem with its light and simple rhythmical structure. The description of the effect of music in its second stanza is particularly fine. The survival of cathedrals with their choirs was a happy accident of the English Reformations. Metre and rhyme scheme both simple.

6   *Rising and falling*: Hooker, in *Ecclesiastical Polity*, V.38, celebrated 'the admirable facility which music hath to express and represent to the mind, more inwardly than any other sensible mean, the very standing, rising, and falling . . . whereunto the mind is subject . . . there is also that carrieth as it were into ecstasies, filling the mind with an heavenly joy and for the time in a manner severing it from the body.' These words seem to have stuck in H's mind and surfaced in this poem.
8   *God help poor Kings*: Just why this phrase occurs here is a mystery, but it obviously denotes supreme pleasure.
9   *Comfort, I'll die*: addressed to music; '*die*' has the meaning 'to languish, pine away with passion' (OED); *post*: ride away 'post haste'. This difficult passage seems to convey that the poet will die one way or another: either of grief by music's departure or happily attaining heaven by travelling in music's company (thanks to Colin Burrow for this elucidation).
12   *You know . . . heaven's door*: Between stanzas 2 and 3 W had:

> O what a state is this, which never knew
> Sickness, or shame, or sin, or sorrow:

> Where all my debts are paid, none can accrue
> Which knoweth not, what means, tomorrow.

Church-lock and key

The common problem of cold and reluctant prayer. In the first stanza he blames himself for it. In the second he catches himself blaming God. In the third he invokes Christ's redeeming blood. As ever, the problem of responsibility between man and God is resolved, or dissolved, by Christ's sacrifice. The dimeter second line of each stanza gives a little lift or kick to the pentameters. The poem owes its modest success to the two similes in its second and third stanzas. Particularly good is the man with cold hands grumbling at the fire, sunk low like H's zeal, while at the same time he rouses it. Sins like stones are stock with H, but here he imagines them in a shallow stream making the running water (Christ's blood) melodious.

Title in W was 'Prayer'. Then, on the cue of 'locks' in the first line, H changed it to the present one. This enabled him to include it in this Church set, with the implied metaphor of the devout man shut out of church standing for his psychological alienation. Christ is then the 'key'.

Between stanzas 1 and 2 W had:

> If either Innocence or fervency
> > Did play their part
> Armies of blessings would contend and vie
> Which of them soonest should attain my heart.

9–10 *for his blood's ... for me*: Genesis 4:10: 'the voice of thy brother's blood crieth unto me from the ground – but here Christ's blood'

9–12 *Yet hear ... loud to be*: W had instead of lines 9–12:

> O make me wholly guiltless, or at least
> > Guiltless so far;
> That zeal and pureness circling my request
> May guide it safe beyond the highest star.

The Church-floor

A double poem. In the first part, H shows us round with genial alle-
gorical confidence. His authoritative tone suggests that he is the rector
(the poem is later than W). In the second, still in allegorical mode, he
relates incidents in cleaning (in CP XIII he insisted 'that the Church
be swept, and kept clean without dust or cobwebs'). The form is ori-
ginal and quietly bold. The first poem has four little three-line stanzas,
metrically diminishing from five feet, to three, to one. In the rhyme
scheme those last lines are made all the odder and plainer by rhyming
across, while emphasized by italics in 1633. So the rhymes go *abw
abx cdw cdx*. It is so pictorial as to verge on being a figure poem. The
second poem is less sharply didactic and formal: a sort of aside from
our guide about difficulties of upkeep. It is of eight lines and a variant
of *ottava rima*: an Italian form in origin. H uses tetrameters, varied
with two dispersed but rhyming pentameters, and a complex rhyme
scheme of *aabccbdd*. The last couplet hands us the allegorical key, in
case we had missed it. It all works, in a precise and positive sense, very
nicely, the complexities suiting the subject.

1   *Mark*: Notice.
8   *Choir*: the raised space at the east end for clergy and choir – but
    can be understood as heaven.
12 *Charity*: 'The very bond of peace and of all virtues' (BCP Collect
    for Quinquagesima), so it comes here, with its synonym *love*, to
    tie up the previous virtues.
15 *weeps*: Changes of temperature cause moisture to gather on mar-
    ble: for H, tears of penitence. Cf. to *Lucus* 1, line 5 and 'Ephesians
    4:30', line 23.
16 *puffing at the door*: It was difficult to prevent dogs following
    people into church. Someone would be put in charge of getting
    them out, with dog-tongs if necessary. Then they would distract
    the worshippers by *puffing at the door*.

The Windows

Not in W, this poem about preaching must belong to H's last years as
Rector of Bemerton. Having been Praelector in Rhetoric and Univer-
sity Orator at Cambridge in his younger days and then having
abandoned these offices, H had reason to reflect on the emptiness of
mere words. Walton (p. 365) relates that H's first sermon at Bemerton

was delivered after 'a most florid manner, both with great learning and eloquence', but that at the end of it he promised to 'be more plain and practical in his future sermons'. In CP VII H insists that 'the character of his sermon is holiness; he is not witty, or learned, or eloquent, but holy' and 'every word is heart-deep'. Here H uses a tight rhyme scheme of *ababb* with a metre of 5, 4, 5, 4, 4 feet. A couplet emphasizes the conclusion of each stanza.

The Windows: H is thinking of stained (annealed) glass with its sacred figures and stories, of which a good deal survived the Reformations (e.g., spectacularly at King's College, Cambridge, familiar to H).

2   *crazy*: full of cracks or flaws; *glass*: pronounced with a short, sharp *a*, American-wise.

6   *anneal*: burn in.

11   *Doctrine and life*: BCP Holy Communion: 'that they [clergy] may both by their life and doctrine set forth thy true and lively Word.'

Trinity Sunday

An ingeniously contrived poem for the Sunday celebrating the three-fold nature of the Christian God – Creator, Redeemer and Spirit – which yet speaks from the heart without impediment. It is all in threes: three stanzas, each of three lines; the three aspects of God in the first stanza; a stanza each for past, present and future; three ways of dealing with sin in the second (prayer, confession and resolution to amend); and in the last stanza three parts of the body, St Paul's three chief virtues from 1 Corinthians 13, and three verbs all beginning with 'r' – three threes! For all its hierographical dexterity, it works well as a simple prayer.

1   *mud*: the dust mixed with water out of which God made man at Genesis 2:7.

Content

H takes his own advice in *The Church-Porch* (stanzas 24 and 25) to keep a 'guard upon himself' and restrain impulses, because

> Who cannot rest till he good fellows [jolly companions] find,
> He breaks up house, turns out of doors his mind.

Psalm 4:4 lies behind it all ('commune with your own heart, and in your chamber, and be still'), but it owes far more to Stoic philosophy of self-awareness and moderation than to Christianity, of which there is no apparent sign. Lines 25–33 are interesting testimony to the aversion to public fame – and publication – which was determinative of the course of his life. Each verse is a sober alternation of pentameters and tetrameters and a quiet rhyme scheme of *abab*. To each of the nine stanzas its metaphor, making a slightly cumbersome collection, in the manner of H's collection of 1,032 *Outlandish* [i.e., foreign] *Proverbs*, published posthumously in 1640. This poem is one of very many similar in the period – the lyric of 'stoic commonplaces'. Cf. Wootton, 'Happy is he born and thought / That serveth not another's will'; Campion, 'The man of life upright'. Poetically, traces its roots to Horace in particular.

8   *in contemplation*: (even) in thinking about it.
15   *let loose to*: aim at.
15–16 *a crown . . . cloister's gates*: A reference to the Holy Roman Emperor Charles V's abdication in 1556 to enter a monastery: a favourite historical precedent at Little Gidding.
17   *This soul*: the 'pliant' and contented one.
19   *tent*: temporary accommodation.
21   *brags*: arrogant boastings.
25   *Chronicle*: record of an eminent life.
28   *rent*: rend, tear.
29   *brunt*: force or shock.
30   *chaw'd*: chewed (up or over).
34   *importune*: accent on second syllable.

The Quiddity

Entitled 'Poetry' in W. This later title puns, meaning both the essence of a thing and a captious quibble in an argument, such as are dismissed in every line except the last two. From self-consciousness as a man in 'Content', H turns to self-consciousness as a poet. For its vivid list of images, this engagingly sprightly poem ransacks the ways of high society, only to negate them one by one: the negations give it its spring, along with its iambics, slowed down by trochees in the last stanza. The last two lines are a quiet triumph. There is the intelligence of describing a poem as a rendezvous of writer and addressee, and the witty gaiety of concluding the poem by stealing a phrase from the secular world which has been so repeatedly put down before: the winner's cry at the end of a card game.

2   *suit*: of clothes.
8   *demesne*: estate.
10   *Exchange . . . Hall*: two London places: the commercial Exchange
     in the City and Westminster Hall with its courts of law.
11   *use*: am working on: poetic composition as waiting on God.

Humility

H's basic thought here is that the traditional virtues are subject to the
sin of pride and need humility to control them – however temporarily.
This intelligent poem is, for H, an unusual mixture of allegory with
fable in the ironical manner of Aesop (a favourite author in elemen-
tary education). It may be modelled on Sidney's poem 'As I my little
flock . . .' in *The Old Arcadia* (circulating in manuscript) in which all
the animals contribute their particular virtues to make a king – which
turns out badly for them because 'thus man their lord became'. Here,
by contrast, each animal presents its particular vice to its opposite vir-
tue. Humility, the Christian virtue, modestly acts as go-between or
usher. It goes well until all the virtues want the glamorous peacock's
feather, the emblem of pride, and fall out with one another. Humility's
tears at this turn of events make the feather bedraggled and turns the
virtues against the beasts – but, in a final and realistic let-down, the
virtues insist on another trial with 'double gifts'. This tart conclusion,
along with all the other twists of irony such as the poor old crow and
the clever fox (accidentally killed or he would have won the day for
the beasts), spices what might otherwise be a stodgy poem with sur-
prises and wry wit. Easy alternate rhyming. Metrically, a run of five
pentameters is followed by a trimeter, a pentameter and another trim-
eter: a distinct improvement on Sidney's duller all-pentameters.

2   *azure*: i.e., heavenly.
10   *Mansuetude*: gentleness.
27   *train*: tail-feathers.
29   *bandying*: getting together.
31   *amerc'd*: fined.
32   *Session-day*: trial day in court.

Frailty

The dilemma of whether to choose the secular career for which his
talents and connections suited him or a life in the Church (Fellows of
Trinity College like him were obliged to be eventually ordained) was

the great crisis of H's life. This poem is set in that quandary and an attempt to take stock of it – poetry as devout self-analysis. The complicated metrics reflect the movements of his mind, its hesitations and anxieties, the number of feet in each stanza going: 5, 2, 5, 2, 3, 3, 5, 2. The accompanying rhyme scheme is *ababccdd*.

1   *silence*: denoting solitary recollection.
6   *Dear*: pun: expensive and beloved.
7   *In all . . . ever tread*: W had:

> Misuse them all the day:
> And ever as I walk my foot doth tread.

9   *abroad*: widely; *Regiments*: regimes.
13   *weeds*: clothes.
17   *brook*: allow.
22   *Babel*: Genesis 11:1–9, the ambitious tower 'whose top may reach unto heaven' built by men, but abandoned when God imposed differences of language, which made cooperative work impossible.

Constancy

Not in W. Arthur Woodnoth, a London businessman, was a friend and useful manager of their affairs to H, the Ferrars at Little Gidding and H's stepfather Sir John Danvers. But he was a worrier and a bore. Should he get ordained? Should he get married? He bothered H in his Bemerton years, even when he was ill (this poem is not in W, so relatively late), with these questions. H tried to settle him down with a sensible letter, written overnight and read to him in the morning (Hutchinson, pp. 380–1). Its advice, particularly to weigh things up objectively and stick to useful employment, is reflected in this poem. So it may well have been written for him, as 'The Bunch of Grapes' all but certainly was. To counter Woodnoth's exaggerated Christian piety H administers a dose of good, Stoic virtue in the fashionable literary form of a 'character'. The trimeters in the first lines and the tetrameters in the fourth are firmly pinned down by decisive pentameters in the middle and at the ends.

8   *look*: transitive.
32–5 *runs bias . . . be so still*: a metaphor from the game of bowls. The bowls or 'woods' are made asymmetrically with a *bias* which swerves them from the straight. A bowler who sees his

bowl running askance from his aim will often *writhe his limbs* in a vain attempt to correct it.

34 *Mark-man*: the man to mark or take notice of.

Affliction (3)

Not in W. H's involuntary sigh *O God!* guides him to Christ's affliction and reassures him of his membership in Christ, whose sufferings (unlike his own in the greater poem 'Affliction (1)') are his main topic here. So his sources are biblical: Romans 8:26: 'the Spirit itself maketh intercession for us with groanings which cannot be uttered'; God moulding man and breathing life into him at Genesis 2:7; 1 Corinthians 12 on Christians as members of Christ's body; 2 Corinthians 1:5: 'the sufferings of Christ abound in us'; 1 Corinthians 15:31: 'I (St Paul) die daily' – which, in view of the foregoing coinherences, H can apply to Christ.

8   *tallies*: accounts (of breaths/sighs).
9–10 *breath to a sigh ... it escape*: sighs were believed to hasten death.

The Star

Not in W. A light-headed spinning out of the metaphorical implications of a shooting star, primarily as a member of Christ's heavenly court. It achieves a certain giddy exhilaration in its penultimate verse. In the last verse the star is like a bee returning to the heavenly hive. Along with five other pieces by H, it was set to music as a part-song by H's contemporary John Jenkins (Oxford, Christ Church MSS 736–8). Certainly it appears (and sounds) as if to be sung. Cf. *Lucus,* 5 ('On Sacred Scripture'), which combines star and bee as here. See also 'Artillery', lines 1–2: 'As I one ev'ning sat before my cell, / Methoughts a star did shoot into my lap.'

Sunday

According to Walton, H on his deathbed 'called for one of his instruments' and, 'having tuned it', sang the fifth stanza of this poem. CP VIII is enthusiastic about Sundays: the parson 'as soon as he awakes on Sunday morning, presently falls to work, and seems to himself as a market-man is, when the market day comes, or a shopkeeper, when customers use to come in.' It is a (somewhat unremittingly) cheerful poem, likening Sundays to the pillars of a palace, the flower beds in a garden, the jewels on a bracelet, a manger for cattle, new clothes and a kind of springboard to heaven. Each verse starts and ends with a bright trimeter, with five tetrameters in between. Lines 43-56 are about the effect of the first Easter on the calendar: the holiness of the old Jewish Sabbath (Saturday), on which God rested from the labours of creation (Genesis 2:2) was transferred to Sunday, the day of Christ's resurrection. To mark this change, H uses the old typology of Samson removing the gates of Gaza, standing for Christ breaking down the gates of death (Judges 16:3), reinforced by the earthquake at Christ's death at Matthew 27:51-2, which caused a resurrection of the Jewish saints of old. This typological compacting is confusing if powerful. Thereafter the imagery is more homely. The change of clothes at line 52 provides a simpler metaphor, and the last verse looks like a happy reference to the children's game of hopscotch in its English ('cat's cradle') version of six squares (the six weekdays).

1-7   *O day . . . the way*: W had:

> O day so calm, so bright:
> The Couch of Time, the balm of tears,
> Th'endorsement of supreme delight,
> The parter of my wrangling fears
> Setting on order what they tumble:
> The week were dark, but that thy light
> Teaches it not to stumble.

2   *this*: (world's).
3   *endorsement*: confirmation.
4   *a friend*: (Christ).
10   *Knocking at . . . thy brow*: Matthew 7:7 'knock, and it shall be opened unto you' – prayer is intended.
11   *worky-days*: weekdays; *back-part*: (of the body, the back or the yard at the back of a house, used for work).
12   *burden*: pun: refrain of a song, repeated after each verse – then in the next line changed to mean 'load'.
14   *release*: (from the week's work).
24   *The other . . . the spare*: H has in mind a building set over arches, in the hollow space under which hucksters could set up stalls, as in many surviving seventeenth-century town halls.
26-8 *They are . . . orders*: W had:

> They are the rows of fruitful trees
> Parted with alleys or with grass
> In God's rich Paradise.

31   *the wife*: the Church as Christ's bride. In the preface to the BCP
     Solemnization of Matrimony marriage signifies 'the mystical
     union that is betwixt Christ and his Church'.
31–2 *Make bracelets . . . glorious King*: W had:

> Make bracelets for the spouse and wife
> Of the immortal only King.

50   *that day*: (the Sabbath – Saturday).
62   *both*: (the poet and Sunday).

Avarice

Not in W. 'The love of money is the root of all evil: which while some
coveted after, they have erred from the faith, and pierced themselves
through with many sorrows' (1 Timothy 6:10) is the text for this little
sermon in the form of a sonnet. Its moral critique is an inductively
Baconian ('whence com'st thou?') inquiry into the origin of money,
rather than specifically Christian or biblical.

7   *destitute*: valueless.

Ana-$\left\{ \begin{array}{c} Mary \\ Army \end{array} \right\}$ gram

In B this tiny hieroglyphical quip or 'pretty conceit' (Puttenham,
p. 82), showing H's regard for Catholic devotion to the Virgin Mary,
was placed between 'Church-music' and 'Church-lock and key'. The
printer of 1633 aptly moved it here, as an introduction to the conflicted
Marian poem which comes next. It depends on The Song of Solomon
6:10: 'Who is she that looketh forth as the morning, fair as the moon,
clear as the sun, and terrible as an army with banners?' – in traditional
Catholic interpretation the answer is Mary. *Lucus* 25 is a more
developed anagram.

To all Angels and Saints

Article 22 of *The Thirty-Nine Articles of the Church of England*
(1563) declared that 'the Romish Doctrine concerning . . . invocation
of saints is a fond thing vainly invented, and grounded upon no
warranty of Scripture.' All the same H, as a warmly ecumenical
soul and a moderate Anglican, hankers after it – his particular love

of Mary as 'Mother of God' no doubt confirmed by his own mother-fixation. He only refrains out of obedience to God's 'prerogative' who 'bids no such thing' and, in the last two lines, says he is very ready to take it up after all if so authorized by Christ. The poem is therefore conflicted, but not anxiously so. Affectionate devotion is its tone and theme. In lines 11–15 H is as happy extolling Mary as the Bible in 'The Holy Scriptures (1)'. In each of its six stanzas a dimeter is sandwiched between two pentameters, giving lightness and rest.

1   *bands*: ranks.
5   *hands*: (ready to offer the crown to God, as in Revelation 4:10).
20   *your*: (angels').
21   *prerogative*: pre-eminent right and power (of God, delegated to kings).
30   *hand*: authorizing signature.

Employment (2)

A remarkable poem with a strong sting in its tail. H is not one for sitting around or snuggling into his fur collar. He gets going, urging himself on with his beloved proverbs and aphorisms. The metre of its six stanzas is a brisk alternation of tetrameters and dimeters rhyming *ababa*. This is the H of 'The Answer': 'eager, hot, and undertaking, / But in my prosecutions slack and small'. Once again, he wishes he were a tree ('Affliction (1)', line 57): this time the ever-productive orange-tree. The last stanza is very dark and cold. It is never the right time. He is like a pedlar whose customer has left him before he could lay out his wares. 'Freeze' in the penultimate line is an aptly chilling improvement on W's 'creep'. In W H's scribe left the space for a title blank. Then H, bitterly, called it 'Employment'. Unrelieved by the slightest trace of Christian comfort, the poem is as bleak as anything by Thomas Hardy.

15   *by the others is oppresst*: As a result of sitting still was oppressed.
20   *advantage*: chance.
21–5   *O that . . . dressèd me*: W had instead:

> O that I had the wing and thigh
> Of laden bees;
> Then would I mount up instantly
> And by degrees
> On men drop blessings as I fly.

29   *So we freeze on*: W had 'Thus we creep on.'

Denial

Another bleak poem. But, reversing the movement of the previous 'Employment (2)', it starts desperately but ends in hope. The form is the thing here. It is suited to the content with striking originality. The feet of the lines of each verse are all metrically unequal: 4, 2, 5, 3, and a joltingly final 1 foot (until the very last line, when it is a nice steady 2). These last lines matter rhyme-wise, too: none of them rhymes at all until the very end when 'chime' rhymes with 'rhyme' (itself!). The problem is unanswered prayer, the failure of the reciprocity which made life worthwhile for H. The psalmist knew about it: 'Hide not thy face from me in the time of my trouble: incline thine ear unto me when I call; O hear me, and that right soon' (Psalm 102:2). H's art at any rate has made the best of it.

24   *nipt*: by frost.
29   *chime*: rhyme and/or harmonize.

Christmas

Like 'Easter' (probably its model) a double poem with the first part more discursive (here a narrative sonnet like 'Redemption') and the second lyrical (rhyming couplets of pentameters with trimeters, flowing along through increasingly long sentences until the final pentameter couplet). It is all equally brilliant and coherent, although the first poem alone is in W and the second was added later. The hunter of the first poem (aristocratic, predatory, lost and exhausted) is matched by the shepherds in the second (nurturing, musical, lively peasants). The pastoral tradition at large and Spenser's *Shepherds' Calendar* (1579) in particular influence the latter. The source is the nativity story in Luke 2: the newborn Jesus laid 'in a manger; because there was no room for them in the inn', announced by angels (not referred to by H) and visited by shepherds, who returned to their work 'glorifying and praising God for all the things that they had heard and seen'. Light, so valued at this midwinter festival, is climactic in both poems. In the first there is the wonderful 'glorious, yet contracted light' from St John's Christmas Day gospel (John 1:4–9). In the second the vivid 'frost-nipt suns look sadly' is challenged by the search for a more 'willing shiner'. No doubt this refers to John 1 again, but the reader is carried away by H's recklessly exhilarated imagining of a twenty-four-hour sun, its beams reciprocally intertwined with his own heart and poem 'Till ev'n his beams sing, and my music shine'. One of his great-est last lines, with its melodically rising vowels.

2   *horse*: body; *I*: mind.
3   *full cry*: hounds in full pursuit, baying.
4   *inn*: Luke 2:7.
6   *expecting*: waiting.
10   *manger*: *Luke* 2:7.
13–14 *Furnish and . . . or grave*: W had:

> Furnish my soul to thee, that being drest
> Of better lodging thou mayst be possesst.

14   *rack*: a kind of manger and an instrument of torture like Christ's cross. *grave*: Christ's sepulchre. An ominous touch of darkness.
26   *candle*: to light the score.
32   *pay*: reward.

Ungratefulness

A happy poem until the last stanza, which is desperate. Theological speculation is not H's forte. In 'Divinity' he treats it as on a par with astronomy. Here he is content to admire (without expounding) two key Christian doctrines: the Incarnation and the Trinity. The latter, though the more 'stately', is too dazzling for present comprehension. It is like a 'cabinet' one cannot get into. The former is an accessibly familiar 'box' because we all have bodies just like that of the divine Christ (note the deft switch from grand 'cabinet' for the Trinity to homely 'box' for the Incarnation). H was fascinated by boxes, their hiding and keeping. Elaborately inlaid or embroidered, they were popular luxury goods and gifts. In 'Evensong' God encloses us in his 'Ebony box' at night; the spring in 'Virtue' is 'A box where sweets com-pacted lie'; Mary in 'To All Angels and Saints' is 'the cabinet where the jewel lay'; in 'Misery' man was once 'A box of jewels'; in 'Sighs and Groans' (next in the collection) God has a 'bitter box' of punishments. This theme shapes the form. Each stanza (room) is a separate box made of one complete sentence – except the last stanza which has two sen-tences, because integrity has been split by an untoward, unfitting extra: 'Sins have their box apart' in man's 'poor cabinet of bone'. And in each stanza pentameters frame and enclose the middle tetrameters and trim-eters fore and aft.

6   *better*: (because higher in heaven).

18   *powder*: (medicinal for filmy eyes).
30   *two for one*: the Trinity and the Incarnation for *a heart*.

Sighs and Groans

Not in W. H is not addressing the sympathetic, suffering Jesus but God the Father, the unpredictable author of his life, death and destiny, and his punitive judge. Hence the abject cringing of those last lines, all negative ('O do not . . . !') except the very last, which is positive. At least H, like the psalmists, is protesting (Psalm 32:4 'thy hand is heavy upon me'; Psalm 88:16: 'Thy wrathful displeasure goeth over me,' etc.). Elsewhere H thinks that groans are highly effective with God – in 'Sion', more so than Solomon's great temple: 'quick, and full of wings'. But here they do not seem to get him anywhere, despite his invocation of Christ's blood in the fourth stanza.

5   *worm*: Psalm 22:6: 'I am a worm, and no man.'
8   *steward*: cf. Luke 16:1–8, the parable of the unjust steward called to account.
10   *magazines*: storehouses.
14   *Egyptian night*: Exodus 10:22: 'there was a thick darkness in all the land of Egypt.'
16   *fig-leaves*: like Adam and Eve in Genesis 3:7.
20   *vial*: bowl, cf. Revelation 15:7: 'vials full of the wrath of God'.
21   *other vessels*: Matthew 26:27–8, the cup given by Jesus to his disciples at the Last Supper, saying 'this is my blood'; Matthew 26:39, the cup of suffering and death accepted by Jesus in Gethsemane; the cup at Holy Communion.
28   *Corrosive*: caustic medicine.

The World

An allegory in which the created world, as God's (Love's) house, is beset by faults and the forces of decay, maintained and refurbished by laws and grace, finally completely ruined and completely rebuilt. This was a great age of ambitious great house building (as by H's stepfather Sir John Danvers at Chelsea on the site of the present Danvers Street) and rebuilding – which, in London, royal proclamations (line 9) tried to control. The allegory of virtues and vices with their attendant constructive and destructive contributions is sustained throughout but saved by H's love of sprightly diction and graphic detail from being laboured. It can be read as a witty contraption or 'toy'.

6   *fashion*: style.
10   *menaces*: threats of penalties.
11   *Sycamore*: a species of fig tree (its leaves used for clothing by
      Adam and Eve in Genesis 3:7). whose roots are a menace to
      buildings.
14   *sommers*: supporting beams.

Coloss. 3:3
Our life is hid with Christ in God

H captures, in Christian terms and with gracefully ingenious means, the
usual way in which we navigate our lives: one eye for the day's business,
another for the fashioning ideal or vision we have for ourselves (Christ
for H). The text of the title is paraphrased and ostentatiously hidden by
being put in italics (the contribution of Buck, the 1633 printer). It runs
obliquely, line by line, through the body of the poem, which goes
straight ahead. So, to H's eye, it is with the sun which goes straight
from east to west daily, but 'doth obliquely bend' as it circles the seasons
of the year. So it is with life, which goes straight through each day, but
overall 'winds towards *Him* [Jesus, H's Master].' It is all of a piece.
Despite its complexity of form on the page, the poem's pentameter
couplets read aloud with fluent conviction, its last sentence a crescendo
six lines long. Altogether a triumph of living art.

8   *Should aim . . . on high*: The archer or marksman closes one eye
      to aim with the other.

Vanity (1)

Not in W. 'Vanity of vanities, saith the Preacher, vanity of vanities; all
is vanity' (Ecclesiastes 1:2). H's beloved St Augustine attacked curios-
ity in *Confessions*, X.55: 'the same motive is at work when people
study the operations of nature which lie beyond our grasp, when there
is no advantage in knowing and investigators simply desire know-
ledge for its own sake.' H's mockery of scientific inquiry would have
grated on his friend Sir Francis Bacon, as well as on modern readers.
As with Augustine, the excuse is the primacy of the knowledge of
God. On the other hand, H is in tune with his brother Edward's reduc-
tion, in his *de Veritate*, of essential knowledge to a handful of innate
'common notions', which God 'embosoms in us' all (line 24). H's sat-
ire is quizzically detached rather than hostile.

1   *fleet*: nimble.
2   *thread*: planets strung on the lines of their orbits.
3   *stations*: positions.
7   *aspects*: relative positions as seen from earth.
14 *destruction*: presumably for the mortal sin of pride.
15 *Chymick*: chemist/alchemist.
17 *callow principles*: naked fledgling elements. The comparison is
    with baby birds in a nest.

Lent

A good-natured but tedious homily in eight stanzas, their pentameter
couplets varied by rhyming trimeters. The Church's season of fasting
from Ash Wednesday until Easter is first enjoined by authority, then
(in case that does not appeal to some people) for its physical and men-
tal benefits. The last three lines are a welcome awakening of H's wit:
the happy scene of feeding poor people at your door preferred to rev-
elling in the parlour because it nourishes your own poor soul.

4   *The Scriptures*: Joel 2:12: 'turn ye even to me . . . with fasting,'
    and Matthew 6:16: 'when ye fast, be not, as the hypocrites, of a
    sad countenance.'
5   *thy Mother*: the Church.
6   *Corporation*: institution with legal status and authority.
20 *motions*: impulses.
31 *Christ's forti'th day*: Christ fasted in the wilderness for forty days
    (Matthew 4:1–2).
35 *Be holy ev'n as he*: 1 Peter 1:15: 'as he which hath called you is
    holy, so be ye holy.'

Virtue

Not in W. The beauty of this little masterpiece on the great old themes
of mortality and immortality is achieved by H's 'utmost art' ('Praise
(2)' line 9) reviving a classical poetic form (cf. Catullus 11 and 51).
The intricacies of its craft only enhance its transparency. H's favourite
word, 'sweet', threads through it: from 'day' to 'rose' to 'spring' and
all it holds; finally to the 'virtuous soul'. Each stanza has its conclusion,
increasingly conclusive as the first three stanzas serially and subtly
increase the grip of 'must die'. Those first three stanzas are connected
by images which slip over the conclusions. The day's tears of dew in
the first become the watery eye of the dazzled gazer in the second.

They are all there in spring's box in the third. The fourth stanza's continuity-with-difference is signalled by its first words: not just 'sweet' as for the first three, but 'Only a sweet . . .' as it focuses on the 'virtuous soul', which has a new kind of simile to itself: the 'season'd timber' which, by being left out, covered from rain, in all weathers through the years after being cut, will be hard and dry enough to be stable and last and last – even when other wood has warped or been turned to charcoal by the fires of the last judgement. So this stanza can have an utterly different conclusion – indeed, a beginning – 'then chiefly lives'.

The sweetness of the first stanza is deliciously sensual. The ear is delighted by the vowels of the first line, springing from their preceding short 'so's, as they ascend the scale like a melody from low 'cool' through open 'calm' to high, pinging 'bright'. The eye is given the quiet spectacle of earth and sky married to each other ('bridal') in luminous response, each revealing the loveliness of the other. In the second stanza the rose – presumably red and carrying erotic associations – is an assault on the eye: a sharp corrective to its sweetness. Two of H's favourite things, boxes (see 'Ungratefulness') and music, furnish the third stanza: the first of these for plenitude, the second for drawing to a close.

2   *bridal*: wedding celebration.
11   *My music . . . your closes*: note the internal rhyme.
15   *coal*: charcoal.

The Pearl (Matt. 13:45)

'The kingdom of heaven is like unto a merchant man, seeking goodly pearls; who, when he had found one pearl of great price, went and sold all that he had, and bought it.' Thus the text of the title, a parable of transcendent, all-inclusive value, which for H is love. It works: above all by giving him a secure standing from which he can view worldly goings-on without the condescending sarcasm of 'Vanity (1)' – indeed with some relish and admiration, and as his own possession ('I know . . .'). This is reflected in the form: nine alternately rhyming pentameter lines enlivened by picturesque wit and sprightly invention, all closed by a simple and direct refrain which, thrice repeated, is finally quite changed (as in the preceding 'Virtue'). It is not exactly a poem of renunciation, rather a praise of love by a process of transcending, like St Paul's famous 1 Corinthians 13 ('the greatest of these is love', Tyndale).

2   *And pipes ... make it run*: a complex metaphor. Perhaps 'head' =
    the brain, and 'pipes' = reading, etc. Or 'head' = the university,
    and 'pipes' = schools.
4   *spun*: on her spinning wheel.
5   *conspire*: plot together what will happen on earth (astrological).
6   *fire*: of the alchemist or smith.
8   *surplus*: excess.
12 *returns*: rejoinders.
13 *vies*: competitions.
14 *glory*: pride.
17 *it*: glory.
25-30 *Have done ... I love thee*: These lively lines, giving welcome
    variety, replace the following catalogue in W:

> Where both the baskets are with all their store,
> The smacks of dainties and their exaltation:
> What both the stops and pegs of pleasure be:
> The joys of Company or Contemplation
>   Yet I love Thee.

smacks: tastes; *stops and pegs*: of a stringed musical instrument.
29 *one to five*: myself against my five senses.
34 *commodities*: wares.
36 *move*: change or develop.
37-8 *labyrinths ... silk twist*: In Greek myth, Theseus found his way
    back to safety from the Minotaur's lair in the Cretan labyrinth
    by following the thread supplied by Ariadne. There is similar
    imagery in *Memoriae Matris Sacrum* 3.10.
39 *did*: past tense – it has already happened, hence his security.

Affliction (4)

The title in W is 'Temptation'. Restless and incoherent anguish is
made real in content and form. The content is remarkable for the var-
iety of metaphors which tumble after one another in rapid succession:
God as hunter (Psalm 38:2: 'thine arrows stick fast in me: and thy
hand presseth me sore'), torture, the unforgettable 'case of knives'('he
would often say, He had too thoughtful a wit: a wit like a penknife in
too narrow a sheath, too sharp for his body,' Walton, p. 350), the
watering pot, the disorderly household and body. The form is as
impulsive, the number of feet in the lines of each stanza going 4, 2, 2,
4, 4, 4. The first four lines rhyme *abba* and the last two lines are a

rhyming couplet. So a stanza consists of a four-line and a two-line part, sometimes separate and sometimes elided. Hope of a steadier existence dawns in the penultimate stanza and is confidently expected in the last, calmer stanza.

4   *wonder*: such as a monster exhibited at a fair.
17   *elements*: of his body: blood, bile, etc.

Man

Psalm 8:4-6 sets the tone:

> What is man, that thou art mindful of him: and the son of man, that thou visitest him?
> Thou madest him lower than the angels: to crown him with glory and worship.
> Thou makest him to have dominion of the works of thy hands: and thou hast put all things in subjection under his feet;
> All sheep and oxen: yea, and the beasts of the field;
> The fowls of the air and the fishes of the sea: and whatsoever walketh through the paths of the seas.
> O Lord our Governor: how excellent is thy Name in all the world!

This poem is Christian renaissance humanism 'in C major – formal, ceremonious praise, without modulations to the minor' (Bloch, p. 259). At the start H introduces God into his train of thought with aristocratic ease. At the end of it, God is the fulfilment of all the previous fulfilments. A happy state of affairs. The completeness of being human is the theme. It is realized in the chiastic metre scheme, the lengths of the first three lines inverted for the second three: 3, 5, 4, 4, 5, 3. So the glorious contents are all tied up in neat metrical parcels. Remarkably, the rhyme scheme is different for each of the nine six-line stanzas. Nine, a trinity of threes, was a symbol of perfection (see H's nine-line poem 'Trinity Sunday'). The amazing variety of rhymings, stanza by stanza, makes for variety in the poem to match the variety of man's endowments, which are its contents: form and content subtly united.

2   *build*: 1 Corinthians 3:9: 'ye are God's building'.
6   *in decay*: used up.
12   *upon the score*: like a musician following his score, rather than autonomously inventing the music.

14–15 *Full of proportions . . . world besides*: Human proportions fit
the universe's (as in lines 22 and 47–8).

23–4 *Herbs gladly . . . acquaintance there*: homoeopathy.

34–6 *All things . . . ascent and cause*: Everything is good for our *flesh*
by its *descent* (lineage) or by *ascent* (raising our *mind* to its
ultimate cause).

39 *Distinguishèd*: separated, as God in creation divided the waters
above (rain) from those below (seas) at Genesis 1:9–10.

53–4 *That, as the . . . servants be*: The more reciprocal and less hier-
archical ending in W is arguably better:

> That as the world to us is kind and free
> So we may be to Thee.

Antiphon (2)

In W the title is 'Ode' (a poem to be sung). An antiphon is sung by two
choirs responding to one another alternately: here, men and angels.
Chorus: all singing together. H fits the content to this form. Men and
angels each have their particular and contrasting reasons for praise, and
all can praise together, too. Britten's musical setting is witty and apt.

15 *take*: in the service of Holy Communion: 'take and eat this [con-
secrated bread] in remembrance that Christ died for thee.'

20 *We have none*: cf. 'Misery', line 31: 'man cannot praise thy name.'

Unkindness

Although this is a spiritual exercise in self-examination, a poem of
penitence, its regret is lightened by vivid images, drawn from social
life, and a shifting metre: the feet of each stanza going 5, 5, 2, 4, 5 and
rhyming economically *abaab*. So it has a quizzical-cum-serious tone.
In H's day 'friends' included all one's kith and kin: supporters and
benefactors (kith) along with one's extended family (kin) in various
relations of unlimited obligation – as the poem attests in every stanza.
H depended on such support in his critical and indecisive years
between giving up Cambridge and taking up Bemerton (1627–30),
when he lived with various 'friends' in this sense. Note the progres-
sions in the last lines of the stanzas, from 'would' to 'could' to
'cannot'.

11   *curious*: fine, elaborate. Probably of marble or various woods.
      Precious rugs were usually spread on a table.
16   *pretendeth*: aspires.

Life

Not in W. Like 'Virtue', a lyric of life's transience. Its mood of serene
resignation, as it meditates on the withering of a bunch of flowers, is
expressed in metres of 5, 5, 3, 5, 5, 3 allowing short, rhyming conclu-
sions (3 and 3) after longer, rhyming runs of thought (5 and 5). The
quality of life, in the end, matters more than its quantity.

1   *posy*: pun: 'poesy' as well as the bunch of flowers.
2   *remnant*: remainder.

Submission

Not in W, but this seems to belong to H's midlife crisis when he was
disappointed of 'his court hopes' (Walton, p. 352; also referred to in
Memoriae Matris Sacrum 7 and 8). He gets over it by reflecting that,
by having his own view (ocular symbolism opens, turns and closes the
poem) of how his life should pan out, he is going back on his previous
surrender to God – and 'perhaps great places' would not be such a
good idea anyhow. H is arguing with himself and with God in alter-
nate 4- and 3-foot lines rhyming *abab* as his thought goes hither and
thither. The briskly practical colloquialism of 'lend me a hand' in the
penultimate line is a nice stroke.

2   'Who made the eyes but I?' God asks him in 'Love (3)'.
4   *design*: project or plan.
8   *degree*: station in life.
12   *Disseise*: deprive.
18   *advise*: argue, deliberate.

Justice (1)

Not in W. The perennial problem of divine justice is indignantly set
out in the italicized (probably by the printers, as usual) pentameters of
the first stanza and ruefully answered with self-criticism in those of
the second stanza. The pentameter lines all divide into 2 feet and 3,
balancing positive with negative reflections. The contradictory enigma
of God is much of a muchness with that of self – not exactly a

solution, more a 'fair enough' in the face of the incomprehensible and unjustifiable. The four lines which are not italicized all rhyme.

1   *skill*: understand.
9   *mean*: are intended for.

Charms and Knots

The title means something like 'spells and riddles'. H loved homely proverbs and here tries his hand at inventing some with enigmatic twists. The result is a ragbag, loosely held together by the inculcation of humility. H omitted four stanzas in the previous W version:

> Who turns a trencher, setteth free
> A prisoner crusht with gluttony.

> The world thinks all things big and tall
> Grace turns the optic, then they fall.

> A falling star has lost its place:
> The courtier gets it, that hath grace.

> In small draughts Heav'n does shine and dwell:
> Who dives on further may find hell.

In the first of these a diner turns his wooden plate over to show he has finished; in the second an optic lens turns things upside down.

1   *a chapter*: of the Bible.
3–4 *A poor man's rod . . . a guide*: Clearer in W:

> A poor man's rod if thou wilt hire
> Thy horse shall never fall or tire.

A poor man's switch or twig is milder than the rich man's riding crop.
5–6 *Who shuts . . . twice told*: Proverbs 19:1: 'He that hath pity upon the poor lendeth unto the Lord; and that which he hath given will he pay him again.'
14   *powder*: hair-powder used in the interests of *pride or lust*.
16   *Ten still . . . go for gains*: The tithe or tenth paid by parishioners to support their church is returned to them in helpful sermons.

17–18 *In shallow water . . . may go*: clearer than in W

> In small draughts Heav'n does shine and dwell:
> Who dives on further may find Hell.

Cf. the polemic against drinking too much in *The Church-Porch*, stanzas 5–7.

Affliction (5)

The first line's easy chattiness with God (very like that of 'Man') introduces a less anguished poem than the others under this title. This is a discursive exercise of reason on the great problem of suffering, making sense of it in terms of biblical history from creation to Christ's incarnation. The poem is cool, in a settled metre of 3, 5, 5, 5, 4, 4; the final 4s rhyming couplets. There are a few great lines (13, 14 and 19) expressing resignation amid the knotty historical paradoxes.

2   *Paradise*: the Garden of Eden.
3   *Ark*: Noah's, a figure for the Church.
7   *At first*: in Paradise.
9   *wanton*: rebellious. Cf. 'The Pulley', lines 18–21.
11   *board*: share food.
16   *the second*: grief (taken up by Christ for *our relief*).
16–17 *double line . . . sev'ral baits*: a metaphor of fishing for the table; *bait* also means food.
17   *either kind*: joy or grief.
18   *mind*: liking.
21   *bow'rs*: artificial pergolas.
24   *bow*: After Noah's flood God set his bow, the rainbow, in the clouds as his promise of no more mass destruction.

Mortification

'In the midst of life we are in death,' according to the BCP Burial Service. As soon as we take our first breath, our dying begins. So 'breath' and 'death' are the rhyming end-words of the third and final lines of every stanza, each of them marking a stage on life's way as some kind of dying. But in the last stanza a soft, retrospective light is shone over all that has gone before: 'all these dyings may be life in death'. The spiritual discipline of mortification was recommended by St Paul, and has been experienced by ascetics, as life-enhancing: 'if ye through the

Spirit do mortify the deeds of the body, ye shall live' (Romans 8:13). So this is one of those endings of H's which transforms what has gone before. The metre of 3, 5, 4, 2 feet in the first four lines of the stanzas swells, then diminishes like life; the 4 then 5 feet of the final two lines enforce the deathly conclusions they describe – except for the last two of all.

1   *decay*: title of the next poem.
2   *sweets*: sweet herbs such as lavender.
5   *clouts*: cloths; *winding sheets*: shrouds.
17 *knell*: tolling of a church bell to announce a death.
21 *circle*: orbit.
23 *dumb*: silent.
29 *chair or litter*: to carry an invalid.
32 *solemnity*: ceremony.

Decay

Not in W. Divine presence is the subject. The first two stanzas are idyllic, the world of the Pentateuch (the first five books of the Old Testament or Hebrew Bible) is described as a golden age – nostalgia in an enchantingly homely key. God was everywhere then, free and easy of access. In the last two stanzas, beginning with an ominous 'But now . . .', God is cabined and confined 'in some one corner of a feeble heart' and even there under pressures which will explode in the conflagration of doomsday. The poem which began so pleasantly in the past ends in horror at the present.

Although the first two stanzas read so smoothly, they are tightly packed with biblical references. Here they are. Angels lodged in *Lot*'s house in Sodom and saved him from that city's destruction (Genesis 19:1–25). *Jacob* wrestled with a mysterious man at the ford Jabbok, who turned out to be God (Genesis 32:22–30). *Abraham* argued ('advised') with God over the fate of Sodom (Genesis 18:23–32). God told *Moses* that he was fed up with the obstinacy of the Israelites: 'now therefore *let me alone*' (Exodus 32:10). Gideon met an angel of the Lord under an *oak* (Judges 6:11). God appeared to Moses in the burning *bush* (Exodus 3:2–6). God spoke to Elijah when he was hiding in a *cave* (1 Kings 19:9). In the Old Testament people often meet up at wells, but for a divine encounter we must go to the New Testament at John 4:6–26, where Jesus reveals himself as Christ to a woman at 'Jacob's *well*' (Genesis 33:19). God revealed himself to Moses on Mount *Sinai* (Exodus 19:20). Aaron had bells on his priestly robe, which rang when he went in or out of the sanctuary (Exodus 28:31–5). By making these one *bell*, H confirms his implicit transposition of the biblical landscape to Wiltshire (not in W, so H probably wrote the poem at Dauntsey or Bemerton).

8–9 *Is my God . . . as we heard tell*: cf. 'Redemption', line 6.
15   *thirds*: Sin and Satan have usurped the other two; *thirds* was also the widow's legal portion of her husband's estate.

Misery

Title in W is 'The Publican', referring to Luke 18. H's restless intelligence shows in this dark and contradictory counterpart to 'Man'. Its length threatens to reduce the indignation of satire to irritability, but it is vivid and acute enough to hold attention. Also its impulsive metre, lines of 4, 5, 4 and 5 feet followed by rhyming 2- and 3-foot lines, carry it along briskly. The last line, turning the general on to the particular, makes all the difference.

4   *His house still burns*: His body is (slowly) consumed.
5   *Man is but grass*: Isaiah 40:6: 'all flesh is grass'.
7   *brook*: stand or bear.
19   *turn*: (away).
25   *quarrel*: argue against.
28   *Dove*: the Holy Spirit (Luke 3:22).
44   *serve the swine*: like the Prodigal Son at Luke 15:15. In W this stanza reads:

> Man cannot serve thee: let him go
> And feed the swine, with all his mind and might:
> For this he wondrous well doth know
> They will be kind, and all his pains requite,
> Making him free
> Of that good company.

good company: the swine (sarcastic), cf. Luke 15:16.
51   *pull'st the rug*: pull up the bedcover.
57   *his*: God's.
62   *winks*: closes its eyes.
66   *rehearse*: recount.
69   *posy*: verse inscribed on a ring as love token; *My pleasure* God's delight.
77   *shelf*: submerged reef.

NOTES TO PP. 97–8   431

Jordan (2)

Title in W 'Invention', imaginative creativity. For the significance of
the later title see note on 'Jordan (1)'. In the first two stanzas, H seems,
justifiably enough, to rejoice in his own poetic skills and fertility. But
in the last stanza poetic self-preoccupation is rebuked. 'A friend' whis-
pers that all this is unnecessary: it could be Sir Philip Sidney, whose
first *Astrophil and Stella* sonnet is also full of poetic self-concern, but
ends with: ' "Fool," said my muse to me; "look in thy heart, and
write." ' When love is the topic, and for H it is the topic of topics, you
should just 'copy out', not invent. Love is simple and has no other
ends in view than love, least of all literary dexterity. It is also a com-
mon experience of writers that exuberant creativity turns out, on
inspection, not to have produced the best results. H calls it bustling.
Line 14, *So did I weave myself into the sense*, may well strike us as a
good thing, a mark of authenticity and the thing which H is particu-
larly good at. It is all the more remarkable, then, that the reciprocity
of love, its preoccupation with the other, decidedly and supremely
matters more.

3   *quaint*: clever.
6   *Decking*: decorating.
8   *sped*: getting along alright.
11   *sun*: pun: the heavenly body and the Son of God.
16   *wide*: of the mark.
18   *expense*: cost, trouble.

Prayer (2)

The last stanza makes clear that the previous three, all beginning with
'Of what . . .', were meditations on prayer as, successively, '*Ease,
Power*, and *Love*'. With its three instances of the first person singular
('I') this last stanza also focuses on the personal lacking from the pre-
vious generalizations, prayer and the poet living happily together in
the reciprocity of a marriage. But its deliberate thought and structure
is altogether no match for the rapturous, headlong list and arresting
conclusion of 'Prayer (1)'.

1   *quick*: lively as well as speedy.
4   *state*: majesty.
15   *curse*: taken on by God in Christ's incarnation: Galatians 3:13.
17   *that which ti'd thy purse*: sin.
24   *ell*: forty-five inches.

Obedience

Bloch, pp. 202–4, refers to Jeremiah 32:9–11 in which the prophet bought a field 'with scrupulous attention to legal custom' as a sign to his fellow Jews of his confidence in the future:

> And I bought the field of Hanameel my uncle's son, that was in Anathoth, and weighed him the money, even seventeen shekels of silver. And I subscribed the evidence, and sealed it, and took witnesses, and weighed him the money in the balances. So I took the evidence of the purchase, both that which was sealed according to the law and custom, and that which was open. And I gave the evidence of the purchases unto Baruch . . . in the sight of Hanameel mine uncle's son, and in the presence of the witnesses that subscribed the book of the purchase.

'What links Herbert's poem to the prophetic tradition,' Bloch writes, 'is both the symbolic action, spelled out in some detail, and the impulse to transmit a message to the community of the faithful, to enact before others the truth he has discovered for himself.' The poem, though allegorical, is in the easy conversational style which H uses with God (see the previous poem, for instance), expressed in lines of 3, 4, 5, 3 and 5 feet: a relaxed and flowing rhythm held together by an economical rhyme scheme of *aabba*.

2 *Convey*: transfer; *Lordship*: ownership.
10 *deed*: legal document.
13 *reservation*: retention of a right.
27 *strange*: extraordinary.
30 *Of what we . . . be withstood*: neither optional nor resistible.
35 *purchase*: 1 Corinthians 6:20: 'ye are bought with a price.'
36 *pass*: convey.
43 *Court of Rolls*: where legal records (rolls of parchment) are kept.
45 *both*: the poet and the 'kind', sympathetic reader.

Conscience

Not in W – nor are any of the poems from here up to 'The Elixir'. The self-examination which H recommended to himself in *The Church-Porch* (line 147: 'Dare to look in thy chest') and practised in 'The Sinner' (lines 1 and 2: 'Lord, how I am all ague, when I seek / What I have treasured in my memory') could turn morbid – and often did with the seriously pious. This is H's spirited counter-attack. In the first stanza conscience is accused of spoiling the pleasures of 'a fair look', delicious food and music – inward brooding shutting one off from the sensual delights of eye and ear which H enjoyed. It also (second stanza) spoils thinking and writing. H's cognitive behaviour therapy for this depressive disorder is Christian: participating in Holy Communion (third stanza) and taking belligerent advantage of Christ's victory over sin (the deliberately aggressive and clumsy metaphor of Christ's cross made into a weapon in the fourth stanza). On Christ as a doctor/medicine, see *Passio Discerpta* 8.

13   *receipt*: recipe or prescription (for the physic/medicine of line 12).

Sion

Not in W. Solomon's temple on Jerusalem's Mount Sion is described in all its gorgeous detail in 1 Kings 5–7. However, even Solomon himself expressed doubts about it when he dedicated it (1 Kings 8:27: 'the heaven . . . cannot contain thee: how much less this house that I have builded?'), and the prophets distrusted its diversion of religion from morals to cult (Amos 5:21–7 and Jeremiah 7). H follows this line in the second stanza of this poem with his characteristically relaxed: 'Yet all this glory, all this pomp and state / Did not affect thee much.' God is concerned with morals and sincerity, not buildings. For the Christian writers of the NT the destruction of the temple by the Romans in 70 CE confirmed it. H's preference for groans in the last stanza (also in 'Gratefulness', 'Longing' and 'Ephesians 4:30') derives from Romans 8:23: 'ourselves also, which have the firstfruits of the Spirit, even we ourselves groan within ourselves, waiting for . . . the redemption of our body.' Groans have the sincerity of the verbally inarticulate – hence H's association of groans with music in the brilliant last stanza. The diction is easy and conversational, the metre stately (5, 5, 4, 4, 5, 5).

10   *ancient claim*: God's promise to David that his son Solomon 'shall build an house for my name' (2 Samuel 7:13); cf. Deuteronomy 16:2, 6 and 11 (Sion as the place chosen by God).

12   *For all thy . . . fabric is within*: 2 Corinthians 6:16: 'ye are the temple of the living God.'

17   *sea of brass*: the enormous bronze basin described in 1 Kings 7:23–6.

Home

Not in W. One of H's poems 'in which outbursts of feeling seem allowed total expression in ways which we are more accustomed to find in drama ... These lines could perhaps not have been written unless *Hamlet* and Donne's poetry had been written first; but they still belong to the small and priceless canon in which spontaneity seems the soul of art' (Vendler, p. 265).

The title hurts, for home is just what in his case H has not got – but pleads for in vain in the two-line refrain which ends each stanza but never loses its urgency (as in 'The Sacrifice', H uses a trimeter refrain to drive home the dull, enduring repetitiveness of grief after the previous discursive pentameters and tetrameters). If only God would show himself to him or 'take me up to thee', his longing for the reciprocity which would make his life worthwhile would be satisfied. He would be at home. But this does not happen. It *had* happened in the incarnation and sacrifice of Christ, which should solve this and all other problems. But (H is more honest than orthodox here) it was long ago: 'He did, he came' at line 22 could hardly be more bitterly laconic. And the present aches with absence. Note the prevailing physicality, climaxing at line 64: 'My flesh and bones and joints do pray.' Cf. the title of *Lucus* 2 ('Patria', 'Homeland').

2   *stay*: H uses its two meanings in this poem: to halt and to remain.

4   *My spirit gaspeth night and day*: Psalm 143:6: 'I stretch forth my hands unto thee: my soul gaspeth unto thee as a thirsty land.'

8   *waste*: expend and lose uselessly.

20   *apple*: traditionally the forbidden fruit eaten by Adam and Eve at Genesis 3:6.

24   *baptis'd*: Christ (Matthew 3:16).

35   *wink*: shut the eyes, excluding the visible world.

41   *flout*: mock.

45–6 *Some may dream ... come to thee*: Life is a happy dream for some, but when they wake up they confront God's reality.

50–51 *no fruitful year ... dreadful day*: The real harvests are spiritual, the real crown of the year doomsday, understood as harvest in Revelation 14.

53   *this knot of man untie*: cf. *Antony and Cleopatra*, 5.2.302–3: 'this *knot* intrinsicate / Of life *untie*.'

55   *pinioned*: bound and hampered.

61   *their old acquaintance*: the poet.

63   *this holy season*: probably Advent, when the coming of Christ is awaited?

66   *Come*: does not rhyme with *pray* (line 64) but *Stay* would. By breaking his own rhyme scheme, H represents his fractured and frustrated condition.

The British Church

Not in W. H's manifesto for his mother church, the Church of England ('Neither too mean, nor yet too gay'), as occupying the middle ground between Catholic Rome (over-dressed and over-kissed) and Genevan Calvinism (under-dressed to the indecent point of nakedness). Conspicuously, H does not distinguish between these three on grounds of doctrine, but of appearance: dress (of which he was always conscious) and ritual (which he valued). His churchmanship is conservatively centrist. Cf. the Scylla and Charybdis imagery of *Musae Responsoriae* 30 and the description of the British Church in *Musae Responsoriae* 39, lines 8–13.

5   *dates her ... thy face*: H dated his letters from Lady Day, the Feast of the Annunciation to the Virgin Mary (pregnant by the Holy Spirit) on 25 March, as the first day of the Christian year – which made sense as the beginning of the Christian era. The Virgin Mary was traditionally a figure for the Church.
10   *Outlandish*: foreign.
13   *hills*: the seven hills of Rome.
19   *valley*: Calvin's lakeside Geneva.
26   *The mean*: the medium or mid-point between opposites.
29   *double-moat*: probably grace and the sea ('Which serves it in the office of a wall, / Or as a moat defensive to a house,' *Richard II*, 2.1.47–8). *Musae Responsoriae* 39, lines 15–16, is also indebted to this scene – perhaps confirming a link between these poems.
30   *none but thee*: triumphant insularity!

The Quip

Not in W, so a later poem in which his own quip at orations in line 19, with its sarcastic double entendre on *in short*, settles matters with his distinguished past as the Cambridge Orator. H is on top form, combining wit and piety with sharp observation of the urban social scene. The form is simple: four sprightly iambic feet to each line of the six four-line stanzas, rhyming *abab*. A quip is a joke at somebody's expense, such as his tormentors here use against the poet; while the Latin *quippe*, meaning 'certainly', ghosts the last line and settles the homesickness of 'Home', two poems before in the collection. This has been led up to by the refrain to the central stanzas.

2   *train-bands*: militia.
3   *lay*: lived.

13   *brave*: showy.
21   *hour*: time (of God's choosing).
24   *home*: as in a nail driven home.

Vanity (2)

Not in W. A double poem in which H reminds himself yet again of the
vanity of earthly pleasures. The first part consists of sober, even plod-
ding, pentameters. In the second part things are livened up with a
complex metre scheme using short lines: 4, 2, 4, 2, 4, 2, 2, 4, 4, 4, 5,
5 feet; and a rhyme scheme of *ababccddeeff*. H is using the content of
a familiar theme to experiment with new form.

4   *embroideries*: embellishments.
7   *betimes*: in good time.
10   *rate*: price.

The Dawning

Not in W, but a poem about Easter morning to match 'Easter'. The
sudden, supernatural joy of Easter after the natural grief of Good Fri-
day, with only a day between, can be hard to adjust to. So here the
poet is still anachronistically sad. But with a witty stroke he reflects
that the risen Christ left his grave-clothes behind (John 20:5–7) so
that (H's inspired and homely guess) we should have a handkerchief
to dry our eyes or bind our wounds. This, then, is a more sober poem
than 'Easter', implying that Christ's resurrection does not solve every-
thing at a stroke. The form embodies the realism of the thought. Amid
the pentameters and tetrameters, the very short and hectoring lines
5 and 13 just after the middle of each stanza are brisk attempts to
buck himself up, which have limited success.

9   *withstand*: resist.
12   *Which . . . raiseth thee*: 'Who takes thee by the hand, that thou
     likewise / With him mayst rise,' 'Easter', lines 3 and 4.

Iesu

Not in W. The title is a common variant of 'Jesus'. 'I' and 'J' were still
interchangeable in H's day and he picks 'I' for the purposes of this
cunningly wrought and deeply felt little poem: so it is in B, though
1633 uses 'J'. Its sources are 2 Corinthians 3:3, where 'the epistle of
Christ [is] . . . written . . . not in tables of stone, but in fleshy tables of

the heart', and the secular tradition of the beloved's name engraved on the lover's heart. The emblem of the name on the heart is first broken, then put together again piece by piece. A trivial domestic accident (reflected in the colloquial language of 'th'other week' and 'I sat me down') is made into a parable of heartbreak and healing. It is a sort of figure poem in the making. Nine pentameter lines, rhyming alternately, conclude satisfactorily with a trimeter.

3   *frame*: structure.
7   *parcels*: portions.
8   *spell*: sort out, make sense of.

Business

Not in W. The continual, bossy self-hectoring is done in a restlessly fractured scheme. There are three rhyming stanzas of four feet to the line, all pushy trochees (accents on the first syllable of each foot). To ginger it up further, these are framed and punctuated by four little rhyming trimeter couplets. Lines 3–14 compare the poet's idleness with the busy-ness of the natural world; lines 15–30 with Christ's work for mankind; lines 31–7 with natural human behaviour. The diction is jerky and aggressive – altogether a deliberately fashioned and deliberately unpleasant poem.

4   *home*: destination.
8   *these*: faults or fears; *those*: tears.
9   *plot*: purpose.
22   *two deaths*: physical and spiritual.
29–30 *any space ... Saviour's death*: No one has time to breathe between sinning and absolution by Christ's death.
32   *cross*: misfortune.

Dialogue

Not in W. Conversations with his divine Master are frequent with H, but here a glance at the alternating roman and italic stanzas (probably a device of Buck, the Cambridge printer of 1633) suggests a particular formality. At Cambridge disputations were a major feature of university life. Undergraduates had to take part in at least four in order to graduate. A question was posed, such as 'Do virtues inhere by nature?' by a Moderator, who then assigned one disputant to speak for and one against. The disputants then spoke in turn, each taking up what the other had said and then challenging it. So it went on until one or

other of the disputants surrendered or 'resigned' or the Moderator
called a halt. Such is the form of this poem: a disputation, without a
Moderator, between the poet and Christ on the question 'What is the
value of being George Herbert?' Is his soul 'worth the having'? It con-
cludes with the poet's desperate resignation. The metre for this
adversarial performance is trochaic (emphasis on the first syllables).
Still more emphatic are the four rhyming lines at the end of each verse.
Each speaker threatens a conclusion, until the shock of the last line
breaks the mould: the poet can no longer hold his ground. The two
uses of 'resign' are axial. The poet uses it to give up at line 24, Christ
(wittier than the poet) to remind him of his own giving up of 'all joys
to feel all smart' in his self-sacrifice at line 28. Once again, H has a last
line which changes everything before. This is not just a device, but a
realistic reflection of how a present moment can reinterpret the past.
There are classical models of this sort of structure as well: cf. Horace,
Odes 3.9 – a love poem which has a similar ironic flavour about the
dubious 'value' of a person, but our longing for them anyway.

4   *waiving*: resigning.
11   *mine*: Christ deftly takes up the poet's inadvertent admission at
      line 7 that he is *thy wretch*.
15   *sold*: Matthew 26:15: Judas sold Christ to the chief priests for
      'thirty pieces of silver'.
20   *savour*: understanding (French *savoir* 'knowledge' or *saveur* 'taste').
28   *resigning*: out of love, not the petulance of line 24.
32   *thou break'st my heart*: Psalm 51:17: 'a broken and a contrite
      heart, O God, shalt thou not despise.' H's desperation is salvific:
      Christ's intention all along.

Dullness

Not in W. The poem mixes sacred and secular tradition, and puts
complaints of sluggishness into a sprightly metre of 5, 3, 5 and 2 feet –
thus making a sustained irony. *Red and white* (line 12) derives
ultimately from Solomon's Song 5:10, 'My beloved is white and
ruddy', but was using a familiar Elizabethan topos. It was a favourite
phrase of Shakespeare's in his early poetry: *Venus and Adonis* (1593),
line 10; *The Rape of Lucrece* (1594), line 65. Also in his play *Love's
Labours Lost* (played at Court in 1597 and published in quarto in
1598), 1.2.9: 'My love is most immaculate white and red.' So H is
taking on, among others, the greatest of English secular poets with a
maturity which makes this poem, in tone and technique, an immense

improvement on his sonnets denouncing secular poetry of 1610 (pp. 197–8). Now he can be ironically critical of himself and more tolerant of his adversaries. Lines 23 and 24 are a little colloquial masterstroke, as he likens his 'dullness' to that of someone vainly looking for some necessary but lost article – in this case, his mind.

3   *quickness*: vitality.
5   *curious*: elaborate.
17   *approaches*: advances; *views*: intentions.
18   *window-songs*: serenades.
19   *pretending*: wooing, aspiring.
25   *clear*: discharge, clarify.

Love-joy

Not in W. The poem is a little scene in a church or house made into a hieroglyphic riddle. The title derives from Galatians 5:22: 'the fruit of the Spirit is love, joy, peace.' The vine is a figure of Israel in the OT (Isaiah 5, etc.) and of Christ in the NT (John 15). As well as having eucharistic significance it was a decorative convention in secular use. See 'The Bunch of Grapes' for another, more elaborate, exploration of this image. The question-and-answer form resembles catechizing, which H praised in CP XXI, admiring 'the singular dexterity of *Socrates* in this kind', and observing that 'at Sermons, and Prayers, men may sleep or wander; but when one is asked a question, he must discover (reveal) what he is.' So here the question of *one standing by* (line 3) about the meaning of 'J' and 'C' evokes H's heartfelt response, which, it turns out, also happens to be theologically correct. So H is simultaneously corrected and confirmed. There is also the ironical self-revelation of H's intellectual bumptiousness in lines 4 and 5: *I* (*who am never loath / To spend my judgement*) (express my opinion). The upshot is that Jesus, H's 'Master', is the sum of all goodness. This poem is the apt source of the George Herbert window in Salisbury Cathedral.

2   *J*: B has 'I' rather than *J* here, and in line 8.
3   *Anneal'd*: stained or enamelled.
5   *spend*: show.
6   *body*: embodiment (in the bunches).

Providence

Not in W. The praise of the natural world by a catalogue of its contents fills Psalm 104. H's genial optimism can only strike post-Darwinian readers as ridiculously complacent, but in its time it was entirely plausible – and very much in agreement with his brother Edward Herbert's philosophy in *De Veritate* (1624), dedicated in the manuscript of 1622 'to my dearest brother George Herbert and my most learned friend William Boswell [his secretary] with this condition, that if there is anything in it which is opposed to good morals or true catholic [i.e., universal] faith, they are to expunge it.' Edward Herbert believed that we know what is good and necessary for us by natural instinct and need no help from philosophers or speculative theologians – and not we alone, but everything:

> It is of the nature of natural instinct to fulfil itself irrationally, that is to say, without foresight. For the elements, minerals and vegetables, which give no evidence of foresight or reason, possess knowledge peculiarly suited to their own preservation.

He was particularly opposed to Calvinism's 'blasphemies against nature ... declaring that it is wholly wicked and corrupt' and proud that his own thinking joined nature and grace together. When H envied trees in 'Affliction (1)' and 'Employment (2)' he was in agreement with his brother's world view. Here he is so on an expansive scale. When he writes in line 29 that 'we all acknowledge both thy power and love' he really means all, because 'all things have their will, yet none but thine' (line 32). 'Each creature hath a wisdom for his good' (line 61). So, for example, pigeons are good at raising their young, sheep and trees fertilize the ground, hot springs cool themselves by boiling, and so on and so on up to the triumphant harmony of the end in which every single thing has its own way of honouring its Creator – as H does by writing the poem. Such is the harmony of creation that 'beasts fain would sing' (line 9) and are allowed to talk (line 21) – perhaps they would even write poetry if they could, but they have to leave that to H. Haydn's *The Creation* is a work two centuries later in the same spirit. H would have loved it.

16 *use*: always do.
22 *yours*: the beasts': they eat with their tongues, but H praises with his.
23 *Pull*: pluck; *you*: the trees. The trees stretch out their hands (branches and twigs) so that we can pluck the fruit. The poet's hand is stretched to write poems, his fruit (cf. 'Employment (2)', line 25; 'Love Unknown', line 6).
35 *puts on*: impels.
53 *engend'red*: born; *prevent*: come before.

58   *twist*: thread.
60   *bowls*: as in the game.
63   *callow*: nestbound.
64   *fledge*: fully feathered.
76   *expressions*: apt words, perhaps juices.
80   *there*: in the things in the previous line.
84   *threat'ned*: challenged; *he*: man.
97   *Hard*: both in themselves and to get.
100   *compare*: are alike in being life-giving.
103   *height*: pride.
108   *from sun to sun*: worldwide.
110   *fire*: originally the property of the gods in the myth of Prometheus.
112   *fuel in desire*: Man has fuel when he desires it, and is fuelled by
      desire.
113   *thou mad'st a sea of wet*: Genesis 2:6 'there went up a mist from
      the earth, and watered the whole face of the ground.'
121   *to*: compared to.
126   *The Indian nut*: the versatile coconut.
130   *help*: protect.
132   *loose . . . bind*: (the bowels).
136   *Sponges, non-sense . . . earth and plants*: Things do not jump
      from one to another, but are linked by intermediary things like
      frogs and bats, etc., which *marry* one species with another.
138   *shiftest hands*: ring the changes.
144   *owes*: owns (God).
148   *twice*: on his own behalf and on the whole world's.

Hope

Not in W. Proverbs 13:12: 'hope deferred maketh the heart sick.' As
ever, H treats allegory with a light touch. But the content is so dense
and enigmatic that a plausible, though not infallible, paraphrase may
be helpful. The basic thought is that we cannot stop hoping, but things
do not turn out as we had hoped; the basic allegory is that Hope is a
personified, independent being – and one of the three chief virtues at
i Corinthians 13:13. So when I tried to set a time by the watch for
Hope to keep to, he gave me an anchor to make me stand still. When
my much-used prayer book showed Hope how faithful I was to the
services of the church on earth, I got a telescope (*optic*) to show me
that the reward of my prayers is very remote and in the heavens.
When I gave Hope a bottle full of my tears to show my grief and peni-
tence, Hope contrariwise gave me *a few green ears* of corn, emblems

of a promising future. I get fed up with all this contradiction of my hopes and call Hope a *Loiterer*, someone who always turns up too late. I expected a wedding ring to bind Hope itself to my hopes – only to discover that Hope has its own ideas.

2   *anchor*: Hebrews 6:19: 'Which hope we have as an anchor of the soul, both sure and stedfast.' Donne gave H a seal-ring engraved with 'the anchor and Christ'. H replied with his Latin poem *In Sacram Anchoram Piscatoris* (p. 486).
5   *vial*: Psalm 56:8: 'put my tears into thy bottle.'

Sin's round

Not in W. The poem is a vicious counterpart to the virtuous circularity of 'A Wreath' (which also, but more elaborately, weaves by repetition) and the start of each stanza takes up the last words of the previous stanza to describe the endless compulsion of sin (generally, but 'masturbatory desire', according to Schoenfeldt, *Prayer and Power*, pp. 242–3). The exclusive use of pentameters reinforces the treadmill effect. The concluding half-rhyme rhymes wholly with the first line, of which it is a repeat. A deliberately depressing poem of self-examination.

2   *ring*: the last word of 'Hope', the previous poem.
4   *cockatrice*: a winged serpent hatched from a cock's egg. Isaiah 59:4–5: 'they conceive mischief, and bring forth iniquity. They hatch cockatrice' eggs.'
5   *draughts*: designs.
8   *Sicilian hill*: the volcano Mount Etna.
9   *vent*: vend or release; *pass them*: (on).
10   *ventilate*: allow to breathe (pun on the previous *vent*).
13   *inventions*: imaginations.
15   *Babel*: Genesis 11:1–9: the great tower built by sinful men before they fell out among themselves.
16   *loiter*: an echo of the previous poem.

Time

Not in W. A realistic encounter, set in everyday life (like 'Death'), in which the author bumps into the traditional figure of time as an old man with a scythe. Time, the reaper, seems to be a hard-bitten old rustic (CP VII: 'country people . . . are thick and heavy, and hard to raise to a point of zeal') Time's 'Sir' suggests inferior social status to his interlocutor (the country parson?): as do his report to him of his clients' complaints, and his patient hearing out of him over 21 lines of orthodox dexterity before having the last, bitter word which reveals the in-denial hypocrisy of the parson-poet's clever reflections. It is all as appropriate to the village scene and its two contrasted characters as it is to the philosophical topic and the collision of poetic imagination with reality. There are close resemblances to 'A Dialogue between Time and a Pilgrim' by H's contemporary Aurelian Townshend. The deflating ending is Time's resounding victory over the poet himself. Both H (in 'Divinity') and his brother Edward (in *De Veritate*) were suspicious of theological speculation.

2   *dull*: blunt; *whet*: sharpen.
4   *at length*: after much use.
7   *Perhaps . . . did pass*: the poet now replies.
9   *hatchet*: a little axe for rough and destructive hacking, in contrast to the delicate and productive work of the *pruning-knife*. John 15:2: 'every branch that beareth fruit, he purgeth [prunes] it, that it may bring forth more fruit.'
22 *rod*: of punishment.
23 *wants*: lacks, is absent from.
26 *Which ev'n eternity excludes*: the paradoxical climax of the poet's evasive rhetorical performance: the length (of the rod in line 22) is an odd quantity if it excludes eternity (or if eternity excludes it? Hard to say).
28 *chafing*: getting cross.

Gratefulness

Not in W. H addresses God in his habitually free and easy way, with the self-irony achieved in these later poems. Social comedy pervades the poem. H is an artful beggar whose persistent nuisance God, pictured as a rich householder, has to put up with. The delicately comic set-up is put in a light metre: stanzas of three four-foot lines capped by one of a mere single foot – very modest. Read aloud and with appropriate expression, both rhyme and metre recede into the background. Gratefulness, the title and the object of the poet's solicitations, is finally revealed as a fundamental attitude and much more than an occasional, polite response. The value of *groans* (line 22) is also asserted in 'Sighs and Groans' and 'Sion' (line 24: 'the note is sad, yet music for a king').

6   *crosst*: denied.
12 *save*: deliver, make good (God's *word* in line 10, i.e., Christ).
23 *country-airs*: folk songs.

Peace

Not in W. Self-irony again, as the poet seeks for peace up various promising but blind alleys before meeting the 'rev'rend good old man', who points him on the right way by telling him the New Testament story in terms of a folk or fairy tale. Allegorical throughout, the poem is enlivened by a very varied metre, each stanza consisting of lines of 5, 2, 4, 3, 5 and 2 feet. The rhyme scheme is *abacbc*, with the *b*s holding things together.

3   *cave*: Elijah heard God's 'still, small voice' in a cave at 1 Kings 19.

7   *rainbow*: the sign of God's covenant of peace after the flood at Genesis 9:13–17.

15   *Crown Imperial*: an English garden flower, which, according to Gerard's *Herbal* (1597), is beautiful but smells in the roots 'loathsomely, like a fox'. Is this a critique of Charles I's monarchy?

22   *Prince*: Isaiah 9:6: 'unto us a child is born, unto us a son is given: and the government shall be upon his shoulder: and his name shall be called . . . the Prince of Peace.'

23   *Salem*: Hebrews 7:1–2: Melchisedec, a type of Christ from Genesis 14, was 'King of Salem . . . which is, King of Peace'.

24   *flock*: John 10:14: Jesus says, 'I am the good shepherd.'

28   *twelve*: the apostles (emissaries) of Christ.

36   *flight*: fleeing away.

39   *bread*: (of Holy Communion).

Confession

Not in W. Remarkable for its depiction of the cruelty of H's God. Two meanings of two key words are at stake here. 'Grief' means physical as well as psychological pain. 'Confession' means admitting to sinfulness in the religious context and, in the secular context, the testimony of a suspect under torture (still a legal recourse in H's time). In the first stanza the psychological pain of the *heart* is announced as the subject, but is described in terms of physical *torture* to extort confession in the second. Religious *confession* comes out clearly as the subject, justifying and explaining the title, in the last stanza. The preceding and penultimate stanza is the turning point: *only an open breast*, cleared by confession, can protect the sufferer from the pangs of conscience by giving them nothing to get a grip on. Unsparing physicality makes the first three stanzas an almost unbearable description of spiritual pain, from which the last three lines provide brilliant relief. The rhym-

ing pentameter couplets which end each stanza fasten securely its
previous lines of 3, 5, 4 and 4 feet rhyming *abab*.

3   *Closets*: small rooms or cabinets.
5   *till*: drawer or other closed compartment.
7   *piercer*: awl.
12   *rheums*: pernicious catarrh.
14   *moles*: see 'Grace', line 13: 'Death is still working like a mole, /
     And digs my grave . . .'
23   *fiction*: a made-up deception.

Giddiness

Not in W. This light-footed poem starts with the same three words as
the preceding, oppressive 'Confession'. The title denotes flighty incon-
stancy and the whole poem is a negative counterpart to the stable and
celebratory humanism of 'Man'. The little hoppity-skippity stanzas
(lines of 5, 3, 5, 2 feet) suit the instability of the subject, which is viv-
idly described in engagingly apt variety.

11   *snudge*: keep snug; *scorns increase*: is improvident.
12   *spares*: scrimps and saves.
15   *partly*: with respect to a part; here, man's mind.
15–16 *crusht the building . . . His mind is so*: fragile.
19   *Dolphin's skin*: the mackerel-like dorado changes colour with its
       environment.
27   *daily*: 2 Corinthians 4:16: 'the inward man is renewed day
       by day.'

The Bunch of Grapes

Not in W. After the splendid irony of the initial outburst, with its com-
monplace fury and blaming, the poem becomes increasingly abstruse.
The basic presupposition for this is that the OT is a prophetic tem-
plate for Christian life. In 'The Holy Scriptures (2)' H rejoices in
skipping from verse to verse of his Bible because, put together, they
'make up some Christian's destiny'.

> Thy words do find me out, and parallels bring,
> And in another [i.e., a story other than my own] make me understood.

So here life is a journey, the Bible its travel guide: particularly its long
account of the wanderings of the Jews from their Exodus from Egypt

until their arrival at the border of Canaan, their Promised Land (line 11: 'Their story pens and sets us down'). They sent spies into Canaan to look it over. The spies came back with a splendid and promising sample: a bunch of grapes so enormous that it took two men to carry it on a staff. Unfortunately, the spies also saw giants in the Promised Land. Their news of these monsters caused the Jews to refuse to go on into their inheritance. So God punished them by sending them back through the wilderness to the Red Sea, where they had begun, before they eventually reached the Promised Land again and possessed it. The third verse is packed with references to incidents along the way of this double journey, climaxing with the big question 'But where's the cluster?' – for us now? It is answered by the Holy Communion service: grapes were first turned into wine by old Noah, then wine was changed into his own redemptive blood by Christ at the Last Supper.

There is a further reference. A friend of H's, who helped him, his stepfather Sir John Danvers and the Ferrar family with their secular affairs, ran a goldsmith's shop in London at the sign of the Bunch of Grapes. He was called Arthur Woodnoth and was a very competent businessman (H made him executor of his will), but he worried continually about the course of his life and whether he should become a clergyman. He plagued H with this question during his Bemerton years. The title of this poem and its theme make it likely that it was written to comfort Woodnoth – like 'Constancy' and the paper H wrote overnight when Woodnoth was staying with him, attempting to settle him down. This paper is printed in Hutchinson, pp. 380–81.

The Bunch of Grapes: Numbers 13:23: 'a branch with one cluster of grapes, and they bare it between two upon a staff'; also Woodnoth's shop sign: see introductory note.

4   *vogue*: tendency; *vein*: humour.
7   *Red Sea*: Numbers 14:25: 'turn you, and get you into the wilderness by the way of the Red sea.'
15   *fires and clouds*: Numbers 14:14: 'thou goest before them, by day time in a pillar of cloud, and in a pillar of fire by night.'
16   *Scripture-dew*: Numbers 11:9: 'And when the dew fell upon the camp in the night, the manna [God-given food] fell upon it.'
17   *sands*: of the wilderness; *serpents*: Numbers 21:6: 'the Lord sent fiery serpents among the people, and they bit the people; and much people of Israel died,' and were presumably buried in *shrouds*; *tents*: Numbers 16:26–7: 'the tents of these wicked men' and the people 'in the door of their tents'.

18 *murmurings*: Numbers 14:2: 'And all the children of Israel mur-
    mured against Moses and against Aaron.'
22 *want*: lack.
24 *Noah's vine*: Genesis 9:20–21: 'Noah began to be an husband-
    man, and he planted a vineyard: And he drank of the wine, and
    was drunken.'
27 *the law's*: (of the OT).
28 *God himself*: Christ; Christ as the 'true vine' (John 15:1) *pressed*
    in the winepress (Reveleation 19:15) of suffering.

Love unknown

Not in W. The self-irony in H's later poems is fully developed here: the
poet beginning with a bore's threat, then going on and on about his
tribulations, which, as the 'dear friend' (the internal voice of the Holy
Spirit?) tells him tersely and then conclusively, he has completely mis-
understood. Without this element of implicit comedy, the bizarre and
even grotesque scenes in the style of the pictorial emblem books of the
day would make up a sorry poem of self-pity – but there is every rea-
son to suppose that a poet as intelligent and sensitive as H was fully
aware of this danger. Pentameter after pentameter, rhyming alter-
nately, the autobiographical narrative is thrice interrupted by the
self-conscious pathos of dimeter phrases in brackets and by the friend's
very succinct comments (only half a line, and that the same each time
apart from telling changes of adjectives) in italics. The upshot,
explained by the Friend in lines 61–70, is that love, unknown to the
sufferer, is repristinated by suffering.

3   *comply*: sympathize.
4   *which may improve*: a sign of the speaker's feebleness.
5   *two lives*: a lease for a father, succeeded by his son; *both*: earthly
    and heavenly life (?).
10–11 *Better ... Than I myself*: Lack of self-knowledge is included
    in the speaker's self-pity.
13 *font*: of baptism.
14–15 *A stream of blood ... remember all*: A melding of three bib-
    lical instances: John 19:34: 'one of the soldiers with a spear
    pierced his [the dead Christ's] side, and forthwith came there out
    blood and water'; Numbers 20:11: 'Moses lifted up his hand,
    and with his rod he smote the rock twice: and the water came
    out abundantly'; 1 Corinthians 10:4: 'that Rock was Christ.'
30 *fold*: of sheep, like Abel the pastor at Genesis 4:4.

45   *To supple hardnesses*: all refers to Holy Communion.
55   *one*: Christ.
60   *another*: Christ.
62   *Master*: Christ.

Man's medley

Not in W. After the cheeriness of 'Man', the gloom of 'Mortification' and the satire of 'Misery', a later poem which strikes a balance with Mozartian poise – the human condition is, after all, a subject worth thinking about in more than one mood (cf. *Hamlet*, 2.2.303–310). The metre of its six stanzas achieves lyrical simplicity by variety: lines of 3, 2, 5, 3, 2 and 5 feet, mixing trochees with iambics as it goes and rhyming *aabccb*. The poem turns and turns again on humanity's double nature, physical and metaphysical, earthly and heavenly.

8   *pretence*: claim.
16   *curious*: delicate.
18–19 *take place / After*: fix his status according to.
30   *two deaths*: physical and spiritual.

The Storm

Not in W. By taking bad weather as a metaphor for psychological disturbance, H describes mental turbulence forcefully, drives it upwards and brings it to the positive outcome of the last couplet. Its final thought is paralleled in the storm scene in Britten's *Peter Grimes*, where Captain Bulstrode advises Grimes: 'There is more grandeur in a storm of wind / To free confession, set a conscience free.' The short dimeter lines give impulse. Cf. also Donne's 'Storm' and 'Calm'.

6   *object*: put them in mind of.
7   *Stars have their storms*: as in the 'civil strife in heaven' in *Julius Caesar*, 1.3.11.
13   *to thy music's wrong*: spoiling God's enjoyment of the celestial music in his heavenly palace.

Paradise

Not in W. Form and content are brought together with extraordinarily artful dexterity. Paradise, the enclosed garden, is here an English orchard tended by the divine gardener with his pruning knife. In

'Time' H figured that Old Father Time's scythe was a pruning-knife to a spiritually disposed person (line 12: 'by thy cutting he grows better'). John 15:2 is the source: 'every branch that beareth fruit, he purgeth it, that it may bring forth more fruit.' The content is an argument for the good effects of suffering and loss – more discursively pondered in 'Love Unknown', but here presented not only much more succinctly, but also by incorporating it right into the fabric of the poem. H uses his own pruning-knife on his work. With it he cuts away at the final words of his iambic rhyming triplets. As Vendler says (p. 220), 'each pruning ... engenders a new word; all together, the poem suggests, our prunings in life give birth to a new language expressive of suffering, composed of words that before the pruning could not have existed.' H perhaps cheats a little: 'ow' and 'frend' are not his usual spelling. But he deals with a painful subject with sustained skill. He brings it to a soberly steady conclusion as masterly as it is modest: *such beginnings touch their end* (but have not acquired it), recalls St Paul's 'I count not myself to have apprehended' (Philippians 3:13) For an excellent parody (in the very best sense) see Vikram Seth's poem 'Lost' in *The Rivered Earth* (London: Hamish Hamilton, 2011, p. 55).

4   *CHARM*: magic spell.
5   *blast*: blight.
7   *START*: a sudden involuntary movement.
10   *SPARE*: refrain from.

The Method

Not in W. Why does God not respond to prayer? He should in theory, being both *Power* (so he *could*) and *Love* (so he *would*). But the answer is practical: methodical self-examination, pictured as a review of H's spiritual journal, shows that God has every reason not to bother with him. Repentance will change it all for the better, the *lament* at the end of the first line changed to the *rejoice* at the end of the last. 'The Method' will work. A busy metre of 2, 4, 4, 2; simple rhyme scheme of *abab*.

3   *rub*: snag.
6   *move*: propose.
9–10 *Go search ... thy book*: like *The Church-porch*, lines 147–8: 'Dare to look in thy chest; for 'tis thine own: / And tumble up and down what thou find'st there'; *turn*: (the pages of).
19   *motions*: good inner impulses.

Divinity

Not in W. The title means theology. The tone of the first three stanzas is unusually sarcastic for H. As a young fellow of Trinity College, Cambridge, H asked his stepfather Sir John Danvers for money to buy some of 'those infinite Volumes of Divinity, which yet every day swell, and grow bigger'. There is a touch of weariness and disaffection from theology in those words. Here he ranks it with astronomy as an unnecessary exercise of speculative or 'discursive' reason – a view shared by his brother Edward. The bitter irony of lines 9–13 derives from St John's account of Christ's crucifixion, to which H so often resorts: the piercing of Christ's side which released blood (the wine of Holy Communion) and water, and Christ's seamless robe. H takes these as pure and simple matters of grace, in no need of complex development. What we really need to know is in lines 17–18 clear and readily accessible to all. H follows it with the sarcasm of lines 19–20. Lines 21–4 assert that obedient participation in Holy Communion *is all that saves*. And in the last stanza the heaven sought by astronomers and theologians is reached by faith, without the help of any *staff of flesh*. It is important that *flesh* here, as always in St Paul's Epistles, is not just bodily matter, but means anything that is not pure spirit, including thinking 'after the flesh' and the 'fleshly mind' (Colossians 2:18).

2   *spheres*: celestial spheres or globes, prestigious pieces of library furniture mapping the courses of the heavenly bodies. H pretends that they are to instruct the stars rather than the astronomers.
3   *clod*: clumsy boor.
12 *curious questions and divisions*: see introductory note.
20 *Who can . . . knots undo*: (fiercely sarcastic).
21 *But he . . . blood for wine*: in Holy Communion.
25 *Epicycles*: movements of planets traced on a celestial globe.

Ephes. 4.30.
Grieve not the Holy Spirit, & c.

Not in W. It was heretical to believe that God the Father had suffered along with Christ, his Son, the former being serenely 'impassible'. This does not seem to trouble H here. Rather, he affirms divine suffering throughout the first three stanzas, then tries vainly to emulate it in the last three. Finding this impossible, he pleads for pardon by Christ's blood. Distress is set in lyrical metres (5, 2, 2, 5, 4, 4 feet per stanza) which carry the thought along with the musicality which surfaces in lines 19–21. Indeed Blow and Jenkins set this poem to music, the lament being a favourite form of seventeenth-century songwriters.

10   *part*: depart (by dying).
16   *sense*: sensitivity.
23   *weep*: by 'sweating' from a change of temperature and humidity. Also at line 15 of 'The Church-Floor'.
24   *bowels*: pun: compassion and/or catgut lute strings.
25   *adjudge*: condemn.
29–30 *But runs ... what shall I*: 'If a clear spring goes on running without stopping, even though I'm not thirsty, will I, who am no crystal (being stained with sin), do any different?' *George Herbert: The Complete English Works*, ed., Ann Pasternak Slater, p. 458.
34   *deserts*: deservings.
36   *store*: abundance.

The Family

Not in W. As the first two stanzas announce clearly, a disorderly household is an allegory, deftly handled as usual with H, for the disordered heart. The countervailing virtues are personified and given capital letters: Peace, Silence, Order and above all Obedience. They are the controlling grown-ups and trusty servants of a household such as that of H's youth at Charing Cross. The last stanza is more rueful than settled. Line 20 is a fine example of H's penetrating perception and verbal economy. The metre is 5, 3, 5, 4; the rhyme scheme is *abab*.

3   *puling*: whining, as a child.
6   *repine*: whinge.
7   *wranglers*: disputatious types.
10   *plays*: cajoles.
13–16 *Humble Obedience ... she doth go*: Obedience is the porter or servant at the door, waiting to take messages and run errands: female because personified virtues always are. Cf. the imagery of *Passio Discerpta* 16 ('On the Sun in Eclipse').
19   *distemper'd*: deranged.

The Size

Not in W. A 'size' was a basic daily ration of food and drink given to needy undergraduates ('sizars') in colleges such as H's Trinity, Cambridge. H was much concerned with temperate diet and translated

Hygiasticon by the complacently octogenarian Paduan virtuoso Cornaro. It was published in 1634 entitled *A Treatise of Temperance and Sobriety*. So here H treats the subject at length: eight stanzas, kept going by a varied metre of 3, 5, 5, 2, 4 and 4 feet, rhyming *ababcc*. He gives it all a haunting ending with recollection of his emblematic dream, partly derived from Psalm 107:30: 'he bringeth them unto the haven where they would be.'

5   *upper*: heavenly (the waters 'above the firmament' of Genesis 1:7); *the low*: the earthly/physical.

7   *fraught*: cargo.

14   *God . . . hungry here*: Matthew 4:2: 'and when he [Jesus] had fasted forty days and forty nights, he was afterward an hungred.'

17   *Lay out*: spend.

21   *Those*: Great joys have to be hoped for; *these* little ones keep some back for later.

22   *on score*: on account.

24   *the rest*: the joys postponed; also repose as at Psalm 15:1: 'who shall rest upon thy holy hill?'

27   *for such doth oft destroy*: Luke 6:25: 'Woe unto you that are full! for ye shall hunger. Woe unto you that laugh now! for ye shall mourn and weep.'

29   *'tice*: entice.

33   *long and bony face*: judging by his portrait by Robert White, a self-portrait of H.

36   *pretender*: suitor.

40   *They would . . . snows destroy*: The rhyme scheme indicates that a line is missing here in B and 1633, damaging the subsequent sense.

42   *seam*: line of stitching shaping a garment.

46   *meridian*: the semicircular line from pole to pole; hence also the brass semicircle or circle holding a globe.

Artillery

Not in W. This odd poem begins with the emblem of a falling star (also in H's Latin poem *Lucus* V lines 3–6; cf. also 'The Star'), standing for a 'good motion' – meaning a stirring of the conscience – hitting the poet. But this fancy is treated realistically. It is a matter of conjecture or 'methoughts', but happened 'one evening' as the poet was sitting out of doors; he shook his clothes to be rid of the incendiary device. The voice of 'one', in italics in 1633, tells him off and provides the correct interpretation. The poet's musings and response follow. He addresses God courteously but firmly. He wants reciprocity between the two of them, each 'shooting' at the other. This is the serious heart of the argument. But although he is corrigible and revokes his refusal, past and present, of divine promptings, 'yet thou [God] dost refuse' the poet's 'tears and prayers'. The word 'refuse' occurs three times, including the long-distance rhyme of line 12 with line 20 – plus the shunning (parrying or avoiding) of line 29. It is the big snag in his relation with his God. Finally the poet resigns himself to it by reflecting that they belong to one another anyhow and infinitely. H is once again treating an obstinate problem with honesty and wit.

5   *one*: someone or other, at line 10 apparently the star.

7   *motions*: promptings.

9   *music in the spheres*: the harmony of the spheres in motion.

18   *Born where ... artilleries use*: See 'Prayer (1)', line 2: 'God's breath in man returning to his birth' and line 5: 'Engine against th' Almighty'.

24   *Thy promise ... thee thy laws*: Psalm 89:34: 'My covenant will I not break, nor alter the thing that is gone out of my lips.'

Church-rents and schisms

Not in W. Another emblematic poem, but much inferior to 'Artillery': no humour or irony, grotesquely mixed metaphors and sustained resentment. Whether it is about church history at large, or (more likely) about the effects of the sixteenth-century reformations and splits in particular, is obscure and debatable. At any rate, H's horror and hatred of this subject is all too evident and makes for an exceptionally bad poem. Cf. *Twelfth Night*, 2.4.110–2, '. . . let concealment like a worm i' the bud / Feed on her damask cheek' (a damask being a rose), and William Blake's lyric 'The Sick Rose' in *Songs of Experience*. The urgency of the address to the mother and the starkly physical, even erotic imagery applied to Mother Church, have points in common with *Memoriae Matris Sacrum* in particular; but also the devotional imagery (of blood, tears, weeping, etc.) of the Latin epigram sequences *Passio Discerpta* and *Lucus*.

1   *rose*: Song of Solomon 2:1: 'I am the rose of Sharon,' applied to the Church; *chair*: of rule and authority.

15   *And made ... fresher than before*: cf. 'Death', lines 13 and 14.

18   *vaded*: in B; 'faded' in 1633.

21   *start*: jump away.
29   *two*: eyes – an unhappily mixed metaphor.
30   *pour it out*: (in tears).

Justice (2)

Not in W. Justice as a quality standing over against humanity in nega-
tive condemnation, justice as a positive force making humanity just:
the change from the first of these to the second, effected by Christ,
converted Martin Luther from a conscience-plagued monk to a free
Christian man and reformer. It is the pattern of this poem. The balan-
cing scales of justice, weighing good and bad, are a classical image,
going back to Homer. Hanging from God's hand, they are the domin-
ant image here: terrifying in the second stanza, happily enabling
reciprocity in the third and fourth. The form of these stanzas fits their
contents: a first line of five iambic feet, shrinking to a couple of
two-foot lines, growing to a couple of four-foot lines, then back to a
final pentameter which restores the balance. The second stanza sees
the scales as 'some tort'ring engine'. The cross comes to mind. In the
third stanza they have become a tilting machine at a well-head, letting
empty buckets down then drawing them up full. Justice is then, in the
last stanza, 'mine' to 'touch / And harp on': no longer an external 'call
on me' but a musical instrument for me to play on. This emblem
works much better than those in 'Artillery'.

5   *through their glass discolour thee*: 1 Corinthians 13:12: 'now we
      see through a glass, darkly.'
9   *beam and scape*: horizontal and vertical members of a cross.
13   *Christ's pure veil*: Hebrews 10:20 'new and living way ...
      through the veil, that is to say, his [Christ's] flesh'.
24   *none*: Romans 8:31: 'If God be for us, who can be against us?'

The Pilgrimage

Not in W. Emblems, somewhat diffuse and forced in 'Love Unknown',
are here so integrated as to seem natural – a part of the landscape. It
is a landscape of the soul – and a bleak one: bitter disappointment in
the fourth stanza and final frustration of all his efforts in the last.
After the excellent plunging-in of the start, we see the pilgrim worried
by it getting late in the day, struggling through a copse, being robbed,
reaching his supposed destination only to find there a brackish pond
infested by midges ('swarming fears'), flinging desperately on and

away – but only to hear a voice in his ears telling him that he will die if he goes on. This truth is resentfully accepted. Shadowing it all are the OT 'strangers and pilgrims on the earth' of Hebrews 11:13 and the NT 'strangers and pilgrims' of 1 Peter 2:11. Iambics, the metre of walking, serve the theme well. Longer lines (pentameters) are followed by shorter ones (dimeters) to mark the starting and stopping along the way – two tetrameters between. See 'Employment (2)' for a comparably heart-sinking ending.

1   the hill: Hebrews 12:22: 'mount Sion ... the heavenly Jerusalem'.
4   cave of Desperation: the Cave of Despair in Spenser's Faerie Queene, 1.9.
17 Angel: Psalm 91:11: 'he shall give his angels charge over thee: to keep thee in all thy ways'; also a gold coin stamped with the image of the archangel Michael.
36 a chair: possibly to carry the moribund as in 'Mortification', line 29, certainly something to rest in.

The Holdfast

Not in W. A sonnet in which the poet makes modest but vain attempts to defend his own spiritual agency against 'one' (a radical Calvinist?) who argues for omnipotent divine agency so exclusively and relentlessly as to reach the brink of nihilism. Understandably, the poet is 'amazed at this, / Much troubled'. Fortunately 'a friend' (a very different character from the oppressive 'one'), intervenes. Nothing has been lost. On the contrary, everything has been saved by Christ (absent from the argument before this point) and is 'more ours by being his': 'more' because sterile theological argument has been superseded by something far more valuable: reciprocal personal relations and mutual possession. 'The heart has its reasons which reason knows nothing of' (Pascal) and H, like his brother Edward, prefers them to discursive, let alone adversarial, theology. H's religion is an affair of the heart, not dogma.

    Holdfast: A securing bolt or clamp; the grip of a limpet. Psalm 73:27: 'it is good for me to hold me fast by God: I have put my trust in the Lord God.' In the last line the holdfast turns out to be Christ.
13 Adam: the primal man of Genesis 1-3. Romans 5:19: 'For as by one man's [Adam's] disobedience many were made sinners, so by the obedience of one [Christ] shall many be made righteous.'

Complaining

Not in W. Suffering under the shadow of divine omnipotence again, H fashions a beautifully turned poem to plead with polite desperation for relief, even by an early death. Human fragility is expressed in short lines which fracture the sense and, in the third stanza, four anguished little questions – 'ejaculations' in the parlance of the piety of the day. An unusual rhyme scheme: the last lines of stanzas 1 and 2 rhyme, as do 3 and 4. Like 'The Pilgrimage', it is in the spirit of Psalm 39: 14–15: 'I am a stranger with thee; and a sojourner, as all my fathers were. O spare me a little, that I may recover my strength: before I go hence, and be no more seen.'

1   *beguile*: deceive.
5   *dust*: Genesis 2:7: 'the Lord God formed man of the dust of the ground'. Cf. 'Denial', lines 16–18: 'O that thou shouldst give dust a tongue / To cry to thee, / And then not hear it crying!'
18   *inch*: Psalm 39:6: 'Behold; thou hast made my days as it were a span long: and mine age is even as nothing in respect of thee' – but an *inch* is even shorter than the psalmist's span (the extent of the arm).

The Discharge

Not in W. Something is discharged when it is over and done with. So why keep worrying about the past and the future? That is the problem. Human accounts (the 'counts' of line 6) are supposed to have been settled by Christ in whom God 'did make / Thy business his' (lines 17–18). But this seems not to have done the trick as it should, for in the seven stanzas which follow this H resorts, not for the first time, to practical wisdom and common sense rather than dogmatic certainty – and ends with the solution as something 'promised' rather than accomplished. In the meantime there are things to do. Shrewd self-management is required and epigrammatically inculcated. The self-awareness and self-irony of the first stanza, so well achieved in these late poems, is sharp and unsparing. The abundant good advice in the poem combines Matthew 6:34 'sufficient unto the day is the evil thereof' with Horace's *carpe diem* ('pluck the day') from his *Odes*, I. The metre is lively: dimeters follow the pentameters, which are often broken in the middle, and there is a good deal of enjambement. The rhyme scheme is thrifty, *abbaa*, allowing the closing tetrameter of each stanza to tie it up neatly.

3   *licorous*: greedy, lustful.
8   *depart*: part with
16   *this*: what follows.
21   *fee*: allotted share.
31   *provide*: look forward.
32   *breaks the square*: goes out of bounds.
40   *a churchyard*: place of burials.
45   *draw the bottom out an end*: unravel a ball of thread or wool.
46   *till night*: (when the dog is unleashed against nocturnal prowlers).

Praise (2)

Not in W. This happy celebration of reciprocity achieved draws on Psalm 116: 1–2: 'I am well-pleased that the Lord hath heard the voice of my prayer; / That he hath inclined his ear unto me: therefore will I call unto him as long as I live.' The first line is addressed to Christ as the 'King of Glory' prophesied in Psalm 24:7–10 and the 'King of Peace' by virtue of his priesthood 'after the order of Melchisedec ... King of Salem, which is, King of Peace' (Hebrews 7:1, 2 and 17). Mutuality is instinct in the form: the pointed and closed 'masculine' rhymes and endings of the longer lines match the softly open 'feminine' ones, with their last syllables unstressed, for the shorter lines. Indeed 'thee' or 'me' ends the shorter lines in every stanza (alternately in the first five) except the next-to-last, which is omitted when the poem is sung as a hymn: a pity, because the Christ-image of God softening, weeping and disagreeing with Justice – humane to the point of being human – is the one to whom the poet appeals and the cause of his praise.

4   *move*: shift, affect, urge.
11   *cream*: a dairy image for his poetry?
15   *alone*: thou only.
21   *tears*: John 11:35: 'Jesus wept.'
24   *dissentedst*: John 8:11: 'Neither do I condemn thee' – Jesus to the woman sentenced according to law for adultery.

An Offering

Not in W. H is hectoring and accusing himself as well as the reader (let's hope, with a certain comic irony) in the first stanza of this double poem. After that it relaxes somewhat, and the second part is a merry little lyric. The change of tone is brought about by the recollection of Christ's sacrificial offering of his blood, now an 'All-heal' medicine. So the 'offering' of the title is probably in the context of the offering of alms by the people in the BCP Holy Communion (also called there 'the oblation'). The first part is all sober pentameters, but the rhyme scheme a spirited *abcbac*. The second part is still livelier with its metre of 2, 2, 3, 2, 2 and 3 feet, rhyming *aabccb*. What threatened to be an offensive – even rude – poem, turns into courtly cheerfulness and warm reciprocity by association with Christ's offering.

2   *fools*: (a gratuitously rude epithet).
6   *two natures*: (human and divine).
10   *deserts*: being deserving.
12   *fence a plague*: fend off or contain a plague, understood as divine punishment, by royal decree or intercession with God.
16   *partitions*: apartments or chambers.

Longing

Not in W. 'Dear prayer' of 'Prayer (2)', celebrated with such delight in its effectiveness in 'Prayer (1)', is, here and now, ineffectual. So, though recalled at intervals amid the bitter complaints, is Christ's great work of salvation. 'The childish repetition of "hear, hear", the repeated poignant self-descriptions, the persistence in demand in spite of all seemliness, are the qualities that make H, in this vein, one of our most accurate poets of expostulation, pain, outcry, wounded hopes and stratagems of emotion' (Vendler, p. 265). For lack of the all-important reciprocity of mutual relation ('I' and 'Thou' are poles apart), the self falls apart and the body is felt as a huddle of separate limbs: in the first two stanzas and still, much later, at lines 75–6 ('ev'ry part / Hath got a tongue'). Complete breakdown is prevented only by hope. 'All thy promises live and bide' (line 68) and at the end the poet is still beseeching. The Book of Job and the Psalms of complaint are models. Short expostulations (just two words) and a fractured metre of 3, 4, 2, 2, 4, 1-foot lines to the stanza have the effect of putting the control and formality of poetry under apt strain from its disordered content.

2   *bones*: Psalm 32:3: 'my bones consumed away through my daily complaining.' Also Psalm 6:2. 'my bones are vexed.'
8–9 *My heart . . . dost curse*: Psalm 102:4: 'my heart is . . . withered like grass'; and Genesis 3:17: 'cursed is the ground for thy [Adam's] sake.'

17   *them . . . they*: mothers.
19   *Bowels*: the seat of compassion: Colossians 3:12: 'bowels of mercies, kindness'.
31   *Lord Jesu, thou didst bow*: John 19:30: Jesus 'bowed his head, and gave up the ghost.'
35-6 *Shall he . . . Not hear*: Psalm 94:9 paraphrased.
45-6 *laid the reins . . . the horse*: allowing the horse to wander by letting the reins rest slackly on it.
52   *interlin'd*: been written between the lines.
54   *nests*: metaphorical: see 'The Temper (1)': 'O let me, when thy roof my soul hath hid, / O let me roost and nestle there.'
65-6 *Were sin alive . . . To bear*: If sin had not been killed off by Christ, then I would just have to bear it.
69   *That*: sin; *wants*: lacks.
70   *These*: promises.
80   *By these . . . my heart*: as in Luke 7:38.
82   *dart*: Psalm 38:2: 'thine arrows stick fast in me.'

The Bag

Not in W. A boisterous exclamation announces a complete change of mood after the pathos of 'Complaining'. Earthbound misery escapes into fantasy as H rewrites, even remythologizes, the story of Christ. His biblical materials are handled with creative freedom. Philippians 2:6-11 (Christ's relinquishing of his divinity to serve and save humanity) is combined with John 13:4, where Jesus 'laid aside his garments' to wash his disciples' feet. This takes up lines 7-18, a dazzling combination of cosmic imagery with the homely business of undressing. Then H returns – he had already treated it in 'The Sacrifice', 'Holy Baptism (1)' and 'Prayer (1)' – to John 19:34, the piercing of Christ's dead body by a soldier's spear (also the subject of *Passio Discerpta* 4). Clearly it was a text dear to him. His treatment of it here is inventive but also gruesome. Christ's body, opened by the wound, serves as a mailbag into which messages can be posted and delivered, on his return to heaven, to his Father. Robust readers may admire this combination of prayer with the physical (very similar to the intense physicality of *Passio Discerpta*), the sacred with the body. Others may need to overcome their understandable squeamishness by letting H's high spirits, evident in the cheery and cheering speech he gives to his Master in lines 31-42, carry them along to the poem's happy ending. The form is secure, each stanza made of four tetrameters flanked by pentameters fore and aft.

6   *close his eyes*: Mark 4:38, where Jesus was 'asleep on a pillow'
      in a storm-tossed boat.
11 *light*: alight, dismount.
13 *tire*: attire.
14 *fire*: lightning.
18 *new clothes*: a human body.
20–22 *He did repair ... cancel sin*: Luke 2:7, when Jesus was born
      'there was no room for them in the *inn*': the first of many *brunts*
      or insults he had to *endure*.
23 *the rest*: his divinity in lines 7–18.
24 *score*: bill (referring to the inn at line 20 and to the inn where the
      good Samaritan left the wounded man and paid the host for him:
      Luke 10:34–5).
25 *returning*: to heaven, because he had just died.
35 *mind*: remember.

The Jews

Not in W. The proliferation of bibles, the OT bound up with the NT
(not just formally but through innumerable interconnections, as cele-
brated in H's two 'The Holy Scriptures' poems and 'The Bunch of
Grapes'), was a good antidote to medieval anti-Semitism. Here H
takes up St Paul's 'continual sorrow' over his Jewish 'kinsmen accord-
ing to the flesh' in Romans 9–11. This is his version of St Paul's 'prayer
to God for Israel ... that they might be saved' at Romans 10:1. He
uses St Paul's image of the Christian Church as a 'scion' or slip of
'wild olive' grafted onto the old olive tree of Israel (Romans 11:17–
24), along with that of the sluices of the irrigation system, which he
saw from his riverside rectory at Bemerton.

2 *scions*: see introductory note.
3 *sluice*: see introductory note. Cf. the aqueduct imagery of *Passio
     Discerpta* 5, also concerned with the depiction of the Jewish people.
5 *not keeping once*: once upon a time – could be a single *once*, but
     more likely referring to the whole OT where Israel frequently
     failed to keep the divine law.
6 *letter*: of the law, lost by inattention to its spirit (Romans 7:6)
     and clinging to its letter.
8 *trumpet*: Joel 2:1: 'Blow ye the trumpet in Zion ... for the day
     of the Lord cometh', taken up in Revelation 8, where seven
     angels have trumpets to announce the stages of the world's end.
     Six trumpets were blown, leaving the seventh for H to long for.
9 *Church ... her face*: Note the Church's humiliation.

The Collar

Not in W. 'He was not exempt from passion and choler', H's brother Edward recalled in his Autobiography – and here it is, punning with a dog-collar and with the Caller who speaks at the end. L. C. Knights confessed that he once thought the poem evasive, finally 'relapsing into the naïve simplicity of childhood'. But for H 'childhood is health' ('Holy Baptism (2)'). And Knights had second thoughts:

> I was wrong. The really childish behaviour is the storm of rage in which the tempestuous desires – superbly evoked in the freedom of the verse – are directed towards an undefined 'freedom'. What the poet enforces is that to be 'loose as the wind' is to be as incoherent and purposeless; that freedom is not to be found in some undefined 'abroad', but, in Ben Jonson's phrase, 'here in my bosom, and at home' (*Explorations*, p. 127).

The freedom of the verse is extraordinary: 32 lines without stanzas and in a metre which jumbles lines of 5, 4, 3, 2 and 1 (at line 16 only) feet any old how, with rhyme-endings which take us to 's' if we use the alphabet. There are Anglo-Latin poems in this sort of 'free verse' from around this time. 'Load' at the end of line 32 just about rhymes with 'abroad' in lines 2 and 28 – which rhymes with the last word of the poem. The last four lines (33–6) both rhyme and are in a metre, selected from the previous chaos, which steadies down to 5, 2, 4 and 3 feet. The marvel of the poem is that it gives form to disorder. Past experience of a shameful tantrum is resurrected complete and whole: so realistically, to be honest, that around half way the reader begins to feel that the poet has got beyond himself (he has), and is even starting to make a fool of himself (he is) – so accurate is H's self-satire. Reciprocity finally supersedes rank individualism.

1   *the board*: the table.
4   *lines*: of verse – spectacularly *free* in this poem.
5   *store*: abundance.
9   *cordial*: good for the heart.
14   *bays*: leaves of the traditional poet's crown.
35   *Me thoughts ... one calling*: 1 Samuel 3:1–8, where God called the child Samuel at night; Job 13:22: 'Then call thou, and I will answer.'

The Glimpse

Not in W. Like 'The Glance', another late poem, this is about the rare comings and prompt goings of delight. But whereas 'The Glance' makes the most of the happy moments, 'The Glimpse' is more concerned with its long absences – and so is sadder. The assonance of the two titles, virtually synonymous, makes them a pair. 'The Glimpse' carries, and is appropriately impeded by, a load of similes for transience and changeability: time itself, music, flowers, quicklime, guests, storage and spinning. The metre of 3, 5, 3, 5, 5 feet works against impulse and being carried away: against longed-for delight, in fact. The frequent trochees (stress on a first syllable) do the same. The rhyme scheme reinforces this pattern: *ababb*.

7   *better time*: pun: a steadier rhythm and a longer stay.
10   *look about*: stay around.
13   *Lime*: gets hotter with water; *they say* refers to some old proverb, perhaps Symphosius *Aenigmata* 75 or, more likely, oral tradition.
19   *did reply*: my heart (line 16) replied.
20   *gentle*: courteous, well-bred.
24   *droppings*: leakages.
27   *stay*: in its other and opposite sense to line 11, of staying away.
30   *thy*: delight's; *court*: of courtiers gathered round their lord.

Assurance

Not in W. The poem dramatizes the healing of H's divided self. His better, more optimistic, self is pitted against the malice of some 'spiteful bitter thought' (those words then shuffled and repeated for vehement emphasis). Its content is revealed in indirect speech in stanza 2: God and the poet are not on the good terms he supposes, even that 'the league between them (agreement or covenant) was broke, or near it.' After resumed invective in stanza 3, stanza 4 has H as a 'little boy asking his father to help in confronting the bullies' (Bloch p. 17) by reminding him that the league between them is all of his doing, not H's, so it is up to him to defend it against the bad thought. Stanzas 4 and 5 (lines 19–30) turn on the use of words: H's lack of them and God's both signing up to the league in his own hand and also guiding H's signature. Stanza 6 appeals to God's power – protesting rather too much and too rhetorically, the reader may feel. This gives H enough gumption to stand up, in the last stanza, to the bad thought and make a couple of jokes at its expense, but the final answer and solution is, as ever, love. The rhyming tetrameters which close each stanza mark off the end of a phase in the argument (with the bad thought in stanzas 1–3, with God in stanzas 4–6, and with the bad thought again but triumphantly in stanza 7).

5   *meet with*: confront, measure up to.
18   *writ thy purpose*: in H's earlier 'Affliction' poems.
39   *bone*: proverbial: a bone of contention, thrown down for dogs to quarrel over: also a bone stuck in the throat.

The Call

Not in W. An intricately crafted jewel of a poem which yet speaks with ardent sincerity. Three appellations or attributes of the divine are announced in the first line of each stanza, then, releasing the possessive 'my' which precedes them all, they are sequentially celebrated for themselves. In the last, love has the final word. There is the utmost economy. Not only is each attribute repeated to be set in motion, but every stanza begins with 'Come' and every subsequent line with 'Such': trochaic starts which set the feet to spring into three iambics. The effect is sheer music, rich content made lightly lyrical.

1   *Come, my . . . my Life*: John 14:6: 'I am the way, the truth, and the life.'
5   *Light*: John 8:12: 'I am the light of the world'; *Feast*: John 6:51: 'I am the living bread,' and Revelation 19:9: 'Blessed are they which are called unto the marriage supper of the Lamb [Christ]'; *Strength*: Psalm 18:1: 'I will love thee, O Lord, my strength.'

Clasping of hands

Not in W. The economy of 'The Call' is here taken to extreme lengths. 'Thine/mine' and 'more/restore' provide all the rhyming line-endings – not to mention 'thine' and 'mine' also providing eleven internal rhymes between them. H's motive is clear enough: reciprocal love is all-in-all. He has taken his cue from the juggling of I and Thou in secular love poetry. But the result is a tongue-and-brain-twister to read aloud, a hall of mirrors on the page: for all its ardour a somewhat obtrusively technical tour de force.

17   *Since thou . . . none of thine*: Mark 15:34, Christ's dying cry from the cross: 'My God, my God, why hast thou forsaken me?'

Praise (3)

Not in W. The sprightliness of this poem suits its title and bounces along on varied line lengths (4, 2, 5, 4, 5, 3 feet, mostly iambic but varied with occasional trochees) and a rhyme scheme of *abacbc* with the *b* rhymes providing lift or spring. 'More' at the end of each and every stanza gives momentum. The content hops from image to image: spinning, running, flying, a horse-drawn cart, angels, devils, weeping, flags on church towers, a wine or cider press, a treasure chest. Agility is the poem's chief quality, 'Wherefore I sing' (line 37) the signature of its bird-like chirpiness.

4   *want of store*: lack of supplies.
10 *two legs*: the law and the prophets of the OT.
11 *twelve*: the apostles of the NT.
12 *twenty then, or more*: a lot of spinning wheels rather than the single one of line 3?
13 *blow*: blast, take against.
15 *teams*: of draught horses; *Albion*: the ancient name of England.
17 *Pharaoh's wheels*: Exodus 14:24–5: God 'troubled the host of the Egyptians, And took off their chariot wheels, that they drave them heavily'.
22 *Devils their rod*: In 'Sin (2)' the Devil 'hath some good in him, all agree' and here enforces God's ruling.
27 *bottle*: Psalm 56:8: 'put my tears into thy bottle: are not these things noted in thy book?'
28 *boxes*: alms boxes in churches, as directed by the BCP.
31 *thou hadst slipt a drop*: John 11:33: 'Jesus wept.'
40 *at use*: with interest; *store*: abundance.

Joseph's coat

Not in W. Mutability is the subject. And the source is the Bible's saga of fortunes reversed and reversed again: the Joseph epic in Genesis 37–50. The patriarch Jacob/Israel 'loved Joseph more than all his children, because he was the son of his old age: and he made him a coat of many colours. And when his brethren saw that their father loved him more than all his brethren, they hated him' (Genesis 37:3–4). They planned his murder but commuted it to selling him to passing merchants, stained his coat in the blood of a kid and showed it to Jacob, who was distraught with grief. Joseph ended up as the governor of Egypt where he wisely stored grain against the coming worldwide famine, which forced his brethren to travel to Egypt for corn. So Joseph became his family's saviour, telling his brethren 'be not grieved, nor angry with yourselves, that ye sold me hither: for God did send me before you to preserve life' (Genesis 45:5): God is the dispenser of anguish and joy. H takes the 'coat of many colours' as the emblem of the alternating happinesses and griefs of the biblical story – and of his own ('Their story pens and sets us down,' 'The Bunch of Grapes', line 11). So far, so good. But H has more: a probing of that mystery of music and the other arts that turn pain into pleasure – even, most movingly, mix them together (see the two instances of *both* and the three-fold *together* at lines 8, 9 and 12) into 'a tune beyond us yet ourselves' (Wallace Stevens, 'The Man with the Blue Guitar'). Such is this poem (a sonnet in which the first and third lines fail to rhyme, thus beginning by enforcing the emotional disjunction which will be mended at the end).

1   *indite*: put into words.
3   *his*: God's.
8   *both*: one grief and smart and my heart; *bier*: stretcher or cart to carry a corpse.
9   *both*: both heart and body.
11   *'ticing*: attracting by an offer of pleasure.
12   *together*: anguish and joy and me.

The Pulley

Not in W. When you pull down on one end of a rope passed over a wheeled pulley, you (paradoxically) pull up anything on the other end. The authority of the account of the creation of man in Genesis 1 notwithstanding, H, with sober boldness, uses this image to invent his own account. The best commentary is by Seamus Heaney in *The Redress of Poetry* (London: Faber, 1995), pp. 11–12:

> . . . a pun on the word 'rest' is executed in slow motion. As in the operation of a pulley, one of the word's semantic loads – 'rest' in the sense of repose – is gradually let down, but as it reaches the limit of its descent into the reader's understanding, another meaning – 'rest' in the sense of 'remainder' or 'left-over' – begins to rise. At the end, equilibrium has been restored to the system, both by the argument and by the rhythm and rhyme, as 'rest' and 'breast' come together in a gratifying closure. But as with any pulley system, the moment of equilibrium is tentative and

capable of a renewed dynamism. The poem can be read as a mimetic ren-
dering of any pulley-like exchange of forces, but equally it presents itself
as an allegory of the relationship between humanity and the Godhead, a
humanity whose hearts, in St Augustine's phrase, 'are restless till they rest
in thee'.

16   *the rest*: everything in lines 6–7, that is, everything other than
      rest!

The Priesthood

Not in W – so probably from H's unsettled years between Trinity Col-
lege, Cambridge and Bemerton. Fellows of Trinity were expected to be
ordained to the priesthood as a matter of course. It opened a career in
the Church and the possibility of marriage. H had taken the prelimin-
ary step of being made deacon in 1624. He postponed ordination to
the priesthood until 1630, when he became Rector of Bemerton. This
poem is set in that postponement and is all about it. Its central stanzas
3–5 (lines 13–30) draw on the image of God as potter which recurs in
the Bible, as at Isaiah 64:8: 'we are the clay, and thou our potter; and
we all are the work of thy hand'; more elaborately at Jeremiah 18:1–6;
more pertinently to this poem at Romans 9:21: 'Hath not the potter
power over the clay, of the same lump to make one vessel unto hon-
our, and another unto dishonour?' The 'vessels unto honour' bring to
H's mind the contemporary fashion, sponsored by Lord Salisbury and
patronized by the king, for imported Chinese blue-and-white porcel-
ain. A fine example of this valuable china carries bunches of grapes in
the magnificent *Cookmaid with Still Life of Vegetables and Fruit* by
Nathaniel Bacon, H's contemporary and the nephew of his friend
Francis Bacon, in Tate Britain, London.

5–6   *my lay-sword . . . holy Word*: Ephesians 6:17 'the sword of the
      spirit, which is the word of God'.
7   *thou art fire . . . hallow'd fire*: Malachi 3:2: God 'is like a refiner's
      fire'; Jeremiah 23:29: 'is not my [God's] word like as a fire?';
      Ezekiel, passim.
14   *fire*: the sacred *fire* of line 7 transposed to the potter's kiln.
17   *boards*: dining tables.
30   *Who bring my God to me!*: Refers to the priest as distributor of
      the consecrated bread and wine at Holy Communion.
32   *To hold the Ark . . . seem to shake*: 2 Samuel 6:6–7, when the
      sacred Ark was being carted to Jerusalem 'Uzzah put forth his
      hand to the ark of God, and took hold of it; for the oxen shook

it. And the anger of the Lord was kindled against Uzzah; and God smote him there for his error; and there he died.'

33   *new doctrines*: the dogmatic protestings of puritan Anglicans?

The Search

Not in W. The restless frustration of H's search for his absconded God is conveyed in fifteen breathless little stanzas, mixing iambic with occasional trochaic in alternating tetrameters and dimeters. It is a biblical theme, common in the Psalms and in the lover's agony at Song of Solomon 3:1 'I sought him whom my soul loveth ... but I found him not', but always – and not least here – fresh in its poignant realism. H's protest is respectful, colloquially clear and witty. The last stanza is a winner: one way or the other, inwardly or outwardly, God defies measurement.

3   *My searches ... daily bread*: Psalm 42:3: 'My tears have been my meat day and night: while they daily say unto me, Where is now thy God?'

4   *prove*: prove true; also bread (previous line) is 'proved' when the dough is set aside for a while so that the yeast in it can work and raise it.

14   *Simper*: twinkle.

31   *covert*: covering; Psalm 88:14: 'Lord, why ... hidest thou thy face from me?'

35   *ring*: ring-fence.

37   *entrenching*: defensive entrenchment.

47   *charge*: accusation against you.

59   *bear the bell*: be the first or leader of a group or flock.

60   *Making two one*: cf. the last line of 'Antiphon (2)'.

Grief

Not in W. A theme repeatedly in his Latin verse: cf. *Alia Poemata Latina* 1 (*In Obitum Henrici Principis*), also *Passio Discerpta* 1 and *Memoriae Matris Sacrum* 1, 9, 10, 16. Desperation is expressed in a series of densely hyperbolic pentameters, alternately rhyming. Their climax is the final, metrically unprecedented and unrhymed, last line. This anti-poem dramatizes H's despair: even of poetry and music and their cult of tears (Dowland's great *Lachrymae* of 1604 come to mind) in the face of real grief. He leaves it all to his rivals, the secular love poets whom he sought to outdo in all his own poetry. They can cope where he can't.

2-4 *come clouds ... nature hath produc'd*: an echo of the storm
     scene in *King Lear* 3.2.1-9? More certainly of Psalm 6:6: 'every
     night wash I my bed: and water my couch with my tears.'
7   *conduits*: channels.
10   *a less world*: the human microcosm.
12   *provision*: accommodation provided for them.

The Cross

Not in W. The poetically unmanageable grief of the previous poem is
here given structure. It is contained or bracketed by two meanings of
the noun 'cross'. The first is a contradiction or frustration of one's
intention. It is stated (line 19: 'things sort not to my will') and
described in painful detail in the first 33 lines of the poem. The second
is the cross willingly accepted by Christ in the last three lines. These
need to be picked over carefully. Line 34 states that the 'dear Father'
of line 31 is the author of the poet's misfortunes, line 35 that 'prop-
erly', appropriately and in the last analysis, they are felt by his Son
who accepted his cross when he said in Gethsemane, 'Father, if thou
be willing, remove this cup from me: nevertheless not my will, but
thine, be done' (Luke 22:42). But these words recur in the Christian's
daily prayer 'Our Father, which art in heaven ... *thy will be done*'
(Matthew 6:10). So, in line 36, they are 'my words', thoroughly
appropriated and familiar by twice-daily repetition. And here the
poet speaks them as his own acceptance of his crosses, the contradic-
tions of his own will. These three last lines thus tie a neat syntactical
knot of mutuality where before there had been diffuse solitary
complaint.

The poem is clearly autobiographically set, but when? Charles (pp.
127-9), plausibly enough, dates it in 1626 when H, as Prebendary of
Leighton Bromswold, set about restoring the ruined, cruciform church
there and raising funds (the 'wealth' of line 5 perhaps) for it. But he
was ill and most of the work was undertaken by the Ferrars, living as
a religious family at nearby Little Gidding. In lines 5 and 6 he could
well be contemplating a Little Gidding of his own at Leighton.

12   *threat'nings*: projects, intentions.
18   *thereof*: of the 'strange and uncouth thing': the cross and/or the
     ruinous church.
23   *sped*: prospering.
27   *fee*: reward.
29   *delicates*: choice foods.

The Flower

Not in W. This supremely beautiful lyric of convalescence was a favourite of Coleridge's. He called it 'a delicious poem', 'especially affecting; and to me such a phrase as "and relish versing" expresses a sincerity, a reality ... and so with many other of Herbert's homely phrases'. He admired the metrics of line 4: its heavy opening succession of iamb, spondee and trochee (ti-tum, tum-tum, tum-ti, reading 'The **late-past frosts tri**butes ...) followed by the lightness of 'of **pleas**ure **bring**'. The shape and rhythm of this line is a miniature of the whole poem's thematic structure. The little two-foot rhyming couplets at the fifth and sixth lines of the stanzas gives them lift. But it is, in its Mozartian way, a serious confrontation of life's bewildering changes, settled by the acceptance of human transience, made possible when concern with power (line 15) is superseded by love (line 43) as the governing principle for God. Most remarkable is H's ability to recapture the bleak past from the standpoint of present happiness. And so is the way in which the apparent and pious finality of line 21 is superseded by a fresh start, addressing the problem of mutability (what is the point of it?) at depth. The resolution renounces religious hubris and affirms reality.

1   *How fresh ... sweet and clean*: Note the rising pitch of the vowels.
2   *returns*: revisitings.
3   *demean*: demeanour and/or estate.
16   *quick'ning*: restoring to life.
18   *chiming*: a set of bells rung in celebration; *passing-bell*: a single bell tolled to announce a death.
21   *spell*: read aright.
25   *Off'ring*: aiming.
28   *My sins ... joining together*: in tears of repentance.
32   *pole*: frozen region.
43   *Lord of love*: as distinct from *Lord of power* (line 15).
44   *glide*: slip away.
45   *prove*: by experience.
48   *store*: abundance.
49   *Paradise*: the secure garden of the spirit.

Dotage

Not in W. The title denotes foolishly excessive affection. Examples of its illusory pleasures are listed in the first stanza, followed by a list of real sorrows in the second and a third stanza condemning human folly's pursuit of the first at the expense of true and heavenly delights. The refrain is cunningly varied. The general effect is smug.

1   *glozing*: flattering; *casks*: empty containers.
2   *night-fires*: will-o'-the-wisps.
3   *Chases in arras*: hunts depicted in tapestry.
4   *mounted*: on horseback; *career*: gallop.
8   *in grain*: ingrained.

The Son

Not in W. This sonnet is a celebration of the unique potential of poetry in English tied to the sun/son pun applied to Christ, which is only possible in 'our language'. English poetry had been defended in the preface to *Tottel's Miscellany* (1557): 'That to have well written in verse, yea and in small parcels, deserveth great praise, the works of divers Latins, Italians and other, do prove sufficiently. That our tongue is able in that kind to do as worthily as the rest, the honourable style of the noble Earl of Surrey, and the weightiness of the deep-witted Sir Thomas Wyatt the elder's verse, with several graces in sundry good English writers, do show abundantly.' Sir Philip Sidney believed that 'truly the English, before any other vulgar language I know, is fit for both sorts' (rhyme and metre). Lines 7–10 are about Christ as the sun, an extension of John 8:12, where he is 'the light of the world'. Lines 11–14 are about Christ as the Son of Man, a title used of him in the Gospels, which denotes both glory and humility.

4   *dress*: prepare.
8   *Chasing the father's dimness*: putting the previous night to flight.
9   *first man in th' East*: Adam in the Garden of Eden.
10   *Western discov'ries*: Christianity travelled west originally and in H's day to America (cf. 'The Church Militant', lines 235–6 and 247).
14   *The Son of Man*: Matthew 16:27: 'the Son of Man shall come in the glory of his Father.'

A true Hymn

Not in W. Ephesians 5:19 and Colossians 3:16 both speak of 'psalms and hymns and spiritual songs' as heartfelt forms of praise. So the title of this excellent poem introduces a lively meditation on heart and diction, sincerity and art, in the making of religious (or any other) poetry. Mutual love is its armature. Human love of God figures in lines 11 and 12, which echo Luke 10:27: 'Thou shalt love the Lord thy God with all thy heart, and with all thy soul, and with all thy strength, and with all thy mind.' But God's love for mankind has the last (italicized in 1633) word in which God himself writes, joining in to round it all off, '*Loved*'. Like many other poets, H starts off with a single phrase which keeps going through his head – here (aptly) the first line, repeated in italics (1633) at line 5. The poem is then made to spin it out, substantiate and accommodate it. The line of thought which results runs in a metric crescendo with a little hesitation in the middle: 3, 4, 3, 5, 5 feet. It is held together by a neat and tidy rhyme scheme using only two rhymes: *abbaa*. The final rhyming pentameter couplets make definite resolutions – most definite and resolved at the very end. The bracketed aside in line 19 is a delightfully acute psychological *aperçu*.

2   *My heart . . . all the day*: Psalm 45:1–2: 'My heart is inditing of a good matter: I speak of the things which I have made unto the King. My tongue is the pen of a ready writer.'
11   *He*: Who? It is left deliberately open, so can (inclusively) be God, the poet, even the (male) reader.
13   *the words only rhyme*: only the words.
15   *make*: make up; *in kind*: apposite, true to type.
20   *God writeth, Loved*: 1 John 4:19: 'We love him, because he first loved us.'

The Answer

Not in W. H's Shakespearean sonnet in answer to his critics. Barnabas Oley in the 'Prefatory View' to CP recalls that in Cambridge 'I have heard sober men censure him as a man that did not manage his brave parts to his best advantage and preferment, but lost himself in an humble way; that was the phrase, I do well remember it.' After twelve lines with his back to the wall, rehearsing and vividly embroidering the things people said against him in his years of uncertainty between leaving Cambridge and settling at Bemerton, the last couplet is more of a conundrum than an answer. Indeed, it leaves the answer to other people: *they that know the rest*. Who are they exactly? Ann Pasternak Slater's answer is plausible: 'the know-alls, the fair weather friends, *flies of estates and sun-shine*, who can tell the speaker so precisely what his shortcomings are, doubtless know his answer better than he does himself' (p. 476). But it could mean those who know him better, even than he knows himself, because they know *the rest*, meaning aspects which his detractors ignore. *Rest* also means heavenly repose, suggesting yet a third possible meaning.

2   *shake my head*: in negative perplexity; *ends*: intentions.
3   *bandy*: get together.
5   *estates*: fortunes.
6   *undertaking*: enterprising.
8   *exhalation*: gas from a dungheap.
10 *pursy*: swollen.

A Dialogue-Anthem

Not in W. Comparison with Donne's grandiloquent Holy Sonnet X, 'Death be not proud', speaks volumes on the difference between the two friends. The title, as with 'Antiphon (1) and (2)', refers to antiphonal church anthems. But its tone of alternating dispute recalls the disputations practised at the universities (H presided over them as Orator at Cambridge). The argument turns on the redeeming death of Christ who 'redeemed us from the curse of the law, being made a curse for us' (Galatians 3:13 and line 6) and by his resurrection caused St Paul to exult: 'Death is swallowed up in victory. O death, where is thy sting? O grave, where is thy victory?' (1 Corinthians 15:54–5).

4   *spell*: understand; *thy King*: Christ.
9   *I shall be . . . better than before*: by entering on eternal life.
10 *Thou so much . . . be no more*: cf. Donne, Holy Sonnet X: 'And death shall be no more, Death thou shalt die,' and Shakespeare, Sonnet 146: 'And death once dead, there's no more dying then.'

The Water-course

Not in W. The bracketed words at the end of each stanza divide the course of its thought into two stark alternatives. Similarly, the irrigation system of the water meadows on the other side of the River

Nadder from Bemerton Rectory had gates and sluices which allowed water to be directed into one *pipe* or channel or the other. H used this as a metaphor here, as in 'The Jews' and similar imagery in *Passio Discerpta* 5. The first stanza ends by combining *Life* with *Strife*, the second with the alternative destinies of *Salvation* and *Damnation*. They are presented as ineluctable, if contradictory, realities. H refrains from further discussion of predestination, the doctrine favoured by radical Puritans. H wrote about it in a letter to Lancelot Andrewes, 'so remarkable for the language and reason of it that after reading it, the bishop put it into his bosom, and did often show to many scholars' (Walton, *Life*, p. 349). This suggests that H's view was moderate. The letter has not survived.

Self-condemnation

Not in W. The poem's admirable and measured condemnation of 'othering', particularly anti-Semitism, is grounded in the Bible as an integration of the Hebrew and the Christian scriptures. As H wrote of *the Jews of old* and *each Christian* in 'The Bunch of Grapes', *Their story pens and sets us down*. He believed in, and always presupposed, the unity of humanity.

2 *For choosing Barabbas a murderer*: Luke 23:18: 'they cried out all at once, saying, Away with this man [Jesus], and release unto us Barabbas.'

6 *That choice*: of line 2.

18 *Judas-Jew*: Matthew 26:14-15: 'Then one of the twelve, called Judas Iscariot, went unto the chief priests, And said unto them, What will ye give me, and I will deliver him unto you? And they covenanted with him for thirty pieces of silver.'

19 *prevent*: anticipate.

22 *snuffs*: the burnt ends of candle wicks, which need to be snipped off for the candle to be bright.

Bitter-sweet

Not in W. This little jewel matches divine with human inconsistency in realistic mutuality. It is a very good example of H's courteous candour, his simplicity of diction, and his skill in putting life's biggest issues into nutshells. The result is a beauty, at once ethical and aesthetic, which is entirely satisfying and entirely Herbertian.

The Glance

Not in W. In 'The Glimpse' the transience of momentary happiness was deplored. Here H makes the best of it. He recalls it with sensual relish in the first stanza; assures himself of its continuing effectiveness in the present in the second; and looks forward to its eternal fulfilment in the third. Each stanza consists of a single long sentence, articulated in a parallel arrangement of line lengths (4, 5, 5, 2; 4, 5, 5, 2 feet) but rhymes *abacbddc*. The dimeters (2 feet) rhyme across three intervening longer lines, lines 2 and 5 across two. So each stanza swells, shrinks, swells and shrinks again: a pattern like breathing which makes the withdrawals and returns of happiness natural. It all presupposes the eye's capacity to communicate feeling: most affectingly in lines 19–21.

8   *take it in*: captivate it.

The 23d Psalm

Not in W. Metrical and rhymed versions of the Psalms in English were made by Wyatt, Sternhold and Hopkins (1562, regularly bound with the BCP for congregational singing), Philip and Mary Sidney and Francis Bacon. Their native Hebrew prosody was not understood until the next century. The Psalms were a constant inspiration to H, but this is his only version of one in *The Temple*. In its middle stanzas a bit clumsy like the Psalms of Sternhold and Hopkins, it is singable by a rural congregation. H's characteristic glosses are his preoccupation with *love* (line 1) and its reciprocity (line 3).

Mary Magdalene

Not in W. H's mother was called Magdalen. H's friend John Donne wrote a sonnet for her, 'To the Lady Magdalen Herbert, Of St Mary Magdalen'. Her devoted son was not to be left behind. In the Bible Mary Magdalene was the sister of Martha and Lazarus, the female disciple who first discovered Christ's empty tomb (Matthew 28:1). She was also the woman 'out of whom he had cast seven devils' and to whom the risen Christ 'appeared first' (Mark 16:9 and John 20:11–17). She came to be identified with the woman of the city, 'which was a sinner', who intruded on Jesus at a dinner party with 'an alabaster box of ointment, And stood at his feet behind him weeping, and began to wash his feet with tears, and did wipe them with the hairs of her head, and kissed his feet, and anointed them with the ointment' (Luke 7:37-38, referred to at John 11:2). Jesus's pharisaical host was offended, but Jesus rejoined that 'Her sins, which are many, are forgiven; for she loved much' (Luke 7:47). This is the story which made her the type of loving repentance and is behind H's disappointingly over-contrived poem (Donne's on this saint is no better). H is hampered by his aversion to the erotic: see line 14.

1   *When blessed . . . Saviour's feet*: The introductory note provides the key to the whole poem.
17   *So to . . . to wash*: her tears.

Aaron

Not in W. H is now, after 1630, a priest rather than hesitating to be one as in 'The Priesthood'. And he is more at home, despite his self-deprecation, with the archetypal priest of the OT than with Mary Magdalene. The source for Aaron's paraphernalia in the first stanza is Exodus 28. The lines swell then shrink: 3, 4, 5, 4, 3 feet. The deftly economical rhyme scheme consists of the same line-ending words in every stanza: 'head', 'breast', 'dead', 'rest' and 'drest'. These happy contrivances, along with trochees varying iambics, make for a mellifluous lyric.

1   *Holiness on the head*: Exodus 28:36: Aaron's mitre had 'Holiness to the Lord' inscribed on it.
2   *Light and perfections on the breast*: Exodus 28:30: 'thou shalt put in the breastplate of judgement the Urim and the Thummim.' The Geneva Bible's marginal note says of these mysterious objects 'Urim figureth light, and Thummim perfection.'
3   *Harmonious bells . . . the dead*: Exodus 28:33-5: 'And beneath upon the hem of it thou shalt make . . . bells of gold . . . and his sound shall be heard when he goeth in unto the holy place before the Lord . . . that he die not.'
9   *Unto a place where is no rest*: hell.
11   *head*: Ephesians 5:23: 'Christ is the head of the church.'
13   *Another music*: other than in line 8.
18   *My only . . . ev'n dead*: Romans 6:6: 'our old man is crucified with [Christ]' and 6:11 'reckon ye also yourselves to be dead indeed unto sin, but alive unto God through Jesus Christ our Lord.'

The Odour. 2 Cor. 2:15

Not in W. The biblical text in the title reads 'For we are unto God a sweet savour of Christ.' H explores its inherent reciprocity (reflected in the exhaling/inhaling form of the stanzas of 5, 4, 2, 4, 5-foot lines, rhyming *ababa*) and makes the most of its adjective *sweet*, already one of his favourite words. He also refers to Song of Solomon 1:3: 'Because of the savour of thy good ointments thy name is as ointment poured forth.' In his preface to *The Temple* Nicholas Ferrar relates that H 'used in his ordinary speech, when he made mention of the blessed name of our Lord and Saviour Jesus Christ, to add, *My Master*'. It was an everyday sort of title compared with Ferrar's own honorifics: ships, colleges, schools, guilds and (particularly relevant here) apprentices all had masters. H rejoices in its sensuous sound, even its taste and smell. And, above all, in the comfortably hierarchical mutual relationship it implies.

2   *Ambergris*: the valuable secretion of the sperm whale, found floating on the sea or gathered from beaches, and used in perfumery and cooking.
7   *into them both*: both words, *my* and *master*.
9   *cordials*: sweet medicines; *curious*: exquisite (delicious).
16   *Pomander*: a sweet smelling, compacted ball of herbs and spices, its perfume enhanced when warmed by the hands (line 20).

The Foil

Not in W. The title puns. A foil could be a thin sheet of metal set under a jewel to intensify its radiance, or something which sets off something else (here the heavens and the earth). So this tiny poem includes the whole universe, plays with thinking of it upside down, then moralizes it (pessimistically).

5   *foil*: 'A thin leaf of some metal placed under a precious stone to increase its brilliancy' *OED*, (5).
6   *virtues*: traditionally angels of the second heavenly sphere.

The Forerunners

Not in W. His white hairs impress upon H the onset of old age and arouse the fear of dementia, depriving him of his poetic powers. In the first two stanzas he steadies himself on the bare poetic minimum (italicized in 1633) of *Thou art still my God*. It returns, to settle matters, in the last stanza. This is like that other all-sufficient fragment 'My joy, my life, my crown' in 'A True Hymn'. In both instances a simple phrase of poetry has therapeutic power because it affirms a relationship of mutual love and trust. Its firmness frees him to wonder what will become of his writing and poetry generally. He is able to recall his high-minded forswearing of secular verse with ironic detachment in lines 14–18. If *sweet phrases* leave him for his worldly colleagues, he chides them as a parent who has washed his dirty children and taken them to church. Will *lovely, enchanting language* leave the church for some love affair? The accurately mimicked parental voice chides again: *Fie, thou wilt soil thy 'broidered coat, / And hurt thyself*. Another anchor of the soul marks the penultimate stanza: *True beauty dwells on high*. It is secure there. It and the poet's words *should* (note!) go together. But if they don't, H still has his 'little phrase' to comfort him in his winter. The whole psychological autobiography is presented in touchingly domestic terms, not least in the last line, and colloquial diction.

1   *harbingers*: the title's forerunners who went ahead of a royal progress, chalking *mark*s on doors of houses to be commandeered for billeting.

3   *dispark*: remove the walls round a park, releasing livestock; also implied by assonance, extinguishing the *sparkling notions* in the next line.

5   *clod*: blockhead.

8   *heart*: as distinct from *brain* (line 3).

9   *pass*: care.

11   *He*: God.

21   *bane*: ruin.

24   *him*: H the poet-priest-musician.

26   *canvas ... arras*: canvas was painted as a cheap substitute for arras tapestry.

31   *you*: the *beauteous words* of line 30.

34   *fee*: payment.

The Rose

Not in W. H answers critics of his withdrawn lifestyle in sprightly trochaic metres, concluding with the emblematic riddle of the title. The poem is a genially defensive display of courteous wit, appropriating the language of his opponents and one of their favourite symbols, in the style of a popular song.

3   *measure*: of goods, etc., and of poetic metre.
4   *size*: allowance of food.
8   *spare*: have and to spare; also, not harm.
10   *meant to say*: almost said.
12   *Who have . . . away*: to God.
18   *purgeth*: CP XXIII recommends 'damask or white roses' for 'loosing'.
19–25 *Purgings . . . If . . . Sweetly . . . So*: note the sequence of initial letters of these four lines.
24   *biteth in the close*: pricks the hand which grasps it in the end.
29   *But I health, not physic choose*: prefer to be healthy rather than need medicine.

Discipline

Not in W. The title means two things: learning by instruction; and the punishment of disorderly persons. To the reader's surprise, although God with his *rod* exercises the latter all too energetically and wildly, it is the poet who exercises the former, instructing God in the fundamental obligation of religion: love. H has done all that is required of him, as the second, third and fourth stanzas make abundantly clear. Now it is for God, not H, to repent and get in line. The trochaic trimeters and dimeters, along with his own irreproachable record, give a sprightly confidence to the poet's corrective instruction of the Almighty. The similarity of the last stanza to the first vindicates the poet's firmness. The appearance of Cupid, the pagan archer-god of love, in lines 17–24, adds zest to this high-spirited and insubordinate poem. He shot God and brought him down to earth by his incarnation in Christ.

11   *by book*: by the book.
12   *thy book*: the Bible.
26   *That which wrought on thee*: Love has power over God, demonstrated by the Incarnation.
31   *Thou art God*: and, by implication, should behave better.

The Invitation

Not in W. H is here the priest, inviting the congregation to 'take, eat and drink' the sacrament of Holy Communion. The BCP itself was insistent about getting the laity to mend their old, catholic ways of leaving it to the priest. It inserted an 'exhortation' in the middle of the service for use 'when [the curate] shall see the people negligent to come to the holy communion'. 'I bid you,' the priest read out to his reluctant congregation, 'in the name of God, I call you in Christ's behalf, I exhort you, as ye love your own salvation, that ye will be partakers of this holy communion ... And whereas ye offend God so sore in refusing this holy banquet, I admonish, exhort and beseech you, that unto this unkindness ye will not add any more. Which thing ye shall do, if ye stand by as gazers and lookers ...' In CP XXII H recommends that the sacrament be celebrated 'duly once a month' (the BCP actually provided for more than that) and includes children who 'are usually deferred too long'. All this informs the repeated *all* in the first line of every stanza.

2   *waste*: destruction. Cf. Philippians 3:19: 'Whose end is destruction, whose God is their belly'.

6   *dainties*: delicacies.

11   *this*: the consecrated wine given to everyone to drink in BCP Holy Communion with the words 'the blood of our lord Jesus Christ which was shed for thee'.

21   *without*: outside; this passage is another reference to the irrigation system of the river at Bemerton, whereby the meadows were flooded or 'drowned' in winter to make them fertile for grazing in spring and summer.

29   *Ev'n in death*: John 13:1 'having loved his own which were in the world, he loved them unto the end.'

36   *Where is All ... All should be*: God 'That All, which always is All everywhere' (Donne, 'La Corona' II, written for H's mother). The second *All* means everyone.

The Banquet

Not in W. As in 'Prayer (1)', a banquet was a dessert of sweetmeats or 'dainties' and fruit, adding festivity to an ordinary meal. This happy poem is set at the moment of eating the bread (Christ's body) and drinking the wine (Christ's blood) and sublimates the 'good cheer' of a secular drinking song. The sacrament stimulates, as it ratifies, H's talent for presenting the spiritual in images full of fresh sensuousness. The metre of 4, 2, 4, 4, 2, 4 feet combines with the *aabccb* rhyme scheme to make a lively poem.

4   *neatness*: daintiness, tastiness; *passeth*: surpasses.

7   *bowl*: for shared drinking, as with 'punch-bowl'.

16-18 *Flowers, and gums ... enemy should win*: Dough is heavy and smelly ('sourdough') unless sweetened and raised (*made a head*) by yeast mixed with sugar or honey.

30 *broken*: The bread was consecrated in BCP by recalling that Christ 'took bread; and when he had given thanks, he brake it, and gave it to his disciples, saying, Take, eat, this is my Body which is given for you.'

41 *court*: (of heaven).

51 *lines and life*: also in 'The Collar', line 4; *lines*: as in writing.

The Posy

Not in W. A posy was a short motto. As in 'A True Hymn', 'The Odour', 'The Forerunners' and 'Antiphon (1)', a little phrase is the poem's seed, containing all that really needs to be said. Here it is 'his own motto, with which he used to conclude all things that might seem to tend any way to his own honour; *Less than the least of God's mercies*' (Ferrar in his preface to *The Temple*). Oley and Walton concur, the latter adding that H applied it to the poems in the 'little book' on his deathbed. According to Puttenham (p. 140), posies 'never contained above one verse ... the shorter the better. We call them posies and do paint them nowadays upon the backsides of our fruit trenchers of wood, or use them as devices in rings and arms and about such courtly purposes.' In 'Misery', line 69, man was originally 'A ring, whose posy was, My pleasure'. Instead of the obvious procedure of giving his 'posy' a line to itself, H breaks it by a line space to bed it into the fabric of the poem in its first stanza and (slightly altered) in the last stanza. Pentameters alternate with dimeters in a simple rhyme scheme of *abab* – simplicity being of the essence.

2 *windows*: 'posies' were often inscribed on windowpanes with a diamond.

9 *Invention*: poetic imagination.

A Parody

Not in W. The poem parodied is a love lyric, printed in Wilcox, p. 634, by William Herbert, Earl of Pembroke, the great patron of literature who appointed H to Bemerton, though he did not live to see H installed there. H's first line is the same as Pembroke's. So it may be a thank you, adapting the Earl's opening lines, metres and sentiments to H's own religious purposes. Whereas the Earl addressed himself to his mistress, H addresses God. So the compliment of imitation is modified to suit H's preference for sacred rather than secular poetry.

The Elixir

From now on, B and 1633 have poems which are also in W. This one is particularly interesting because we have it in three successive versions: that written by H's scribe in W; H's revisions of it in his own hand, also in W; and B/1633. It is worth taking them in order. Words cancelled by H are struck through, his substitutes put in italics.

Perfection   *The Elixir*

    Lord teach me to refer
    All things I do to thee
That I not only may not err
    But also pleasing be

    A man that looks on glass
    On it may stay his eye
Or if he pleaseth, through it pass
    And then the heav'n espy.

    ~~He that does ought for thee~~
    ~~Marketh that deed for thine:~~
~~And when the Devil shakes the tree,~~
    ~~Thou say'st, this fruit is mine.~~

    All may of thee partake
    Nothing can be so ~~low~~   *mean*
Which with his tincture (for thy sake)
    Will not ~~to Heaven grow~~   *grow bright & clean*

    A servant with this clause
    Makes drudgery divine:
Who sweeps a ~~chamber~~ for thy laws   *room, as*
    Makes that and th'action fine

    ~~But these are high perfections.~~   *This is the famous stone*
    ~~Happy are they that dare~~   *That turneth all to gold:*
~~Let in the Light to all their actions~~   *For that which God doth*
                         touch and own
    ~~And show them as they are.~~   *Cannot for less be told.*

H gave the scribe of W a poem entitled 'Perfection', which sets out to show that anything which is 'referred' to God can *partake* of his perfection and *grow* up to *Heaven*. But in the last stanza he seems to lose his nerve and his way. It starts with *But*, then congratulates those who boldly *dare* to let divine Light in on *all their actions*. What has gone wrong? Something fundamental: the poem is about human religious aspiration, which H had learned to distrust (see 'The Flower', lines 29–31), rather than the power of divine love to transfigure and transform, which he valued supremely. So, not only does that last stanza go. So does the third, with its note of human initiative – and, alas, with it the picture of the scrumping devil. *To heaven grow* at the end of the fourth stanza goes out, too – 'Off'ring at heav'n, growing and groaning thither' in 'The Flower' never worked. The whole upward movement is at fault and must be cancelled, even reversed, so that earthly matters (*mean* or ordinary rather than *low* now) can, in a ringing phrase, *grow bright and clean* – just where they are and without uplift. So much for H's negative revisions. But there is a powerful positive change in his revision of the last stanza. When H's brother Edward was in Florence he saw – it seems to have been a highlight of his visit – 'that nail which was at one end iron, and the other gold, made so by virtue of the tincture into which it was put'. Here is that *tincture* in the fourth stanza. And in the new last stanza it appears in its solid form as the much and vainly sought philosopher's stone, also known as 'The Elixir', which is now an alternative title to *Perfection*.

In B/1633 the first stanza of W is tightened up and straightened out, vague 'referring' changed to seeing and doing. The second stanza is new: God is there already (*prepossess'd*) so it is not for us to go at things like a bull at a gate. The third stanza is the limpid second from W. The fourth is as H revised it in W. So are the fifth and the sixth. The alternative title in W wins. Unsparing self-criticism, of the man as of the poet, has resulted in the complete simplicity of a poem which has become a popular hymn (omitting, alas, the rude *beast* of the second stanza).

8 *his*: its.
15 *his*: its; *tincture*: quintessence, tincture or soul of a thing: here with the particular meaning in the brackets. 'All things that are, though they have sev'ral ways, / Yet in their being join in one advice / To honour thee', 'Providence', lines 145–7 – a view shared by Edward Herbert in his *De Veritate*.

A Wreath

Word for word as in W, so an early poem, but so good as to need no revision. The uses of repetition to bind a poem were familiar to H's predecessors and contemporaries, Donne's sacred sonnets, 'La Corona', being an example familiar to H because given by its author to H's mother. Pindar several times compared his song to a wreath or garland; and the image of weaving or wreathing is used to denote the complexity of the song itself. But this poem takes the prize for sheer intricacy – and grace. The weaving of words is what it is all about: its subject and its action as well as its sustained technical method. A word in one line is repeated in the next. 'Give' at the end of line 11 links to the same word at the end of line 2, 'praise' at the end of the final line to the same word at the end of the first line. The same applies to 'ways' with lines 3 and 10, and 'live' with lines 4 and 9. So ends not only meet, but tangle: as they should in a wreath. And within that circularity, line is twisted with line. Nor is it all mere repetition. The second instance of a word corrects or extends the first, giving impetus throughout. That 'simplicity' should end the long sentence which runs from lines 1 to 8 and then recur at line 9 may seem ironical at the heart of such a complicated performance. And it is – but at the same time sincere and, when the poem is read aloud, true of its effect. The intricate prosody comes from a simple heart and reads aloud like ordinary speech.

Death

The poems from here on to the end are a series taken from W, keeping its order. Death is cheerfully encountered in the ordinary way of things as an old acquaintance, previously repellent and misunderstood but now looking much better than he did before. Once gruesome, 'our Saviour's death' has made him 'fair and full of grace', socially not only acceptable but welcome. The courteous and genial tone, touched with comedy and so evident in the wonderful fourth line, contrasts strongly with the bullying mockery of Donne's more famous 'Death be not proud'.

11   *fledge*: young birds which have grown their feathers and can fly away and leave the *shells*: of their eggs behind.
12   *extort*: (tears).
16   *request*: demand.
22   *Half that we have*: (our bodies).
24   *down*: soft feathers.

Doomsday

H again treats a grandiose apocalyptic subject, the resurrection of the dead at the end of time, with cheerful familiarity. The first line of each stanza is a refrain echoing Dowland and the clown Feste's song in *Twelfth Night*, 2. 4.51: *come away* (as we would say, 'come on'). It announces a lyrical mood: all in gay and easy rhyming couplets, with two impulsive dimeter lines followed by four trochaic tetrameters giving a bouncy beat. The first stanza shows H's comic talent, in the last everyone joins in the final music.

8   *Make this the day*: addressed to God, inviting him to get on with it.
10   *trumpet*: 1 Corinthians 15:52: 'the trumpet shall sound, and the dead shall be raised incorruptible'.
12   *Cure Tarantula's raging pains*: 'Such as are stung by the Tarentula [spider] are best cured by music,' Greene, *Philomela* (1615).
15   *confession*: (by opening themselves up).
17-18 *Flesh's stubbornness ... to the grave*: Obstinate *flesh* may have taught the *grave* to hang on to what it has got.
29   *consort*: musical ensemble.

Judgement

The iambic pentameters of the first and third lines of each verse instil a more serious mood than that of the preceding 'Doomsday'. But their weight is relieved by two iambic dimeters and a tetrameter at the end. The sources are biblical and ominous: Daniel 7:10, 'the judgment was set, and the books were opened', and Revelation 20:12: 'I saw the dead, small and great, stand before God; and the books were opened: and another book was opened, which is the book of life: and the dead were judged out of those things which were written in the books, according to their works.' H seems to have transposed this cosmic scene to the terrors of the schoolroom, the master calling for his pupils' exercise books. Some of the boys can, he hears tell (he is not certain about it for himself), draw the master's attention to immaculate pages and so *excel* in *merit*. They are justified by works. Not so H. He will not hand in his own book but *thrust a Testament into thy hand*. This is the Christian New Testament, which tells on page after page of Christ's taking human sins or, in schoolroom terms, *faults* upon himself. H is justified by grace and his graceful and resourceful wit triumphs over dread. The last line deserves pondering.

Heaven

H got from Ovid, *Metamorphoses* III the myth of the origin of the echo. Echo was a woodland nymph, punished by Juno for failing to report on her husband Jupiter's amours. Her powers of speech were reduced to only being able to repeat the last word or two of anything she heard. Her body died and only her copy-cat voice was left to haunt her native woods and wilds. She haunted poets, too. Echo poems were written by Sidney and H's brother Edward among others, but none as good as H's, of which Vendler (p. 227) writes that 'the verses are ... a radical endorsement of the human: in our yearning, we speak God's language. When we find words of the right sort to ask about the divine – words like "delight", "enjoy", "pleasure", and "persever" – God can do nothing better than answer us in our own vocabulary.' In other words, such words invite a perfect reciprocity: like Echo's, but fulfilling and not merely redundant. So over lines 4–12 Echo changes from a nymph among the forest's leaves to the voice which speaks from the leaves of the Bible to answer H's opening question about the 'delights on high': from a responsive nymph to the book which answers his deepest questions.

8   *Bide*: wait.
14 *Light*: Psalm 4:7: 'Lord, lift thou up: the light of thy countenance upon us'; and the Psalms and the Bible passim, especially Revelation 22:5: 'there shall be no night there; and they shall need no candle, neither light of the sun; for the Lord God giveth them light.'
16 *Joy*: Psalm 16:12: 'in thy presence is the fulness of joy.'
17 *pleasure*: Psalm 16:12: 'at thy right hand there is pleasure for evermore.'
18 *Leisure*: Revelation 14:13 and BCP Burial Service: 'Blessed are the dead which die in the Lord, even so saith the Spirit, for they rest from their labours.'
20 *Ever*: Revelation 22:5: 'and they shall reign for ever and ever'.

Love (3)

Here is one of the greatest poems in the English language. Simone Weil considered it 'the most beautiful poem in the world' (S. Petrement, *Simone Weil: A Life* (London: Mowbrays, 1976), p. 330). Seamus Heaney (p. 14) writes that 'that immaculate ballet of courtesy and equilibrium in "Love" (3) represents a grounded strength as well as a perfect tact.' In W it is followed by *Finis* (the end) with flourishes on either side, suggesting that H himself thought it his ultimate poem. Its biblical seed is 1 John 4:8: 'God is love.' God as the maker of man speaks in the second stanza and in the second line H is a son of the ur-man Adam, made of *dust* and *guilty* of disobedience. In the third stanza God is man's redeemer who *bore the blame*. But we only have to suppose that H had written 'God' where he actually wrote 'Love' for the poem's secret to be revealed by the contrast. Love is not only at home in the dinner-party allegory, but also – and more – the final resolution of all H's doubts of his own self-worth and his God's benevolence. Heaney's 'grounded strength' resides in the realistic domestic setting, the guest displaying all the diffidence and self-deprecation recommended by etiquette books of the time, the host countering it with 'perfect tact'. The difference between the two of them is shown by the contrast of *quick-eyed Love* and *I cannot look on thee*. But it was set in the very first line. *Love bade me welcome* gets alert sprightliness from the light syllables which spring from its stresses. *Soul drew back* is all stresses, making a heavy drag. Thereafter, Love speaks in short, monosyllabic sentences, the guest at more length – until the final stanza, when Love has two of the longer iambic pentameters and the guest's riposte is reduced, first to one of the shorter trimeter lines, and then to the silent obedience and enjoyment of the last line with its satisfying rhyme and marvellous modesty. This is a dialogue which ends all dialogue in the perfect reciprocity of holy communion.

2   *dust*: Genesis 3:19: 'dust thou art, and unto dust shalt thou return.'

3   *quick*: lively, alert.

9   *unkind*: unnatural.

12   *eyes . . . I*: a pun (Love is witty, humorous).

15   *who bore the blame*: Isaiah 53:11: 'he shall bear their iniquities', and Hebrews 9:28: 'Christ was once offered to bear the sins of many.'

17   *sit*: H was uncertain about whether communicants should receive sitting or kneeling: In CP XXII 'the Feast indeed requires sitting, because it is a Feast; but man's unpreparedness asks kneeling.' Here he prefers the former, along with more puritan Anglicans and to suit his allegory. *Meat*: food.

18   *eat*: Mark 14:22, etc., and BCP Holy Communion: 'Jesus took bread, and blessed, and brake it, and gave it to them, and said, Take, eat, this is my body.' *The 23 Psalm*: 'thou dost make me sit

and dine.' Song of Solomon 2:3–4: 'I sat down under his shadow with great delight, and his fruit was sweet to my taste. He brought me to the banqueting house, and his banner over me was love.'

Glory be . . . towards men: The three lines under *Finis* are not in W, but were added on the next page between double ruled lines in B, and printed as two lines on the same page in 1633. They quote Luke 2:14, the song of the angels at Christ's birth.

The Church Militant

Although included in *The Temple*, this long and trying poem is separated from 'Love (3)' and its colophon by five blank pages in W, by one in B, and by a band of ornament in 1633. It is something else: apparently a survey of Church history from Noah (the OT is included) to the contemporary English colonization of America's eastern seaboard. The overall scheme is Christianity's progress from east to west, like the sun. The chronological order often goes into reverse to pick up antecedents. At line 103 it starts all over again in Babylon as Sin, the Church's enemy, takes over as protagonist until the future Judgement Day, foreseen near the end at line 269. There are pauses for set pieces within the hectic narrative: lines 107–23 are a satire on Egyptian polytheism; lines 161–224 satirize Roman Catholicism generally and the papacy in particular; lines 235–62 are an apology for the Virginia Company, chartered in 1606, in which H's friends and relations were to be involved. At line 236 religion is *ready* to go to America and at line 247 it *shall* flee there. The first expedition sailed in 1607 when H was a scholar at Westminster. Dating the poem at this time is not favoured by most commentators, but it fits its character as a piece of jejune juvenilia, far below any of H's later work in quality. The company was dissolved in 1624 and H's lines 235–6 caused the Cambridge University authorities to hesitate over the printing of *The Temple* in 1633. The poem is in relentless rhyming pentameter couplets, occasionally varied by an ineffectual refrain and a rogue triplet at lines 267–9. The rhymes are often so odd as to be comical: *Solomon* with *religion* at lines 20–21; *Anthony* with *history* at lines 41–2; *profess* with *offices* at lines 173–4, etc. It is a beginner's work, immature in thought and technique. Its dandified wit and sarcasm in the manner of Donne's *Satires* of the 1590s (another possible indication of an early date) and its in-jokes for the learned make it unrewarding for the general reader. It is meant to be funny. Its obscurities are a far cry from the simplicity prized by the mature H. Generically, this is an epyllion, closest, in the Latin verse, to *Lucus* 32 ('The triumph of Death'). Most of the features indicated are typical of late Elizabethan/Jacobean epyllia – e.g., an extravagant style, a rather 'knowing' or ironic tone, and several set pieces. Other examples of epyllia are Milton's *In Quintum Novembris* and Jonson's 'On the Famous Voyage' (*Epigrams* 133).

11   *vine*: Isaiah 5:7: 'the vineyard of the Lord of hosts is the house of Israel, and the men of Judah his pleasant plant.'

15   *Noah's shady vine*: Noah 'planted a vineyard' (Genesis 9:20).

19   *Where th' Ark . . . Abraham began*: obscure because a muddle – of Noah's Ark with the Ark of the Covenant, and Moses's chest containing the Tablets of the Law, which, after many adventures, came to rest in Solomon's temple. *Abraham*: his descendants?

26   *Rending . . . partition-wall*: Matthew 27:51, when Christ died 'the veil of the temple [concealing the Ark] was rent in twain from the top to the bottom; and the earth did quake'; also Ephesians 2:14: Christ 'hath broken down the middle wall of partition between us'.

32   *Listens*: pays attention to what is . . . .

37   *prove*: experience.

38   *Wonders of anger*: the plagues of line 40 and Exodus 8–11.

41   *Holy Macarius and great Anthony*: fourth-century hermits.

43   *Goshen*: Exodus 8:22, the part of Egypt occupied by the Jews and exempt from the plagues; Exodus 10:22–3: 'thick darkness' over Egypt, but 'all the children of Israel had light in their dwellings'.

44   *Nilus*: the Nile.

52   *fisher's net*: Matthew 4:19, Jesus to his disciples: 'I will make you fishers of men.'

54   *to spell Christ-Cross*: A cross preceded the alphabet on the horn-books which taught children their letters from its 'criss-cross-row'. The philosophers have to go back to their lessons.

56   *Ergo*: 'Therefore' in Latin.

60–62 *Before the other . . . their foes*: in W:

> Before the other two were in their prime.
> From Greece to Rome she went, subduing those
> Who had subdued all the world for foes.

65   *his*: Adam's, representing mankind.

67   *The great heart*: of the Roman warrior of line 63.

72   *Giving new names ... to the year*: the Christianization of the Roman calendar.

74   *Who were ... in Alexander's stem*: Constantinople/Byzantium, the eastern Christian imperial capital after the dissolution of the empire of Alexander the Great.

81   *Germany*: the seat of the western Holy Roman Empire from the tenth century.

90   *higher victory*: the uniting of church and state in the reformation of Henry VIII.

93   *Constantine's British ... of old*: Constantine, the first Christian Emperor, had a British mother and was proclaimed Emperor at York in 306.

95   *a sheet of paper*: the (spurious) 'Donation of Constantine' giving power and land to the Church.

98   *old meridian*: the sun's zenith and the line from pole to pole passing through England.

103 *Babylon*: the tower of Babel (Genesis 11) and the capital city of sin in Revelation.

112-13 *Adoring garlic ... which he may eat*: cf. Donne, *Of the Progress of the Soul* (1611-12), lines 427-8: 'onions are / Gods to them.'

131 *became a poet*: wrote oracles in verse.

132 *sublimate*: bichloride of mercury, a violent poison.

134 *pull*: draw lots.

147 *Disparking*: expelling.

159 *Rock*: Matthew 16:18: 'thou art Peter, and upon this rock I will build my church' (the title deed of the papacy). W has here:

> Traditions are accounts without our host.
> They who rely on them must reckon twice
> When written truths shall censure man's devise.

163 *wear a Mitre*: Sin becomes the Pope.

169 *a handsome picture by*: Papal patronage of painting.

174 *Christ's three offices*: prophet, priest and king.

177 *petty deities*: the saints.

200 *cloisterers*: monks and nuns.

201-4 *Who without spear ... the Pope's mule*: in W:

> Who brought his doctrines and his deeds from Rome
> But when they were unto the Sorbonne come,
> The weight was such they left the doctrines there
> Shipping the vices only for our sphere.

207 *Janus*: the two-faced Roman deity.

215 *Old and new Babylon*: the original city and the code-name of Rome in Revelation 14 onwards.

234 *The spacious . . . Jewry to be seen*: Ezra 3:12, the temple rebuilt in Jerusalem after the exile was not as fine as the original, nor the recently reformed churches as the original, nor OT Jewry as the spacious world as first created.

236 *the American strand*: see introductory note.

247–8 *Then shall Religion . . . ev'n as we*: When religion is totally corrupted in Europe it will *to America flee*. This passage on the fall of Europe and the rise of America is interestingly paralleled in the final section of Book 5 of Abraham Cowley's *Plantarum Libri Sex*, a major Latin didactic work of the 1660s.

258 *But lends . . . our desolation*: the plundering of American gold by European adventurers, which the *grace* of the Christian gospel will repay.

265 *one*: (empire).

272–3 *Thus also Sin . . . power and skill*: in W

> Like Comic Lovers ever one way run:
> Thus also sin and darkness constantly
> Follow the Church and sun where ere they fly.

277 *where judgement shall appear*: Revelation 7:2: the last judgement is announced by an 'angel ascending from the east'.

L'Envoy

An envoy concludes a poem with an address to its dedicatee or reader. Here H finishes off *The Church Militant* with a prayer to God to see off Sin, the protagonist of the final two-thirds of the poem. Although this poem is in W, its first line is the same as that of 'Praise (2)', which is not. The pentameter couplets of *The Church Militant* are forsaken in favour of lighter tetrameter couplets, to which a trimeter couplet was added in B and *FINIS* in 1633. These additions obscure the fact that in W, H's scribe wrote *Finis* after 'Love (3)', making it the conclusion of H's own *The Church* (from which the anticlimactic *The Church Militant* and 'L'Envoy' are separate).

9 *thy flesh*: Ephesians 5:30: 'we [Christians] are members of his [Christ's] body, of his flesh, and of his bones.'

16 *discharge*: get rid of; *behind*: left over.

ENGLISH POEMS IN THE WILLIAMS
MANUSCRIPT NOT INCLUDED
IN *THE TEMPLE*

The Holy Communion

In B and 1633 this discursive poem of eight stanzas (two tetrameter couplets, both followed by trimeters which rhyme together) is superseded by the better double poem of the same title. The trouble with this poem is there at the start. H wants to *know* exactly how the bread and wine become the body and blood of Christ, whereas in the double poem he takes that devoutly for granted and interprets it with happy metaphors – and in the final stanza calls it *this ease*. There is nothing easy about this one as H tacks laboriously from stanza to stanza, penultimately asserting the dualism of flesh and spirit which was the problem all along. Granted that the nature of the sacrament was hotly and divisively disputed among the reformers of the previous century, and continued to be, H does nothing to alleviate it in this poem, and, apart from the engagingly outspoken lines 6–9, was right to drop it.

2   *these gifts*: the bread and wine.
6   *creature*: created matter or the poet himself.
18   *more*: longer (by being indirect).
25   *Impanation*: the divine Christ becoming bread, in parallel with his *Incarnation*.
34   *glorious*: heavenly.
36   *they deceive*: The stars 'oftentimes do miss' ('The Holy Scriptures (2)', line 13) as astrological guides.
41   *meres*: boundaries.
42   *pole*: position.
45   *pledge*: BCP Holy Communion, prayer after communion: 'we offer and present unto thee, O Lord, ourselves, our souls and bodies'.

Love

A well-made poem. The rhyme scheme is *abc, abc*. The feet per line go 4,5,4, 4,5,4. So they match in shape with slight but telling variation. Its intimacy – we catch H washing, troubled and then happy – combine with its gentle self-irony to make it endearing and enjoyable. There seems to be no good reason why it did not make it into B and

1633, unless H disapproved of the last stanza with its clever prayer telling God that in subduing man *thou dost no more, than doth the grave*, and hanging on to his desire to *o'ercome thee and thy Love* – which it would do God credit to allow. In 'The Thanksgiving' and 'The Reprisal' H admitted defeat – a more orthodox option. Here his ultimate concern with love results (as it tends to do) in sailing near the wind.

14   *Great waves . . . my breast*: Mark 4:37–8: 'And there arose a great storm of wind, and the waves beat into the ship, so that it was now full. And he [Christ] was in the hinder part of the ship, asleep on a pillow.'

24   *short of*: behind, lower than.

Trinity Sunday

In W this poem follows the other poem with the same title which made it into *The Temple*. The proximity was fatal. 'Trinity Sunday' in B and 1633 is a prayer: a little masterpiece of ingenuity and sincerity. This is a disquisition, also playing with numbers, but diffusely and ineffectually. The lack of an addressee and the preoccupation with arithmetic obscure the argument (not much of an argument), which seems to be that *one, / Is none*, two is better but not satisfactory, and three is the unity of all in one. The metre and rhyme scheme are both so complex as to seem muddled: 2,1,2,2,2,4,3,2,3,4,2,4,2,4,3,2,5, 2,1 and *aabbccdddeffgghjehj*.

12   *the first Thief*: Satan or Adam.

Even-song

Like the other 'Evensong' in B and 1633, for which this may have been a trial run, here is a poem of private devotion rather than the public BCP Evening Prayer. The diminishing lengths of its lines, from five to four to three feet, suit the fading of the light. The first three stanzas are wistful, then anxious. The fourth stanza begins a meditation on Psalm 139:10–11: 'If I say, peradventure the darkness shall cover me: then shall my night be turned to day. Yea, the darkness is no darkness with thee, but the night is a clear as the day: the darkness and light to thee are both alike.' At 1 Kings 8.12 Solomon, dedicating the temple, said that 'the Lord said that he would dwell in the thick darkness.' The multiple paradoxes result in obscurity.

7   *his*: the sun's.
11   *Fouling her nest*: by nocturnal emission?

The Knell

This is a meditation on death, announced by the tolling or 'knell' of a church bell. It may well take its cue from Donne's famous Meditation 17 in *Devotions Upon Emergent Occasions* (1624): 'The bell doth toll for him that thinks it doth; and though it intermit again, yet from that minute, that that occasion wrought upon him, he is united to God . . . I am involved in Mankind, therefore never send to know for whom the bell tolls; it tolls for thee.' Who *thy servant* is in the second line, the person dying or the poet, is left open, in tune with Donne's inclusive humanity. The sound of the bell is imitated by the short, measured two-foot lines, its reverberation in the poet's mind by the pentameters.

3   *wishly*: longingly.
5   *offers*: (in sacrifice).
11   *Disbanded*: Turned loose (from the army).
17   *Juleps*: cooling medicinal drinks; *Cordials*: heart-warming ditto.

Perseverance

H's anxiety about his poetry and his own salvation is expressed in stanzas of three urgent pentameters followed by a tetrameter. The trochees increase in the final stanzas (lines 11, 13, three times with the present participles in line 15, redressed by the two trochaic 'thou's in line 16). H is afraid that his poems may help others, but condemn him (? by their self-revelations) and that his 'many crimes and sins' may divorce him from God. With the last stanza the poem's gathering force bursts into desperate gestures and assertions. Why did H not include so strong a poem in his final collection? Perhaps because it was too strong, too revealing of his inward terrors.

1   *expressions*: squeezings out.
3   *move*: in the sense of feel moved.
12   *banns*: of marriage, referring to line 10.

POEMS FROM IZAAK WALTON'S
THE LIFE OF MR GEORGE HERBERT

Sonnets

Walton relates that H 'in the first year of his going to Cambridge sent his dear mother for a New-year's gift' a letter with two sonnets. The letter reproved 'the vanity of those many love-poems, that are daily writ and consecrated to Venus' and declared his own 'resolution to be, that my poor abilities in poetry shall be all and ever consecrated to God's glory'. The date, then, is 1610. In 1609 Shakespeare's *Sonnets* were published and Donne sent the first fruits of his own religious poetry to H's mother: the '*La Corona*' sequence of sonnets, with a dedicatory poem. Reaction against Shakespeare and emulation of Donne may have stimulated H to write these priggish poems in sonnet form. They are technically elaborate with much enjambment, crowds of metaphors and a barrage of hectoring rhetorical questions. In 'Jordan (2)' H is critical of his early efforts in religious verse with their 'thousands of notions' and 'trim invention'. The last three lines are disgusting and go beyond ordinary prudishness.

3   *other flames*: by which they were executed.
4   *livery*: uniform.

6   *Roses and lilies speak thee*: Song of Solomon 2:1: 'I am the rose of Sharon, and the lily of the valleys.'

To my Successor

Walton relates that, having finished the restoration of his rectory at Bemerton, H 'caused these verses to be writ upon, or engraven in the mantle of the chimney in his hall'. They do not survive there.

ADDITIONAL ENGLISH POEMS

To the Right Hon. the L. Chancellor (Bacon)

This poem survives in manuscript in the British and Bodleian libraries. Francis Bacon became Chancellor in 1618 and published a first instalment of his encyclopaedic *Instauratio Magna* in 1620: the multi-faceted 'diamond' referred to in the poem. H had known Bacon, a frequent visitor to his stepfather's house and garden at Chelsea, for some ten years. In 1620 H was elected University Orator at Cambridge: the summit of his academic career. As Orator he expressed the University's thanks for Bacon's gift of his book in his Latin poem 'In Honorem', etc. (p. 340). This English poem is on a more intimate level and accompanied H's return gift to Bacon, which H calls 'a blackamoor', meaning his Latin poem *Aethiopissa ambit Cestum Diuersi Coloris Virum*, the complaint of a negro maid wooing 'a man of a different colour' (p. 342). This Latin poem appears to be an entirely secular love lyric, but draws on the words of King Solomon's black lover in Song of Solomon 1:5-6: 'I am black, but comely, O ye daughters of Jerusalem . . . Look not [down] upon me, because I am black, because the sun hath looked upon me.'

12   *factious*: partisan (because black, like the blackamoor maid in the accompanying Latin poem).

A Paradox: That the Sick are in better State than the Whole

Another poem to survive in manuscript in the British and Bodleian libraries. It takes and speaks from the invalid's side (*ours* at line 7) and reads as an ocasional poem to comfort and divert him or her in lively stanzas, ending with decisive pentameters. The paradoxes are mostly far-fetched, more witty than substantial, but the insight into the moral ambivalence of sick-visiting in the last stanza is shrewd and gives the poem a lift at the end.

4   *want*: lack.
12   *Mediocrity*: a middling state betwixt and between.
16   *better fate*: tears of joy.
38   *Plaints*: complaints.

To the Lady Elizabeth Queen of Bohemia

Inscribed 'G. H.' in a manuscript in the British Library. James I's daughter Elizabeth was Queen of Bohemia for little more than a year. She was married to Frederick, protestant Elector (of the Holy Roman Emperor) Palatine (the Rhineland) in 1613. In 1619 the Bohemians deposed their king and elected Frederick to succeed him: an affront to the catholic Emperor which resulted in Elizabeth and Frederick being defeated in battle, losing everything and having to live in exile in Holland. Elizabeth became a heroine of the protestant cause, particularly in Cambridge where H had been Orator since 1620, succeeding Sir Francis Nethersole who had accompanied Elizabeth to Bohemia. So this is a public, courtly poem, one among many such addressed to Elizabeth, by a rising star of a protestant university.

3   *Jointure*: property given to a wife in a marriage settlement.
8   *two clods of earth*: Bohemia and the Rhineland; *ten spheres* concentrically making up the whole universe.
13   *optic*: telescope, Holland being famous for the manufacture of lenses.
16   *foil*: see H's poem 'The Foil', p. 169.
17   *tiffany*: fine silk.
27   *hale*: tug.
29   *When sense is made by comments*: commentary is needed for intelligibility.
42   *Children*: Elizabeth had plenty, including Charles I's general Prince Rupert of the Rhine and Sophia the future mother of George I.
47   *Eagle's wings*: the heraldic imperial eagle.
48   *Harpies*: plundering, birdlike monsters.
50   *Purgatory*: the region between hell and paradise believed in by catholics but not protestants.
51   *Paris garden*: a bear-baiting pit among the theatres of Southwark.
62   *habitable sea and brinish strand*: Holland.

L'Envoy

This follows on from the previous poem, with the same addressee.

2   *David's tree*: Psalm 1:3: 'he shall be like a tree planted by the waterside: that will bring forth his fruit in due season.'
10   *Main*: open sea.

THE LATIN VERSE

MUSAE RESPONSORIAE
THE MUSES' REPLY

This accomplished sequence of forty epigrams, preceded by three dedicatory poems, is a response to a long polemical poem the *Anti-Tami-Cami-Categoria* (the punning title is hard to translate, but amounts to something like: *Anti-Oxford-Cambridge-Accusations*) by Andrew Melville (1545–1622), a Scottish religious reformer. Melville's poem was prompted in particular by the opposition of Oxford and Cambridge to the Millenary Petition of 1603. This was a request from a number of Puritan divines that the English Church should abandon various liturgical practices, which they considered unscriptural and too close to Roman Catholicism; these included the use of the cross at baptism, as well as confirmation, the marriage ring, the surplice and elaborate music to accompany worship.

The second edition of Izaak Walton's *Life* (1675) reports that H wrote the poems of *Musae Responsoriae* while a schoolboy at Westminster School. Since Melville's poem certainly dates from the time of the Millenary Petition, and H was at Westminster School from 1605 to 1609 (aged 12 to 16) it is possible that H at least began the sequence during that period. However, Melville's poem was not published until 1620 and it is likely that H returned to his work, or began it, in that year. Most details of the sequence fit this later date: the dedicatory poems are appropriate to the early 1620s (when the future Charles I was still Prince of Wales and Lancelot Andrewes was Bishop of Winchester), but the sequence shows no awareness of Melville's death in 1622. It is possible that some of the sharper and more invective epigrams are of an earlier date, and were tempered by H with the more mature and nuanced pieces (such as 36 and 37) as he shaped them into a sequence in the early 1620s. H's collection was not published until 1662.

Although the purpose of H's sequence is to counter Melville's arguments, the tone is on the whole fairly respectful, with little ad hominem attack. What emerges most clearly is H's love and respect for the Anglican rites, especially church music, and his own poetic discernment and ambition. This is the most metrically varied of all H's collections, perhaps to make a point about the range of expression and emotional nuance made possible by Anglican ritual. The most common metrical form, as in each of H's collections of epigrams, is the elegiac couplet (a dactylic hexameter followed by a pentameter); but the full range of metres is very wide, including hendecasyllables, iambic trimeters and iambic distichs, as well as an ambitious range of lyric metres (alcaics, sapphics, glyconics, third archilochian, 'lesser' asclepiad and the third asclepiad – see the Appendix on metrical forms). The metrical variety of the collection, and the incorporation of a wide range of lyric forms, gives the sequence an Horatian feel in counterpoint to its essential identity as a book of epigrams.

To the Most Venerable and Most Mighty Monarch
James by the Grace of God King of Great Britain,
France and Ireland, Defender of the Faith, &c.
George Herbert

Metre: elegiac couplets. It is conventional to begin a poetry collection
with thanks and offering to a noble or royal patron. Here H appropri-
ates several conventional tropes of panegyric – for instance, calling
James I *Caesar* and comparing him to the sun – but applies them to a
single vivid and unusual image: life emerging, under the influence of
the sun, from the mud of the Nile shore. The mud is H's latent talent,
capable of producing poems when exposed to the sun and wind of the
king's favour. The comparison is both flattering and arresting; but it
also retains a kind of pride: the Nile mud has to be *fertile* for the sun's
rays to work upon it. H returns to the image of the Nile – associated
this time with God, rather than the king – in the final poem of the col-
lection (40), evidence of its careful structure and arrangement.

2   *sun*: Horace compares Augustus to the sun in the praise poems
       of his fourth book of *Odes*. *Odes* IV was a particularly influen-
       tial model upon later Latin panegyric.

To His Most Glorious Highness, Charles,
Prince of Wales, and Prince of Youth

Metre: hendecasyllables.

3   *May you . . . a lenient eye*: This line reworks Tibullus, 2.1.80.
5-6   *bookworms . . . black moths*: Worms and moths – both of which
       destroy parchment and paper – are mentioned in a similar con-
       text by Martial (*Epigrams*, 14.37); their destruction of literary
       works is associated with envious resentment and the threat of
       obscurity.

To the Most Reverend Father in Christ
and Lord, the Bishop of Winchester, &c.

Metre: elegiac couplets. The Bishop of Winchester at this date was
Lancelot Andrewes (1555-1626), famous for his scholarship and the
intricate style of his sermons. Theologically, he was Anglican, steering
a middle course between the Puritan and Catholic positions, and as
such an appropriate dedicatee for this collection. In 1601 Andrewes

was appointed dean at Westminster Abbey, with overall responsibility for Westminster School; he left to become Bishop of Chichester in 1605, at the end of H's first year. There is also evidence that H consulted Andrewes around the time that he was appointed Orator in 1620.

3   *empty numbers*: 'Numbers' here refers to poetic metre. H personifies his own poetry book, which, aware of its poetic shortcomings, is ashamed to stop at Andrewes's door. H perhaps also refers to Andrewes's talent for serious prose (in contrast to his own for poetry).

EPIGRAMS IN DEFENCE OF THE DISCIPLINE OF OUR CHURCH

1. To the King
The Reason for Writing Epigrams.

Metre: elegiac couplets. A dedication to the monarch early in a book of epigrams is a feature of both classical and early modern epigram collections (compare, for example, the fourth poem of both Martial's and Ben Jonson's *Epigrams*).

5   *Cathars*: The Cathars were Christian dualists with a popular following in southern Europe from the twelfth to the fourteenth centuries. Ferociously persecuted as heretics by the Catholic Church, they disappeared by the middle of the fourteenth century. In texts of H's time, however, *Cathars* is often used, as here, as a denigrating term for the Puritans; *your books*: James I wrote several works of poetry, theology and on the theory of kingship. Jonson's *Epigrams* (1616) also address James as both monarch and author: 'How, best of kings, dost thou a sceptre bear! / How, best of poets, dost thou laurel wear!' (*Epigrams*, 4.1–2).
6   *crumbs*: The Latin word here, *analecta*, is used twice by Martial in similar contexts.

2. To Melville

Metre: elegiac couplets. This gracious and witty poem tacitly acknowledges what a reader might find unseemly: the attack upon a senior scholar by a young student. (Melville was almost sixty when he wrote the *Anti-Tami-Cami-Categoria*, and seventy-five in 1620; the poems of this collection date to H's mid-to-late twenties at the latest, and some may be considerably earlier.) W. Hilton Kelliher comments that in this epigram H 'borrows and then restores the elder's years as a duellist returns a defeated adversary's weapon' (in J. W. Binns, *The Latin Poetry of English Poets* (London: Routledge, 1974), p. 31). Note also the shared imagery of youth and age that links this poem to the second dedicatory poem, to Charles, Prince of Wales.

3. To the Same.
On the Monstrosity of the Phrase
Anti-Tami-Cami-Categoria

To the same: i.e., Melville.
Metre: elegiac couplets. This epigram plays on the extravagant and rather awkward title of Melville's poem, which has four components: *Anti-* ('against'), *Tami-* (the River Thames, which runs through Oxford), *Cami-* (the River Cam, which runs through Cambridge) and *Categoria* (Greek: 'accusation'). In response, H offers two possible titles for a collection of replies, both of which imitate the rhyme between the two middle elements: *Anti-furi-Puri-Categoria* (line 8), in which *furi-* means 'furious' or 'raging' and *Puri-* stands for 'Puritans'; and *Anti-pelvi-Melvi-Categoria* (line 10) in which *pelvi-* is short for *pelvis*, another word for *pollubrum*, a wash bowl or basin, and *Melvi-* stands for Melville himself.

9   *And since . . . the Royal altar*: Among other rituals, Melville was
     opposed to the ceremonial washing of hands at the altar, using a
     ritual basin, which was practised by Lancelot Andrewes, Dean of
     the Chapel Royal (hence the mention of the royal altar).
10   *Anti-Basin-Melville-Accusations*: See introductory note above
     on this coinage. The choice of words in the Latin phrase
     Anti-pelvi-Melvi-Categoria creates a rhyme (*pelvi-Melvi*) which
     suggests 'pell-mell'.

4. Division of the Anti-Tami-Cami-Categoria

Metre: elegiac couplets. H analyses Melville's poem under three headings. He sets aside two of them – on sacred authors and the worship of God himself – as being points of agreement. The tone of this poem is noticeably jocular (rather than aggressive) and, in fact, rather respectful.

5. On the Type of Metre

Metre: elegiac couplets. H makes fun of Melville for writing his long polemical poem on ritual practice and religious conduct in sapphics, a metrical scheme inherited from the female poet Sappho. (Though sapphics are also the second most common metre in Horace's *Odes*, and were widely used by neo-Latin lyric imitators of Horace in the Renaissance – see the Appendix on metrical forms.) H's mocking list of alternative suggestions draws attention to the marked metrical variety of his own collection. The poem includes many terms with erotic, romantic or feminine connotations, implying that Melville's choice of metre is unmanly and aimed principally at women.

4   *propped on heroes' lofty feet*: The *lofty feet* of heroes refers to hexameter, the metre used in epic poetry. The pun on *pedes* (both literal 'feet' and the 'feet' or unit-divisions in a line of poetry) is a commonplace of Latin poetry.

5   *mournful elegiacs*: i.e., elegiac couplets, the metre of this poem, as well as most of H's collection. It was the most commonly used metre for Latin epigram in the period, and despite its characterization here as *mournful*, was not confined to poems of mourning or lament (the modern sense of 'elegiac'); *sharp iambic*: The various iambic metres, all based upon a short followed by a long syllable, include iambic trimeters, iambic dimeters and various combinations and variations of these. H gives examples of most of these in the course of the collection. Iambic metres are associated with poetry of insult and invective, both in the ancient Greek authors Archilochus and Hipponax, and the imitation of these forms by Catullus and Martial in their epigrams and Horace in his *Epodes*.

6. On the Bewitched Gorgon

Metre: elegiac couplets. This epigram alludes to the full title of Melville's poem, which includes the phrase *Contra larvatam geminae Academiae Gorgonem*: 'Against the ghostly Gorgon of the two Universities'. Melville characterizes Oxford and Cambridge combined as the Gorgon Medusa, with flashing eyes that turn men to stone, and hair made of snakes. H suggests a wilful misinterpretation of Melville's title, using a learned reference to read 'Gorgon' as meaning 'Pallas Athene', goddess of wisdom and learning (see note on line 4). Cf. H's treatment of the Gorgon in his ode on the death of Prince Henry in 1612 (included in *Other Latin Poems*).

4   *Pallas*: Pallas Athena is described as having 'the face of the Gor-
     gon' in Sophocles' play *Ajax* (line 450). The epithet refers to
     Athena's *aegis*, her shield, which bore an image of the Gorgon.
     Athena helped Perseus to kill the Gorgon Medusa.

7. On the Pride of the Bishops

Metre: elegiac couplets.

4   *panelled ceilings*: The resonant Latin word *laquearibus*, meaning
     a panelled or coffered ceiling, is associated in Latin literature
     with grand royal or noble palaces – including Dido's palace in
     the *Aeneid* (1.726) and the houses of the great in Horace, *Odes*
     2.16.11. H uses a related word (with ironic humour) to describe
     his humble cottage in *Memoriae Matris Sacrae*, 7.22.
5   *Sun*: Note that the king is compared to the sun in the first dedica-
     tory poem to the sequence. James I was a keen supporter of the
     episcopacy.

8. On the Two Universities

Metre: iambic distichs (iambic trimeter followed by iambic dimeter).
In this poem, as in epigram 6, H characterizes and defends the uni-
versities as patrons of scholarship and the arts. The second half of
the poem is an early example of the telescope being used metaphori-
cally. For the characterization of Melville as a beast, which bites
and kicks, compare Ben Jonson, *Poetaster* (1601), 'Apologetical Dia-
logue', in which Jonson describes his attempts to keep his work 'Safe
from the wolf's black jaw and the dull ass's hoof' (line 226). H's
imagery subtly casts Melville as hostile to poetry as well as to the
universities.

2   *black tooth*: A 'black tooth' is a conventional attribute of the
     poet of satire or invective; cf. Horace, *Epode* 6.15.
4   *double throne of the Muses*: i.e., the two universities, Oxford
     and Cambridge.
6   *kicks*: The detail of kicking casts Melville as a ferocious animal,
     another trope of the invective poet (cf. Horace, *Epode* 6, in
     which the poet is characterized as a fierce dog or bull).
11   *Belgian telescope*: The Latin word for telescope, *perspicillum*, is
     first recorded in 1610 and was used by Francis Bacon in his
     Novum Organum (1620). Milton uses the imagery of the tele-
     scope in *Paradise Lost* (3.588–90, 5.261–3).

9. On the Sacred Rite of Baptism

Metre: elegiac couplets. This epigram is concerned with Melville's opposition to the practice of posing questions to the child who is presented for baptism, which are answered on his or her behalf. The Latin text plays upon the literal meaning of *infans*, 'infant' or 'young child', as 'one who does not speak'. H wrote two English poems on 'Holy Baptism'.

3–4 *Land which . . . everlasting God*: These lines seem to allude to the idea of baptized Christians as heirs of the kingdom of God.
15 *promise of heaven*: The word here means literally 'bail', hence the reproach of the final line.

10. On the Sign of the Cross

Metre: iambic trimeter. Melville rejected the use of the sign of the cross in baptism, as it is not mentioned in scripture. H makes two main points in reply: (1) Tertullian compared every Christian at the font of baptism to a fish, and (2) when swimming, the natural position of the arms forms a cross. Donne makes the same point in his poem 'The Crosse', line 19: 'Swimme, and at every stroake, thou art thy Crosse.'

11. On the Oath to the Church

Metre: elegiac couplets. This short epigram revolves around a Latin pun. The word *articulus* can mean both 'article' (as in the sacred articles, to which those who took the oath to the church subscribed) and 'joint'. Gout (*podagra*) – a painful and disfiguring disease of the joints in the foot – is a common theme of Latin satire and epigram, in which it is typically associated with the rich and self-indulgent. (See, for instance, Horace, *Satires*, 2.7.15, and *Epistles*, 1.131; Martial, *Epigrams*, 1.99.2, 9.92.9.)

12. On the Purification after Childbirth

Metre: elegiac couplets. This epigram addresses the custom of women attending church for a ceremony of purification shortly after the birth of a child – another of the rites opposed by Melville. In a remarkably personal and psychologically interesting move, H suggests that Melville's opposition to this practice and his lifelong religious ardour are both an attempt to make up for the loss of his own mother's prayers. Melville's mother died, shortly after his father, when Melville was only about two years old. H's own intense relationship with his mother is the subject of his memorial sequence for her, *Memoriae Matris Sacrum*.

9–10 *If everyday dishes . . . holy praise*: The point here is that if we
are expected to give thanks each time we eat, how much more
should we give thanks for the birth of children.

13–14 *So when the wife . . . birth to her children*: These lines allude
to the narrative of the Fall in Genesis 3.

13. On the Priestly Beauty of the Antichrist

Metre: elegiac couplets. Melville refers to the priestly beauty of the Antichrist in lines 47–8 of his poem.

14. On the Surplice

Metre: sapphics. This piece in sapphics (the same metre as Melville's original poem) defends the Anglican use of the surplice, a long white linen or cotton tunic worn by clergymen.

4   *black teeth*: a typical characteristic of the envious attack; see
Horace, *Epode* 6.15, and the notes on poem 8 above.

5   *better urn*: an allusion to the myth told in *Iliad* 24, that two jars
or urns stand in the palace of Zeus, one full of good fortune, the
other of evil.

13–14 *From all the creatures . . . for man to follow*: A marginal note
here indicates that sheep and doves are meant, with a reference
to Columella, *De Re Rustica*, describing a preference for white
wool and white doves. See also Matthew 10:16.

20   *And triumphs in its whiteness*: The final line is a multiple pun:
Albion albo. Albion is 'England', *albo* is 'white', but the line
refers also to the alb – a long white form of surplice.

15. On the Biretta

Metre: hendecasyllables. Melville had also opposed the wearing of the biretta, a cap with three or four peaks or corns, considered Romish in style. H defends it (in preference to the skullcap) on the grounds of its shape and position, which, he ironically suggests, would be more 'cooling' to the overheated brains of Melville and his party than the closely fitting skullcap.

16. Against the Puritan

Metre: elegiac couplets.

3   *Hellas*: Greece.
6   *This is the only . . . suits your nose*: Kelliher (ibid., p. 30) sug-
     gests that this is an allusion to Melville's Scots accent. However,
     several contemporary texts refer to the nasal speech of the Puri-
     tans. See for instance Ben Jonson, *The Case is Altered* (1609), in
     which Aurelia says: 'but learne to speak i'the nose, and turne
     puritan presently' (1.5). In an unpublished poem, written in
     response to H's death in 1633 and titled 'On Mr Herberts Devine
     poeme the church', John Polwhele used a similar motif to char-
     acterize Anglican versus Puritan styles of worship: 'Where is
     most Catholique Conformitie / Without a nose-twange spoylinge
     harmonie' (Bodleian MS Eng. poet. f. 16, f.11).

17. On Bishops

Metre: 'lesser' asclepiad (asclepiad line repeated). The rather weak end-
ing to this epigram argues that even if bishops are an imperfect
institution, it is better to have just a few than to have every presbyter
ranking as a bishop. In 1617 Lancelot Andrewes had visited Scotland
with James I in an effort to persuade the Scottish church of the bene-
fits of episcopacy over Presbyterianism.

11   *O blind people*: Milton's lines on corrupt clergy make a useful
     comparison: 'Blind mouths! that scarce themselves know how to
     hold / A sheep-hook, or have learned aught else the least / That
     to the faithful herdsman's art belongs!' (*Lycidas*, lines 119-21).

18. To Melville: On the Same

Metre: elegiac couplets. Weavers, tailors and other craftsmen were
particularly associated with Puritanism at this time. See also the fol-
lowing poem.

19. On the Puritan Weaver

Metre: elegiac couplets.

6   *both those Texts*: This depends on an ambiguity in Latin between the 'text' of scripture, and the 'text' of woven fabric. (*Textus* means literally 'woven'.)

20. On Magical Whirling

Metre: iambic trimeter. Melville's poem compares the priest's words to an infant at baptism to the noise of a screech owl (since words addressed to a young baby are without meaning to him) and sacred music to the clash of Phrygian cymbals. Melville's vocabulary is drawn from ancient descriptions of witchcraft, especially of the witch Canidia in Horace, *Epode* 5. H repeats some of these key terms in a way meant to make Melville's accusations seem ridiculous; he plays in particular on the Puritan reputation for noisy prayer and preaching.

21. To the Brothers

Metre: elegiac couplets. The *brothers* in question are both Roman Catholic friars and Puritan brethren.

22. On Spots and Stains

Metre: iambic trimeter. H's little parable is essentially a version of Matthew 7:3: 'And why beholdest thou the mote that is in thy brother's eye, but considerest not the beam that is in thine own eye?'

23. On Sacred Music

Metre: alcaics, the most common metre of Horace's *Odes*. This particularly rich and ambitious poem lies at the heart of *Musae Responsoriae*. Its length, allusive sophistication and personal tone demonstrate H's particular investment in the question of sacred music, which is here aligned very closely with poetry. (On this, see also the English poem 'Church-music'.) The poem combines classical (Orpheus, Amphion) and Christian (David) aetiologies of music and song, and the landscape that responds to that song is likewise both classical (the rivers Tiber and Po at lines 43–4) and biblical (the River

Jordan, line 42). A rich array of allusions, as well as the choice of metre, relate the poem to Horace in particular, with echoes of two of Horace's major odes of poetic confidence and inspiration.

1   *Deucalion*: a reference to the myth of the flood, inflicted by Zeus, which Deucalion and his wife Pyrrha alone survived. Afterwards, they repopulated the earth by scattering stones which grew into men and women. This opening image is closely connected to that found at *Memoriae Matris Sacrum* 12. Cf. also the *man of stone* in the first poem of *Lucus*: the power to overcome a stony heart is associated by H with both God and music.

4   *Rocks and useless crags*: The Latin phrase here is a close imitation of a line from Horace, *Odes* 2.20.24. The Horatian phrase is the very last line of his second book of *Odes*, and the imitation here appears in the same metrical position. Horace's poem describes the poet's metamorphosis into a bird, an image of his immortal power.

14   *shaken*: The Latin word here, *percussa*, meaning 'struck' or 'shaken', can also be used in Latin for the onset of poetic inspiration; *tortoise-shell*: that is, a lyre made from a tortoiseshell.

15   *Amphion*: The walls of Thebes rose magically at the sound of Amphion's song. Amphion and his tortoiseshell lyre are described at Horace, *Ars Poetica* 394–6.

23   *To where do you call me*: A similar phrase is found in one of Horace's most famous odes about poetic inspiration, *Odes* 3.25.1, addressed to Bacchus.

25   *wonderful thumb*: The thumb was used in tuning the lyre.

28   *new guest*: This is a version of the motif of 'katasterism', widely used in panegyric poetry, in which a human character is raised on their death to the heavens and transformed into a star or a constellation. Here H imagines his own soul borne to the stars (that is, heaven) under the inspiration of music.

29–32 *Moses . . . to the Lord*: For Moses' song of triumph, see Exodus 15.

33–6 *What is this . . . better world*: For a similar sequence of vivid metaphors, cf. 'Prayer (1)'.

42   *Jordan itself . . . in amazement*: Joshua 3 recounts how the waters of the Jordan were divided so that the priests bearing the Ark of the Covenant could pass through on dry land.

47–8 *To make more . . . your pulpits*: A reference to the Puritan preference for preaching rather than music, strongly resisted by Hooker in *Of the Laws of Ecclesiastical Polity* (1597).

24. On the Same

Metre: elegiac couplet. Melville had described the singing of hymns as *mugitus*, a word used of the lowing of cattle. H responds that he would rather *low* (like a cow) than *rudere*, a word used of the roaring of lions and (in Ovid and the satiric poet Persius) the braying of an ass. The latter is probably what is meant here, as asses are associated with folly.

25. On the Use of Rites

Metre: glyconics. The glyconic line is the basis of many metrical arrangements, including the asclepiad and sapphic stanzas. Neither Horace nor Catullus used a sequence of pure glyconic lines as H does here, but repeated glyconics are found in Seneca's tragic choruses (e.g. *Hercules Furens*, 875–94). Cf. also Richard Crashaw's long poem in glyconics, *Bulla*.

The guiding metaphor of this poem describes the rites and rituals of the English Church as her clothing; and clothing as a feature that both distinguishes civilized men (like the Romans on their arrival in Britain) from savages, and also protects vulnerable women from rape. It uses the conventional image of the Church as the 'bride of Christ', but in a particularly vivid way: the Puritan bride, left naked, is vulnerable to assault by other men. H explores the same idea in the English poem 'The British Church'.

5–6 *Living without . . . he cried*: The Latin of these lines is marked by particularly heavy alliteration.
19–22 *For scripture . . . and naked*: Hutchinson identifies the scriptural passages alluded to here: that the debtor should be allowed to retain his clothes (Deuteronomy 24:13), but that clothes that do not belong to him should be given to the naked (Ezekiel 18:7). The Church, it is implied, is such a debtor (to God), but she should not be stripped of the clothes that are properly hers (i.e., in H's view, the use of sacred rites).

26. On the Wedding Ring

Metre: elegiac couplets. The water imagery of this poem continues in the following piece. The metaphorical association between a literal storm or flood (such as the biblical flood, the end of which was marked by the rainbow) and the destructive powers of erotic passion is a classical commonplace, found for instance in Horace, *Odes* 1.5.

3–4 *If you disapprove ... of heaven's water*: See Genesis 9.13–17 for
       the rainbow appearing to Noah after the flood as a mark of
       God's covenant with man never to flood the world again.
5   *For that image ... from ours*: This line is borrowed, only slightly
       altered, from Horace, *Satires* 2.3.320, in which Horace's slave
       Damasippus offers Horace various unflattering comparisons
       that reflect his own folly.

27. On the Pure and the Worldly

Metre: iambic distichs (iambic trimeter followed by iambic dimeter).
On the pure and the worldly: The Latin title of the poem, *De Mundis
et mundanis*, puns upon the similar words *mundus* ('pure' or 'clean')
and *mundanus* ('of the world', so in a religious context 'wordly' or
'irreligious').

3   *worldly man and the Puritan*: The two characters are dubbed
       Cosmicos and *Catharus*. *Catharus*, literally 'a Cathar', is regu-
       larly used to mean a Puritan. *Cosmicos* is the Latin form of the
       Greek word for *mundanus*, 'wordly'.

28. On the Lord's Prayer

Metre: Third Archilochian (iambic trimeter, followed by a dactylic
hemiepes and an iambic dimeter). Classical texts would usually print
the second and third lines of each stanza as a single line, to form
couplets.

4   *Sevenfold*: The Lord's Prayer has seven verses. The shield of Ajax
       (line 5) was made of seven layers. Cf. Shakespeare, *Antony and
       Cleopatra*: 'The seven-fold shield of Ajax cannot keep / The bat-
       tery from my heart,' says Antony (5.15.38–9).

29. On a Certain Puritan

Metre: elegiac couplets. The poem mocks the enthusiastic style of
Puritan preaching, and suggests that it can be self-indulgent and
self-important.

2   *savage armpit goat*: The *goat* that lives in the armpit – a refer-
       ence to the sharp and unpleasant smell – is found at Catullus
       69.6 and Ovid, *Ars Amatoria* 3.193, in a similar phrase to H's
       line.

30. On the She-Wolf of the Vatican Brothel

Metre: iambic trimeter. In Duport's 1662 publication of *Musae Responsoriae*, this poem was followed by the anagram epigram reproduced as *Lucus* 25.

4   *Charybdis ... Scylla*: two monsters (or nautical obstacles) either side of the strait between Italy and Sicily. In the *Odyssey* Odysseus is forced to choose between them. H describes how the Anglican Church steers a path between the extremes of Roman Catholicism and Puritanism in 'The British Church'.

31. On the Laying on of Hands

Metre: iambic trimeter. This short piece centres on the similarity between two related Latin words: *impositio*, the term used for the 'laying on' of hands in a healing rite, and *imponere*, which can mean 'impose', 'inflict' and even 'cheat' or 'trick' (as in the modern English 'imposture'). In the Book of Common Prayer laying on of hands is part of the rites of confirmation and the ordination of priests and bishops.

32. The Frenzy of the Petitioning Ministers: In the Comic Mode

Metre: iambic trimeter. *The Frenzy ... Comic Mode*: The term *raptus* in the title suggests divine inspiration of the most violent – especially Bacchic – type. The final word of the title is a Greek term meaning 'in the comic mode', a reference to ancient comedy. The Roman numerals in the poem identify each of the five 'acts' in the drama. The implication is that the behaviour of Puritans is both ridiculous and predictable.

7-8   *Then he breaks out ... Roams the woods*: The initial disapproval and secretive plotting, followed by loss of control and the mention of roaming the woods suggests in particular the story of the *Bacchae*, in which Pentheus opposes the cult of Dionysus, but is finally seized by the god himself. In his frenzy he ranges wildly in the forest and is finally torn to pieces by female followers of Bacchus, including his own mother.

9-10   *he dashes off ... back on again*: H's mini-drama has a gentler conclusion: the Puritan simply destroys his clothes (or the clothes of his soul) in his enthusiasm and returns to Holland for repair.

Puritans were particularly associated with Calvinist Holland, and (because many Dutch immigrants were tailors or weavers) with those professions also alluded to here.

33. On the Enumeration of Authors

Metre: elegiac couplets. Hutchinson notes: 'The Oxford resolution against the Millenary Petition contained the boast that "there are at this day more learned men in this kingdom than are to be found among all the ministers of religion in all Europe besides." Melville replied with a catalogue of Protestant divines on the Continent and at home.'

3   *Martyr*: Peter Martyr Vermigli (born Piero Mariano, 1499–1562), an Italian theologian who converted from Roman Catholicism to Protestantism and was an influential figure in Reformation theology. *Calvin*: John Calvin (1509–64), French theologian whose thought led to the Calvinist movement. *Beza*: Theodore Beza (1519–1605), French theologian and scholar, a follower of Calvin and another important Reformation figure. *Bucer*: Martin Bucer (1491–1551), an early Protestant reformer, originally a Dominican, who left the order after meeting Luther.

5   *Whitaker*: William Whitaker (1548–95), an important Anglican theologian and Master of St John's College, Cambridge.

15 *Constantine*: Constantine the Great, Roman Emperor 306–37 CE. The first emperor to convert to Christianity, after a vision of the Cross before his victory against Maxentius at the Milvian Bridge in 312 CE. He proclaimed tolerance of all religions throughout the Empire.

17 *man from Hippo*: St Augustine of Hippo (354–430 CE), early Christian theologian and Bishop of Hippo (in present-day Algeria).

19 *Ambrose*: Aurelius Ambrosius (c. 340–97 CE), archbishop of Milan, noted in particular for his correspondence with and influence upon St Augustine. He is believed to be the author, with Augustine, of the Latin hymn 'Te Deum Laudamus'. The following line puns on his name, which means 'ambrosia', the sweet food of the classical gods.

23 *James*: James I, the monarch at the time.

27 *Apostolic Succession*: The Latin term *Ordo* denotes the Apostolic Succession; the same word is used again in the following line, meaning 'battle array', the arrangement of an army.

31-2 *One day . . . destroyed them all*: These lines are taken from
Ovid, *Fasti* 2.235-6, with the single substitution of *Catharos*
('Puritans') for *Fabios* ('the Fabii').

34. *On the Holy Greed for Gold*

Metre: elegiac couplets. H's collection as a whole follows roughly the
order of Melville's poem, and here he addresses its closing sequence,
on excessive luxury and display in church worship. The title *De auri
sacrâ fame* quotes the first line of the last stanza of Melville's poem
('Quid fames auri sacra?', 197).

2   *Aeacus*: mythical king of Aegina, renowned for his justice in life,
who became one of the judges in the Underworld after his death.
H addresses Melville ironically as 'Aeacus' to draw attention to
his judgemental pronouncements.

3   *mackerel*: an image of poems being reused to wrap spices or fish
is a trope of classical satire and invective, suggesting that the work
is worthless and deserves only to be discarded. The closest parallel
here is Martial 3.1.9 (which also names *scombris*, 'mackerel').

35. *To Scotland. An Exhortation to Peace*

Metre: elegiac couplets. The 'heat' (as well as the noise) of Puritan
preaching and worship is a theme throughout H's collection. Cf. 29 on
the sweating Puritan preacher. Here the motif is creatively juxtaposed
with Scotland's reputation for cold weather.

3   *Antiperistasis*: a Greek word used in philosophy for any process
in which one quality heightens the force of another, opposing
quality: here the cold of Scotland is imagined to fuel the heat of
Puritan excess.

36. *To the Innocent Who Have been Led Astray*

Metre: elegiac couplets. Here H is at pains to distinguish between the
Puritan leaders – of whom he disapproves – and the innocence and
genuine piety of their followers.

37. *To Melville*

Metre: hendecasyllables. This interesting poem appropriates Horace's
rhetoric of satiric impotence (found particularly in the *Epodes*) to

stress H's essential respect and good intentions towards Melville. In combination with the previous poem, 36, it marks a relaxation in the closing stages of the sequence. Kelliher describes the poem as 'a minor masterpiece of ironic compliment' (ibid., p. 30). He also points out that the good-humoured tone of the poem is rare in religious debate of the time. The combined declaration of savage satirical power and the decision not to employ it is described in similar terms to that of Ben Jonson's 'Apologetical Dialogue' to *Poetaster* (1601), especially lines 144–66.

5   *city*: Edinburgh.

8   *Which no signature debased*: This line refers to the signing of the Millenary Petition.

12   *toothless*: Satire or invective is traditionally 'sharp-toothed' or 'biting' (see Horace, *Satires* 1.4.93 and the 'black tooth' of poems 8.2 and 14.4). To be 'toothless' is therefore to be without true aggressive intention or effect. Compare Jonson, 'Apologetical Dialogue' to *Poetaster*, lines 61–3: 'I can profess I never writ that piece / More innocent, or empty of offence. / Some salt it had, but neither tooth nor gall.'

17   *Athens*: the universities of Oxford and Cambridge.

19–20   *I would by now . . . crackling Greek one*: These lines combine the Roman Muses (*Camoenis*) and the Greek ones. H knowingly declares that of course he *could* destroy Melville if he wished to, but has chosen not to.

25   *paper . . . smeared*: The Latin phrase here, *charta . . . delibuta*, is a more polite version of a famous phrase from Catullus' invective, *cacata charta*, meaning pages smeared with excrement, or used as toilet paper (Catullus 36.1).

27   *Hercules*: Hercules was unwittingly poisoned by a cloak soaked in the blood of the centaur Nessus, who had been shot by Hercules using arrows tipped in the poison of the Lernaean Hydra. Hercules' wife Deianira gave him the cloak believing it would secure his fidelity to her.

33–41   *I have not used . . . Although you deserve it*: These lines list some of the insults directed at the Anglicans in Melville's poem. Several of these feature in poem 20.

40   *Berecynthian*: Berecynthus is a mountain in Phrygia, sacred to the goddess Cybele. 'Berecynthian' thus suggests the worship of Cybele, marked by the beating of drums.

43   *Caesar is . . . only sober man*: The poem ends with a perhaps respectful, perhaps ironic comparison between Melville and Caesar.

38. To the Same

Metre: elegiac couplets.

39. To His Most Serene Majesty

Metre: hexameter. This penultimate poem addressed to the king is one of the most substantial of the collection, and the only piece in hexameters, the metre of epic poetry. Its opening depiction of the peculiar blessedness and perfection of British Christianity is particularly memorable.

1   *trifles*: The Latin word, *nugas*, suggests trivial and insignificant poems. The word is repeated at the close of the poem (line 38, *nugis*) where it is associated specifically with poetry. The repetition suggests both that others' poetry (especially Melville's) is artistically insignificant compared to his own, and (in the closing movement of the poem) that H's own pleasure in and mastery of verse should be secondary to his devotion to his king and his religion. This ambiguity in his attitude to his art is typical of H; see the notes on *Memoriae Matris Sacrum* 4 (which uses the related verb *nugor*) and 19.

8–13 *Everywhere . . . its fullest form*: This description of the admiration of the British church by her neighbours, by the angels and even Christ himself bears comparison with the passage in Milton's *In Quintum Novembris* in which the Devil expresses his envy of English worship (lines 25–47). Although not published until 1645, *In Quintum Novembris* is one of Milton's early poems, a tour de force of mock-epic hexameters on the Gunpowder Plot of 1605. See also the notes on *Lucus* 32 (*The Triumph of Death*), H's own attempt at mock-epic hexameter verse.

15–16 *Set these lands . . . jewel in a box*: The imagery of these lines is reminiscent of the famous description of England's 'sceptred isle' in Shakespeare's *Richard II* (2.1). H's English poem 'The British Church', which covers similar ground, also alludes to this scene (see note on line 29 of that poem).

40. To God

Metre: Third asclepiad (glyconic followed by a lesser asclepiad). Many poetry collections of the period end with a final hymn to God, even if the collection itself is not concerned with religious or devotional matters (e.g., the final poem of Jonson's *Forest* (1616)). This poem combines the rich fullness of God with motifs of divine inspiration, associating both the poet and the collection (and, by implication, its viewpoint) with God himself.

The first and last lines of the poem imitate Horace, *Odes* 4.3 (1–4 and 24). The final line quotes the last line of Horace's poem, but replaces the Latin word *spiro* ('breathe') with *scribo* ('write'). *Odes* 4.3 is itself a major poem of gratitude for the gift of inspiration (addressed in Horace's case to his Muse). H's choice of metre contributes to the imitation, as *Odes* 4.3 is also in the third asclepiad, a relatively unusual metre.

9   *Nile*: This image of the Nile's fertility links this poem with the
     first dedicatory poem preceding the collection, where it is also a
     metaphor for poetic creativity (though there applied not to God,
     but to James I). Compare also the evocation of the River Thames
     in spate at *Memoriae Matris Sacrum* 18.

LUCUS
THE SACRED GROVE

The Latin title of this collection, *Lucus*, means a 'wood' or 'grove' and often specifically a thicket of trees sacred to a deity. The habit of naming a collection of varied poems a 'wood' (in Latin, *silva*) has its origin in the five collections of *Silvae* written by the Latin imperial poet Statius in the reign of Domitian in the late first century CE. Statius' *Silvae* are occasional poems, principally of praise and celebration of the emperor and his ministers, their culture, achievements and lifestyle. Several Renaissance and early modern authors revived the use of wood or woodland words as titles for collections of poetry, but the most significant model for H is that of Ben Jonson, whose best-known verse collection is *The Forest* (1616). The choice of the term *lucus* (rather than simply *silva*) adds a suggestion of religious feeling appropriate to the content of H's collection. There is no direct evidence for the date of *Lucus*, although poems 26–8, on Pope Urban VIII, must date from after the Pope's election in August 1623, and probably quite soon after.

The form of these poems, most of which are brief and address particular points of doctrine, devotion or morality, are best understood as epigrams; although *Lucus* 32, 'Triumphus Mortis' ('The Triumph of

Death'), at 101 hexameter lines, in which Death himself speaks, is closest to an epyllion or mock-epic fragment. The precedent for the inclusion of this poem here is perhaps also to be found in Jonson, whose collection of *Epigrams* (1616) concludes with a not dissimilar piece of mock-epic (*Epigrams* 133, 'On the Famous Voyage'). The Latin poems on the Gunpowder Plot by Campion ('De Pulverea Coniuratione') and Milton ('In Quintum Novembris') are also comparable in tone and style to this interesting longer piece.

Even generous readers of H have mostly found *Lucus* unrewarding. Kelliher remarks that 'few poems will compete with the English as a record of H's daily communings with God' (ibid., p. 35). Modern – that is, post-romantic – tastes tend to find the formalized wit and wordplay of early modern epigrams unappealing, or at least not the 'stuff of poetry'. *Lucus* has also been criticized for its random assembly of apparently only loosely related pieces, probably the product of several years' work, of 'no single theme or clearly definable structure' (Kelliher, ibid., p. 39). This is perhaps unfair: there are multiple links of theme and imagery between these poems and their cumulative effect adds up to more than the sum of their parts. The collection should be read as a sequential whole.

Thematically, the collection ranges across religious, moral and patriotic themes. Classical allusions are indebted in particular to moralizing Latin authors (Martial, Horace, Juvenal, Seneca and Persius) as well as, of course, to the Bible.

Note on metres: Most of these poems are composed in elegiac couplets (a dactylic hexameter followed by a pentameter). This is one of the most widespread and versatile of Latin metres, particularly frequently used in Renaissance and early modern Latin verse, for poetry of all kinds and on a great variety of themes. Other metres found in this collection are hendecasyllables (an eleven-syllable metre found in the epigrams of Catullus and Martial) and iambic trimeters (also commonly used for epigrams). Finally, the mock-epic 32 *Triumphus Mortis* is in hexameters, the epic metre of Homer and Virgil, as well as, for instance, Catullus' own 'mini-epic', poem 64.

1. *Man, a Statue*

Metre: elegiac couplets (a dactylic hexameter followed by a pentameter), the most common metre for epigrams, but one also associated with personal address of various kinds (e.g., dedicatory poems and love elegies).

This unusual opening poem replaces several conventional opening gambits – such as an address to a Muse, a patron or dedicatee – with a prayer to God, requesting not inspiration but some softening of the heart (perhaps an openness to poetic inspiration?) which is reimagined as a partial reversal or at least limitation of the effects of the Fall. These effects – of human sin – are imagined as a kind of metamorphosis from flesh, or earth, to stone. The central image is probably indebted to Ezekiel 36.26: 'I will take away the stony heart out of your flesh, and I will give you an heart of flesh.' The emotional tone of this short piece is complex: in a manner typical of H's English poetry, it suggests both intense dependence on and devotion to God, alongside a hint of frustration and resentment, much as one might feel towards a recalcitrant lover.

Man, a Statue: The title of the poem plays with the implications of the key term 'image'. In Latin *imago* can mean various kinds of likeness or copy, including a statue or a mask.

1   *Image of God*: Genesis 1.27: 'So God created man in his own image.' The Latin word *imago* is the term used in the Vulgate at this point. In interpreting *imago* in this context as a statue, H is perhaps also thinking of the account at Genesis 2.7 of God forming Adam by shaping the earth. H adds to the familiar idea of man as the 'image of God' by specifying that he is *saxea* – a stony image, one made of rock (not the earth or clay implied in the Genesis story). As the second line makes clear, the idea is that the original softness of man has become stony, 'hardened over' at the Fall.

3   *Coral flowers*: Ancient authorities believed that coral was a plant that hardened into something resembling stone when it was removed from the water. (Pliny, *Natural History*, 32.2.11).

4   *Adam*: H is perhaps mindful here of the etymology of 'Adam' as 'of the earth'. The transition of earth to stone is one of progressive hardening, here an image of sinful separation from God.

5   *You who ... marble to weep*: Here H turns to address God, as creator of all things, directly. For the motif of weeping marble see 'The Church-Floor', lines 13–15, which also relates the weeping of marble to the cleansing of sin, as well as 'Ephesians 4:30', line 23.

6   *heart*: H ends his plea by focusing not on his body as a whole, but specifically on his heart (*cor*). The motif of a heart as hard as (or harder than) stone is a common one, introduced often in erotic or romantic contexts. Generally in such contexts the

speaker enjoins a beloved to soften towards him, not to be 'too hard'; whereas here H asks God to allow his own (H's) heart to remain, at least, not harder than stone.

2. Homeland

Metre: elegiac couplets. The relationship between the title of this poem (*Patria*, 'homeland', 'native land' or 'the land of one's fathers') and its content is oblique. But the yearning theme of the poem compares the flame that sends sparks up to the sky to the mind confined to the body but sending up prayers to heaven. The point of the title seems to be the yearning for heaven – the land of one's heavenly father – while limited to one's bodily state. The imagery is rather aggressive: the mind is compared first to a flame and then to a sharpened spear point, turned upon the body and ultimately capable of boring *right through*. Rather similar imagery – though in a much more extensive form – can be found in Richard Crashaw's 'The Flaming Heart'. Cf. also the imagery of flame and fire in H's own 'Love' (II).

1   *As the slender . . . up to heaven*: The way in which a flame seems to aspire upwards is a common source of imagery. Fire in general is also a common image for passionate feeling.
6   *bore . . . right through*: The translation here represents a single Latin word, *perterebrare*. It is a very strong and concrete term, used in classical sources only in the most literal sense of boring stone, and it has a technical feel in Latin. As such, it suggests the force and precision of the assault of the mind upon the body, but also the considerable resistance that the body creates.

3. On Stephen, Stoned

Metre: elegiac couplets. The phrasing of the title is striking. Not 'on the stoning of Stephen', but 'on Stephen who has been stoned'. There is a thematic connection here with the first poem on the 'stony' state of sinful man, and perhaps also on the stony resistance of the flesh implied by the term *perterebrare* (*bore right through*) in the last line of the previous poem. *Stephen*: the first martyr, a deacon of the early church in Jerusalem, who was stoned to death for his teachings (Acts 5–7).

1   *flint*: Henry Vaughan's collection of verse *Silex Scintillans* (Part I: 1650; Part II: 1655) means 'The Sparking Flint'.

4. On Simon Magus

Metre: elegiac couplets. *Simon Magus*: Simon Magus or Simon the Magician was a Samaritan convert to Christianity. When he saw others receiving the Holy Spirit from the apostles Peter and John, Simon offered money to receive it too (Acts 8). Peter reproached him for his offer, and the sin of simony (paying for position or influence in the church) is named after him. Simon's story is told in the chapter immediately following those that recount the story of Stephen, so the two epigrams here follow the order of the Book of Acts, as well as offering rival models, positive and negative, from the early church.

5   *And so will you buy Heaven?*: This couplet works with a kind of pun on heaven (meaning salvation) and heaven (meaning the sky, with all its individual stars). H suggests that Simon should start his bidding with a single star – i.e., he implies that he has misunderstood the kind of *heaven* that he is attempting to purchase. At the same time, the example is itself ridiculous – however rich you are, no one can buy even a single star – demonstrating Simon's ignorance and folly.

8   *If you cast them . . . upon your head*: In Latin this line conceals a punning joke that is hard to translate. The phrase *in caput ipsa ruit* can mean both 'it collapses on [your] head' – i.e., the head of the person who threw it upwards; or 'it [a coin] comes down heads'. The point seems to be that Simon, a mercenary man, ought to understand and appreciate the nature of coins, if not of salvation.

10   *Image of God*: Note the link to the opening line of the first epigram. There is a play here on the appearance of everyday coins, which typically incorporate an image of a ruler or monarch.

5. On Sacred Scripture

Metre: hendecasyllables. Each line has eleven syllables. This metre is associated in particular with the epigrams of Catullus and of Martial, and was extremely widely used in neo-Latin epigrams on all subjects from the sixteenth century onwards. This interesting poem combines two strong images – of swallowing a star or a bee – to characterize the action of the Holy Scriptures within the mind and body of the poet. It is noticeable that both these motifs have overlaps with conventional imagery of poetic inspiration. Note also the continued language of physical penetration in H's experience of the divine.

4–5   *Could it be . . . a falling star*: A similar image is found in 'Artillery', lines 1–2: 'As I one ev'ning sat before my cell, / Me thoughts a star did shoot into my lap.' Cf. 'The Star', which also combines the images of a star consumed or internalized by the poet with the image of a bee ('To fly home like a laden bee / Unto that hive of beams / And garland-streams', lines 30–32).

7   *disreputable lodging*: The idea of the body as an unworthy residence for a divine star is also found in H's English poem 'The Star': 'Take a bad lodging in my heart', line 6.

8   *the honey*: The Scriptures are compared to honey in 'The Holy Scriptures (1), line 2: 'Such ev'ry letter, and a hony gain'.

9   *the house*: i.e., the honeycomb.

13   *narrow lanes*: The term here translated as *narrow lanes* (*angiportus*) has a disreputable feel in Latin literature, used of the location of sordid sexual assignations in both Catullus 58.4 and (perhaps in reminiscence of Catullus) in Horace, *Odes* 1.25.10. The intimate action of scripture in these lines is similar to the description of Hebrews 4:12, where the word of God is 'a discerner of the thoughts and intents of the heart'.

14   *And the byways . . . as it flees*: This rather striking line in Latin (*Et flexus fugientis appetitûs*) suggests that human 'appetite' or 'desire' flees from the Scriptures as they pursue it within the recesses of the author's own body. This ironically transfers a typically erotic image of pursuit (cf. Horace, *Odes* 4.1.38–40) to the rout of desire itself.

6. On the British Peace

Metre: elegiac couplets. This is the only poem to introduce a markedly patriotic – rather than religious – note. It is perhaps significant that it is placed later in the sequence than epigram 2 ('Homeland'), which refers not to England but to heaven. No other epigram has such particular reference to the time and place of H's writing, though epigrams 10 and 26–8 concern the Pope of the day. Note that here, too, English foreign policy is endowed with religious significance.

2   *rest of the earth . . . in wickedness*: The unrest afflicting other lands is probably the Thirty Years' War, which began in 1618, with full hostilities under way by 1620. James I pursued a peaceful foreign policy and England remained largely uninvolved in the conflict.

3   *waves*: *fluctus*. This commonly bears the metaphorical meaning of commotion or disturbance in Latin, especially war or unrest (cf. e.g., Horace, *Epodes* 2.2.85, of the civil war).

8   *move upon our waters*: The image of Christ 'moving' upon the waters alludes to both Genesis 1:2: 'And the Spirit of God moved upon the face of the waters' and John 6.19: 'they [the disciples] see Jesus walking on the sea.'

7. Avarice

Metre: elegiac couplets. This is the first epigram on an abstract idea, here the sin of greed. See also epigrams 16 (on love) and 19 (on affliction). As is often the case, H also composed an English poem on the same theme ('Avarice'). Epigrams of this sort, which rely upon subtle distinctions of grammatical form and Latin word order for their concise wit, are particularly resistant to close translation. In this example, the effect of the poem depends partly upon a pun between *aurum* ('gold') and *avarus* ('greedy' or 'a greedy man'). For all the *aurum* in the poem, it turns out that it is the *avarus* who possesses it least of all.

8. On the Washing of the Apostles' Feet

Metre: elegiac couplets. This is a typical example of the early modern satisfaction in discerning signs of divine providence in pre-Christian myth, history or (as here) scientific beliefs. Here the travels of the apostles spreading the Gospel around the world are compared to that of the sun – the apostles themselves are compared to suns in H's English poem 'Whitsunday'. The Latin epigram is weakened, however, by the lack of close correspondence: while the sun bathes itself in the water before travelling on, in this image it is Christ – whom we might expect to be linked to the sun – who bathes the feet of the apostles. The episode to which the title refers is found in John 13.

9. On Luke the Doctor

Metre: elegiac couplets. This epigram suggests that Christ chose a doctor (St Luke) as his disciple as an emblem of how his life and teaching was to 'cure' the ill effects of the apple that led to the Fall. The detail of an unripe apple suggests the homely advice of a sympathetic doctor ('It's best not to eat fruit that's not yet ripe').

10. The Title of the Pope

Metre: elegiac couplet. This epigram is a comment upon the motto *nec deus nec homo* ('neither God nor man'), supposedly adopted by the Papacy. In fact, there is no evidence that it was used to describe the Pope. The phrase appears in a distich composed for inscription on a medieval crucifix, where it refers to the painting of Christ (as opposed to Christ himself). It is also one of the *Adagia* of Erasmus (4.8.76).

11. Payment of Tribute

Metre: iambic trimeters. This epigram refers to Matthew 17:24–7, in which Simon Peter is asked if Jesus pays the tax to the temple. On saying that he does, Jesus tells Peter to cast a line in the water, saying that money sufficient for both their taxes will be found in the fish's mouth, as then proves to be the case. The poem also refers to the episode recounted in three of the Gospels (Matthew 22:15–22, Mark 12:13–17 and Luke 20: 20–6), where Christ is asked about the legality of Jews paying taxes (or 'tribute') to Caesar (Tiberius, the Roman emperor of the day). Jesus replied: 'Render unto Caesar what is Caesar's, and unto God what is God's.' The *you* of the poem is Christ himself.

12. The Storm while Christ Sleeps

Metre: elegiac couplets. Like many of these short epigrams, the poem is based upon wordplay. In particular, the word used for the rising of the storm (*surgit*) is closely related to that used at the end of the same line for the awakening of Christ (*resurgis*). The term also suggests resurrection.

13. The Good Citizen

Metre: iambic trimeters. Another short poem that particularly resists translation. The epigram depends partly upon a pun on the meaning of the adjective *bonus*, different parts of which can mean simply 'good', good men or people, 'the good' and also 'goods' (in the sense of properties or possessions). Both the verbs in lines three and four, *interverteret* ('purloin', 'defraud' or 'spend') and *possidet* ('possess', 'occupy', 'own' or 'settle') can refer to financial transactions. Humility is personified as a woman.

14. On Peter's Shadow

Metre: iambic trimeters. The title and first line allude to Acts 5:15: 'they brought forth the sick into the streets, and laid them on beds and couches, that at the least the shadow of Peter passing by might overshadow some of them.' The verbs of line 1 (*produxit*, 'brought forth') and line 2 (*reduxit*, 'brought back') are closely related, emphasizing the reciprocity.

15. Martha: Mary

Metre: Elegiac couplets. This miniature poetic dialogue imagines a conversation between Martha and Mary. The story of Christ's visit to their house is told in Luke 10:38–42. Kelliher comments on H's 'flair for illuminating religious truths by means of homely pictures' (ibid., p. 42). The glimpse of domestic life bears comparison with the more sustained description of *Memoriae Matris Sacrum* 2.

2   *light a fire in the hearth*: The last three words of this line (*luceat igne focus*) are borrowed from a popular passage in the Roman elegiac poet Tibullus (1.1.6).

3   *my furniture*: The form of this phrase in Latin perhaps alludes to a well-known phrase from the Roman satirist Persius: 'Dwell with yourself: get to know how scant your own furniture is' (Persius, *Satires* 4.52). The same word for *furniture* (*supellex*) is found in both. Persius was widely admired in the seventeenth century for his philosophical tone and content, which was considered to be particularly compatible with Christianity. The allusion here is appropriate: Martha is too concerned with the cleanliness of her literal furniture at the cost of considering the furniture of her heart.

16. Love

Metre: Elegiac couplets. This unusual short poem stands out for its vivid depiction of the dangers of intellectual curiosity when it leads to excessive credulity and anxiety. H wrote several English poems on love, but none with similar content to this piece. The allure – and ultimate pointlessness – of knowledge of all kinds is vividly described in 'Vanity (1)'.

6   *But why . . . IN LOVE*: The question and answer here allude to a famous line from Ovid's love elegies: 'He who does not wish to

become idle, should fall in love' (*Amores* 1.9.46). What is meant by this sluggish idleness – uninvigorated by passionate love – is described in H's 'Dullness', which like this poem employs the language of romantic or erotic love for religious purposes.

17. On a Proud Man

Metre: iambic trimeters. This poem belongs to the epigrammatic trad-ition, amply demonstrated by Catullus and Martial, of short poems addressed to 'types' who exemplify particular moral and social virtues and vices (here the sin of overweening pride). See also epigrams 21 and 22.

18. On the Same

Metre: elegiac couplets. Compare the imagery of the first epigram of the collection, in which sin transforms man from the earth of his ori-ginal shaping into rigid rock.

19. Affliction

Metre: elegiac couplets. Compare H's four English poems of the same title 'Affliction (1), (2), (3) and (4)'. In this epigram the waters over which Christ walked are a metaphor for human cares and affliction.

20. On Vainglory

Metre: iambic trimeters. The Latin of this poem is marked by some unusual vocabulary, as well as the compressed language and rapid shifts of imagery that are typical of many of H's English poems; Kel-liher (ibid., p. 42) compares it to 'The Collar'. *Vainglory* is one of the vices discussed by Aristotle, and the poem as a whole adopts an Aris-totelian approach, recommending the 'golden mean' or middle path between extremes of behaviour. The whole poem is very much in the spirit of the long English piece *The Church-Porch*.

    On vainglory: The word for *vainglory* (literally, 'empty glory') is Greek.

7   *Round and firm*: Here a single Latin word, *rotundus* (literally, 'rounded'), alludes to a well-known line from Horace's *Satires*, describing the wise and virtuous man as one who is 'whole in him-self, smooth and round' – so smooth that troubles simply slip off

the surface without gaining any purchase (Horace, *Satires* 2.7.86). Jonson alludes to the same passage in *Epigrams* 98 ('To Sir Thomas Roe'): 'He that is round within himself, and straight, / Need seek no other strength, no other height; / Fortune upon him breaks herself, if ill, / And what would hurt his virtue makes it still' (lines 3–6); *handle*: H here follows the suggestion of his first image. If virtuous self-sufficiency is suggested by a smooth, round surface that repels attack, then logically some sort of projection increases vulnerability – hence the detail of a handle. H was perhaps also thinking of the classical comparisons of man to a fragile or imperfect clay vessel, found both in Persius and Seneca.

15   *curd ... rennet*: The point here is that curd is thick and heavy; rennet runny and thin – both extremes to be avoided.

21. *On the Glutton*

Metre: elegiac couplets. Greed and gluttony are typical targets of Latin satire in both classical and neo-Latin versions. H translated Cornaro's *Treatise of Temperance and Sobriety* (published in *Hygiasticon* (1634)).

22. *On the Wicked but Eloquent Man*

Metre: elegiac couplets.

1   *rags of Baucis*: The Latin phrase *pannusia Baucis* is borrowed from Persius, *Satires* 4.21. Philemon and Baucis were a poor but virtuous elderly couple who unwittingly hosted Zeus and Hermes and were rewarded for their hospitality. But the point here (as in Persius) is simply that Baucis is an emblem of poverty.

4   *Charon*: the ferryman of the Styx. In other words, an eloquent tongue without virtuous deeds will lead to Hell.

23. *Consolation*

Metre: elegiac couplets. As Hutchinson points out, this poem owes a good deal to Seneca, *Epistles* 24.19–20, a famous passage in which Seneca claims that 'we die every day'. The image of the water clock, measuring time drip by drip, is also drawn from that passage. This deft, but ultimately conventional epigram may be compared to varied motifs of consolation found in H's collection in memory of his mother, *Memoriae Matris Sacrum*.

24. On Angels

Metre: hendecasyllables. This poem takes as its subject the scholastic idea (found in Aquinas) that while human knowledge is subject to the limitations of sensory perception, angels benefit from immediate apprehension. The working of the mind upon the sensory images it receives is compared to the grinding of grain in a mill. The image bears comparison with the description of learning and reason, compared to spinning and the working of a press in 'The Pearl'.

25. *Rome. Anagram*
{
Frontier. Maro.
Branch. Shoulder.
Delay. Love.

Metre: elegiac couplets. This anagrammatic elegy plays upon six Latin words made of the same letters: *oram* (the accusative singular form of the word for a border or boundary), *Maro* (one of the names of the poet Virgil), *ramo* (the dative or ablative singular form of the word 'branch' or 'bough'), *armo* (the dative or ablative singular form of the word for 'shoulder'), *mora* (meaning 'delay') and *amor* (meaning 'love'). Poetic anagrams of this kind often seem remote from modern poetic taste, but they are a common feature of early modern collections and anthologies, both in English and the vernacular. *The Temple* includes the English couplet 'Anagram on the Virgin Mary' (playing upon 'Mary' and 'Army') as well as 'Paradise' which makes uses of a similar word-game. This particular poem was originally included in *Musae Responsoriae*, though it may have been composed even before that. There is evidence that Herbert's piece was popular and circulated quite widely, but it is easy to find many pieces of this sort at the time. A similar poem (though from the Jesuit perspective) is, for example, found on page 23 of *Bernardi Bauhusii è Societate Iesu Epigrammatum Selectorum Libri V* (Antwerp, 1616).

10   *Fabius:* Quintus Fabius Maximus, appointed dictator by the Romans to deal with Hannibal's invasion of Italy, pursued a policy of delay.

26. Response of Pope Urban VIII

Metre: elegiac couplets. This imagined 'response' is to epigram 25, the anagram on Rome. As well as the central anagrammatic transformation of Rome (*Roma*) into Love (*Amor*) the poem also works with a pun on *everto* ('overturn' or 'destroy') and *inverto* ('turn upside down', 'upset').

Pope Urban VIII (elected in August 1623) was a keen composer of Latin poetry. Hutchinson notes that H 'allows the Pope to have the better of the exchange'.

27. *Response to Urban VIII*

Metre: elegiac couplets. This epigram plays upon the meaning of the adjective *urbanus* ('urbane' or 'witty').

28. *To Pope Urban VIII*

Metre: elegiac couplets. Pope Urban VIII wrote Latin poetry. Cardinal Bellarmine (d. 1621), a major figure of the Counter-Reformation, was involved in theological controversies with both Lancelot Andrewes and James I.

2   *Pierian*: The Pierian spring in Macedonia is sacred to the Muses; here the adjective means lords who are also poets.

5   *Helicon*: Mount Helicon in Boetia is a mountain sacred to the Muses; in particular, the Hellenistic poet Callimachus described a dream in which he encountered the Muses on Helicon. Here the mountain stands for poetry in general.

29. *Reasonable Sacrifice*

Metre: elegiac couplets. *Reasonable sacrifice*: The title is a Greek phrase composed of elements found in Romans 12:1: 'I beseech you therefore, brethren, by the mercies of God, that ye present your bodies a living sacrifice, holy, acceptable unto God, which is your reasonable service.'

2   *turf*: The Latin word *caespes* can mean 'turf', 'earth' and 'altar'. The phrase *living turf* is borrowed from Horace, *Odes* 3.8.4, where it describes an altar. H has pointedly reappropriated the phrase to describe the human body, the 'sacrifice' of the title and of the biblical passage to which the title refers.

30. *On Thomas Didymus*

Metre: hendecasyllables. The poem addresses doubting Thomas, who did not believe in the resurrection of Jesus until he had seen and touched Christ's wounds for himself. H pursues the idea of probing the 'inwardness' of Christ, beginning with the 'inside' of his body, and adding the images of *marrow* and finally of the inner security of a resting place and citadel. For the imagery here, compare the English poem 'The Bag'.

8   *roaring lion*: The final line alludes to 1 Peter 5:8: 'Be sober, be vigilant; because your adversary the devil, as a roaring lion, walketh about, seeking whom he may devour.'

31. On the Sundial

Metre: Elegiac couplets. The poem compares the combination of light and shade necessary to a functioning sundial to the human blend of soul and body. The image also suggests man's temporal existence.

32. The Triumph of Death

Metre: hexameter. Hexameter verse, the metre of Homer and Virgil, is associated strongly with epic, although it was also used for didactic and satirical poetry, and for verse letters. This short fragment in florid epic style – to some comic effect – is an example of the early modern enthusiasm for mock-epic or epyllion ('mini-epic'), a trend evident both in English and in Latin (cf. the Gunpowder Plot poems of Milton (*In Quintum Novembris*) and Campion (*De pulverea coniuratione*) and mock-epic pieces, such as Jonson's 'On the Famous Voyage' (*Epigrams* 133)). The use of classical names and epithets, especially in the opening lines, establishes the mock-epic register.

   The poem as it is included here is an adaptation of an earlier piece entitled *Inventa Bellica*, recorded in at least two contemporary manuscripts. The earlier version does not present Death himself as the speaker, as this poem does.

   The Triumph of Death gives an ironic account of the origins of warfare, beginning with a brawl at a country festival. This passage is similar to an account of the origin of satiric and invective verse in Horace, *Epistles* 2.1.139–55. The centrepiece of H's poem is the quite detailed description of the construction and effect of the cannon (lines 51–84), which has several points in common with part of Milton's *Paradise Lost*, Book VI, especially VI.578–94. The fascination with gunpowder and the 'technology of death' is typical of a large number of sixteenth- and seventeenth-century Latin poems, not least the large amount of British Latin verse produced in the aftermath of the foiled Gunpowder Plot (1605). In his *Novum Organum* (1620) Francis Bacon claimed that gunpowder, printing and the mariner's compass were three inventions that had changed the world. H inveighed against war in his oration 'On the Return of Prince Charles from Spain' (1623).

2   *Emathian river*: a reference to the Battle of Pharsalia in 48 BCE, when Caesar defeated Pompey; *Daunia*: i.e., Apulia, where Hannibal defeated the Romans at Cannae in 216 BCE.

8   *its branches – Death*: probably a reference to Cain's murder of Abel with a wooden club.

9   *Flora*: goddess of spring and flowers.

13 *Turns up his nose*: This phrase is borrowed from Horace, *Satires* 2.8.64, where they describe a man who sneers at everything.

14 *Ucalegon*: Ucalegon appears in the *Aeneid* 2.312. The insertion of this unusual name here contributes to the mock-epic effect.

14–15 *words / Like slingshots*: The Latin phrase is also used by Cicero to describe particularly effective phrases.

16–17 *anger / Makes a weapon*: A similar description of improvised weapons among country people is found in Virgil, *Aeneid* 7.506–10.

18 *Bacchus*: Bacchus, the god of wine, *nourishes brawls* because men are more likely to fight when they are drunk. Cf. *The Church-Porch*, lines 25–36.

21–2 *Treacherous wine ... itself provided*: The point here is that wine both 'provides the blood' – that is, rouses men's anger and urge to fight – and, ironically, deprives them of it when, as a result, they are wounded and bleed.

23 *Tisiphone*: one of the Furies, also mentioned in line 71.

27 *Bellona*: Roman goddess of war.

32 *at the tilt*: Tilting at the quintain was still practised at this period.

36 *when iron is torn from deep in the earth*: The process of mining is often employed as a motif of excessive human greed and ambition; H himself makes the association in his English poem 'Avarice'.

40 *ballistas*: siege engines in the form of a sling; *onagres*: a military engine that hurls larges tones; *Scorpio*: a military engine that hurls darts. Literally, a 'scorpion'.

41 *Catapult*: here referring specifically to a large siege engine that hurls arrows, stones and other missiles; *Sicilian master*: Archimedes of Syracuse devised engines of war to defend his city against the Romans in 214 BCE.

44 *Holy Tityrus*: Tityrus is the name of a shepherd-poet in Virgil's *Eclogues* (and many pastoral poems, both Latin and vernacular, which imitate Virgil). Here the name is used to denote the shepherd boy David, who defeated Goliath and went on to become

both poet and king; *Idumaean enemy*: Here refers to Goliath, the giant Philistine killed by David with his slingshot (1 Samuel 17).

45   *Arviragus*: Arviragus is mentioned at Juvenal, *Satires* 4.126 and his (probably mythical) story is told in Geoffrey of Monmouth's *Historia Regum Britanniae* (*c.* 1138).

47   *Demetrius*: Demetrius, the king of Macedonia, known as the 'besieger of cities' for his attack on Rhodes with giant siege engines.

55   *curule's chair*: a stool of crossed legs supporting a central seat, without back or arms, on which senior Roman magistrates sat.

58   *coffered ceilings*: The word for *coffered* here is a distinctive term associated with grandeur (cf. the description of Dido's palace in the *Aeneid* 1.726). H uses a related word, without irony, to describe the grandeur of bishops in *Musae Responsoriae* 7.4; *Orcus*: i.e., the Underworld.

59   *Mephis*: probably a personification of the sulphurous odours of hell.

60   *Acorn*: The *glans* ('acorn') meant here is a bullet. Primitive man was often depicted as eating coarse food with clumsy table manners: he is described as 'belching acorns' in Juvenal, *Satires* 6.10.

63   *lictor*: Lictors were Roman civil servants who served and guarded magistrates. Here bullets are imagined as the lictors of Pluto, god of the Underworld.

65   *distaffs and the threads of life*: The three Fates are conventionally depicted spinning the threads of life.

66   *Atropos*: one of the three Fates.

71   *Tisiphone*: one of the Furies, also mentioned in line 23.

76   *Erebus*: Hell.

82   *Cocytus*: a river in the Underworld.

83   *Pilot*: Charon, the ferryman on the River Styx. He is exhausted from having to carry so many dead.

86   *Aetna*: Mount Etna in Sicily. Zeus trapped the monster Typhon beneath Etna, and the forges of Hephaestus were also said to be located beneath the volcano. Here Aetna seems to denote a fiery enemy of heaven, a kind of conflation of the monster Typhon and the volcano itself.

88   *Cacus*: a fire-breathing giant and son of Vulcan; *Ixion*: Punished by Zeus, Ixion was bound for ever to a wheel of fire.

90   *Monk*: either Friar Bacon, traditionally the inventor of gunpowder, or perhaps the German monk Berthold Schwartz.

96   *our strength*: The speaker is still Death himself.

96   *Jesuit*: A Spanish Jesuit, Mariana, in his *De Rege et Regis Institutione* (1599), defended tyrannicide, as did the Italian Jesuit

Cardinal Bellarmine and the English Jesuit Henry Garnett, who
was executed for his role in the Gunpowder Plot (1605).

99   *blood of kings:* This may allude to the assassinations of Henri III
(1589) and Henri IV (1610).

33. *The Triumph of the Christian. Against Death*

Metre: iambic trimeter. This short poem is presented as a concise
'reply' to Death's argument in the previous poem.

1   *Truly? ... whatsoever:* The line ends with two exclamations:
hercle aedepol, literally 'By Hercules! By Pollux!' The idiomatic
meaning is simply one of strong assertion: 'truly indeed', 'there's
no doubt whatsoever'; but the reference to Hercules and Pollux –
both mythical heroes of remarkable courage and physical
prowess – adds to the irony of the address to Death here.

34. *To John, Leaning on the Breast of the Lord*

Metre: hendecasyllables. The striking – even shocking – imagery of
this epigram has parallels in other neo-Latin pieces, in particular Rich-
ard Crashaw's epigram on Luke 11:27, published in his *Epigrammata
Sacra* (*Sacred Epigrams*) of 1634, in which he imagines Mary, the
mother of Christ, drinking from her son's side as he had drunk from
her; a tamer version of a similar conceit is found among the *Carmina*
of the Jesuit poet François Remond (*Carmina,* Vienna, 1617). It seems
likely that Crashaw's poem was influenced by H's epigram.

    To John ... the Lord: Note the Greek term, an adjective meaning
literally 'upon the breast'. Hutchinson points out that the term seems
to be coined by H, but based upon a phrase in John 21:20, describing
the disciple John, 'who leaned upon his [Christ's] breast at supper'.

7–9   *Then, if enough ... fall and die:* The closing image of the poem
is difficult to interpret. The *thrones* in question seem to be the
breasts of Christ himself, but one of the constellations is also
named the *throni Caesaris* ('thrones of Caesar'). The couplet
seems to be working with an allusion to the end of Horace, *Odes*
1.1, which has a similar rhetorical structure, though in a very
different context. Horace's poem ends: 'If you [Maecenas, his
patron] should include me among the lyric bards / I shall strike
the stars with my uplifted head' (*Odes* 1.1.35–6), an irreverent
suggestion that he may attain immortality or even be trans-
formed into a star by virtue of his literary fame. H's point seems

to be that if he is blessed by grace he may even touch the breast
of Christ at his death – and thereby reach heaven and immortal
life. As so often in H's Latin poetry, the undoubted piety of the
sentiment is combined with an allusive register that suggests
powerful poetic ambition.

35. To the Lord

Metre: elegiac couplets. This elaborate address to the Lord finds vari-
ous ways to ask for one thing: to see God. For a prayer as the close to
a *silva*-style collection of various pieces, cf. the final poem of Jonson's
1616 collection *Forest*, 'To Heaven', which addresses God directly.

1   *Hyblas*: Hybla in Sicily was famed for its honey. In fact, there
    were many ancient towns called Hybla in Sicily, so the phrase *a
    hundred Hyblas* may be a learned joke.

1–2 *Christ, fine . . . and its peace*: The extravagant juxtapositions of
    attributes in the opening couplet are reminiscent of many of H's
    English poems. Cf. 'Prayer (1)'.

3   *grant that I should see you*: A kind of pun lurks in the Latin
    phrase *sine te cernam*; *sine* is here a verb in the imperative,
    meaning 'grant that . . .', but the phrase *sine te* recurs in line 6,
    this time as a preposition, where it means *without you*.

PASSIO DISCERPTA
THE PASSION IN PIECES

A series of Latin poems of uncertain date that meditate upon Christ's
suffering and death, comparable to the English poem 'The Sacrifice'.
Unlike *Lucus*, the poems of this collection have a clear chronological
order, following the events of the Passion in the Gospel accounts. The
devotional seriousness of the collection is plain, but (as in most of H's
Latin verse) the style is marked by wit and wordplay. The intense
physicality of the sequence also has points in common with H's poems
in memory of his mother, *Memoriae Matris Sacrum*. Kelliher remarks
that 'nothing quite like H's sequence is to be found in Anglo-Latin
sacred verse before his time' (ibid., p. 35).

    The title *Passio Discerpta* describes the composition of the collec-
tion: a series of short poems on different aspects of Christ's suffering,
hence 'The Passion in Pieces' or 'Scattered'; but it also alludes to the
physical violence of the episode, since *discerpta* can mean 'torn apart',
'rent' or 'mangled'.

As in *Lucus*, the majority of these poems are written in elegiac couplets (a dactylic hexameter followed by a pentameter). A handful, however, are in other metres, including iambic trimeters (three poems), hendecasyllables (two poems) and one example of iambic distichs.

1. To the Dying Lord

Metre: elegiac couplets. This opening poem imagines that the ink of the written collection replaces H's helpless tears as he contemplates the crucifixion: the ink is both more efficacious (as it can write the verse) and, with its dark colour, a more fitting marker of the author's own sinfulness. H's collection in memory of his mother, *Memoriae Matris Sacrum*, begins with a similar motif. Cf. also the association between ink and sin in 'Good Friday': 'My heart hath store, write there, where in / One box doth lie both ink and sinne' (23–4).

The combination of strong devotional feeling with an artful awareness of the architecture of the poetry collection is typical of H.

2. On the Sweat of Blood

Metre: elegiac couplets. The poet addresses the bloody sweat itself. Imagining himself present at the crucifixion, he offers himself as a possible host for the sweat as it leaves Christ. The intensely physical imagination of this rather extraordinary conceit finds parallels in several of H's poems (cf. *Lucus* 34, 'To John, leaning on the breast of the Lord'), as well as contemporary religious poets such as Crashaw.

1   *other aspect*: i.e., Christ in his divine, rather than human aspect. The point is that Christ as God is without limit; but that his human body – to which his blood and sweat was confined – was of ordinary human scale.

4   *mob*: The Latin word *turba* is a derogatory term for a crowd. It refers here to the crowd at the crucifixion.

3. On the Same

Metre: elegiac couplets. Once again, Christ's blood is personified.

4. On the Pierced Side

Metre: elegiac couplets. The detail is taken from the narrative of the crucifixion in John 19:34: 'But one of the soldiers with a spear pierced his side, and forthwith came there out blood and water.'

5. On the Spitting and the Mockery

Metre: iambic trimeter. A difficult but interesting piece, which moves – rather queasily to modern taste – from the flowing water (that is, saliva) of the men who spit at Christ to the waters of life that Christ's death represents for those who believe in him. (We also remember the water and blood that flowed from his side when pierced by the spear in the previous poem.) At the end of the poem, Christ's body, which is earlier characterized as a 'sacred course' for the waters of life, is described as an aqueduct for the Gentiles: that is, a reliable source of clean water for a large population.

7   *Fig Tree:* The image of the Jewish people as a cursed fig tree alludes to Matthew 21:19: 'And when he [Jesus] saw a fig tree in the way, he came to it, and found nothing thereon, but leaves only, and said unto it, Let no fruit grow on thee henceforward for ever. And presently the fig tree withered away.' At 21:21 Jesus compares the withered fig tree to those who have no faith. The dry and withering fig tree of the Jewish people is implicitly contrasted to the Gentiles – that is, future Christians – who flock to the aqueduct bearing the waters of life.

6. On the Crown of Thorns

Metre: elegiac couplets. This striking poem begins with a powerful paradox, which, as Kelliher remarks, 'seems almost blasphemous until it is recognized as a lament' (ibid., p. 38). H is working here with the conventional image of Christ as the head and the church as the body (see Ephesians 5:23 and 30). For the poet, Christ's suffering represents salvation – characterized here as a garland of roses. Cf. 'The Thanksgiving', lines 13–14: 'Shall thy strokes be my stroking? thorns, my flower? / Thy rod, my posie? crosse, my bower?'

7. On the Reed, the Thorns, the Bowing Down and the Scarlet

Metre: elegiac couplets. This poem is based upon several details of the mockery of Christ before his crucifixion, according to the accounts in Matthew and Mark, including clothing him in a robe of scarlet or purple (like an emperor), putting a crown of thorns on his head and a reed in his hand, and pretending to bow down and revere him (Matthew 27:28–30; Mark 15:17–20). The poem is spoken by Christ himself, like H's English poem 'The Sacrifice'.

8. On the Slaps

Metre: hendecasyllables. See in particular Mark 14:65: 'And the servants did strike him with the palms of their hands.' For the conceit, cf. 'The Thanksgiving': 'Shall thy strokes be my stroking? thorns, my flower? / Thy rod, my posy? cross, my bower?' lines 13–14. H often incorporates medical imagery; cf. *Lucus* 9 ('On Luke the Doctor') and the sixth poem of *Memoriae Matris Sacrum*.

9. On the Whip

Metre: elegiac couplets. The whipping of Christ before the crucifixion is described at John 19:1, Mark 14:65 and Matthew 27:26.

10. On the Divided Garments

Metre: iambic trimeter. In each of the gospel accounts, Christ's garments are divided by lot at the crucifixion.

11. On the Good Thief

Metre: elegiac couplet. Christ was crucified between two thieves. In St Luke's account, one of these (the 'good thief') asked Jesus to remember him, and Jesus replied: 'To day shalt thou be with me in paradise' (Luke 23:43).

12. On Christ about to Ascend the Cross

Metre: iambic trimeter. In Luke 19 the publican Zacchaeus, a small man, climbs a sycamore tree in order to see Jesus.

13. Christ on the Cross

Metre: elegiac couplets.

1.   *balm*: opobalsama is balm or the sap of the balsam-tree. Christ is also compared to ointment or balm at 8.2; *healed world*: The expression here is similar to that at 9.1, where Christ is described as the hope of the world which is not 'healed' but *flagellati* – 'whipped' or 'under the lash'.

3–4.   *Those drips . . . assaults of blood*: The flow of Christ's blood is extended to Christ himself, who is described as a river. The adjective *iugem* in the final line, meaning everlasting or perpetual, is used particularly of running water in classical Latin. We can compare similar imagery of Christ as water in the fifth poem of this collection. H imagines himself drinking from Christ's side in *Lucus* 34.

14. On the Nails

Metre: Elegiac couplets.

2   *So that your ... of the lesser*: This difficult and compressed line refers to Christ's double nature as both God (his *better* nature) and man (his *lesser* nature). The crucifixion is understood as an essential element of the incarnation – something that Christ as man had to endure in order for mankind to benefit from the incarnation.

3–4   *Now you are ... his own crook*: a striking intervention of the poet's own speaking voice, as if he were himself holding the wood and the nails. Christ as the 'Good Shepherd' is a conventional image derived from the gospels; but the detail here is unusual: Christ is caught by his own hook or crook. (A *falx* is usually a pruning-hook or scythe, but seems to refer here to a shepherd's crook.) We find a similar image in Andrew Marvell's 'Damon the Mower' poems – cf. 'And there among the grass fell down, / By his own scythe, the Mower mown' ('Damon the Mower', lines 79–80).

15. On the Bowed Head, John 19

Metre: Elegiac couplets. The conceit of this poem is a kind of gruesome answer to Matthew 8:20: 'And Jesus saith unto him, The foxes have holes, and the birds of the air have nests; but the Son of man hath not where to lay his head.' The reference in the title is to John 19:30, describing the moment of Christ's death: 'he said, It is finished: and he bowed his head, and gave up the ghost.' The arresting effect of this combination – the torment of the crucifixion as a kind of bed or couch – has something in common with Marvell's famous line from 'An Horatian Ode upon Cromwell's Return from Ireland', describing in this case the execution of Charles I: 'Nor called the Gods with vulgar spite / To vindicate his helpless right, / But bowed his comely head, / Down as upon a bed,' lines 61–4.

16. On the Sun in Eclipse

Metre: iambic distichs (iambic trimeter followed by iambic dimeter). This poem is an allegory of the eclipse, in which the sun is a household porter whose master, Christ, must deny to his household the life and light that he lacks himself at the crucifixion. The eclipse of the sun, earthquake, opened graves, split rocks and the torn veil in the Temple (see following poems) are all described as taking place in the immediate aftermath of the crucifixion.

17. The Opened Tombs

Metre: elegiac couplets. Matthew 27:51–2 describes the opening of the tombs at the moment of Christ's death, as well as an earthquake (see the following poem), the tearing of the veil in the temple (see poem 19), and the splitting of rock (see poem 20).

18. The Earthquake

Metre: elegiac couplets. This deceptively simple poem imagines Christ nailed to the cross to be somehow 'fixed' to the entire world and able to move it with him – hence the subsequent earthquake. The final couplet adds the evocative suggestion that the earth *flees* from the nails as Christ himself could not.

3   *Foolish men . . . as it flees*: The Latin of this line is particularly good, with a careful counterpoint between words suggesting fixity (*stolidi*, 'foolish men' and *figite*, 'fix' or 'nail') and flux (*fugientem*, the earth 'as it flees').

19. The Torn Veil

Metre: hendecasyllables. This rapidly running metre gives an impression of urgency. This poem characterizes Jewish worship as the childhood of man's relationship to God, now superseded by the maturity of Christian salvation.

1   *Circumcised Man*: The noun *verpus* (*circumcised man*) appears several times in classical Latin literature as an insulting term for a Jew (e.g., Catullus, 47.4, Juvenal, 14.104 and Martial, 7.82.8).
5   *single city*: i.e., Jerusalem.
9   *phylacteries*: indicative of Jewish worship.

11   *emerged from puberty*: The Latin phrase here is borrowed from
      Terence's comedy *Andria* (1.1.24). It is a Latin imitation of a
      Greek idiom.

20. *The Cleft Rocks*

Metre: elegiac couplets.

1–4   *Humanity was . . . no man had made*: The first four lines of this
      poem play repeatedly with the Latin verb *facio* ('to make') and
      related terms: Adam and Eve were originally 'made' (*factus*, 1) in
      a pure and whole state, without flaws. Their human clay,
      smashed by the Devil, is described as *fictile opus* ('a work of
      clay', line 2). In line 4, the golden calf made (*facta*) and wor-
      shipped by Aaron (Exodus 32) is contrasted to the tablets bearing
      the Ten Commandments that Moses received directly from God
      (and therefore *infectas*, not made by man).
8   *But grind . . . lighten all losses*: The closing image of the 'grind-
      ing' of hearts to make a powder that heals all perhaps also
      alludes to Exodus 32: in his fury at the worship of the golden
      calf, Moses broke the tablets bearing the Ten Commandments,
      burnt the golden calf 'and ground it to powder' (Exodus 32:20).
      See also Psalm 51:17: 'a broken and a contrite heart, O God,
      thou wilt not despise'.

21. *On the Harmony of the World with Christ*

Metre: elegiac couplets.

3–4   *Take this man . . . mine instead*: The final couplet refers to Pla-
      to's doctrine of the *World-Soul*. H suggests that insofar as there
      is such a thing, the soul of the world is Christ himself – but also
      that Christ and his world are so profoundly in harmony that
      any Christian soul demonstrates the truth of Christianity. H
      ends with an irreverent suggestion to Plato that he should
      exchange his theory (of the *World-Soul*) for H's own: that is, for
      Christianity – or perhaps the verse collection of which this is the
      final word. The effect is humorous, but allows H to end his col-
      lection of devotional poems not, in fact, with Christ, but with
      himself: the last word is *meam*, 'mine'.

MEMORIAE MATRIS SACRUM
A SACRED GIFT IN MEMORY OF MY MOTHER

This fine collection of Latin and Greek verse in memory of H's mother is often described as the best of his Latin poetry. It was apparently composed in June 1627 in the weeks following Lady Danvers's death at the beginning of the month. It was published later that summer alongside John Donne's 'Sermon of Commemoration for the Lady Danvers'. In it we find the metaphorical distinction of H's English religious poetry applied unstintingly to his experience of bereavement.

Memoriae Matris Sacrum is rewarding both for the quality and variety of the poetry and for the picture of H himself that emerges in glimpses of his home life, especially in poems 7 and 19. The collection is strikingly varied – in the style and form of the poems themselves – but also unified by the central theme of bereavement, as well as by its literary sophistication and self-aware exploration of the relationship between H's grief and his literary gifts. It is marked by vividly sensuous imagery, applied in particular to his mother's physical presence – in life (2), in death (5) and in the form of a tormenting apparition (7) – and to the linked motifs of pregnancy, birth and breastfeeding, but also to H's own physical experience (as in 6). In particular, H associates giving birth both with his mother's delivery of himself as a baby and with his own labour and delivery of these poems.

Memoriae Matris Sacrum is the only one of H's Latin collections to have a modern edition with translation and full commentary. Freis, Freis and Miller's recent edition (hereafter FFM) has much to offer, especially for those with a little Latin who wish to follow the text closely.

I

Metre: elegiac couplets. The metaphorical texture of this opening poem is typically dense, combining tears, the Thames and the Muses' spring of poetic inspiration, and then adding ash – the ash of the burning poet himself – to the water to create the ink of the written collection. Similar elements can also be found in the opening poem of *Passio Discerpta* and in the English poem 'Good Friday'.

1   *Ah mother . . . weep for you*: The language of the opening line is
     condensed: we are to imagine the poet drawing water from a
     spring to feed his tears; but it is also a question about poetics:

inspired poets drink from the Muses' spring on Helicon, and H seems to be asking which source or poetic model he should look to in composing this collection of lament.

4   *And I dryer*: The phrase *siccior ipse* perhaps incorporates an echo of Virgil, *Eclogues* 5.44: *formosi pecoris custos formosior ipse*, 'I, the guardian of a beautiful flock, still more beautiful myself.' That passage is the last line of the epitaph for Daphnis, the shepherd poet. The allusion suggests grief and a pastoral setting, but also H's poetic power and ambition.

5   *still burning*: The image of the poet consumed by fire belongs to the language of passionate love. Cf. Jonson's 'The Hourglass' (in which the poet is burnt to ashes by love and his ashes are then used to mark the time).

8   *delivers*: The last word of the Latin line, *parit*, is used of a woman giving birth. By turning to poetry, H transforms his lost mother into verse, but also becomes a 'mother' himself; *Mother: now . . . these Metres*: This line depends in Latin on a kind of pun that is hard to translate: the line begins with the word *Mater* ('Mother') and the penultimate word is *Metra* ('Metres' or 'Measures' – that is, poetry). In other words, H has rearranged the letters of 'mother' to make 'metres' – a concrete demonstration of the process of 'making poetry' out of his grief. For this kind of effect, cf. the anagrams of *Lucus* 25 and 'Anagram of the Virgin Mary' in *The Temple*.

2

Metre: iambic trimeter. The most substantial poem in the collection, this piece is described by Kelliher as 'one of the finest memorial poems in Anglo-Latin verse' (ibid., p. 50). Its portrait of Lady Danvers combines the domestic abilities of a skilled mistress with intellectual acuity and unfailing moral fibre.

This is a surprisingly embattled poem: the final verse paragraph (52–65) turns from praise to attack, as H confronts the ignorant who criticize his praise. His fighting spirit is apparently inherited from his mother, who tackles daily prayer (17) and the challenge of an unexpected guest (27–8) with courageous verve.

1   *Cornelias . . . Sempronias*: Cornelia, the daughter of Scipio Africanus, a Roman general famous for defeating Hannibal, was the mother of both Sempronia and the brothers Tiberius and Gaius Gracchus (the 'Gracchi'). Cornelia and Sempronia were

considered embodiments of feminine self-control, piety and loy-
alty. H may also be remembering Propertius, *Elegies* 4.11, on the
death of a later Cornelia, wife of Aemilius Paulus, who is also
depicted as an archetype of Roman womanly virtue.

11   *proud edifice of turrets*: i.e., an elaborate hairstyle. The image
carries a suggestion of identification between a fine woman and
a proud city.

13   *Babel*: the tower of Babel, see Genesis 11.1–9.

17   *assailed*: The Latin verb *adorta* is quite strong, with a suggestion
of military attack, especially combined with the characterization
of the prayers as 'keen' or 'sharp' and 'fiery'. Similar powerful
language recurs in lines 27–8.

30   *Pallas*: Athena, severe goddess of wisdom and war.

34   *Catos*: Cato the Elder and Cato the Younger, Roman statesmen
of the first and second centuries BCE, were famous examples of
unswerving moral principle.

37   *harmony of sense and expression*: This idea is central to ancient
aesthetics, especially poetics. Cf. 'A True Hymn'.

41   *Pactolus*: The Pactolus is a gold-bearing river in modern Turkey.
The move from writing to dust to sand perhaps also remembers
that sand was scattered on freshly written pages to dry the ink.

44–9 *A brief foretaste ... anticipate the measure*: These lines are
marked by their use of rhyme, not usually a feature of H's Latin
verse; *measure*: The image here is again of music: the praises of
his mother are imagined as music that is echoed and anticipated
by heaven.

45   *Reliever*: The Latin word here, *Subleuatrix*, is unclassical. It is
used of the Virgin Mary in medieval Latin.

47   *balm*: H returns rather often to images of balm. Cf. *Passio Dis-
cerpta* 8 and 13, in both cases of the healing comfort of Christ.

51   *lesser stars*: i.e., the myriad of minor stars visible in the night sky.

55–6 *Should I ... tinkling proclamations*: These lines – the mute poet
contrasted to the noisy world, loud with tinkling praises of his
mother – perhaps allude to 1 Corinthians 13. The implication is
that H's praise of his mother, unlike that of others, is rooted in
love for her.

57   *my mother's urn*: H is asking whether he alone is forbidden from
grieving publicly for his mother, but the expression – and the
implied image of penetrating or reopening his mother's burial
urn – is rather remarkable.

58   *rosemary*: Rosemary was used at funerals on account of its
strong scent, and was associated with remembrance of the dead;

cf. Ophelia in *Hamlet* (5.4): 'There's rosemary, that's for remembrance.'

59   *my tongue*: H's reference to 'bringing back' his tongue for his mother perhaps implies that he returned to Latin verse in the aftermath of her death in 1627 after a considerable break. The latest datable poems in *Lucus* are addressed to Pope Urban III, elected in August 1623.

63   *smear the pages*: The Latin phrase here alludes to Horace, *Satires* 1.4.36, in a passage characterizing weak and worthless poets.

3

Metre: elegiac couplets. H imagines the sunbeams, which seem to offer a link between himself on earth and his mother in heaven, as a kind of ladder, an image probably influenced by Jacob's vision of a ladder between heaven and earth (Genesis 28).

1   *Phoebus*: Phoebus Apollo here represents the sun.

10   *Weave and twist . . . where she is*: There is marked alliteration in this final line, an aural version of the twist and weave of the sunbeams as they form a rope or ladder. For a similar image (and the yearning quality), cf. the end of 'The Pearl. Matthew 13:45' ('Yet through these labyrinths, not my grovelling wit, / But thy silk twist let down from heaven to me; / Did both conduct, and teach me, how by it / To climb to thee') and 'Matins' ('Then by a sun-beam I will climb to thee').

4

Metre: 'third asclepiad', a glyconic followed by an asclepiad line. This metre is used by Horace in twelve odes, as well as by the Greek lyricists. A relatively unusual metre, confined to lyric poetry, it is not used for epigrams. It is chosen here with care: H's poem is a self-conscious discussion of the generic choices appropriate to his grief.

The poem begins with a worry that lyric poetry is an inappropriate vehicle for praise and lament of his mother, who is now in heaven. As it develops, H argues that his own mortal state on earth is transformed and made heavenly by the glorious task of praising his mother: by implication, his poetry is similarly transformed and transcendent.

Sir John Danvers's garden at Chelsea was famous. In 1609 H's mother married Danvers – a man only ten years older than H and the same age as his eldest brother – and H spent a good deal of time at the

Chelsea house. Throughout this collection, H associates the garden's loss of his mother's nurturing care with his own grief and desolation.

1   *Why do I trifle my time on a reed?*: The opening line has several connections with programmatic statements in classical poetry. In his first poem Catullus dismisses his own verse as *nugas* ('trifles'), the noun to which H's verb *nugor* is related. *Calamo*, a reed, denotes the pipe of pastoral poetry; but also the 'reed pen' itself (compare 'On the death of fairest Queen Anne', line 8, which is explicitly about writing, not song).

3   *a narrow garden*: The detail *tenui* ('narrow'), describing the garden, continues the allusions to classical poetics. *Tenuis* is often used in Roman poetics to imply a small-scale style, rather than the grand ambition of epic or tragedy. The point is that the 'small-scale' genre of lyric poetry seems inappropriate now that his mother has been removed from the narrowness of earthly life to the eternal proportions of heaven. Cf. the 'short and narrow verged shade' of Marvell's 'The Garden' (line 5).

8   *shed my skin*: This striking phrase is borrowed from Horace, *Epodes* 17.15, where it describes metamorphosis.

9   *sphere*: This image of strength and virtuous self-sufficiency is similar to that at *Lucus* 20.5–7. The lines in *Lucus* are indebted to Horace, *Satires* 2.7.86, on true freedom.

10   *fingers*: H imagines himself playing a musical instrument as he sings (the 'reed' of the opening line) as he sings.

14   *into another*: H's mother not only gave birth to him – gave him the world – but also taught him by her faith and example, hence giving him the hope of heaven.

16   *paired flutes*: The *pares tibiae* or double flute was used for dramatic performances in the ancient world and is also associated with pastoral poetry. Here there may also be an allusion to the unusual metre, composed of two quite distinct lines.

5

Metre: elegiac couplets. In this tender and surprising poem H addresses the plants and flowers of his mother's garden (see headnote to poem 4). Pastoral poetry traditionally associates lists of flowers with lament as well as courtship: cf. the 'catalogue' of flowers in Shakespeare's *Hamlet* (5.4), *A Winter's Tale* (Perdita, 4.4) and Milton's *Lycidas* (lines 142–50). Just as the blossoming garden came to stand for H's

mother and all her virtues in life, so the plants and flowers now repre-
sent her death.

The poem is particularly effective in its combination of conven-
tional elegiac motif and a sense of overwhelming personal sorrow
(that H cannot bear to see the garden blossom without his mother)
with a grounding in pragmatic reality: gardens do fade and run to
weed if they are not maintained.

6

Metre: alcaic stanzas, the most common metre in Horace's *Odes*.
H reproaches his doctor for his futile attempts to cure him of his grief.
The poem is marked by its use of strong language, which applies both
to physical illness (fever, swelling) and, metaphorically, to poetic
inspiration. H's self-depiction in this poem is strikingly feminine: he is
'widowed' of his own mother in line 12 (with a word usually used of
women), his own mother is 'inside' him in line 16, and that image is
converted explicitly to one of pregnancy and labour in lines 19-20.
Cf. the close of poem 1. The poem is also a memorable description of
the physiological effects of profound grief.

1   *Galen*: a famous Roman doctor, used here to denote a doctor in
     general. H addresses Luke as a doctor in *Lucus* 9 and describes
     Christ's healing power in medical terms in *Passio Discerpta* 8, as
     well as the English poem 'Time'.

12   *Then death ... all the more*: If H does not die in a holy state he
     risks never being reunited with his mother in heaven. The word
     he uses to describe his deprivation here, *viduabor*, is used usually
     of women who have lost a spouse, as if H feels he is 'widowed'
     of his own mother.

13-16 *But see how ... my leaping vein*: The language of heat here –
     especially the phrase *ardore scribendi* (*the ardour of writing*) – is
     appropriate to poetic inspiration as well as fever. H's mother and
     the 'heat' of his inspiration are closely associated, and described
     as being 'in his veins'.

17-20 *If I should be ... are not safe*: This remarkable description of
     H as a woman in the final stages of pregnancy, labouring to give
     birth to his praise of his mother, is also influenced by the vocabu-
     lary of inspiration: inspired poets may be described as 'filled'
     with inspiration in a similar way.

22   *combination*: The Latin word here is *crasis*, a Greek term which
     is used linguistically to denote the combining of two adjacent

vowels or dipthongs into one long vowel or dipthong, for instance at a word division. This technical term adds to the association between H's grief and his poetic skill.

21–4 *My condition . . . heal my heart*: Here H admits that his response to the situation – that is, his need to resolve his grief poetically – is unusual.

7

Metre: hexameter. This strange poem addresses an image of H's mother. He longs for this image to reveal the true face of his mother – to be really his mother – and imagines his joy if it did so and his readiness to live quietly with her for the rest of his life, setting aside other ambitions. The poem closes with an inventive version of the 'praise of rural retreat' motif, popular in poetry of H's day. The garden of H's cottage is here associated closely with Lady Danvers's garden in the fifth poem.

1 *maternal Guardian Spirit*: FFM insist that this must be a demon. I think it is more likely that we are meant to imagine an actual cloud or fog here, somehow resembling his mother, given that the image is described with the terms *nebulas* (line 2) and *nubi* (line 5) and is described as being *heavy with rain* (line 5). The summer of 1627 was wet, and several other poems in the collection seem to allude to the weather (of. 9, 10, 11 and 18).

4 *With breasts . . . as he gapes*: Powerful imagery of breastfeeding – or rather specifically the desire to suckle – is also found in *Lucus* 34, in which H imagines himself suckling from Christ himself.

7 *Juno*: The wife of Jupiter, hence queen of heaven. Here referring to H's mother.

8 *spring dawn*: i.e., a clear sunrise, without clouds.

11 *Astraea*: Astraea, daughter of Themis and goddess of justice, was the last of the immortals to leave the earth at the end of the Golden Age.

13 *tongue of her Balance*: As goddess of justice, Themis is often depicted with a pair of scales. The 'tongue' is the pointer of the balance.

16 *Sun's team*: the horses of the sun, which draw it through the heavens. A metaphorical way of saying that the poet would spend the whole of every day with the spirit, if it assumed the appearance of his mother.

17–21 *And I would . . . its paling stars*: H imagines how he would be prepared to renounce worldly pursuits and ambitions for the chance to be with his mother again. Minerva, goddess of wisdom, represents intellectual ambitions.

19   *bearded dreams*: These dreams are 'bearded' because they are old or long cherished by the poet.

22   *little cottage*: H's cottage is *laqueata*, 'fretted' or 'coffered' with beams. This resonant word is found in Horace, *Odes* 2.16.11, which goes on to endorse the moral and psychological benefits of a modest life without worldly ambition. The register of the word itself, however, is apparently misplaced: both in Horace and in Virgil (*Aeneid*, 1.726, of Dido's palace) what is 'coffered' is the majestic ceiling of a palace or fine villa, not a humble cottage. The combination of this term with just 'ten roofbeams' is probably intended to be a humorously ironic touch: a bit like calling your self-assembly porch a 'portico'. H uses a related word, without irony, to describe the grandeur of bishops at *Musae Responsoriae* 7.4 and the awesome architecture of the Underworld in *Lucus* 32.58.

26   *impervious to clumsy feet*: As in the description of the 'narrow garden' in poem 4 (line 3), the description of this garden employs terms that can also be applied to poetry. Narrow, exclusive paths, closed to all but a few, are associated with the aesthetics of small-scale, finely wrought poetry – contrasted with the grander, more public and political genre of popular epic (a distinction prevalent in classical Latin poetry, itself in imitation of the Hellenistic poet Callimachus). See also the beginning of the following poem.

27   *nosegay*: The Latin word *fasciculus*, a small bundle, can also be used of a packet of letters or books (e.g., Horace, *Epistles* 1.13.12). The choice of words suggests that the flowers of H's garden are his poetry.

28   *fed daily on the smoke*: In the *Iliad* the gods feed on the smoke of sacrifice.

29–30   *Only don . . . listless appearance*: H recognizes that his comforting fantasy depends upon suspending his awareness of reality and of his mother's absence.

33–4   *And lest . . . a similar fate*: The remaining 'children' of the garden (*foetus*, literally babies or offspring) are the flowers. The 'growing joys' H imagines for himself and his mother are described as children growing (*crescentia*) among the flowers of the garden. The flowers of this garden might also be understood to be the poems of the collection itself, as well as H's nine brothers and sisters. The metaphor imagines a rural retreat for H and his mother that is strikingly close to marriage.

8

Metre: iambic distichs (an iambic trimeter followed by an iambic dimeter). This is the same metre as *Passio Discerpta* 16 and Horace, *Epodes* 2. The imagery of this poem blends in a memorable way Callimachean poetics – which prefers the small-scale and exclusive path of finely wrought poetry to the broad and popular ways of more ambitious genres – with biblical imagery of the 'path of righteousness'. This is a poem about literary choices and vocation, as well as religious calling in the face of suffering. Kelliher considers it 'the finest, as it is the briefest, lyric that he ever published' (ibid., p. 47); FFM call it 'a particularly powerful example of Herbert's ability to use constrained metrical forms to create an extraordinary range of emotion and thought without ever abandoning simplicity and lucidity of surface' (FFM 110).

4   *mingled my wine with gall*: Before the crucifixion, Jesus is given wine mixed with gall (Matthew 27:34). This passage is also reminiscent of Christ's prayer in the garden 'take away this cup from me' (Mark 14:36, also Luke 22:42).

7–8   *At length someone . . . in my ear*: This motif of divine intervention is borrowed from classical sources, where it has a particularly poetic resonance: at the beginning of Virgil's *Eclogue* 6 the poet-shepherd Tityrus is about to sing of kings and battles (that is, epic) when Apollo pulls his ear and tells him to 'keep his sheep fat, but his Muse [i.e., his poetry] thin'. This passage is an imitation of Callimachus, who recounts a similar guiding encounter with Apollo as the principle behind his small-scale poetry. See also Milton, *Lycidas*, lines 76–7: 'But not the praise / Phoebus repli'd, and touch'd my trembling ears.'

9   *This was . . . your Lord*: See Mark 10:39: 'And Jesus said unto them, Ye shall indeed drink of the cup that I drink of; and with the baptism that I am baptized withal shall ye be baptized.'

9–10 *This was once . . . approve the Vintage*: For the direct statement and its acknowledgement, compare the end of 'Love' (III): 'You must sit down, says Love, and taste my meat: / So I did sit and eat' (lines 17–18) and 'The Collar': 'But as I raved and grew more fierce and wild / At every word, / Me thoughts I heard one calling, *Child!* / And I replied, *My Lord*' (lines 33–6).

9

Metre: elegiac couplets. A deeply self-conscious poem, H returns to
the association between the water of weeping and ink that we have
already seen in poem 1, as well as in the first poem of *Passio Dis-
cerpta*. To this is added in this instance the water of the seas on which
the king will fight. H mentions contemporary politics only to set it
aside: the poem is an elliptic kind of *recusatio* (literally, 'refusal') in
which a poet claims inadequacy to tackle the 'grander' themes of epic
or political poetry. Once again H's aesthetic choices of poetic genre
are linked to his personal grief: because he is grieving, he does not care
about the king's exploits.

The imagery throughout is marked by difficulty and obstruction:
the sun is obscured, eyes are dimmed with weeping, the fleet is ham-
pered by storms, even the passage of time itself is slowed by water, and
finally writing itself is obstructed by tears that threaten to dissolve the
ink. The overall effect is of an enormous personal struggle.

1   *Mother*: The Latin word used here, *Genitrix*, is a rather grand
    term, applied to Venus (as mother of Aeneas and the Romans) in
    the *Aeneid* 1.590 and by Lucretius 1.1, as well as to earth as the
    universal mother in Lucretius 2.599. Cf. H's address to the
    Church as mother in 'The British Church (1)'.

6   *dimming eyes*: The Latin phrase means literally 'failing cheeks'.
    The adjective *occiduis* is more properly applied to the sun itself,
    as it is a common word for 'setting'.

7   *the King ... deeds of daring*: Buckingham sailed from Stokes
    Bay to relieve La Rochelle on 27 June 1627, just a few weeks
    after Lady Danvers's death.

11 *Tillius*: Count Tilly was the commander of the army of the Cath-
    olic League. He defeated Christian IV of Denmark at Lutter on
    27 August 1626.

14 *excess of water*: Hutchinson points out that this line, and the
    following poem, suggest it was a particularly wet summer. The
    cloud of poem 7 perhaps reinforces this impression.

18 *waters*: i.e., the ink.

10

Metre: hendecasyllables.

1–4   *gloomy south ... stressed unfairly*: Evidently Britain's gloomy
        climate was already a trope of travel writing in the seventeenth
        century.
9   *two Gaelic lands*: Scotland and Ireland.
10   *Wales*: H was born at Montgomery in Wales.
11   *All three ... an earlier age*: The idea seems to be that the rain
        across the land is the tears of an earlier age, held in the sky and
        now released in honour of Lady Danvers.

11

Metre: elegiac couplets. H compares his mother's stabilizing influence
upon him to the roots of an oak tree, to the grafting of one tree upon
the stock of another, and then to the rock to which a sea creature
firmly clings. There is a striking intimacy to all these images, amount-
ing even to a kind of unity in the image of grafting. 'Affliction (5)' also
uses the metaphor of trees in a storm. In the *Dictionary of National
Biography* entry on H, Helen Wilcox notes the marked 'restlessness'
of his life, with the early loss of his father and repeated moves through-
out his early years. The final lines of poem 11 are striking in their
implicit poetic ambition: Odysseus and Achilles are figures of great suf-
fering, but the phrasing of the final line in particular associates H not
only with Achilles but also with the author of the *Iliad*, Homer himself.

10   *Polypus*: A sea creature that is fixed firmly to a rock.
13–14 *second Ulysses ... second Iliad*: In these lines H aligns himself
        with the hero first of Homer's *Odyssey* (Odysseus, famed for his
        long journey home from Troy) and then of Homer's *Iliad* (Achil-
        les, whose glory is dependent upon his early death, and whose
        grief and anger at the loss of first his partner Briseis, and then his
        closest friend Patroclus, structure the *Iliad*).

12

Metre: choliambic, a variation of iambic trimeter, associated particu-
larly with satirical and invective poetry. As befits invective, this poem
attacking the callousness of Stoics includes quite crude and strong
vocabulary. For the note of invective towards those who criticize his
grief, compare also the final paragraph of the second poem.

1   *prowling crag*: Rock is also related to impervious sinfulness in
     the opening poem of *Lucus*.
2   *Stripped of . . . in bones*: The image here is perhaps indebted to
     the 'valley of dry bones', Ezekiel 37:1-14. There the bones are an
     image of the house of Israel, all hope lost, revived only by the
     Lord.
3   *Molossian hounds*: wolf-dogs of famed ferocity, used by Epirot
     shepherds to guard their sheep. For Molossian hounds in an
     invective context, see Horace, *Epodes* 6.
4   *peels*: *Glubat*, literally to 'peel' or 'husk', often has an obscene
     meaning in Latin, referring to male masturbation or fellatio.
6-8 *Medusa . . . Pyrrha*: Medusa turned men into stone, whereas
     Pyrrha repopulated the earth after the flood by throwing stones
     that became men (see Ovid, *Metamorphoses* 1.383-93).
10   *Tiger*: The capitalized Latin, *Tigris*, is a pun: both a female tiger
     and the River Tigris. Diogenes, who brought Stoicism to Rome
     in the second century BCE, was thought to have been born in
     Seleucia on the Tigris.

13

Metre: elegiac couplets. In this brief epitaph H applies once again the
language of passionate victory to his mother's virtuous life.

14

Metre: elegiac couplets. The first in a series of five short Greek poems,
showing the influence of poems from the *Greek Anthology* and in par-
ticular the *Anacreonta*, a collection of Greek lyric poetry fashionable
in H's day. The celebratory diction of this piece connects it closely to
the previous poem and the one that follows. For detailed comments
on H's Greek verse, see Blair and FFM.

15

Metre: iambic trimeter. Returning to the imagery of the garden, H
imagines his mother, at her death, gathering together all the scents of
her flower-garden and sweeping on ahead, leaving behind her a faint,
scented trace of the path to heaven. For the garden imagery, cf. poems
5 and 7.

2   *cultivated field of God*: The Greek phrase is found in 1 Corinthians 3:9 – God's field is the church.

16

Metre: anacreontics, a light metre used in short pieces of Greek lyric. The opening four lines of this poem are an imitation of poem 29 of the *Anacreontea*. The conceit of the poem is that two eyes are not enough to weep for such a woman as Lady Danvers. H imagines himself as Argos, the mythical giant with many (often a hundred) eyes, one to weep for each of his mother's virtues. Argos also appears, in a similar context, in the poem on the death of Queen Anne included in the *Alia Poemata Latina* ('On the death of the fairest Queen Anne', line 5).

17

Metre: hexameter. This hexameter poem is modelled upon several influential Greek poems of pastoral lament, especially those by Bion, Moschus and Theocritus. All of these models are written in hexameters and feature a refrain – found here in lines 1, 8 and 15. Once again, the final paragraph of the poem returns to the imagery of Lady Danvers's garden, as in poems 5, 7 and 15. In this poem in particular, elements drawn from Hellenistic Greek poetry are combined with reminiscences of the grander register of Homer and Pindar.

9–10   *Their hearts . . . terrible grief*: cf. Homer, *Iliad* 9.9 where Agamemnon is 'stricken in his heart with great grief'. There is a pun on 'struck' in this line.

17   *like the sun*: H compares his mother to the sun, more usually an image of God or the king (as in the prefatory poem to *Musae Responsoriae*, addressed to James I, and its final poem, 40, a hymn to God).

20   *Sirius*: the Dog Star, which marks the hottest period of the summer.

23   *measuring out*: another play upon the 'measures' of poetry itself. The words with which H measures out his mother's life are the lines of his poetry. Cf. a similar play in the last line of the first poem. Examples of this motif in H's English poetry can be found in 'Good Friday', 'Judgement' (lines 11–15), 'Longing' (lines 10–12, 80–82) and 'Frailty' (lines 17–24).

18

Metre: elegiac couplets. This short poem is densely Homeric, indebted to the descriptions of the River Scamander in spate (in the *Iliad* 5.599, 18.403 and 21.235). A succession of unusual words and constructions are drawn directly from Homer. At first the Thames during a storm at night threatens to burst its banks, and with it the order of nature itself (H may have been remembering how Scamander rises up and fights Achilles directly in the *Iliad* 21). But in the final couplet respect for H's mother prevents the river from flooding, although its stormy state is considered appropriate to passionate grief.

19

Metre: elegiac couplets. This coda to the collection is a kind of reverse of the poetic motif of *recusatio* (or 'refusal' poem, in which a poet explains why he will not or cannot write the sort of poetry that a patron hopes for or expects). H claims that he had intended to give up poetry, but was forced to return to it by his Muse, who demanded compensation for her distress at his mother's death. His deferral to the Muse of both his distress and his longed-for conversation with his dead mother – his Muse has managed to catch her in heaven, by bribing the Fates, presumably in the fashion of Orpheus – is touching.

1   *reed pipes*: The reed pipe as a symbol for lyric poetry appears also at the first line of poem 4.

8   *trivial poems*: Hutchinson and FFM disagree about the interpretation of this final line: is *stulta* a vocative exclamation addressed to the Muse ('stupid woman!') or a characterization of the poems H has written ('foolish things')? Hutchinson remarks that 'the poet would hardly condemn his tributes to his mother as foolish things'. But H quite often dismisses the writing of poetry in general – not just this poetry – as being of doubtful moral value, and his modesty here mirrors, for instance, *nugor* in the opening line of poem 4. Cf. 'The Posy' for another statement of doubt about the importance and value of writing poetry compared to religious devotion. For the opposite argument – though applied to H specifically – see 'The Quiddity' and poem 6 of this collection. In both cases the argument is one of psychological or spiritual utility for H in particular.

ALIA POEMATA LATINA
OTHER LATIN POEMS

These mostly occasional poems are not a collection in their own right, but simply an assembly of those of H's Latin verse which was not included in any of the collections. The order follows that given in Hutchinson, which is chronological insofar as that can be determined. The eighth piece, *Aethiopissa ambit Cestum Diversi Coloris Virum*, was widely circulated and appears in many contemporary manuscript collections and personal miscellanies.

On the Death of Henry, Prince of Wales

Metre: hexameter. Henry, the eldest son of James I, died of typhoid fever on 6 November 1612, aged only nineteen. H, also nineteen at the time, wrote this piece and the following ode, in response. They were the first of his poems to be printed.

The imagery of flowing water runs throughout the poem; cf. the imagery of tears and ink in *Passio Discerpta* 1, and of Christ as a pure stream in *Passio Discerpta* 5 and 13.

1   *Parnassian*: Parnassus is a mountain near Delphi, sacred to Apollo and home of the Muses.

2   *ivy*: Ivy is associated with the inspired poet, as for instance in Horace, *Odes* 1.1.29.

4   *Cyrrha*: one of the peaks of Parnassus; *Libethra*: a city close to Olympus where Orpheus was buried by the Muses.

8   *sisters*: the Muses. The winged horse Pegasus is said to have struck the ground with his hooves on Mount Helicon. From these marks, four springs burst forth, from which were born the Muses.

22   *Philomela*: The daughter of Pandion, she was transformed into a nightingale after being raped and mutilated by Tereus, her sister's husband; *Dido*: Queen of Carthage, who loved Aeneas and killed herself after he left her to sail on to Italy and found Rome. Dido and Philomela are conventional examples of unfortunate women, here considered lucky in comparison to the Prince and his subjects.

33   *blast of gunpowder*: an allusion to the Gunpowder Plot (1605). The Latin phrase here is similar to that found in H's description of gunpowder in *Triumphus Mortis*, poem 32 of *Lucus*.

37   *without your sun*: i.e., Prince Henry was England's 'sun'. Comparisons between a monarch and the sun are a common motif in political panegyric.

43   *The rivers rest in their course*: The Latin phrase here is an adapted quotation of Virgil, *Eclogues* 8.4, where it describes the response of nature to the song of Damon and Alphesiboeus.

[Ode Appended to the Previous Poem]

Metre: alcaics. This interesting and accomplished ode takes the form of a hymn to Athena, followed (unusually) by Athena's reply. The first portion of the poem asks – in a roundabout way – why so powerful a goddess as Athena, who was strong enough to defeat the Giants and the Gorgon, has not intervened to save Prince Henry. Athena's reply suggests that Henry is transformed from earthly fruit to a subject for heavenly (i.e., eternal) song.

The ode offers both a comforting motif of salvation (Henry lives for ever in heaven) and also a powerful statement of poetic ambition. Both parts of the poem – the prayer to Athena and her reply – allude to related episodes of the same myth: Athena's assistance to Perseus in his battle with the Gorgon Medusa, and the creation of poetry or song as a direct result of that battle. Pindar's *Pythian* 12 relates how Athena invented piping in imitation of the sound of the Gorgons as they lamented for Medusa after Perseus had beheaded her. (For a similar reworking of the myth of *Pythian* 12, see Ben Jonson's early ode, *Uncollected Verse* 48.) The Gorgon also appears in *Musae Responsoriae* 6.

3–4 *Camoenae ... Pieria and the Muses of Latium*: Note the blend here of Greek and Roman terms for the Muses.

9   *Hydra*: The Lernaean Hydra was a mythical beast in the form of a snake, killed by Hercules as one of his twelve labours.

11   *Minerva*: the Latin title for Athena.

12   *Aegis*: the shield of Athena, bearing the head of the Gorgon Medusa.

15   *Ajax*: Athena was hostile towards the lesser Ajax and his ship was ruined on his return from Troy.

17   *Gorgon*: Medusa, also killed by Hercules with the assistance of Athena.

20   *Enceladus*: one of the Giants. In the battle between the Giants and the Olympian Gods, Athena hurled the spear that wounded Enceladus; *Rhoecus*: another of the Giants.

24   *Bellona*: Roman goddess of war.
33   *tibia*: literally, a shin bone, but commonly used for a pipe or flute.

On His Birthday and Good Friday
Falling on the Same Day

Metre: elegiac couplets. In 1607 Good Friday fell on H's birthday, 3 April (he was fourteen) and again in 1618 and 1629. Hutchinson suggests that 1618 is the most likely date for this poem. Cf. a similar occasion for Donne's poem 'Upon the Annuntiation and Passion falling upon one day. Anno Dñi 1608'.

10   *brother*: The Latin word in fact means 'coeval', one of the same age as myself.

On the Death of the Fairest Queen Anne

Metre: elegiac couplets. Anne of Denmark, the wife of James I, died on 2 March 1619. This minor and quite early poem is interesting for its foreshadowing of several themes that recur in H's more mature Latin work.

4   *slender renown*: H compares his 'slight' or 'slender' fame to Anne's power and glory. But the word for 'slight', *tenuis*, is an important term in Latin poetics, with strong positive connotations of unassuming but highly fashioned, small-scale verse (in comparison to, for instance, epic poetry). See also the note on *Memoriae Matris Sacrum* 4 (line 3).
5   *Briareus*: the son of Uranus and Gaea. According to Hesiod, he has a hundred arms and fifty hands; *Argus*: a giant with many eyes (often a hundred). Cf. *Memoriae Matris Sacrum* 16 – also in a mourning context.
9-10 *For the praises ... upon the Ocean*: The point seems to be that the praise of Anne, like the stars, will endure for ever; whereas the grief of her people is only fleeting. Cf. Beaumont and Fletcher, *Philaster* (1611): 'All your deeds / Shall be in water writ, but this in Marble' (*v. iii. 91*).

To the Author of Instauratio Magna

Metre: elegiac couplets. This is the first of three poems addressed to Francis Bacon, whom H knew well. *Novum Organum*, the second part of *Instauratio Magna*, was published on 12 October 1620.

Comparison between the Office and the
Book of the High Chancellor

Metre: elegiac couplets. In a letter dated 4 November 1620 H, writing
as Orator of the University of Cambridge, thanked Bacon for the gift
of his book to the university. The poem depends partly on a piece of
wordplay that is hard to translate: the Latin word *munus* means both
'duty' or 'public office' and also 'gift'. So Bacon benefits those living
today by his *munus* as Lord Chancellor; and the men of the future by
the *munus* of his book donated to the university.

In Honour of the Illustrious Lord Verulam, Viscount
St Alban, Keeper of the Great Seal, After the
Publication of His Instauratio Magna

Metre: iambic trimeters. Hutchinson describes this poem as 'the most
famous of H's Latin poems'. It was printed in four separate books
within twenty-five years, and also appears in several manuscript col-
lections. Bacon was made Viscount St Alban on 27 January 1621, but
was deprived of the Great Seal on the 1 May that year. The poem must
therefore date from between those two points.

Syntactically, it is simply a list of epithets and noun phrases describ-
ing Bacon's attributes and characteristics, carried off with the kind of
poetic creativity and verve that distinguishes some of H's most effect-
ive English pieces, e.g., 'Prayer (1)'.

4   *Inductive Method*: Book II of the *Novum Organum* discusses
     improvements to the method of inductive reasoning, the prin-
     ciple by which arguments should begin from established facts
     rather than theories.

5   *Arts*: The title of MA refers to the Latin Magister artium, 'master
     of arts'.

12   *Steward*: The Latin word *Promus*, meaning a steward or the per-
     son in charge of a storehouse, probably alludes to Bacon's
     personal collection of adages and proverbs, *A Promus of Formu-
     laries and Elegancies*; *Router of Idols*: In Book I of *Novum
     Organum* Bacon refutes the idols of the tribe, the cave, the mar-
     ketplace and the theatre.

18   *Herculean Stagirite*: Aristotle, who is falling because, it is
     implied, Bacon's work has displaced him.

23   *hive of Honey*: a common image in H, often associated with
     divinity. Cf. the first line of *Lucus* 35 (*To the Lord*).

26   *mustard-seed*: This final comparison probably alludes to the parable of the mustard seed (Matthew 13:31–2; Mark 4:30–32; Luke 13:18–19), in which Christ compares the kingdom of God to the mustard seed, on the grounds that it is smaller than other seeds, but produces a plant larger than all other herbs. H suggests that Bacon's project is a scientific equivalent of the kingdom of God.

An Ethiopian Girl Woos Cestus, a Man of a Different Colour

Metre: elegiac couplets. This popular Latin poem is reproduced in several contemporary manuscript collections, and appears to have initiated a vogue for similar pieces in both English and Latin. The erotic motif of darkness is probably indebted at least in part to the Song of Solomon, 1.5: 'I am black, but comely.' It is strikingly unlike H's other poetry and is the only straightforward 'love poem' attributed to him (although his religious poems and poetry of mourning both make considerable use of erotic motifs). It was sent to Bacon along with an English poem dedicating it to him, and playing on the 'blackness' of ink, and of the girl in the poem. This perhaps supports its authenticity – see the remarks on H's 'ink' imagery in the first poems of both *Passio Discerpta* and *Memoriae Matris Sacrum*. For further comment on this piece and the tradition it inaugurated, see Gilmore.

While He Seeks the Infanta

Metre: elegiac couplets. Prince Charles visited Spain in 1622/3 to woo the Infanta (on this episode see Drury 118–24). James I visited Cambridge on 12 March 1622/3. Hutchinson has some detailed notes about the authenticity of this poem. The translation is Herberts's own.

In the Latin text, the Prince seeks *Infantem* (the Infanta herself, rather than the 'Spain' of his English translation) and James the Granta (the Cambridge river, here representing Cambridge itself). Both the Infanta and Cambridge (and therefore by extension H himself, who is in Cambridge) are sought after, one by the prince, one by the king. The question posed by the poem is which of these loves is the greater? H's answer is that Cambridge's love for the king is greater than that of the Infanta for the prince, because the intellectual distance between 'us' – that is, between H and the others who receive him in Cambridge – and the king is even greater than the voyage undergone by the prince to Spain.

On the Death of the Incomparable Francis, Viscount St Alban, Baron Verulam

Metre: elegiac couplets. Bacon died on 9 April 1626 and this poem first appeared in a memorial volume for him printed later that year.

5   *Flora*: Goddess of plants and flowers, associated with the spring; *Philomela*: daughter of Pandion, she was transformed into a nightingale after being raped and mutilated by Tereus, her sister's husband. (See above note 7 to *In Obitum Henrici Principis*.) The nightingale's song is thus characterized as a lament. Her attendance here is connected to the detail of Bacon's tongue in the next line, since Philomela's tongue was cut out after the rape to prevent her from explaining what had happened to her.

6   *tongue*: The conceit is that Bacon's tongue alone is to be buried: he can no longer speak in person, but the rest of his work shall endure.

On the Sacred Anchor of the Fisherman, G. Herbert

Metre: iambic trimeters, elegiac couplet, hendecasyllables and hexameter. These Latin lines are, at least in origin, an answer to John Donne's Latin poem 'To Mr *George Herbert*, with one of my Seal[s], of the Anchor and Christ'. Shortly before his death Donne had made several seal, engraved with the figure of Christ crucified on an anchor (the emblem of hope), which he sent to his friends. The poem exists in more than one version: for further discussion of its textual history, see Hutchinson. Part of the poem appears to date from after Donne's death in 1631 and may not be by H. The very varied metrical arrangement of the poem is quite different from H's usual practice.

[Another version]

When H died, this verse was found wrapped up with the seal that Donne had given to him.

Index of Titles

Index of First Lines

PENGUIN CLASSICS

THE COMPLETE POEMS
ANDREW MARVELL

'Thus, though we cannot make our sun
Stand still, yet we will make him run'

Member of Parliament, tutor to Oliver Cromwell's ward, satirist and friend of
John Milton, Andrew Marvell was one of the most significant poets of the
seventeenth century. *The Complete Poems* demonstrates his unique skill and
immense diversity, and includes lyrical love-poetry, religious works and biting
satire. From the passionately erotic 'To his Coy Mistress', to the astutely political
Cromwellian poems and the prescient 'Garden' and 'Mower' poems, which
consider humankind's relationship with the environment, these works are
masterpieces of clarity and metaphysical imagery. Eloquent and compelling, they
remain among the most vital and profound works of the era – works by a figure
who, in the words of T. S. Eliot, 'speaks clearly and unequivocally with the voice
of his literary age'.

This edition of Marvell's complete poems is based on a detailed study of the extant
manuscripts, with modern translations provided for Marvell's Greek and Latin
poems. This edition also includes a chronology, further reading, appendices, notes
and indexes of titles and first lines, with a new introduction by Jonathan Bate.

Edited by Elizabeth Story Donno

With an introduction by Jonathan Bate

PENGUIN CLASSICS

THE COMPLETE POEMS
JOHN MILTON

> 'I may assert Eternal Providence
> And justify the ways of God to men'

John Milton was a master of almost every type of verse, from the classical to the
religious and from the lyrical to the epic. His early poems include the devotional
'On the Morning of Christ's Nativity', 'Comus', a masque, and the pastoral elegy
'Lycidas'. After Cromwell's death and the dashing of Milton's political hopes,
he began composing *Paradise Lost*, which reflects his profound understanding of
politics and power. Written when Milton was at the height of his abilities, this great
masterpiece fuses the Christian with the classical in its description of the Fall of
Man. In *Samson Agonistes*, Milton's last work, the poet draws a parallel with his
own life in the hero's struggle to renew his faith in God.

In this edition of the *Complete Poems*, John Leonard draws attention to words
coined by Milton and those that have changed their meaning since his time. He
also provides full notes to elucidate biblical, classical and historical allusions and
has modernized spelling, capitalization and punctuation.

Edited with a preface and notes by John Leonard

THE STORY OF PENGUIN CLASSICS

Before 1946 ... 'Classics' are mainly the domain of academics and students; readable editions for everyone else are almost unheard of. This all changes when a little-known classicist, E. V. Rieu, presents Penguin founder Allen Lane with the translation of Homer's *Odyssey* that he has been working on in his spare time.

1946 Penguin Classics debuts with *The Odyssey*, which promptly sells three million copies. Suddenly, classics are no longer for the privileged few.

1950s Rieu, now series editor, turns to professional writers for the best modern, readable translations, including Dorothy L. Sayers's *Inferno* and Robert Graves's unexpurgated *Twelve Caesars*.

1960s The Classics are given the distinctive black covers that have remained a constant throughout the life of the series. Rieu retires in 1964, hailing the Penguin Classics list as 'the greatest educative force of the twentieth century.'

1970s A new generation of translators swells the Penguin Classics ranks, introducing readers of English to classics of world literature from more than twenty languages. The list grows to encompass more history, philosophy, science, religion and politics.

1980s The Penguin American Library launches with titles such as *Uncle Tom's Cabin*, and joins forces with Penguin Classics to provide the most comprehensive library of world literature available from any paperback publisher.

1990s The launch of Penguin Audiobooks brings the classics to a listening audience for the first time, and in 1999 the worldwide launch of the Penguin Classics website extends their reach to the global online community.

The 21st Century Penguin Classics are completely redesigned for the first time in nearly twenty years. This world-famous series now consists of more than 1300 titles, making the widest range of the best books ever written available to millions – and constantly redefining what makes a 'classic'.

The Odyssey continues ...

The best books ever written

PENGUIN CLASSICS

SINCE 1946

Find out more at www.penguinclassics.com